Autobiography:
Essays Theoretical
and Critical

Autobiography:
Essays Theoretical and Critical

Edited by James Olney

Princeton University Press
Princeton, New Jersey

*The editor dedicates
his part in this volume to
Georges Gusdorf,
mentor and friend*

Contents

Preface

The essays in this volume have been selected with an eye both to excellence and to variousness. There are many voices now engaged in the dialogue on autobiography as the introductory essay and the bibliography demonstrate; it has been my intention in editing this collection not to establish any critical "line" but to provide a forum for as many different voices as possible. I decided early on not to extract from books but to include only complete, self-contained works of essay length and only those essays representing a distinctive voice, with a minimum of repetition or overlap. About half of the essays are original and half are reprints. I wish to thank the Information Service of the British Library, the Reference Division of Perkins Library, Duke University, the Interlibrary Loan Department of James E. Shepard Library, North Carolina Central University, and the following individuals for various kinds of advice and assistance rendered during the preparation of this volume: Germaine Brée, Elizabeth W. Bruss, Thomas Cooley, James M. Cox, Catherine Dammeyer, James Goodwin, Janet Gunn, Georges Gusdorf, Joanna Hitchcock, William Howarth, Ernst Manasse, Barrett Mandel, Ernest D. Mason, Roger Porter, Louis Renza, Robert Sayre, Daniel Shea, Michael Sprinker, and Albert Stone.

There is no theory that is not a fragment, carefully prepared, of some autobiography. —Paul Valéry

Autobiography:
Essays Theoretical
and Critical

Autobiography and
the Cultural Moment:
A Thematic, Historical, and
Bibliographical Introduction

James Olney

Writing about autobiography in a context of literary studies involves one immediately, irremediably, and uncomfortably in
paradox. Autobiography is both the simplest of literary enterprises
and the commonest. Anybody who can write a sentence or even
speak into a tape recorder or to a ghostwriter can do it; yet viewed
in a certain light it might fairly be seen as a very daring, even
foolhardy, undertaking—a bold rush into an area where angels
might well fear to tread. Is it not foolish to imagine that one's life
can be, or should be, transformed into a piece of writing and
offered up to the general public for consumption? Nevertheless,
whatever reasons one might find why autobiography should be
practised by no one, recent publishing history offers plentiful evidence that it is practised by almost everyone. Perhaps this is so because there are no rules or formal requirements binding the pro-
spective autobiographer—no restraints, no necessary models, no
obligatory observances gradually shaped out of a long developing
tradition and imposed by that tradition on the individual talent who
would translate a life into writing.

But if autobiography is the least complicated of writing performances, it is also the most elusive of literary documents. One never
knows where or how to take hold of autobiography: there are simply no general rules available to the critic. Indeed, in many cases,

© 1980 Princeton University Press *Autobiography: Essays Theoretical and Critical*
0-691-06412-1/80/0003-025$01.25/1 (cloth)
0-691-10080-2/80/0003-025$01.25/1 (paperback)
For copying information, see copyright page

having somehow or other taken hold, it is only by an act of faith that one can sustain the claim or the belief that it is autobiography that is being held. In talking about autobiography, one always feels that there is a great and present danger that the subject will slip away altogether, that it will vanish into thinnest air, leaving behind the perception that there is no such creature as autobiography and that there never has been—that there is no way to bring autobiography to heel as a literary genre with its own proper form, terminology, and observances. On the other hand, if autobiography fails to entice the critic into the folly of doubting or denying its very existence, then there arises the opposite temptation (or perhaps it is the same temptation in a different guise) to argue not only that autobiography exists but that it *alone* exists—that all writing that aspires to be literature is autobiography and nothing else.

In addition to being the simplest and commonest of writing propositions, autobiography is also the least "literary" kind of writing, practised by people who would neither imagine nor admit that they were "writers." But it is also (or can be and often has been) the most rarified and self-conscious of literary performances: the mere mention of Nabokov's *Speak, Memory* and Roland Barthes' recent book, *Roland Barthes par Roland Barthes*—where the phrase "by Roland Barthes" is as much a part of the title as is "Roland Barthes"[1]—should suffice to demonstrate this. And I doubt that many people would want to argue that earlier autobiographers such as St. Augustine, Montaigne, or Rousseau were precisely lacking in self-consciousness or were without literary awareness and literary value, even though the tormented, hyperconscious modern self may not have existed in their days. Moreover, although it is widely practised by self-proclaimed nonscribblers, autobiography exercises something very like a fatal attraction for nearly all men and women who would call themselves "writers." The daring venture of writing their own lives directly as well as indirectly seems to have an overwhelming appeal for all such.

Here all sorts of generic boundaries (and even lines dividing discipline from discipline) are simply wiped away, and we often cannot tell whether we should call something a novel, a poem, a critical dissertation, or an autobiography. In *Beyond Good and Evil*, Nietzsche remarked, "Little by little it has become clear to me that

[1] See Elizabeth Bruss's reference to these two works in her essay in this volume; cf. also Philippe Lejeune, "Autobiography in the Third Person," *New Literary History* 9 (1977): 49, notes 27 and 28.

every great philosophy has been the confession of its maker, as it were his involuntary and unconscious autobiography," and much the same could be claimed—indeed has been claimed—about psychology and history, lyric poetry and even literary criticism. Are we to call the last four books of Augustine's *Confessions* (which offer a commentary on the account of the creation in Genesis) philosophy, theology, hermeneutics, exegesis—or autobiography? What about Montaigne's *Essais* or Pascal's *Pensées*? Or consider R. G. Collingwood's *Autobiography*, which he says is "the story of [my] thought," but which sports such typical chapter titles as "The Decay of Realism," "The History of Philosophy," "The Need for a Philosophy of History." What is this—history, philosophy, autobiography? Or again, recall W.E.B. DuBois's *Dusk of Dawn*, which is subtitled "The Autobiography of a Race Concept": Is it sociology or autobiography, science or literature?

I fear that it is all too typical—indeed it seems inevitable—that the subject of autobiography produces more questions than answers, more doubts by far (even of its existence) than certainties. Paul Valéry claimed that *La Jeune Parque*, the longest of his poems and one of the most obscure, was his true autobiography and I, for one, believe him (see my essay in the present collection) just as I believe the argument that I advanced a few years ago that T. S. Eliot's *Four Quartets* is his spiritual autobiography. Where does this leave us? It leaves us at least with the perception that what is autobiography to one observer is history or philosophy, psychology or lyric poetry, sociology or metaphysics to another. Further on I will argue that literary criticism, too, can be seen as autobiography reluctant to come all the way out of the closet—that the literary critic, like Nietzsche's philosopher, is a closet autobiographer—and that this accounts in part for the very remarkable increase in interest that literary critics have shown in the subject over the past twenty years or so. At the moment, however, I want to consider the history of autobiography and the history of critical/theoretical—that is, "literary"—discussions of autobiography.

The first autobiography was written by a gentleman named W. P. Scargill; it was published in 1834 and was called *The Autobiography of a Dissenting Minister*. Or perhaps the first autobiography was written by Jean-Jacques Rousseau in the 1760s (but he called it his *Confessions*); or by Michel de Montaigne in the latter half of the sixteenth century (but he called it *Essays*); or by St. Augustine at the turn of the fourth-fifth century A.D. (but he called it

his *Confessions*); or by Plato in the fourth century B.C. (but he wrote
it as a letter, which we know as the seventh epistle); or . . . and so
on. Priority depends on whether we insist upon the word: if we
refuse to call a book an autobiography unless its author called it
that, Scargill's latter-day entry bears away the honor, for the word
was fabricated toward the end of the eighteenth century at which
time three Greek elements meaning "self-life-writing" were combined to describe a literature already existing under other names
("memoirs" and "confessions," for example). Or if we are not
hypernominalists (and in fact I know of no one who would stick at
the word, so that as far as I am aware the present occasion is the
first time Scargill's name has been brought forward in this regard)
then priority depends on the rigor and twist of definition we give to
"autobiography" and to all three parts of the word: "auto-" "bio-"
"graphy." What do we mean by the self, or himself (*autos*)? What
do we mean by life (*bios*)? What significance do we impute to the
act of writing (*graphē*)—what is the significance and the effect of
transforming life, or *a* life, into a text? Those are very large, very
difficult questions, and prudence might well urge that we give the
Rev. Mr. Scargill the palm and call it a day, for if we go back beyond him and beyond the authority of the word on the title page—
saying *this* is an autobiography[2]—we shall find matters not only to

[2] There is a special irony attaching to Scargill's claim to priority—the irony that,
although his title page affirms that this is an autobiography and although it is true
that the author's genuine identity was that of a dissenting minister, this is not an
autobiography but what the DNB calls "a romance." The historical moment that
saw publication of Scargill's *Autobiography* also saw a number of earlier works republished under the new title of "autobiography": *Autobiography. A Collection of the
most instructive and amusing lives ever published, written by the parties themselves: with . . .
compendious sequels carrying on the course of events to the death of each writer*. 34 vols.
(London, 1826-1833). The same month (October 1834) in which Scargill's *Autobiography* was published, Jack Ketch's memoirs were republished, edited, and retitled by
Charles Whitehead: *Autobiography of a Notorious Legal Functionary* (London, 1834).
   Also in 1834 (but in what month I am uncertain: the Preface is dated "Geneva,
May 1834") Cochrane and McCrone of London published, in two volumes, *The
Autobiography, Times, Opinions, and Contemporaries of Sir Egerton Brydges, Bart. R.J.
(Per legem terrae) Baron Chandos of Sudeley, etc.* Brydges' work is a very curious performance, a misshapen, lumpy ragbag of a book, yet thoroughly complacent in its
high self-regard. There is certainly a bit of autobiography in it, but also a good bit
more of the times, opinions, and contemporaries of the Baronet. Although Sir Egerton's book is undoubtedly an autobiography in part and of sorts, I prefer Scargill's
claim because the irony and paradox that the first *Autobiography* should have been
something other than autobiography seems to me too nice to abandon. In 1833 a
seventeen-page piece entitled "Autobiography of a Scottish Borderer" appeared in

be much more complicated than we had expected but agitated and controversial as well. The presence of controversy is evident in the fact that every one of the writers mentioned (as well as others) has had his champion(s) as the first—or at least the first *true*—autobiographer. This is one of the paradoxes of the subject: everyone knows what autobiography is, but no two observers, no matter how assured they may be, are in agreement. In any case, wherever and on whatever grounds we may wish to assign priority and to whatever books we may be willing to grant the title the practice of autobiography has been with us for a long time, and it is with us in generous supply today.

The same is not true, however, of a theoretical and critical literature about autobiography. That literature began, in effect, in 1956, which is not even yesterday but only about an hour ago as such matters must be judged. It is as if autobiography were a normal and natural human activity—and lately even a necessary human activity—while criticism of it is a moral perversion (I have heard it so described) and a simple nuisance. But if critical and theoretical writing about autobiography really is a perversion, it is well on its way to becoming a naturalized and normalized perversion and well on its way to becoming acceptable in polite scholarly society by the mere number of people—and respectable people too—engaged in it. Literary journals nowadays devote special numbers to the question of autobiography—*Sewanee Review, New Literary History, Genre, Modern Language Notes,* and *Revue d'histoire littéraire de la France,* to mention only the first that come to mind; so many sessions of the annual MLA meeting concern themselves with autobiography that it is impossible to attend them all, and a recent American Studies Association meeting brought together twenty-five or thirty people, all in one way or another "authorities" on the subject; books on autobiography appear regularly from university presses, dissertations are even more regularly announced in the MLA bibliography, and recently it has seemed to me that hardly a day has gone by that an essay treating of the subject has not come across my desk. Of course, there are some particular reasons (the present volume being one) why these essays, once produced,

---

Fraser's Magazine signed simply "H." A certain aura of romance seems to hover about the piece (it may be more than mere coincidence that Brydges wrote for *Fraser's* also), and the seventeen-page length that requires it to settle for inverted commas removes the piece from serious contention for the italic-type authority of *Autobiography*.

should appear on my desk just now—but these reasons do not explain why the essays (and so many of them) should have been produced in the first place, or at just this moment in time. Why was it not proper to produce literary studies of autobiography twenty-five years ago? Why is nothing else as proper, as vital today? These are the questions I want to consider in the remainder of this essay, but before examining them we might get some insight into the questions themselves if we survey the kinds of critical attention devoted to autobiography, the recurrent themes of that criticism, and the varieties of approach offered to the subject over the past twenty years or so.

In the beginning, then, was Georges Gusdorf. True, Gusdorf is a massively learned man and he had by way of background the work of Wilhelm Dilthey, in whose historiography and hermeneutics (or in what he called, more generally, the "human studies") autobiography occupied a central place as *the* key to understanding the curve of history, every sort of cultural manifestation, and the very shape and essence of human culture itself. And Gusdorf also had as background the work of Georg Misch, disciple, literary executor, and son-in-law of Dilthey, who produced a *History of Autobiography*, which was a true life's work—three volumes, each divided into two huge parts, thus forming six massive tomes, 2,868 pages long, yet coming no closer to the present than the Renaissance, and terminated only by Misch's death.[3] True also that two years before Gusdorf's "Conditions et limites de l'autobiographie," Wayne Shumaker published *English Autobiography: Its Emergence, Materials, and Forms* and that as long ago as 1909 Anna Robeson Burr published *The Autobiography: A Critical and Comparative Study*. But the latter has no real significance apart from its early date—a harbinger of a false dawn (there are good reasons in the book itself, I believe, why the dawn was a false one)—and Shumaker's book, while an intelligent and penetrating work in its own right, is at one and the same time restricted in its theoretical scope and rather diffuse in its

[3] Misch's work, as Gusdorf says with more regret than some might be able to muster, was "malheureusement inachevé"; but students and disciples of Misch carried his work on after his death, producing one more volume, two more tomes, another 1,000 pages, and bringing the *Geschichte der Autobiographie* up to the nineteenth century. The *History*, all of which was published under Misch's name, thus occupies four volumes, eight tomes, and nearly 4,000 pages, and it traces the subject from prehistoric Babylonia and Assyria to the late nineteenth century.

treatment. Between Anna Robeson Burr and Wayne Shumaker, J. Lionel Tayler (in 1926) and A. M. Clark (in 1935) made brief excursions into the territory of autobiography and produced a pair of genial and pleasant exercises but hardly anything more profound than that characterization would suggest. Thus, it is only with Gusdorf's essay (one of a dozen or so on related topics forming a Festschrift in honor of Fritz Neubert) that all the questions and concerns—philosophical, psychological, literary, and more generally humanistic—that have preoccupied students of autobiography from 1956 to 1978 were first fully and clearly laid out and given comprehensive and brilliant, if necessarily brief, consideration.

When I say that it all begins with Gusdorf's essay, however, I would not be understood to mean that subsequent critics stumbled across "Conditions et limites de l'autobiographie" or came upon Dilthey or Misch and suddenly realized that here was a real subject that had previously been unrecognized or neglected. What happened was quite different and very much more interesting. As a case in point perhaps I may be permitted to offer a small part of my own autobiography, which I believe will serve to demonstrate the falsity of a simplistic, cause-effect understanding of literary history.

My interest in autobiography was not at first specifically literary but was an ad hoc response to a course called "Concepts of Man," in which I read, with a group of honors students, a number of autobiographies. At the same time I was deeply engaged in reading and discussing four modern writers: Joyce, Lawrence, Yeats, and Eliot. What I came to feel was frequently the case was that works in the one group were works of art that presented themselves as autobiographies (Montaigne's *Essays*, Newman's *Apologia*), while works in the other group were autobiographies that presented themselves as works of art (Joyce and Lawrence in all their works, Yeats in the *Collected Poems*, Eliot in *Four Quartets*). Now this was no great perception; it had certainly been brought forward often enough in the cases of Joyce, Lawrence, and Yeats. What was somewhat more interesting was a case such as Tolstoy where *A Confession* and *The Death of Ivan Ilyich* present themselves as virtually the same work—metaphoric representations of one and the same experience and consequent vision—while bearing titles that would identify the one as an autobiography, the other as a piece of fiction and a work of art; or the case of Newman where the *Gram-*

mar of Assent and virtually everything Newman wrote—whether novel, poem, polemical essay, or saint's life—has a strong odor of autobiography about it.

When I began (in about 1966) to write what eventually became *Metaphors of Self* it never occurred to me to look for critical works on autobiography for the simple reason that I did not think of what I was doing as a study of autobiography; I thought of it as a study of the way experience is transformed into literature (which I suppose could be another way of describing autobiography)—as a study of the creative process, a humanistic study of the ways of men and the forms taken by human consciousness. In West Africa (where I spent the years 1967 to 1969 and where I wrote a large part of the book in first draft) my conception of the subject no doubt began to clarify and focus itself around autobiography and its status as literature, but the book situation being what it was, there was no way, no matter how much I might have desired it, that I could lose my innocence with regard to critical works on autobiography. In England, where I spent the last four months of 1969 revising and rewriting my manuscript, I finally lost my critical virginity, but I still did not come across Gusdorf's essay (it has never been easily available). It was only when the manuscript was submitted to Princeton University Press in early 1971 that a reader remarked that I should be aware of Gusdorf; I read his essay, found it obviously brilliant, and made some revisions and additions to about five or six pages of manuscript.

In translating "Conditions et limites de l'autobiographie" into English for the present volume, I have been repeatedly astonished at the overwhelming similarities between that essay and my book, and after reading the translation, Professor Gusdorf responded in kind: "I have the impression that the translation is all the better for the reason that the thought is not at all foreign to you. These ideas are yours also. The thesis of *Metaphors of Self* even turns up, toward the end of the essay, in regard to . . . a critical school that worked out an interpretation of literature by attempting to draw out significant complexes characteristic both of a life and a work. These 'complexes' are also keys to the autobiography—'metaphors.' " It is my assumption that many critics of the autobiographical mode have had experiences very much like my own—that is to say, they worked out ideas about autobiography and then found themselves both anticipated and confirmed in Gusdorf (or Misch or Dilthey), but there is one more, later detail in this complex of anticipation, confirmation, and interrelationship that I would like to mention. In 1975 Gusdorf published a second, long essay ("De l'autobiographie initiatique à l'autobiographie genre littéraire") in which not only the ideas and the general argument but even specific details, examples, and turns of phrase are identical to those that I deployed in *Metaphors of Self*, but I know for a certainty that Professor Gusdorf was entirely unaware of my book in 1975—as unaware as I was of his essay in 1969.

Now this excursion into my autobiography can come to an end, but what I wish to say through this brief personal narrative is that within a few years of one another (and I believe quite independently) a number of people turned their critical attention to autobiography, found the same, new kind of interest in it and read it in the same, new sort of way, and that this number of people who share something of a common interest and understanding is increasing—has in the past few years increased—very rapidly. Which brings me back to the questions, Why? Why now? Why not earlier? In light of the experience I have just narrated, we cannot reply that it is a matter of simple cause and effect or of influence and imitation—that the work of Dilthey, Misch, or Gusdorf is the cause and the work of subsequent writers the effect. I am convinced that it was something more deeply embedded in the times and in the contemporary psyche, something more pervasive in the intellectual and spiritual atmosphere that caused and continues to cause a great number of investigators, thinkers, and critics to turn their attention to the subject of autobiography. Let us, however, again take up the thread of the history of critical thought on the subject.

In the same year that "Conditions et limites de l'autobiographie" appeared, H. N. Wethered published a little book called *The Curious Art of Autobiography*, which is interesting mostly for its title and the coincidence of date with Gusdorf's essay. A much more important book was Roy Pascal's *Design and Truth in Autobiography* (1960), which asks whether in discovering or imposing a design the autobiographer is not playing fast and loose with truth: Is there such a thing as design in one's experience that is not an unjustifiable imposition after the fact? Or is it not perhaps more relevant to say that the autobiographer half discovers, half creates a deeper design and truth than adherence to historical and factual truth could ever make claim to? This is obviously an interesting and important question (which Gusdorf treats with customary acuity) and one that orients Pascal's book toward a view of autobiography as a creative

act—a guest, albeit still a rather shadowy one and probably unin-
vited, at the literary feast. However, Pascal shows a somewhat un-
fortunate tendency to receive books into the canon or to cast them
into outer darkness according to an uncomfortably narrow definition that leads him to approve some as "real" or "true" autobiographies while rejecting others as not "real" or not "true." Nevertheless, his book remains an important event in the history I am
tracing. Interestingly, at the beginning of the book Pascal records
something of an autobiographical impetus behind his work, which
is significant because in this particular instance at least autobiography and criticism of autobiography are drawn into much the
same orbit.

Early on in this history in progress, a number of writers attempted to establish the moment when a modern autobiographical
consciousness and self-consciousness began to insinuate itself into
culture and the creative act and began to make its presence felt in
literature. I have already mentioned one of these works, *English Autobiography: Its Emergence, Materials, and Forms* (1954), and in the
twenty or so years following the appearance of Shumaker's book
there were six or eight more books and a number of articles that
focused their attention on this same historical moment (the
seventeenth and eighteenth centuries) and philosophical/psycholog-
ical/literary phenomenon: *Every Man a Phoenix: Studies in Seventeenth-Century Autobiography*, by Margaret Bottrall (1958); *The Beginnings of Autobiography in England*, by James M. Osborn (1959);
Defoe and Spiritual Autobiography, by George A. Starr (1965); *Versions of the Self: Studies in English Autobiography from John Bunyan to
John Stuart Mill*, by John N. Morris (1966); *The Eloquent "I": Style
and Self in Seventeenth-Century Prose*, by Joan Webber (1968); *British
Autobiography in the Seventeenth Century*, by Paul Delany (1969);
L'autobiographie en France, by Philippe Lejeune (1971); and, to a certain extent, two recent books, *Imagining a Self: Autobiography and
Novel in Eighteenth-Century England*, by Patricia Meyer Spacks
(1976); and *Autobiographical Acts: The Changing Situation of a Literary Genre*, by Elizabeth W. Bruss (1976). Articles by (among
others) Barrett J. Mandel, Roger J. Porter, Jacques Voisine, Karl J.
Weintraub, Philippe Lejeune, and Robert Bell[4] concern themselves

---

[4] For all these, see the Bibliography. Karl J. Weintraub has now (1978) extended
his important article, "Autobiography and Historical Consciousness," into an
equally important book, *The Value of the Individual: Self and Circumstance in Autobiography*, a work that performs in English (and in 400 pages as against 4,000) much the

with the dawning self-consciousness of Western man that found literary expression in the early moments of modern autobi-ography—those moments when secular autobiography was slowly developing out of spiritual autobiography and when autobiography as a literary mode was emerging out of autobiography as a confes-sional act. All the foregoing books and articles (and there are a good many more than those I have mentioned) look to the historical, psychological, and social origins of a literary act that has been ex-tended, altered, and redesigned in subsequent centuries but that for all its inward and outward transformations has still retained some sort of constant essence: it remains, in some way that we may agree to recognize, the act of autobiography.

In the hands of other critics, autobiography has become the focalizing literature for various "studies" that otherwise have little by way of a defining, organizing center to them. I have in mind such "studies" as American Studies, Black Studies, Women's Studies, and African Studies. According to the argument of these critics (who are becoming more numerous every day), autobi-ography—the story of a distinctive culture written in individual characters and from within—offers a privileged access to an experi-ence (the American experience, the black experience, the female experience, the African experience) that no other variety of writing can offer. I am anticipating myself somewhat now, but I would suggest that this special quality of autobiography—that is, that au-tobiography renders in a peculiarly direct and faithful way the ex-perience and the vision of a people, which is the same experience and the same vision lying behind and informing all the literature of that people—is one of the reasons why autobiography has lately be-come such a popular, even fashionable, study in the academic world where traditional ways of organizing literature by period or school have tended to give way to a different sort of organization (or disorganization). This new academic dispensation brings to-gether a literature that is very rich and highly various, heteroge-nous in its composition—a literature so diverse that it cries out for

---

same service as Misch's monumental work in German. *The Value of the Individual* offers a lucid and comprehensive history of the emergence of the elements and types of autobiography, at the same time analyzing the historical and cultural conditions under which that emergence became possible, perhaps even inevitable. For the mo-ment, and I should think for the foreseeable future, this book is the definitive English-language treatment of autobiography as an epiphenomenon and mirror of cultural history.

some defining center; such a center autobiography has been felt to provide. To understand the American mind in all its complexity—so goes the argument—read a variety of American autobiographies; moreover, since many of the autobiographies were written by the same people who produced the fiction, drama, and poetry of the nation, the student who sees autobiography as the central document possesses something very like a key to all the other literature as well. James M. Cox pushes the argument one step further with the claim that in writing the autobiography of the American nation (the Declaration of Independence), Thomas Jefferson also wrote the script of its subsequent history.

Whether or not the foregoing is the explanation for academic interest in autobiography (in fact, I do not think it is anything approaching a complete explanation), it cannot be disputed that the interest exists, that it is very intense, and that it has been especially apparent in all the "studies" mentioned earlier. Robert F. Sayre, who wrote one of the earliest and most intelligent books on American autobiography in a literary context—*The Examined Self: Benjamin Franklin, Henry Adams, Henry James* (1964)—has also produced the definitive bibliographical article on the uses of autobiography for those trying to sort through that mixed bag that goes under the name of American Studies, "The Proper Study—Autobiographies in American Studies" (1977). In "Autobiography and the Making of America" Sayre goes on to make clear the analogical significance of autobiography in the building of a nation and in the building of character. Daniel Shea's *Spiritual Autobiography in Early America* (1968) is a fine and thorough study of the most characteristic orientation toward their experience adopted by American autobiographers before Franklin (Shea also considers Franklin and some writers after him). Franklin himself, as something approaching an archetypal American autobiographer, has been the subject of numerous essays and chapters of books including "Autobiography and the American Myth," by William C. Spengemann and L. R. Lundquist (1965); "Autobiography and America," by James M. Cox (1971); "Form and Moral Balance in Franklin's Autobiography," by Morton L. Ross (1976); and "Three Masters of Impression Management: Benjamin Franklin, Booker T. Washington, and Malcolm X as Autobiographers," by Stephen J. Whitfield (1978). Post-Franklin American autobiography has recently received insightful treatment from Thomas Cooley in *Educated Lives: The Rise of Modern Autobiography in America* (1976) and from Mutlu Konuk

Blasing in *The Art of Life: Studies in American Autobiographical Literature* (1977). One hears, furthermore, that a number of books on American autobiography are in the making—in particular a much anticipated book by Albert E. Stone, who has already given us both a very useful bibliographical article, "Autobiography and American Culture" (1972), and a wide-ranging essay on varieties of violence in American life and American autobiography, "Cato's Mirror: The Face of Violence in American Autobiography" (1977).

Even more than American Studies, Black Studies courses and programs have been organized around autobiography—in part, no doubt, because (as John Blassingame has pointed out) black history was preserved in autobiographies rather than in standard histories and because black writers entered into the house of literature through the door of autobiography. From Frederick Douglass to Malcolm X, from Olaudah Equiano to Maya Angelou, the mode specific to the black experience has been autobiography; and of recent times the critical literature has more than kept pace with the primary literature. In black autobiography and criticism of it, we have something akin to a paradigm of the situation of autobiography in general. It is very doubtful that Equiano, Douglass, and Malcolm X saw their works as texts that might be studied in literature courses, yet the past few years have seen literary analyses devoted to all three; and Douglass and Malcolm X are firmly established authors in courses that find themselves, comfortably or not, within departments of English as opposed to departments of History or Social Science.

If black autobiography is a paradigm, the history of Maya Angelou's *I Know Why the Caged Bird Sings* is a paradigm of a paradigm. Until fairly recently, black writing in general was barely mentioned as literature—if mentioned at all it was usually in some other context—and until very recently, autobiography received much the same treatment. Moreover, women writers have not always been given due consideration as makers of literature. But here we have an autobiography by a black woman, published in the present decade (1970), that already has its own critical literature. Is this to be attributed solely to the undoubted quality of Maya Angelou's book? Surely not. And here is a most striking sign of the critical/cultural times: *her autobiography was Maya Angelou's first book*. It is not so astonishing that fifty years after their publication Henry James's autobiographical volumes should come in for critical discussion as works of literature in their own right; there was, after all, a whole shelf of novels that preceded *A Small Boy and Others* and *Notes of a Son and Brother*, and James acknowledged that he had much the same ultimate design in his fiction and his autobiography: the tracing of the evolution of individual consciousness. But the case is quite different with Maya Angelou, and we can only conclude that something like full literary enfranchisement has been won by black writers, women writers, and autobiography itself when we contemplate the fact that already in 1973 Sidonie Smith was publishing "The Song of a Caged Bird: Maya Angelou's Quest after Self-Acceptance," two years later George Kent was offering "Maya Angelou's *I Know Why the Caged Bird Sings* and Black Autobiographical Tradition," and a year after that Liliane Arensberg was talking to us about "Death as Metaphor of Self in *I Know Why the Caged Bird Sings*." This is a striking phenomenon and one that should give pause to students of literary history and cultural forms.

Black autobiography in general has been well served of late by two books—Sidonie Smith's *Where I'm Bound: Patterns of Slavery and Freedom in Black American Autobiography* (1974) and Stephen Butterfield's *Black Autobiography in America* (1974)—as well as by numerous articles including Warner Berthoff's "Witness and Testament" (1971), Michael G. Cooke's "Modern Black Autobiography in the Tradition" (1973), John W. Blassingame's "Black Autobiographies as Histories and Literature" (1973-1974), Houston A. Baker, Jr.'s "The Problem of Being: Some Reflections on Black Autobiography" (1975), Elizabeth Schultz's "To be Black and Blue: The Blues Genre in Black American Autobiography" (1975), Paul John Eakin's "Malcolm X and the Limits of Autobiography" (1976), Roger Rosenblatt's "Black Autobiography: Life as the Death Weapon" (1976), James M. Cox's "Autobiography and Washington" (1977), and Albert E. Stone's survey of recent developments in Afro-American autobiography, "After *Black Boy* and *Dusk of Dawn*: Patterns in Recent Black Autobiography" (1978). This dry list of titles that appear in such places as *New Literary History*, *Yale Review*, *Criticism*, *Sewanee Review*, and in an anthology of critical pieces on Romanticism published by Cornell University Press may serve to indicate the literary respectability that discussion of black autobiography has attained.

As several recent bibliographical publications attest, Women's Studies courses have a sizeable autobiographical literature to draw on, but theoretical and critical writing is for the most part yet to come. Patricia Meyer Spacks has published the most notable and

enlightening work on women autobiographers both in essays—
"Reflecting Women" (1973) and "Women's Stories, Women's
Selves" (1977)—and in books—*The Female Imagination* (1975) and
*Imagining a Self: Autobiography and Novel in Eighteenth-Century Eng-
land* (1976). That women's autobiographies display quite a different
orientation toward the self and others from the typical orientation
to be found in autobiographies by men is established in Mary G.
Mason's "The Other Voice: Autobiographies of Women Writers."
Women who write out their inner life in autobiographies, Patricia
Meyer Spacks says, "define, for themselves and for their readers,
woman as she is and as she dreams," which is a fine way of pointing up the importance of those autobiographies for the somewhat
undefined field of Women's Studies. In African Studies as in
Women's Studies extensive critical discussion is yet to be given to
the considerable volume of autobiographies available. One book
exists—James Olney's *Tell Me Africa: An Approach to African Literature* (1973)—and a handful of essays mostly on individual autobiographies such as Camara Laye's *L'enfant noir*, Peter Abrahams' *Tell
Freedom*, and Ezekiel Mphahlele's *Down Second Avenue*.

In addition to providing the subject for philosophical and historical studies and besides the uses to which American Studies, Black
Studies, Women's Studies, and African Studies have put it, autobiography has also been subjected to a certain amount of generic criticism: various writers have attempted to draw generic boundaries
around autobiography, defining it as a specifically *literary* genre,
telling what autobiography is and what it is not, which works are
autobiographies and which are something else, what we can expect
from an autobiography and what an autobiography can expect
from us. Elizabeth W. Bruss's *Autobiographical Acts* (1976) is undoubtedly the most distinguished book of genre criticism in English, and Philippe Lejeune's *Le pacte autobiographique* (1975), the
most distinguished book in French.[5] Like critics who adopt a
generic approach to other literary modes, genre critics of autobiography frequently attempt to contain their subject with an array of
graphs, tables, arrows, pointers, and other schematic devices
(Lejeune's text is strewn with them at the outset), and they tend
toward a quasi-legalistic language of contracts, rights, obligations,

[5] Lejeune published the first chapter of his book under the title "Le pacte autobiographique" in *Poétique* in 1973 and the last chapter, originally presented as a
paper at a Sorbonne colloquium on autobiography, under the title "Autobiographie
et histoire littéraire" in *Revue d'histoire littéraire de la France* in 1975.

promises, expectations, and pacts. (At the Sorbonne colloquium to which he presented his second paper on autobiography, Georges Gusdorf complained bitterly of Lejeune's murdering to dissect, for Gusdorf viewed it as an act of critical *hubris*, an act of violence and arrogance, committed against the distinctive essence of autobiography—its *humanness*.) Lejeune's definition of autobiography is: "A retrospective account in prose that a real person makes of his own existence stressing his individual life and especially the history of his personality" (*Le pacte autobiographique*, p. 14). With such a definition as this and with the tools of graphs and tables in hand, the critic can readily determine what is and what is not an autobiography and can analyze at great length the work certified as generically genuine. In his final chapter Lejeune escapes somewhat from the self-imposed rigidities of generic definition when he makes the intelligent point that one should not think of a specific genre as an isolated or isolable thing but should think in terms of an organic system of genres within which transformations and interpenetrations are forever occurring.

Other critics who would like to draw some sketchy lines that would indicate something of the peculiar nature of autobiography have been reluctant to define or to impose rigid schemata and so have resorted to descriptive accounts and to generally rather loose classifications and categories. Jean Starobinski's "The Style of Autobiography" (1971) commences as a genre study but concludes with something quite different: a consideration of style as a metaphoric representation of the present writing self and, at the same time, of the past written self. Stephen Spender's common-sense view in "Confessions and Autobiographies" (1955)—the view of a poet who has also produced an autobiography—distinguishes autobiography from biography, which is a distinction that I imagine every writer on autobiography would feel it necessary to maintain. In a relatively early essay, "The Dark Continent of Literature: Autobiography" (1965), Stephen A. Shapiro argues that in theme, structure, and intention autobiography is frequently indistinguishable from other varieties of literary art. Similarly, in "Some Principles of Autobiography" (1974), William Howarth demonstrates the variousness of the art, offers loose groupings of several different kinds of autobiography, and suggests that the reader should be prepared to be flexible in response to this mode because of the mode's own flexibility. This is something of the same demonstration and lesson provided by Francis R. Hart in "Notes for an Anatomy of

Modern Autobiography" (1970), a study that examines a considerable number of modern autobiographies in an attempt to discover what the characteristics of the modern mode are and what different varieties there might be. Roger J. Porter's sensitive "Edwin Muir and Autobiography: Archetype of a Redemptive Memory" (1978) explores the shadowy area where psychology, literature, and myth intersect, and at the same time he provides a responsive, delicate reading of Muir's profoundly moving *Autobiography*.

Erik H. Erikson, working at the cutting edge of psychology and history in "Gandhi's Autobiography: The Leader as a Child" (1966; included in *Life History and the Historical Moment*), has some very useful and penetrating things to say about the stages of life and psycho-history, and he shows how as students of autobiography we should fix autobiographical events in the moment of writing and in the history of the writer and his time. As Erikson makes brilliantly clear and as I have also tried to demonstrate in this volume, it is memory that reaches tentacles out into each of these three different "times"—the time now, the time then, and the time of an individual's historical context. (The title of the final version of Frederick Douglass's autobiography, *The Life and Times of Frederick Douglass*, demonstrates precisely these three points of reference.) Now that I have briefly sketched the history and themes of theoretical and critical writing on autobiography, I want to turn back to the central questions, Why? Why now? Why not earlier?

Much of the early criticism of the autobiographical mode was directed to the question of *autos*—how the act of autobiography is at once a discovery, a creation, and an imitation of the self (it was on this issue that Gusdorf's two essays and my own book crossed paths so frequently). Here I think we come at one of the most important explanations for the critical turn toward autobiography as literature, for those critics who took *autos* for their primary focus tended to be very free in their understanding of *bios*, seeing it as the entire life of the individual up to the time of writing, the psychic configuration of the individual at the moment of writing, the whole history of a people living in this individual autobiographer, or any combination of these and various other possible senses of *bios*. This shift of attention from *bios* to *autos*—from the life to the self—was, I believe, largely responsible for opening things up and turning them in a philosophical, psychological, and literary direction.

It is a curious fact that biography has been an admissible subject in literary studies for quite a lot longer than autobiography, but is it not an astonishing proposition and a fearful paradox to say that someone writes someone else's life? F.S.L. Lyons is writing the authorized life of W. B. Yeats; Richard Ellmann wrote the life of James Joyce: or, more astonishing and fearful still, Edgar Johnson has written the "definitive" life of Charles Dickens. Can this be? Can a life be written? The question is neither idle nor meaningless. The tradition that a life can be written goes back a long way, of course. In his "Life of Theseus," Plutarch says in passing, οὕτως ἐμοὶ περὶ τὴν τῶν βίων τῶν παραλλήλων γραφήν ("so in the writing of my Parallel Lives"), but the antiquity of the tradition in no way lessens its fearfulness, for in his use of the dative of possession Plutarch appropriates the lives to himself: "*my* Parallel Lives." *Emoi* (to me, for me, therefore mine) replaces *autou* (of him, his), and Theseus is nowhere in the picture. Can Edgar Johnson similarly refer to "my life" (incidentally lived by Dickens, but "mine" now by the act of writing)? These questions that trouble the art of biography do not disappear when the individual who lived the life undertakes to write it—on the contrary, they become rather more complex and demanding.

Prior to the refocusing from *bios* to *autos* there had been a rather naive threefold assumption about the writing of an autobiography: first, that the *bios* of autobiography could only signify "the course of a lifetime" or at least a significant portion of a lifetime; second, that the autobiographer could narrate his life in a manner at least approaching an objective historical account and make of that internal subject a text existing in the external world; and third, that there was nothing problematical about the *autos*, no agonizing questions of identity, self-definition, self-existence, or self-deception—at least none the reader need attend to—and therefore the fact that the individual was himself narrating the story of himself had no troubling philosophical, psychological, literary, or historical implications. In other words, the *autos* was taken to be perfectly neutral and adding it to "biography" changed nothing (which is why librarians and bibliographers, being good, simple souls and devoted to systems of classification that go back far beyond the time when the study of autobiography came into vogue, like to view autobiography as nothing other than a subdivision of biography—which is itself classified as a variety of history).

One consequence of this assumption was that the only terms that could be brought to bear in a critical discussion of autobiography would reflect no more than the critic's view of the content narrated—"charming," "scandalous," "touching"—a direct response to the recollected life as transmitted through the unclouded, neutral glass of the *autos*. Thus in 1909 W. D. Howells called autobiography "that most delightful of all reading," and as late as 1964 Bonamy Dobrée was saying that "autobiographies are the most entrancing of books." Or if a more critical judgment were to be brought in, it could only be in terms of the author's truthfulness: Did he, for whatever reason, deliberately and consciously alter details in that body of historical facts that lay there in a clear and objective light to be recovered accurately by the author's memory and to be transmitted faithfully to the reader as the *bios* of this autobiography? What Gusdorf and others argued, however, was that the *autos* has its reasons and its truth (which, in terms of historical fact, may well be false) that neither reason nor a simple historical view of *bios* can ever know. It is revealing that Gusdorf's first book was entitled *La découverte de soi*, for in that book, in his two essays on autobiography, and in all of his writing in what he terms "les sciences humaines" he has been concerned with what he calls "le problème de la connaissance de soi"—consciousness of self, or self-knowledge. "La question," he has written to me privately, "me préoccupe depuis toujours," and it is that same preoccupation, I believe, that has led so many critics, at much the same cultural moment, to autobiography as a subject of the most vital interest for philosophers, psychologists, and theorists and historians of literature.

It was this turning to *autos*—the "I" that coming awake to its own being shapes and determines the nature of the autobiography and in so doing half discovers, half creates itself—that opened up the subject of autobiography specifically for literary discussion, for behind every work of literature there is an "I" informing the whole and making its presence felt at every critical point, and without this "I," stated or implied, the work would collapse into mere insignificance. In a certain paradoxical way, this is what I understand James M. Cox to mean by his "recovering literature's lost ground through autobiography" (I use the term "paradoxical" because the way he recovers lost ground from, for example, history is to secure the self and its reality by attaching it irrevocably to history—its own history and the making of history). The encroachments of history on literature will only end, he implies, when we succeed in fastening the *autos* down—in history, in public and visible acts, with all the subsequent history that follows upon those acts. It is my understanding that Cox is as determined as Gusdorf or anyone else to secure the self and thereby to secure added territory for literature.

The *bios* of an autobiography, we may say, is what the "I" makes of it; yet as recent critics have observed, so far as the finished work is concerned, neither the *autos* nor the *bios* is there in the beginning, a completed entity, a defined, known self or a history to be had for the taking. Here is where the act of writing—the third element of autobiography—assumes its true importance: it is through that act that the self and the life, complexly intertwined and entangled, take on a certain form, assume a particular shape and image, and endlessly reflect that image back and forth between themselves as between two mirrors. But at this point, as French critics tell us (for example, Jacques Derrida, Michel Foucault, Roland Barthes, Jacques Lacan, and American adherents like Jeffrey Mehlman and Michael Ryan who have been quick to learn the lesson), the text takes on a life of its own, and the self that was not really in existence in the beginning is in the end merely a matter of text and has nothing whatever to do with an authorizing author. The self, then, is a fiction and so is the life, and behind the text of an autobiography lies the text of an "autobiography": all that is left are characters on a page, and they too can be "deconstructed" to demonstrate the shadowiness of even their existence. Having dissolved the self into a text and then out of the text into thin air, several critics (with the *hubris* peculiar to modern criticism?) have announced the end of autobiography. A few years ago it was the demise of the novel; now it is autobiography's turn. Has criticism of autobiography thus come full circle? Did it will itself and its subject into existence twenty-odd years ago through a belief in the reality of the self, and has it now willed itself and its subject out of existence again upon discerning that there is no more there than, as Michael Sprinker puts it, "fictions of the self"?

In her intriguing "Eye for I," Elizabeth W. Bruss adopts rather a different tactic from Sprinker's: she *assumes* that which he argues—that is, she takes it for granted that autobiography as we know it is at an end, and with this presumed agreement in hand she turns her attention to autobiography as we do not know it. As to the *autos*, what she says is not that the self is altogether a fiction or a delusion and every emanation of it a deconstructible text but that its ability to say "I" in a written text and to have any authority for that assertion has been of late so thoroughly compromised philosophically and linguistically and so thoroughly complicated literarily that the very basis on which a traditional autobiography might be commenced has simply been worn away. It is something revealing that Elizabeth Bruss speaks in the past tense of how "we were apt to regard autobiography," our regarding it thus being a matter of yesterday and last year. Louis A. Renza, on the other hand, has nothing to say about the transformations or conclusions of a literary genre. He would have it that autobiography as an act producing a text accessible to appropriation by readers has never been possible, neither in the past nor now, though of course many people have been sufficiently deluded that they thought it possible and so have commenced texts destined sooner or later to break down into a sort of perpetual beginning and a fragmented, stuttering incoherence. Is it all past tense, then, both with autobiography and criticism of it—the former a mere stuttering and the latter no more than a babbling about stuttering?

I do not believe so, but I do think that the direction taken in the performances of structuralist, poststructuralist, and deconstructionist critics is a revealing one, for, however much they talk about genre or linguistics or deep-lying structures, what they are still troubling about is the self and consciousness or knowledge of it, even though in a kind of bravura way some of them may be denying rather than affirming its reality or its possibility. And this is the crux of the matter, the heart of the explanation for the special appeal of autobiography to students of literature in recent times: it is a fascination with the self and its profound, its endless mysteries and, accompanying that fascination, an anxiety about the self, an anxiety about the dimness and vulnerability of that entity that no one has ever seen or touched or tasted (unless perhaps G. M. Hopkins, who was modern but not postmodern: "that taste of myself, of *I* and *me* above and in all things, which is more distinctive than the taste of ale or alum, more distinctive than the smell of walnutleaf or camphor").

If this is indeed the case—that it is the lure of the self quite immediately and doubly revealed that has drawn students of literature to autobiography—then critics of the autobiographical mode have felt much the same pressure as contemporary thinkers in other areas, and they have reacted to it in much the same way. Historiographers have come to recognize and to insist that the *autos* of the historian is and must be present in the writing of history; phenomenologists and existentialists have joined hands with depth psychologists in stressing an idea of a self that defines itself from moment to moment amid the buzz and confusion of the external world and as a security against that outside whirl. The study of how autobiographers have done this—how they discovered, asserted, created a self in the process of writing it out—requires the reader or the student of autobiography to participate fully in the process, so that the created self becomes, at one remove, almost as much the reader's as the author's. (Consider what happens in John Stuart Mill's *Autobiography*. It was in reading Marmontel's *Mémoires* and giving his full participation and assent to the process of self-creation occurring in that autobiography that he discovered new possibilities in himself, shed tears, and began to emerge from the depression previously crushing him.) This is the double thrust of Barrett J. Mandel's "Full of Life Now," an article that I take to be a highly original treatment of the phenomenology of reading, which is a subject of great current interest (Wolfgang Iser and Stanley Fish, in their different ways, have contributed much) and of vast importance.

There are various reasons why literary critics did not appropriate the autobiographical mode earlier than they did. First, there is the dual, paradoxical fact that autobiography is often something considerably less than literature and that it is always something rather more than literature. In some tangled, obscure, shifting, and ungraspable way it is, or stands in for, or memorializes, or replaces, or makes something else of someone's life. If part of the function of criticism is to judge (and surely it is), then it is not just a joke to say that judging an autobiography to be "bad" is very nearly the same as judging a life to be "bad." We all know that we are saying something about the character of Malcolm X, for example, when we judge his *Autobiography*; and this case reveals the real situation in a particularly acute way since we cannot argue that it is only or primarily a literary text that we are tying so intimately to Malcolm X's life, for he did not, of course, stand as sole or ultimate authority for that literary text. Yet the question and its obvious answer remain: Which of us does not *know* that he or she is offering judgment of Malcolm X's moral character in offering a presumably literary judgment of *The Autobiography of Malcolm X* by Alex Haley? The writer of an autobiography is doing something other, something both less and more than creating an artifact accessible to objective, critical analysis and evaluation when he chooses to write directly about himself and his life. Autobiography, like the life it mirrors, refuses to stay still long enough for the genre critic to fit it out with the necessary rules, laws, contracts, and pacts; it refuses, simply, to be a literary genre like any other.

A second, related reason for the neglect of autobiography as a subject of literary study is that critics of twenty-five years ago insisted that for satisfying aesthetic apprehension a work must display (in Stephen Dedalus's phrase) "wholeness, harmony, and radiance." Now some autobiographies may display a certain radiance and a few may strive for and achieve some sort of harmony, but no autobiography as conceived in a traditional, common-sense way can possess wholeness because by definition the end of the story cannot be told, the *bios* must remain incomplete. In effect, the narrative is never finished, nor ever can be, within the covers of a book. (This might be qualified by remarking that in a sense, conversion narratives achieve a kind of completeness by recording the death of the old individual—as it were, the Old Adam—and laying that individual to rest within the confines of the conversion narrative.) Furthermore, by its very nature, the self is (like the autobiography that records and creates it) open-ended and incomplete: it is always in process or, more precisely, is itself a process.

A third reason why a body of critical literature did not grow up alongside autobiography is that autobiography is a self-reflexive, a self-critical act, and consequently the criticism of autobiography exists *within* the literature instead of alongside it. The autobiographer can discuss and analyze the autobiographical act as he performs it: St. Augustine, Montaigne, Rousseau, Henry James are forever talking about what they are doing even as they do it. This is markedly different from the constraints of fictional verisimilitude under which the novelist operates. Certainly the novelist can comment on, theorize about, analyze and criticize his fiction if he so desires—but he must go outside the work to do it and thereby surrender a large part of his privileged status as the creative consciousness in which this fiction comes into being. In order to talk about his fictions, Henry James had to write the "prefaces" to the New York edition, but in *A Small Boy and Others* and *Notes of a Son and Brother* it is as if the critical, theoretical prefaces had found their way into the text of the narrative, allowing the author (who is also the hero and enfolding consciousness) to comment in his own voice on the origins of the tale, the problems it presented in conception and composition, and the means discovered to overcome those problems. Until very recently it would have been impossible to compile a collection of theoretical and critical essays such as the present one, but from St. Augustine on a compiler could have put together a vast collection of critical, theoretical pieces drawn from and reflecting on autobiographies and the creative process that has brought them into being.

I remarked earlier that the student and reader of autobiographies—the literary critic who has taken them up so avidly in the past twenty years—is a vicarious or a closet autobiographer, and it is precisely because he is able to participate fully if vicariously in the self-creation going on in autobiography that the reasons outlined above for the previous neglect of autobiography have more recently been turned on their heads to become positive reasons for making autobiography a central concern in literary studies. Two contributors to the present volume have remarked to me, quite independently of one another, that they would never consider writing their autobiographies—but if I am right in my conception of the acts of reading and criticism, then of course they do not need to: their autobiographies have already half emerged in the act of living and writing about the autobiographies of others. It is my thorough persuasion that there is a large element of autobiographical determination in each of these views of what constitutes autobiography, what its present state is, and whether or not it is possible at all. I suggest that a reading of Elizabeth Bruss or Michael Sprinker, of Germaine Brée or James Cox, of Barrett Mandel or Louis Renza—with due attention to style as Jean Starobinski describes it—will reveal a half-obscured, half-emergent autobiography that has been profoundly implicated in determining the particular critical or theoretical attitude being expressed.

As I pointed out earlier, criticism has always found its place within the creative act of autobiography, and now writers on autobiography have reversed that proposition to bring the creative act of autobiography, clandestinely perhaps, into their criticism. The open-endedness of autobiography that requires readers to continue the experience into their own lives thus becomes a virtue for recent critics rather than the defect that the New Critics would have felt it to be. As Germaine Brée demonstrates so persuasively, this is one reason why Michel Leiris has recently and rapidly been elevated into a modern classic: his autobiographic quest, far from concluding or being closed, remains open-ended, turns back on itself, and in its circularity, becomes endless. Just as Leiris "fears and loathes the fact and idea of death," so his quest fears and loathes conclusion and so also his readers fear and loathe conclusion. Germaine Brée, John Sturrock, Henri Peyre, Jeffrey Mehlman, and Philippe Lejeune (in both *Lire Leiris* and *Le pacte autobiographique*) have all given shrewd readings to Leiris as *the* modern autobiographer. As Rousseau was the classic autobiographer of his time, so Leiris seems well on the way to becoming that for our time (if one can speak of a classic in the contemporary world and if one can apply the word to an art that is, as Germaine Brée says, "antiautobiographic"). It may well define the mood of our time and our temperament that we should take an endless, open-ended, labyrinthine antiautobiography for our classic autobiography. If the student of autobiography is, as I believe, a vicarious autobiographer, he does not want, indeed cannot allow, the work to be whole, complete, finished, and closed. Not until he abandons *his* autobiography—giving up his *autos*, his *bios*, and the *graphē* (which is in the reading as well as the writing) that unites and brings the *autos* and the *bios* to being—can he ever assent to that eventuality.

This, then, is my answer—and the essays in the present volume I offer as widely various evidence in support of that answer—to the questions "Why?" "Why now?" "Why not earlier?"

Conditions and Limits
of Autobiography

Georges Gusdorf

Translated by James Olney

Autobiography is a solidly established literary genre, its history traceable in a series of masterpieces from the *Confessions* of St. Augustine to Gide's *Si le grain ne meurt*, with Rousseau's *Confessions*, Goethe's *Dichtung und Wahrheit*, Chateaubriand's *Mémoires d'outre tombe*, and Newman's *Apologia* in between. Many great men, and even some not so great—heads of government or generals, ministers of state, explorers, businessmen—have devoted the leisure time of their old age to editing "Memoirs," which have found an attentive reading public from generation to generation. Autobiography exists, unquestionably and in fine state; it is covered by that reverential rule that protects hallowed things, so that calling it into question might well seem rather foolish. Diogenes demonstrated the reality of movement simply by walking, and thus brought the scoffers over to his side in his dispute with the Eleatic philosopher who claimed, with reason as his authority, that it was impossible for Achilles ever to overtake the tortoise. Likewise, autobiography—fortunately—has not waited for philosophers to grant it the right to exist. However, it is perhaps not too late to ask ourselves some questions about the significance of such an undertaking and about the likelihood of its accomplishment in order to sort out the implicit presuppositions of autobiography.

First of all, it is necessary to point out that the genre of autobiography seems limited in time and in space: it has not always existed

"Conditions and Limits of Autobiography" translated by James Olney originally appeared as "Conditions et limites de l'autobiographie" by Georges Gusdorf in *Formen der Selbstdarstellung: Analekten zu einer Geschichte des literarischen Selbstportraits*, ed. Günther Reichenkron and Erich Haase. Copyright © 1956 by Georges Gusdorf. Reprinted by permission of the author and the publisher, Duncker & Humblot.

nor does it exist everywhere. If Augustine's *Confessions* offer us a brilliantly successful landmark right at the beginning, one neverthe-less recognizes immediately that this is a late phenomenon in West-ern culture, coming at that moment when the Christian contribu-tion was grafted onto classical traditions. Moreover, it would seem that autobiography is not to be found outside of our cultural area; one would say that it expresses a concern peculiar to Western man, a concern that has been of good use in his systematic conquest of the universe and that he has communicated to men of other cul-tures; but those men will thereby have been annexed by a sort of intellectual colonizing to a mentality that was not their own. When Gandhi tells his own story, he is using Western means to defend the East. And the moving testimonies collected by Westermann in his *Autobiographies d'Africains* convey the shock of traditional civiliza-tions on coming into contact with Europeans. The old world is in the process of dying in the very interior of that consciousness that questions itself about its destiny, converted willy-nilly to the new life style that whites have brought from beyond the seas.

The concern, which seems so natural to us, to turn back on one's own past, to recollect one's life in order to narrate it, is not at all universal. It asserts itself only in recent centuries and only on a small part of the map of the world. The man who takes delight in thus drawing his own image believes himself worthy of a special interest. Each of us tends to think of himself as the center of a living space: I count, my existence is significant to the world, and my death will leave the world incomplete. In narrating my life, I give witness of myself even from beyond my death and so can preserve this precious capital that ought not disappear. The author of an au-tobiography gives a sort of relief to his image by reference to the environment with its independent existence; he looks at himself being and delights in being looked at—he calls himself as witness for himself; others he calls as witness for what is irreplaceable in his presence.

This conscious awareness of the singularity of each individual life is the late product of a specific civilization. Throughout most of human history, the individual does not oppose himself to all others; he does not feel himself to exist outside of others, and still less against others, but very much *with* others in an interdependent ex-istence that asserts its rhythms everywhere in the community. No one is rightful possessor of his life or his death; lives are so thor-oughly entangled that each of them has its center everywhere and its circumference nowhere. The important unit is thus never the isolated being—or, rather, isolation is impossible in such a scheme of total cohesiveness as this. Community life unfolds like a great drama, with its climactic moments originally fixed by the gods being repeated from age to age. Each man thus appears as the possessor of a rôle, already performed by the ancestors and to be performed again by descendants. The number of rôles is limited, and this is expressed by a limited number of names. Newborn children receive the names of the deceased whose rôles, in a sense, they perform again, and so the community maintains a continuous self-identity in spite of the constant renewal of individuals who constitute it.

It is obvious that autobiography is not possible in a cultural landscape where consciousness of self does not, properly speaking, exist. But this unconsciousness of personality, characteristic of primitive societies such as ethnologists describe to us, lasts also in more advanced civilizations that subscribe to mythic structures, they too being governed by the principle of repetition. Theories of eternal recurrence, accepted in various guises as dogma by the majority of the great cultures of antiquity, fix attention on that which remains, not on that which passes. "That which is," according to the wisdom of Ecclesiastes, "is that which has been, and there is nothing new under the sun." Likewise, beliefs in the transmigration of souls—beliefs to be found throughout the Indo-European sphere—grant to the nodes of temporal existence only a sort of negative value. The wisdom of India considers personality an evil illusion and seeks salvation in depersonalization.

Autobiography becomes possible only under certain metaphysical preconditions. To begin with, at the cost of a cultural revolution humanity must have emerged from the mythic framework of traditional teachings and must have entered into the perilous domain of history. The man who takes the trouble to tell of himself knows that the present differs from the past and that it will not be repeated in the future; he has become more aware of differences than of similarities; given the constant change, given the uncertainty of events and of men, he believes it a useful and valuable thing to fix his own image so that he can be certain it will not disappear like all things in this world. History then would be the memory of a humanity heading toward unforeseeable goals, struggling against the breakdown of forms and of beings. Each man matters to the world, each life and each death; the witnessing of each about himself enriches the common cultural heritage.

The curiosity of the individual about himself, the wonder that he feels before the mystery of his own destiny, is thus tied to the Copernican Revolution: at the moment it enters into history, humanity, which previously aligned its development to the great cosmic cycles, finds itself engaged in an autonomous adventure; soon mankind even brings the domain of the sciences into line with its own reckoning, organizing them, by means of technical expertise, according to its own desires. Henceforth, man knows himself a responsible agent: gatherer of men, of lands, of power, maker of kingdoms or of empires, inventor of laws or of wisdom, he alone adds consciousness to nature, leaving there the sign of his presence. The historic personage now appears, and biography, taking its place alongside monuments, inscriptions, statues, is one manifestation of his desire to endure in men's memory. Famous men—heroes and princes—acquire a sort of literary and pedagogical immortality in those exemplary "Lives" written for the edification of future centuries.

But biography, which is thus established as a literary genre, provides only an exterior presentation of great persons, reviewed and corrected by the demands of propaganda and by the general sense of the age. The historian finds himself removed from his model by the passage of time—at least, this is most often true, and it is always true that he is at a great social distance from his model. He is conscious of performing a public and official function similar to that of the artist who sculpts or paints the likeness of a powerful man of the day, posed most flatteringly as determined by current conventions. The appearance of autobiography implies a new spiritual revolution: the artist and the model coincide, the historian tackles himself as object. That is to say, he considers himself a great person, worthy of men's remembrance even though in fact he is only a more or less obscure intellectual. Here a new social area that turns classes about and readjusts values comes into play. Montaigne had a certain prominence, but was descended from a family of merchants; Rousseau, no more than a common citizen of Geneva, was a kind of literary adventurer; yet both of them, in spite of their lowly station on the stage of the world, considered their destiny worthy of being given by way of example. Our interest is turned from public to private history: alongside the great men who act out the official history of humanity, there are obscure men who conduct the campaign of their spiritual life within their breast, carrying on silent battles whose ways and means, whose triumphs and reversals also merit being preserved in the universal memory.

This conversion is late in coming insofar as it corresponds to a difficult evolution—or rather to an *in*volution of consciousness. The truth is that one is wonderstruck by everything else much sooner than by the self. One wonders at what one sees, but one does not see oneself. If exterior space—the stage of the world—is a light, clear space where everyone's behavior, movements, and motives are quite plain on first sight, interior space is shadowy in its very essence. The subject who seizes on himself for object inverts the natural direction of attention; it appears that in acting thus he violates certain secret taboos of human nature. Sociology, depth psychology, psychoanalysis have revealed the complex and agonizing sense that the encounter of a man with his image carries. The image is another "myself," a double of my being but more fragile and vulnerable, invested with a sacred character that makes it at once fascinating and frightening. Narcissus, contemplating his face in the fountain's depth, is so fascinated with the apparition that he would die bending toward himself. According to most folklore and myth, the apparition of the double is a death sign.

Mythic taboos underline the disconcerting character of the discovery of the self. Nature did not foresee the encounter of man with his reflection, and it is as if she tried to prevent this reflection from appearing. The invention of the mirror would seem to have disrupted human experience, especially from that moment when the mediocre metal plates that were used in antiquity gave way at the end of the Middle Ages to silver-backed mirrors produced by Venetian technique. From that moment, the image in the mirror became a part of the scene of life, and psychoanalysts have brought out the major role that this image plays in the child's gradual consciousness of his own personality.[1] From the age of six months, the human infant is particularly interested in this reflection of himself, which would leave an animal indifferent. Little by little the infant discovers an essential aspect of his identity: he distinguishes that which is without from his own within, he sees himself as another among others; he is situated in social space, at the heart of which he will become capable of reshaping his own reality.

[1] Cf. in particular the research of Jacques Lacan: "Le stade du miroir comme formateur de la fonction du Je," *Revue française de psychanalyse* 4 (1949).

The primitive who has not been forewarned is frightened of his reflection in the mirror, just as he is terrified by a photographic or motion-picture image. The child of civilization, on the other hand, has had all the leisure necessary to make himself at home with the changing garments of appearances that he has clothed himself in under the alluring influence of the mirror. And yet even an adult, whether man or woman, if he reflects on it a little, rediscovers beyond this confrontation with himself the turmoil and fascination of Narcissus. The first sound image from the tape recorder, the animated image of the cinema, awaken the same anguish in the depths of our life. The author of an autobiography masters this anxiety by submitting to it; beyond all the images, he follows unceasingly the call of his own being. Thus with Rembrandt, who was fascinated by his Venetian mirror and as a result endlessly multiplied his self-portraits (like Van Gogh later)—witnessings by himself about himself and evidence of the impassioned new disquiet of modern man, fierce to elucidate the mystery of his own personality.

If it is indeed true that autobiography is the mirror in which the individual reflects his own image, one must nevertheless acknowledge that the genre appeared before the technical achievements of German and Italian artisans. At the edge of modern times, the physical and material appeal of the reflection in the mirror bolsters and strengthens the tradition of self-examination of Christian asceticism. Augustine's *Confessions* answer to this new spiritual orientation by contrast to the great philosophic systems of classical antiquity—Epicurean, for example, or Stoic—that contented themselves with a disciplinary notion of individual being and argued that one should seek salvation in adhering to a universal and transcendent law without any regard for the mysteries (which anyway were unsuspected) of interior life. Christianity brings a new anthropology to the fore: every destiny, however humble it be, assumes a kind of supernatural stake. Christian destiny unfolds as a dialogue of the soul with God in which, right up to the end, every action, every initiative of thought or of conduct, can call everything back into question. Each man is accountable for his own existence, and intentions weigh as heavily as acts—whence a new fascination with the secret springs of personal life. The rule requiring confession of sins gives to self-examination a character at once systematic and necessary. Augustine's great book is a consequence of this dogmatic requirement: a soul of genius presents his balance sheet before God in all humility—but also in full rhetorical splendor.

During the Christian centuries of the Western Middle Ages, the penitent, following in the footsteps of Augustine, could scarcely do anything but plead guilty before his Creator. The theological mirror of the Christian soul is a deforming mirror that plays up without pity the slightest faults of the moral personality. The most elementary rule of humility requires the faithful to discover traces of sin everywhere and to suspect beneath the more or less appealing exterior of the individual person the horrid decay of the flesh, the hideous rotting of Ligier Richier's *Skeleton*: every man is uncovered to reveal a potential participant in the *Dance of Death*. Here again, as with primitives, man cannot look on his own image without anguish. It was to require the exploding of the medieval Romania— the breakdown of its dogmatic frame under the combined thrust of the Renaissance and the Reformation—before man could have any interest in seeing himself as he is without any taint of the transcendent. The Venetian mirror provides the restless Rembrandt with an image of himself that is neither twisted nor flattering. Renascent man puts forth on the oceans in search of new continents and men of nature. Montaigne discovers in himself a new world, a man of nature, naked and artless, whose confessions he gives us in his *Essays*, but without penitence.

The *Essays* were to be one of the gospels of the modern spirituality. Freed of all doctrinal allegiance, in a world well on its way to becoming secularized, the autobiographer assumes the task of bringing out the most hidden aspects of individual being. The new age practises the virtue of *individuality* particularly dear to the great men of the Renaissance, champions of free enterprise in art as in morals, in finance and in technical affairs as in philosophy. The *Life* of Cellini, artist and adventurer, testifies to this new freedom of the individual who believes that all things are permitted to him. Beyond the rediscovered disciplines of the classical period, the Romantic era, in its exaltation of genius, reintroduced the taste for autobiography. The virtue of individuality is completed by the virtue of *sincerity*, which Rousseau adopts from Montaigne: the heroism of understanding and telling all, reenforced even more by the teachings of psychoanalysis, takes on, in the eyes of our contemporaries, an increasing value. Complexities, contradictions, and aberrations do not cause hesitation or repugnance but a kind of wonderment. And in a profoundly secular sense, Gide repeats the Psalmist's exclamation: "I praise thee, O my God, for making me a creature so marvellous."

Recourse to history and anthropology allows one to locate auto-biography in its cultural moment.[2] It remains to examine the undertaking itself, to clarify its intentions, and to judge of its chances for success.[3] The author of an autobiography gives himself the job of narrating his own history; what he sets out to do is to reassemble the scattered elements of his individual life and to regroup them in a comprehensive sketch. The historian of himself wishes to produce his own portrait, but while the painter captures only a moment of external appearance, the autobiographer strains toward a complete and coherent expression of his entire destiny. The catalogue of Bredius lists sixty-two portraits of Rembrandt accepted as authentic and painted by himself at all ages in his life. The constantly renewed attempt shows clearly that the painter is never satisfied: he acknowledges no single image as his definitive image. The total portrait of Rembrandt is to be found on the horizon of all these different visages of which it would be, in a sense, the common denominator. While a painting is a representation of the present, autobiography claims to retrace a period, a development in time, not by juxtaposing instantaneous images but by composing a kind of film according to a preestablished scenario. The author of a private journal, noting his impressions and mental states from day to day, fixes the portrait of his daily reality without any concern for continuity. Autobiography, on the other hand, requires a man to take a distance with regard to himself in order to reconstitute himself in the focus of his special unity and identity across time.

At first sight there is nothing startling in this. If one accepts that each man has a history and that it is possible to narrate this history, it is inevitable that the narrator should eventually take himself as narrative object from the moment that he entertains the notion that his destiny holds a sufficient interest for himself and everyone else. The witness of each person about himself is in addition a privileged one: since he writes of someone who is at a distance or dead, the biographer remains uncertain of his hero's intentions; he must be content to decipher signs, and his work is in certain ways always related to the detective story. On the other hand, no one can know better than I what I have thought, what I have wished; I alone have the privilege of discovering myself from the other side of the mirror—nor can I be cut off by the wall of privacy. Others, no mat-

[2] For more details one might refer to the work, unfortunately not finished, of Georg Misch: *Geschichte der Autobiographie*, tome 1 (Teubner, 1907).

[3] See also André Maurois, *Aspects de la biographie* (Paris, 1928).

ter how well intentioned, are forever going wrong; they describe the external figure, the appearance they see and not the true person, which always escapes them. No one can better do justice to himself than the interested party, and it is precisely in order to do away with misunderstandings, to restore an incomplete or deformed truth, that the autobiographer himself takes up the telling of his story.

A great many autobiographies—no doubt the majority—are based on these elementary motives: as soon as they have the leisure of retirement or exile, the minister of state, the politician, the military leader write in order to celebrate their deeds (always more or less misunderstood), providing a sort of posthumous propaganda for posterity that otherwise is in danger of forgetting them or of failing to esteem them properly. *Memoirs* admirably celebrate the penetrating insight and skill of famous men who, appearances to the contrary notwithstanding, were never wrong: Cardinal de Retz, leader of a hapless faction, unfailingly wins back after the event all the battles he had lost; Napoleon on Sainte Hélène, through his intermediary las Cases, gets even with the injustice of events, hostile to his genius. One is never better served than by oneself.

The autobiography that is thus devoted exclusively to the defence and glorification of a man, a career, a political cause, or a skillful strategy presents no problems: it is limited almost entirely to the public sector of existence. It provides an interesting and interested testimony that the historian must gather together and criticize along with other testimonies. It is official facts that carry weight here, and intentions are judged by their performance. One should not take the narrator's word for it, but should consider his version of the facts as one contribution to his own biography. Private motives, the obverse of history, balance and complete their opposite, the objective course of events. But for public men it is the exterior aspect that dominates: they tell their stories from the perspective of their time, so that their methodological problems are no different from those of the ordinary writing of history. The historian is well aware that memoirs are always, to a certain degree, a revenge on history. Reading Cardinal de Retz's memoirs one cannot understand at all how it was that he made such a magnificent mess of his career; a clear minded biography would not be overawed by this victim who puffs himself up as a victor but would reestablish the facts, making use of elementary psychology and necessary cross-checking.

The question changes utterly when the private face of existence assumes more importance. In writing his *Apologia pro vita sua*, Newman attempts to justify in the eyes of contemporary opinion his movement from Anglicanism to Roman Catholicism. But with their temporal reference, social and theological occurrences have relatively little significance. The dispute takes place for the most part in the interior domain: here, as in Augustine's *Confessions*, it is the history of a soul that is told to us. External and objective criticism might well pick out an error in detail here and there or a bit of cheating, but it does not reach to the heart of the matter. Rousseau, Goethe, Mill are not content to offer the reader a sort of *curriculum vitae* retracing the steps of an official career that, for importance, was hardly more than mediocre. In this case it is a question of another truth. The act of memory is carried out for itself, and recalling of the past satisfies a more or less anguished disquiet of the mind anxious to recover and redeem lost time in fixing it forever. The title of Jean Paul's autobiographical writing, *Wahrheit aus meinem Leben*, expresses well the fact that the truth in question shows forth from within the private life. Moreover, memories of childhood and youth are very numerous, including among them many masterpieces, for example, Renan's *Souvenirs d'enfance et de jeunesse* or Gide's *Si le grain ne meurt*. Now an infant is not yet an historical figure; the significance of his small existence remains strictly private. The writer who recalls his earliest years is thus exploring an enchanted realm that belongs to him alone.

Furthermore, autobiography properly speaking assumes the task of reconstructing the unity of a life across time. This lived unity of attitude and act is not received from the outside; certainly events influence us; they sometimes determine us, and they always limit us. But the essential themes, the structural designs that impose themselves on the complex material of exterior facts are the constituent elements of the personality. Today's comprehensive psychology has taught us that man, far from being subject to ready-made, completed situations given from outside and without him, is the essential agent in bringing about the situations in which he finds himself placed. It is his intervention that structures the terrain where his life is lived and gives it its ultimate shape, so that the landscape is truly, in Amiel's phrase, "a state of the soul."

From this the specific intention of autobiography and its anthropological prerogative as a literary genre is clear: it is one of the
means to self knowledge thanks to the fact that it recomposes and
interprets a life in its totality. An examination of consciousness limited to the present moment will give me only a fragmentary cutting
from my personal being without guarantee that it will continue. In
recounting my history I take the longest path, but this path that
goes round my life leads me the more surely from me to myself.
The recapitulation of ages of existence, of landscapes and encounters, obliges me to situate what I am in the perspective of what I
have been. My individual unity, the mysterious essence of my
being—this is the law of gathering in and of understanding in all the
acts that have been mine, all the faces and all the places where I have
recognized signs and witness of my destiny. In other words, autobiography is a second reading of experience, and it is truer than the
first because it adds to experience itself consciousness of it. In the
immediate moment, the agitation of things ordinarily surrounds
me too much for me to be able to see it in its entirety. Memory
gives me a certain remove and allows me to take into consideration
all the ins and outs of the matter, its context in time and space. As
an aerial view sometimes reveals to an archeologist the direction of
a road or a fortification or the map of a city invisible to someone on
the ground, so the reconstruction in spirit of my destiny bares the
major lines that I have failed to notice, the demands of the deepest
values I hold that, without my being clearly aware of it, have determined my most decisive choices.

Autobiography is not simple repetition of the past as it was, for
recollection brings us not the past itself but only the presence in
spirit of a world forever gone. Recapitulation of a life lived claims
to be valuable for the one who lived it, and yet it reveals no more
than a ghostly image of that life, already far distant, and doubtless
incomplete, distorted furthermore by the fact that the man who
remembers his past has not been for a long time the same being, the
child or adolescent, who lived that past. The passage from immediate experience to consciousness in memory, which effects a
sort of repetition of that experience, also serves to modify its significance. A new mode of being appears if it is true, as Hegel
claimed, that "consciousness of self is the birthplace of truth." The
past that is recalled has lost its flesh and bone solidity, but it has
won a new and more intimate relationship to the individual life that
can thus, after being long dispersed and sought again throughout

the course of time, be rediscovered and drawn together again beyond time.

Such is doubtless the most secret purpose in every exercise in Memories, Memoirs, or Confessions. The man who recounts himself is himself searching his self through his history; he is not engaged in an objective and disinterested pursuit but in a work of personal justification. Autobiography appeases the more or less anguished uneasiness of an aging man who wonders if his life has not been lived in vain, frittered away haphazardly, ending now in simple failure. In order to be reassured, he undertakes his own apologia, as Newman expressly says. Perhaps Cardinal de Retz is ridiculous with his claim to political insight and to infallibility, since he lost every game he played; but it may be that every life, even in spite of the most brilliant successes, knows itself inwardly botched. So autobiography is the final chance to win back what has been lost—and we must acknowledge that Retz, as after him Chateaubriand, knew how to play this game masterfully, in such a way that he seemed to the eyes of future generations a conqueror much more than would have been the case had the obscure intrigues he enjoyed pursuing turned out well for his faction. Retz, the writer and memorialist, compensated for the failure of Retz, the conspirator; the task of autobiography is first of all a task of personal salvation. Confession, an attempt at remembering, is at the same time searching for a hidden treasure, for a last delivering word, redeeming in the final appeal a destiny that doubted its own value. For the one who takes up the venture it is a matter of concluding a peace treaty and a new alliance with himself and with the world. The mature man or the man already old who projects his life into narrative would thus provide witness that he has not existed in vain; he chooses not revolution but reconciliation, and he brings it about in the very act of reassembling the scattered elements of a destiny that seems to him to have been worth the trouble of living. The literary work in which he offers himself as example is the means of perfecting this destiny and of bringing it to a successful conclusion.

There is, then, a considerable gap between the avowed plan of autobiography, which is simply to retrace the history of a life, and its deepest intentions, which are directed toward a kind of apologetics or theodicy of the individual being. This gap explains the puzzlement and the ambivalence of the literary genre. The man who sets about writing his memoirs imagines, in all good faith, that he is writing as an historian and that any difficulties he may discover can be overcome through exercise of critical objectivity and impartiality. The portrait will be exact, and the sequence of events will be brought out precisely as it was. No doubt it will be necessary to struggle against failures of memory and temptations to fudge the truth, but a sufficiently strict moral alertness and a basic good faith will make it possible to reestablish the factual truth as Rousseau claimed in some celebrated pages at the beginning of his *Confessions*. Most authors who recount themselves ask no other questions: the psychological problem of memory, the moral problem of the impartiality of the self to itself—these are not insurmountable difficulties. Autobiography appears as the mirror image of a life, its double more clearly drawn—in a sense the diagram of a destiny.

Now, one is aware of the recent revolution in historical methodology. The idol of an objective and critical history worshipped by the positivists of the nineteenth century has crumbled; hope for an "integral resurrection of the past" nourished by Michelet has come to seem meaningless; the past is the past, it cannot return to dwell in the present except at the cost of complete falsification. The recall of history assumes a very complex relation of past to present, a reactualization that prevents us from ever discovering the past "in itself," as it was—the past without us. The historian of himself finds that he is caught up in the same difficulties: returning to visit his own past, he takes the unity and identity of his being for granted, and he imagines himself able to merge what he was with what he has become. The child, the young man, and the mature man of yesterday are gone and cannot protest; only the man of today can speak, which allows him to deny that there is any division or split and to take for granted the very thing that is in question.

It is obvious that the narrative of a life cannot be simply the image-double of that life. Lived existence unfolds from day to day in the present and according to the demands of the moment, which the individual copes with the best he can using all the resources at his disposal. Life is a dubious battle in which conscious schemes and projects mingle with unconscious drives and with the desire to give up and to strive no more. Every destiny opens its way through the undetermined variables of men, circumstances, and itself. This constant tension, this charge of the unknown, which corresponds to the very arrow of lived time, cannot exist in a narrative of memories composed after the event by someone who knows the end of the story. In *War and Peace*, Tolstoy has shown the immense difference there is between a real battle lived from minute to minute by the agonized participants largely unaware of what is happening even if they enjoy the security of being staff officers and the narrative of the same battle put in fine logical and rational order by the historian who knows all the turning points and the outcome of the conflict. The same time gap exists between a life and its biography: "I don't know," Valéry wrote, "if anyone has ever tried to write a biography and attempted at each instant of it to know as little of the following moment as the hero of the work knew himself at the corresponding instant of his career. This would be to restore chance in each instant, rather than putting together a series that admits of a neat summary and a causality that can be described in a formula."[4]

Thus the original sin of autobiography is first one of logical coherence and rationalization. The narrative is conscious, and since the narrator's consciousness directs the narrative, it seems to him incontestable that it has also directed his life. In other words, the act of reflecting that is essential to conscious awareness is transferred, by a kind of unavoidable optical illusion, back to the stage of the event itself. At the beginning of a recollection of his childhood, the novelist François Mauriac protests against the notion "that an author retouches his memories with the deliberate intention of deceiving us. In truth, he is yielding to necessity: he must render stationary and fixed this past life which was moving. . . . It is against his own will that he carves out of his teeming past these figures that are as arbitrary as the constellations with which we have peopled the night."[5] In short, a kind of Bergsonian critique of autobiography is necessary: Bergson criticizes classical theories of volition and free will for reconstructing a mode of conduct after the fact and then imagining that at the decisive moments there existed a clear choice among various possibilities, whereas in fact actual freedom proceeds on its own impetus and there is ordinarily no choice at all. Likewise, autobiography is condemned to substitute endlessly the completely formed for that which is in the process of being formed. With its burden of insecurity, the lived present finds itself caught in that necessary movement that, along the thread of the narrative, binds the past to the future.

[4] Paul Valéry, *Tel Quel II* (Paris, 1943), p. 349. Cf. this remark of the same author: "The person who confesses is lying and fleeing the real truth, which is nothing, or unformed, and in general blurred."

[5] François Mauriac, *Commencements d'une vie* (Paris, 1932), Introduction, p. xi.

The difficulty is insurmountable: no trick of presentation even when assisted by genius can prevent the narrator from always knowing the outcome of the story he tells—he commences, in a manner of speaking, with the problem already solved. Moreover, the illusion begins from the moment that the narrative *confers a meaning* on the event which, when it actually occurred, no doubt had several meanings or perhaps none. This postulating of a meaning dictates the choice of the facts to be retained and of the details to bring out or to dismiss according to the demands of the preconceived intelligibility. It is here that the failures, the gaps, and the deformations of memory find their origin; they are not due to purely physical cause nor to chance, but on the contrary they are the result of an option of the writer who remembers and wants to gain acceptance for this or that revised and corrected version of his past, his private reality. Renan expressed it very well: "Goethe," he remarks, "chooses, as title of his Memoirs, *Truth and Poetry*, thereby showing that one cannot compose his own biography in the same way one would do a biography of others. What one says of oneself is always poetry. . . . One writes of such things in order to transmit to others the world view that one carries in oneself."[6]

One must choose a side and give up the pretence of objectivity, abandoning a sort of false scientific attitude that would judge a work by the precision of its detail. There are painters of historical scenes whose entire ambition in painting a battlefield is to represent in the most minute detail the uniforms and the weapons or to render an exact topographical map. The result is as false as it could well be, while Velásquez's *Rendición de Breda* or Goya's *Dos de Mayo*, even though they swarm with inaccuracies, remain wonderful masterpieces nonetheless. An autobiography cannot be a pure and simple record of existence, an account book or a logbook: on such and such a day at such and such an hour, I went to such and such a place . . . A record of this kind, no matter how minutely exact, would be no more than a caricature of real life; in such a case, rigorous precision would add up to the same thing as the subtlest deception.

One of Lamartine's finest autobiographical poems, *La vigne et la maison*, evokes the house in Milly in which the poet was born, the facade of which is decorated with a garland of woodbine. An historian has discovered that there was no vine growing against the

[6] Ernest Renan, *Souvenirs d'enfance et de jeunesse* (Paris, n.d.), Preface, pp. ii-iii.

house in Milly during the poet's childhood; only much later, after the poem was written and in order to reconcile poetry and truth, did Madame de Lamartine have a climbing vine planted. The anecdote is symbolic: in autobiography the truth of facts is subordinate to the truth of the man, for it is first of all the man who is in question. The narrative offers us the testimony of a man about himself, the contest of a being in dialogue with itself, seeking its innermost fidelity.

Any autobiography is a moment of the life that it recounts; it struggles to draw the meaning from that life, but it is itself a meaning in the life. One part of the whole claims to reflect the whole, but it adds something to this whole of which it constitutes a moment. Some Flemish or Dutch painters of interior scenes depict a little mirror on the wall in which the painting is repeated a second time; the image in the mirror does not only duplicate the scene but adds to it as a new dimension a distancing perspective. Likewise, autobiography is not a simple recapitulation of the past; it is also the attempt and the drama of a man struggling to reassemble himself in his own likeness at a certain moment of his history. This delivering up of earlier being brings a new stake into the game.

The significance of autobiography should therefore be sought beyond truth and falsity, as those are conceived by simple common sense. It is unquestionably a document about a life, and the historian has a perfect right to check out its testimony and verify its accuracy. But it is also a work of art, and the literary devotee, for his part, will be aware of its stylistic harmony and the beauty of its images. It is therefore of little consequence that the *Mémoires d'outre-tombe* should be full of errors, omissions, and lies, and of little consequence also that Chateaubriand made up most of his *Voyage en Amérique*: the recollection of landscapes that he never saw and the description of the traveller's moods nevertheless remain excellent. We may call it fiction or fraud, but its artistic value is real: there is a truth affirmed beyond the fraudulent itinerary and chronology, a truth of the man, images of himself and of the world, reveries of a man of genius, who, for his own enchantment and that of his readers, realizes himself in the unreal.

The literary, artistic function is thus of greater importance than the historic and objective function in spite of the claims made by positivist criticism both previously and today. But the literary function itself, if one would really understand the essence of autobiography, appears yet secondary in comparison with the anthropological significance. Every work of art is a projection from the interior realm into exterior space where in becoming incarnated it achieves consciousness of itself. Consequently, there is need of a second critique that instead of verifying the literal accuracy of the narrative or demonstrating its artistic value would attempt to draw out its innermost, private significance by viewing it as the symbol, as it were, or the parable of a consciousness in quest of its own truth.

The man who in recalling his life sets out to discover himself does not surrender to a passive contemplation of his private being. The truth is not a hidden treasure, already there, that one can bring out by simply reproducing it as it is. Confession of the past realizes itself as a work in the present: it effects a true creation of self by the self. Under guise of presenting myself as I was, I exercise a sort of right to recover possession of my existence now and later. "To create and in creating to be created," the fine formula of Lequier, ought to be the motto of autobiography. It cannot recall the past in the past and for the past—a vain and fruitless endeavor—for no one can revive the dead; it calls up the past for the present and in the present, and it brings back from earlier times that which preserves a meaning and value today; it asserts a kind of tradition between myself and me that establishes an ancient and new fidelity, for the past drawn up into the present is also a pledge and a prophecy of the future. Temporal perspectives thus seem to be telescoped together and to interpenetrate one another; they commune in that self-knowledge that regroups personal being above and beyond its own time limits. Confession takes on the character of an avowal of values and a recognition of self by the self—a choice carried out at the level of essential being—not a revelation of a reality given in advance but a corollary of an active intelligence.

The creative and illuminating nature thus discerned in autobiography suggests a new and more profound sense of truth as an expression of inmost being, a likeness no longer of things but of the person. Now this truth, which is too often neglected, nevertheless constitutes one of the necessary references for understanding the human realm. We understand everything outside of us as well as ourselves with reference to what we are and according to our spiritual capacities. This is what Dilthey, one of the founders of modern historiography, meant when he said that universal history is an extrapolation from autobiography. The objective space of history is always a projection of the mental space of the historian. The poet Novalis had a presentiment of this well before Dilthey: "The historian," he says, "constructs historic beings. The facts of history provide the matter which the historian molds in giving it life. Thus history too yields to the general principles of creation and organization, and apart from these principles there is no true historical construction—nothing but scattered traces of chance creations in which an aimless genius has been at work."[7] And Nietzsche, for his part, affirmed the necessity of feeling "as his *own* history the history of all humanity" (*The Gay Science*, section 337).

We must, therefore, introduce a kind of reversal of perspective and give up thinking about autobiography in the same way as we do an objective biography, regulated only by the requirements of the genre of history. Every autobiography is a work of art and at the same time a work of enlightenment; it does not show us the individual seen from outside in his visible actions but the person in his inner privacy, not as he was, not as he is, but as he believes and wishes himself to be and to have been. What is in question is a sort of revaluation of individual destiny; the author, who is at the same time the hero of the tale, wants to elucidate his past in order to draw out the structure of his being in time. And this secret structure is for him the implicit condition of all possible knowledge in every order whatsoever—hence the central place of autobiography, especially in the literary sphere.

Experience is the prime matter of all creation, which is an elaboration of elements borrowed from lived reality. One can exercise imagination only by starting from what one is, from what one has tried either in fact or in wish. Autobiography displays this privileged content with a minimum of alterations; more precisely, it ordinarily fancies that it is restoring this content as it was, but in giving his own narrative, the man is forever adding himself to himself. So creation of a literary world begins with the author's confession: the narrative that he makes of his life is already a first work of art, the first deciphering of an affirmation that, at a further stage of stripping down and recomposing, will open out in novels, in tragedies, or in poems. The novelist François Mauriac is doing no more than repeating an intuition well-known to many writers

---

[7] *Blütenstaub*, section 92. In *Novalis Werke*, ed. Gerhard Schulz (München, 1969), p. 345.

when he says: "I think that every great work of fiction is simply an interior life in novel form."[8] Every novel is an autobiography by intermediary—a truth that Nietzsche extended even beyond the limits of what would properly be called literature: "Little by little it has become clear to me that every great philosophy has been the confession of its maker, as it were his involuntary and unconscious autobiography."[9]

We might say then that there are two guises or two versions of autobiography: on the one hand, that which is properly called confession; on the other hand, the artist's entire work, which takes up the same material in complete freedom and under the protection of a hidden identity. After Sophie's death, Novalis kept a private diary for some time in which he recorded his moods from day to day and in a bald style; and at the same period there was coming to birth within him the *Hymnes à la nuit*, one of the masterpieces of Romantic poetry. Neither the poet nor his fiancée is named in the *Hymnes*; nevertheless it is certain that the *Hymnes* have the same autobiographical content as the *Journal*—they represent a chronicle of the experience of Sophie's death. Likewise, Goethe took the trouble to write his memoirs; but his work throughout, from *Werther* right up to *Faust* Part II and the *Marienbad Elegies*, unfolds as one massive confession. "There is not, in the *Affinities*," he confided to Eckermann, "a single episode that was not lived, although no episode is presented just as it occurred."

But it is pointless to multiply examples. Critics have decided to range writers' works in chronological order and to search in each of them for an expression of a real situation, thus acknowledging the autobiographical character of all literary creation. To understand *A la recherche du temps perdu*, it is necessary to recognize Proust's autobiography in it; *Green Henry* is Gottfried Keller's autobiography, just as *Jean-Christophe* is Romain Rolland's. The autobiographical key allows for a correlation of the life with the work. This correlation is not, however, as simple as that, for example, between a text and its translation. Here our earlier observations again assume their full importance.

[8] Mauriac, *Journal II* (Paris, 1937), p. 138. Cf. Maurois, *Tourguéniev* (Paris, 1931), p. 196: "Artistic creation is not a creation *ex nihilo*. It is a regrouping of the elements of reality. One could easily show that the strangest narratives, those which seem furthest from real observation, such as *Gulliver's Travels*, the *Tales* of Edgar A. Poe, Dante's *Divine Comedy* or Jarry's *Ubu Roi*, are made from memories."

[9] Friedrich Nietzsche, *Beyond Good and Evil*, section 6.

With the literary artist it is not really possible to detect in the life itself a kind of truth that exists before the work and comes to be reflected in it—directly in autobiography, more or less indirectly in novel or poem. The two simply are not independent: "The great events of my life are my works," Balzac said. Autobiography is also a work or an event of the life, and yet it turns back on the life and affects it by a kind of boomerang. Psychoanalysis and other depth psychologies have made us familiar with the idea already implicitly contained in the practice of the sacrament of confession that in becoming conscious of the past one alters the present. As Sainte-Beuve remarked in the case of the writer, "Writing is liberation." After self-examination a man is no longer the man he was before. Autobiography is therefore never the finished image or the fixing forever of an individual life: the human being is always a making, a doing; memoirs look to an essence beyond existence, and in manifesting it they serve to create it. In the dialogue with himself, the writer does not seek to say a final word that would complete his life; he strives only to embrace more closely the always secret but never refused sense of his own destiny.

Here again, every work is autobiographical insofar as being registered in the life it alters the life to come. Better still, it is the peculiar nature of the literary calling that the work, even before it has been realized, can have an effect on being. The autobiography is lived, played, before being written; it fixes a kind of retrospective mark on the event even as it occurs. One critic has observed that reading the correspondence of Mérimée gives the impression that his way of living the episodes he describes is already affected by the account that he will give of them to his friends. Likewise, Thibaudet defends Chateaubriand against those who accuse him of having falsified his Memoirs: "His way of arranging his life after the event is consubstantial with his art. It is not deformation but formation from within. We cannot separate his falsehoods from his style." We can only "see his personality and his life as a function of his work and also its consequence—as, at one and the same time, the cause and the effect of his style."[10]

Style should be understood here not only as a principle of writing but as a line of life, a "life style." The truth of the life is not different in kind from the truth of the work: the great artist, the great writer lives, in a sense, for his autobiography. This could easily be dem-

---

[10] Albert Thibaudet, *Réflexions sur la critique* (Paris, 1939), pp. 27, 29.

onstrated in the case of Goethe or of Baudelaire, of Gauguin, of Beethoven, of Byron, of Shelley, and of many others among the greatest artists. There is a romantic life style as there is a classical, a baroque, an existentialist, or a decadent life style. The life, the work, the autobiography appear thus like three aspects of a single affirmation, united by a system of constant intercourse. A single acquiescence justifies the venture of action or the venture of writing, so that it would be possible to discern a symbolic correlation between them and to bring out the gravitational centers, the inflectional points of a destiny. In this correlation, theoreticians of *Formgeschichte* [Form History][11] have found the starting point for a method of literary and artistic interpretation that is specially concerned to lay bare those essential themes that will render the man and the work intelligible. Chronological order, which is altogether external, thus seems illusory; literary history makes room for what Bertram, in Nietzsche's case, calls a personal "mythology" organized around leitmotifs of the total, integral experience: the knight, Death and the Devil, Socrates, Portofino, Eleusis—those overwhelming ideas that Bertram finds leaving their deep impress on Nietzsche's work as on his life.

In the final analysis, then, the prerogative of autobiography consists in this: that it shows us not the objective stages of a career—to discern these is the task of the historian—but that it reveals instead the effort of a creator to give the meaning of his own mythic tale. Every man is the first witness of himself; yet the testimony that he thus produces constitutes no ultimate, conclusive authority—not only because objective scrutiny will always discover inaccuracies but much more because there is never an end to this dialogue of a life with itself in search of its own absolute. Here every man is for himself the existential stakes in a gamble that cannot be entirely lost nor entirely won. Artistic creation is a struggle with the angel, in which the creator is the more certain of being vanquished since the opponent is still himself. He wrestles with his shadow, certain only of never laying hold of it.

[11] Cf. Paul Böckmann, *Formgeschichte der Deutschen Dichtung* (1949) for the literary application of *Formgeschichte* (trans. note).

Full of Life Now

Barrett J. Mandel

> The forms are many in which the unchanging
> seeks relief from its formlessness.
> —Samuel Beckett, *Malone Dies*

There are many myths and misconceptions about autobiography. I would like to look at two of them. First, there is the misconception that autobiography, even if it is not life *per se*, represents recollections or memories of the past. Second, one often hears that autobiography is essentially fictional.

Strictly speaking, autobiography is not a recollection of one's life. Of course, everyone has recollections and memories. Memories are common phenomena—familiar, comfortable, inevitable. They are also spontaneous and natural. An autobiography, on the other hand, is an artifact, a construct wrought from words. Memories do not make an autobiography; they constitute what William Earle, in his exceedingly illuminating book of the same title, calls "the autobiographical consciousness."[1] Simply put, the autobiographical consciousness is that consciousness which thinks about itself—its present, past, and future.

In putting itself before the mind as its "object" of attention, consciousness most often aspires to obscure the truth of one's actual being. (By "being" I refer not to the evanescent ego or everyday consciousness but to the true subject underpinning the "I" of the ego—the entity known to Sartre as the "unreflected consciousness," to Spiegelberg as the "pure ego," to Bergson as "*élan vital*,"

[1] *The Autobiographical Consciousness: A Philosophical Inquiry into Existence* (Chicago, 1972).

to Heidegger as *Entwurff*, and to Francis Hart as the "restricted I . . . with reference to an implicit totality.")[2] It is everyday consciousness that "naturally" separates inner from outer reality, thus falsifying existence. Consciousness, and not the true self, flashes pictures before the eye, pictures we take to be the real me—my true story. It is customary to believe that we see the truth about ourselves in the mirror of our thoughts. Drawing from the existential insights of Heidegger, Marcel, Husserl, and Merleau-Ponty, Earle points out that *myself* and its story are products of the mind. Since the mind is the only part of us that is conscious and conscious of itself, we mistakenly assume that this consciousness is conterminous with who we are. Actually the conscious mind is rooted in the unseen (but not unseeing) being—the *source* of consciousness. Autobiographies, like all works of art, emanate ultimately from the deeper reality of being.

For Earle consciousness is the "great liar": it lies as much to itself as to others. "If consciousness were not a liar, it would have no problems, particularly that of self-lucidity." Earle goes on to show that the consciousness can lie only because, in fact, it knows the truth. "It could not lie to itself, since it would not be aware of what it had to lie about."[3] Thus, it is one thing to hold memories in consciousness and another thing to write—that is, to compose the truth of one's life in words. This composing process inevitably draws its truth—through tone, style, mannerisms, and insights—from one's being.

Experience proves that writing from the pictures in one's mind is valueless. It is similar to trying to recall an image of the Parthenon so precise that it allows one to count the number of columns it contains. The so-called picture is there, but the columns cannot be counted. If one is to write about the Parthenon convincingly, its picture must be bypassed. Indeed, in a crucial sense such a picture is not the beginning or source of writing, but a false start or dead end. A writer relying on memory pictures usually winds up crumpling

---

[2] These authors treat the subject of "being" in many places and at length. See for example Martin Heidegger, *Being and Time*, trans. John Macquarrie and Edward Robinson (New York, 1962); Henri Bergson, *L' Evolution créatrice* (Paris, 1939); Francis R. Hart, "Notes for an Anatomy of Modern Autobiography," *New Literary History* 1 (1970); Herbert Spiegelberg, "Husserl's Phenomenology and Existentialism," *The Journal of Philosophy* 57 (1960): 62-74; Jean-Paul Sartre, *The Transcendence of the Ego* (New York, 1957), pp. 35-54.

[3] Earle, *The Autobiographical Consciousness*, p. 40.

pages and suffering frustration.[4] On the other hand, if the picture is transcended so that a true experience of being can fuel the writing, the real essay will rise from a source of subjectivity unknown to the questing ego with its interminable carrying on, its pictures, and the like. In this respect, I can "remember" whatever I like about my life and then find as I write my autobiography that the truth which ultimately discloses itself has little to do with these initial memories.

"Pictures from the past"—memories—usually occur in one's thoughts unbidden. I am going about my business when something happens and I "get" a memory. Whenever a certain tune plays on the radio, it triggers a memory of the high-school prom. Or I may not notice that I am noticing a button on someone's coat because what I do notice I am noticing is that I am remembering my grandmother pressing me, as a child, to her bosom, pinching my skin with her button. This always happens when I don't notice that I am noticing that kind of button. Or, my eye glances up at my index cards and my mind glides to a weekly card game played by the grownups in the early forties. Something happens *now* and a memory is triggered. What happens now is unpredictable, while the memory is hinged to the mysterious, fleeting present more than to the past. The picture never develops to a new stage, it does not elaborate itself, does not clarify through successive reappearances, ends abruptly as time goes on, leads nowhere. The truth is not in these pictures, but *behind* them. The pictures—part of a survival mechanism—are there to *prevent* self-discovery.

Richard Wright (*Black Boy*) provides a striking example of how memories of the past are nothing but themselves—not useful as insights into past experiences. For a quarter of a century after the occasion on which he had seen his father leave his mother and go off with another woman, Wright's mind was afflicted by a useless, painful recollection. "Many times in the years after that, the image of my father and the strange woman, their faces lit by the dancing flames, would surge up in my imagination so vivid and strong that I felt I could reach out and touch it; I would stare at it, feeling that it possessed some vital meaning which always eluded me." For twenty-five years (during which time he did not write an autobiography), he was plagued intermittently by this memory or picture in the mind, and he mistakenly assumed that it possessed a meaning

---

[4] For a more extensive discussion of this point of view, see Barrett Mandel, "Losing One's Mind: Learning to Write and Edit," *College Composition and Communication* 29 (1978): 362-368.

that he was obliged to figure out. Actually it meant nothing but itself.

What we have here is a recurring picture that came to mind whenever something in the physical reality of Wright's life triggered the memory of his father and the woman. Wright never solved the mystery. In fact, his sense that there was a mystery to be solved was part of and literally linked to the recurring picture: each time the image reappeared, the notion of the mystery arose and departed intact, unsolved. Both merely evaporated, dissolved once and for all when, twenty-five years later, Wright visited his much aged father. Later still, Wright created his brilliant autobiography, letting the meaning of the years apart from his father rise from the experience lying *beneath* his familiar memories: "We were forever strangers, speaking a different language, living on vastly distant planes of reality."[5] Everyone has pictures about his or her life; some people abandon them sufficiently so that they can write middling autobiographies; others—far fewer—trust themselves to let the truth of their experience illuminate the deeper relevance of these pictures in the context of their total existence. It is the *context* disclosed through writing that is the autobiography.

Moving to my second point, it is my contention that autobiography is not fiction—it is not in principle doomed to a limbo where the autobiographer, because he or she cannot put life or even memories onto the page, must resort to writing fiction. This is the notion currently held by most critics who have struggled with the problem. In *Anatomy of Criticism*, Northrop Frye states that autobiographies are inspired by an impulse undifferentiated from the impulse that produces fiction. "We may call this very important form of prose fiction the confession form."[6] Patricia Meyer Spacks articulates the same position in her article, "The Soul's Imaginings: Daniel Defoe, William Cowper." In speaking about Cowper's *Memoir* (and by clear implication about any autobiography), Spacks writes:

> Selecting, repressing, interpreting his experience, according himself importance as a unique personality, he exercises his fantasy by making himself into something very like a fictional character. . . . Reading his work may provide the same imagi-

[5] *Black Boy* (New York, 1966), p. 42.
[6] *Anatomy of Criticism* (Princeton, 1957), p. 307.

native complexities as experiencing a novel; the presumed difference in authorial intent between fiction and factual records
makes little necessary difference in effect, though it poses
knotty philosophic and literary questions.[7]

Of course it is true that autobiographers use techniques of fiction, but such usage does not turn an autobiography into a fiction
any more than Dvořák's use of folk motifs turns the *New World
Symphony* into a folk song. At every moment of any true autobiography (I do not speak here of autobiographical novels) the author's
intention is to convey the sense that "this happened to me," and it
is this intention that is always carried through in a way which, I
believe, makes the result different from fiction. Despite the autobiographer's use of fiction techniques, the intention itself always
speaks through very clearly. Moreover, critics always overlook the
converse view that a novelist may use devices of autobiography:
first person narration, use of protagonist/narrator, facts drawn
from history, local color. Still, the intention in most novels is perfectly clear: the novelist's use of autobiographical devices serves an
end that is purely fictional. No one takes *Robinson Crusoe* for autobiography; no one takes Robin Maugham's *Escape from the Shadows*
for fiction. A reader who at first mistakes fiction for autobiography
or vice versa feels cheated. One wants to know whether the book is
one or the other: it makes a difference in terms of how the book is
to be read.

All genres readily borrow from other genres and modes: *Sons and
Lovers* borrows techniques from autobiography, but no one denies
that it is ultimately fiction; H. G. Wells' *Experiment in Autobiography*, because it borrows devices from fiction, is viewed as a kind
of fiction. But here is the point we are overlooking. Certainly autobiographies and fiction are to some degree similar. After all, as
James Joyce knew so well, any human verbalizing is a process that
by its very nature fictionalizes experience. (Beckett's Moran says,
"It seemed to me that all language was an excess of language.") But
we can accept Joyce's pronouncements on language and still distinguish between the kind of basic human fictionalizing that we label
"fiction" and the kind that we label "fact." Regardless of the
rootedness of both novels and autobiographies in a process that
binds them together, the very simple point that critics have been

[7] *PMLA* 91 (1976): 425.

missing in their zeal to deal with the "knotty philosophic and literary questions" is that autobiographies and novels are finally totally distinct—and this simple fact *every reader knows*.

It is academic sleight of hand to say that books which stand perfectly well on their own as paragons of style and form are not what they appear to be. Holding autobiography up to the standard of fiction does an inevitable disservice to the former. According to Spacks, "The level of dependability involved in the provision of evidence differs in autobiographer and novelist, and not to the advantage of the recorder of fact. The novelist's knowledge of his character necessarily sets the standard of completeness" (426). But is it not true that "completeness" rests not in the work of literature but in the reader? A work of literature is completed by the satisfied reader no matter what it accomplishes theoretically in its own self-containment. A reader looking for qualities of self-penetration and self-discovery in a context that stamps itself as disclosing the real world would find a novel to suffer from the disadvantage of incompleteness: *Robinson Crusoe* simply cannot do what Cowper's *Memoir* does.

In their perplexity about autobiography, critics have seized upon the idea that autobiographies, because they are not real life and not what we usually categorize as nonfiction, must in fact be fiction (read: "failed" fiction). E. B. Vitz, for instance, tells us that autobiographers present *masks* influenced by the literary tradition. "From a purely literary standpoint, then . . . there is little difference between [autobiography and fiction]."[8] Others tell us that linear cause and effect replace the complexities of real life: the autobiography, we are told, is a story; therefore, it is fiction. And it is mediocre fiction because it does not have the flexibility of the novel or the story. But in fact, a genre that has produced Mill's *Autobiography*, Goethe's *Dichtung und Wahrheit*, and Gosse's *Father and Son* is so manifestly not fiction that one has to be a special pleader to relegate such classics to an inferior status within the fictional mode. Asserting, however, that autobiography is not fiction cannot suffice: even the obvious needs to be validated.

As I have indicated, the problem results from leaving out readers, without whom we are left with a false dichotomy: fiction/ nonfiction. We find books cut adrift from the very subjectivity that gives them their reality and without which they are left embalmed

---

[8] "The *I* of the *Roman de la Rose*," *Genre* 6 (1973): 51.

forever in dry logic and academic rules, neat but unconvincing. The point is that fiction is fiction *for a subject*. Autobiography is autobiography *for a subject*. No amount of logic brought to bear to prove that because autobiography is not life it is actually fiction will convince any reader that autobiographies can or should be read as fictions. It is a total denial of the reader's experience. It is simply a fact that readers turn to autobiography for the kind of satisfaction that one derives from reading something true rather than fabular.

It would also be misleading to label autobiography nonfiction. To call autobiography nonfiction and novels fiction implies that autobiographies are not some particular thing and that novels are, in fact, something. By splitting literature into fiction and non-fiction—an illusion passing itself off as self-evident reality—we have created fiction at the heart of literary activity, relegating autobiography and other forms of writing to merely "something else." But there is nothing inherent in the forms themselves requiring such a ranking.

Both autobiographers and novelists intend us to take their words as true. The truth is the goal of all serious writing. There is long-standing agreement among cultivated people that fiction can reveal truth, and that is why serious people such as Bellow, Baldwin, Hawkes, and Lessing write novels. That is also why universities have courses in literature. Autobiographies are not essentially fabular; they are experiential: an autobiography shares experience as its way of revealing reality. The kind of truth inherent in fiction and autobiography is released by a reader choosing one genre rather than the other. (I mean choosing in two senses: the literal choice of taking the book down from the shelf and also the choice of opening up one's mind to the kind of book that presents itself.) Each satisfies according to the needs and expectations of a particular reader at a particular moment. As in all art, the response of a subject is required for the unleashing of the intrinsic powers of the specific art form.

The autobiography (as a genre) embodies truth when the reader seeks confirmation of his or her own perceptions of reality in terms of those experienced by another mortal; the novel (as a genre) embodies truth when the reader seeks to satisfy his or her need for confirmation that there is value in playing, fantasizing, creating shape and order for their own sake. When I feel a need to put myself in touch with what I call the "real world," I do not read *The House of Mirth*; when I feel a need to lose the real world for one of imagination, order, and illusion, I do not read Abelard's *History of My Calamities*. To deny any of this, it seems to me, would be to deny the obvious. And yet, by implication, it has often been denied. The truth of literature is created as much by the reader as by the author.

But the question about the difference between autobiography and fiction is even knottier. While I know that fiction/nonfiction is a false dichotomy and that truth is to be found in both autobiographies and novels (depending on what I seek to satisfy in myself at a given moment), I am also aware that this explanation does not plumb deep enough. For in both autobiography and fiction "falsehood" resides too. Some autobiographers, of course, come right out and admit that they are telling lies, thereby achieving a deeper honesty. (Mary McCarthy comes to mind.) Others do not. But as I read Schweitzer's *My Life and Thought*, part of my mind never forgets that he has to be distorting, misremembering, enhancing, perhaps even lying. Likewise as I read *Catch-22*, I am always noticing that life is *not* like that: the book is too funny to be true, too artfully organized to be like life. What is actually happening as I turn my attention from novel to autobiography is that my need for satisfaction remains constant while the books before me shift and alter in their ability to provide this satisfaction. Novel reading goes false; I turn to autobiography. Autobiography suddenly seems too simplistic, I turn to the "deeper" truth of fiction. By my always knowing that the autobiography (however true) is at some level false and that the novel or play, however make-believe, is at some level true, I allow for the shift to occur every time my need for satisfaction (which is constant) requires it. In other words, because I know at some level that novels (poems, plays) are both false and true and that autobiographies (history, biography) are both true and false, *I*, as reader, am empowered to give them each room enough to change into what they have to become so that I can experience satisfaction with each. I can create the autobiography as true or false. It requires my presence in order to reflect reality.

By employing devices of the other genre, both fiction and autobiography achieve their goal by suggesting the presence of the other. That is why the dichotomy between fiction and nonfiction is false: It precludes the subject who can discern the presence of potentiality, the presence of the other. Somewhere tucked up in my response to Schweitzer is my awareness that this writer is *pretending* that the words he is writing are equivalent—like a mathematical "equals" sign—to what happened in his life. I am always vaguely aware that Schweitzer knows that he is pretending—that he is falsifying to some degree by leaving things out, sacrificing certain facts so as to get at the essence, pretending to remember dialogue of years earlier so as to create a sense of its reality—and that he achieves this by using various writing techniques designed to stimulate belief. By the same token, I am always indistinctly cognizant that novelists such as Bellow and Heller are *pretending* that they have nothing to do with Henderson or Yossarian, pretending that these characters do not arise out of the real experience of the authors in their day-to-day lives, pretending that, in fact, they are not authors at all but just men paring their nails. After all, what does fiction mean? What is it? Fiction alleges that the "created thing" lives apart from the real experience of its author, that it has its own reality and is not connected to the reality of, for example, the person sitting at the typewriter surrounded by crumpled pages of discarded manuscript. Autobiography does the opposite: it pretends to be the whole life of its author. What I am saying is that while I am reading either autobiography or fiction I never totally forget that each is a pretense, a construction, an illusion. And since I actually participate in the creation of the validity of the form, I quite often find myself experiencing satisfaction rather than resistance to the autobiography or novel before me.

On the other hand, at the moment when I find myself thinking that the author believes that what he or she is saying is totally true and not a kind of pretense, I experience a loss of satisfaction and fall out of the world of the book and into my own room again. For me this happens with *Mein Kampf* and *The Fountainhead*, books in which the authors take themselves too seriously. What I mean is that I lose satisfaction the moment I sense that an author thinks he has the *truth* and forgets that he is at least as wrong as he is right, that his work contains as much fiction as reality, that he is playing as much as speaking in earnest, constructing as well as intuiting. Hitler forgets that his "life" is a product of his mind. Rand thinks she is talking about reality when she imprints her mind on the world of experience. I cannot participate in the creation of something that does not remember it is a pretense, a perspective, an angle.

On the other hand, I experience profound satisfaction when I read Hannah Tillich's *From Time to Time* or Garcia Marquez's *One Hundred Years of Solitude*. In these works I always sense that the au-

thors know they are creating, playing. Take, for example, the closing words (before the Postlude) of *From Time to Time*. Here Tillich
is aware that the book that purports to be her life (something that
presumably happened) requires her conscious constructive presence
and full effort *now*: "I decided to look at my own life and try to
come to an awareness of what I had lived. I insisted that I could go
back to time and place of any experience in my life and find it there
untarnished, living again as it was, remembering its sweetness and
sorrow. This I have tried to do."[9] One can almost imagine the vi-
brant old woman wandering in a child's book of life-sized three
dimensional pop-up scenes from her life.

Readers turn to autobiography to satisfy a need for verifying a
fellow human being's experience of reality. They achieve satisfaction when they feel strongly that the book is true to the experience
of the author and when they are aware, to a lesser degree, that the
book is an achievement of literary construction, making use of pretense as a way of highlighting its opposite, reality.

I would like to examine a short biographical passage from Edmund Gosse's *Father and Son* in order to exemplify the points of
view that autobiography is neither memory nor fiction. Gosse had
been brought up by his father as one of the Plymouth Brethren, a
small devout band of Christian fundamentalist dissenters. Keeping
within the strictures against frivolity, the elder Gosse had upset the
young child Edmund by expressing disinclination to allow his son
to accept an invitation to a party. The elder Gosse sanctimoniously
suggested that the two of them kneel and pray for guidance, all
along assuming (according to Edmund) that the matter was already
closed.

> As I knelt, feeling very small, by the immense bulk of my
> Father, there gushed through my veins like a wine the deter-
> mination to rebel. Never before, in all these years of my voca-
> tion, had I felt my resistance take precisely this definite form.
> We rose presently from the sofa, my forehead and the backs of
> my hands still chafed by the texture of the horsehair, and we
> faced one another in the dreary light. My father, perfectly
> confident in the success of what had really been a sort of incan-
> tation, asked me in a loud wheedling voice, "Well, and what is
> the answer which our Lord vouchsafes?" I said nothing, and so
> my Father, more sharply, continued, "We have asked Him to

[9] *From Time to Time* (New York, 1973), p. 243.

direct you to a true knowledge of His will. We have desired Him to let you know whether it is, or is not, in accordance with His wishes that you should accept the invitation from the Browns." He positively beamed down at me; he had no doubt of the reply. He was already, I believe, planning some little treat to make up to me for the material deprivation. But my answer came, in the high-piping accents of despair: "The Lord says I may go to the Browns." My father gazed at me in speechless horror. He was caught in his own trap, and though he was certain that the Lord had said nothing of the kind, there was no road open for him but just sheer retreat. Yet surely it was an error in tactics to slam the door.[10]

The passage is certainly autobiographical—a perfect little gem. It is not life. In life Edmund would not have known his father's thoughts (with or without a wheedling voice). He would not have remembered exactly what his father said so many years earlier. In life a young child could not know that his father "was already . . . planning some little treat." Furthermore, in life there is no time for even knowing the meaning of what is happening for oneself, let alone for another. Only in retrospect can the author say, "Never before, in all these years of my vocation, had I felt my resistance take precisely this definite form." At the time of the incident Edmund would have been too immersed in his despair and triumph to know what he *now* knows about forms. The passage also creates an illusory sense of time: it is not the time the event had to have taken in reality. There are leaps in time, for instance, between his father's last words and his hasty retreat through the doorway.

In addition, this passage from Gosse's autobiography is not a simple recollection—it is not a memory that occurs in the mind at moments when something in the physical universe triggers a picture from the past. Rather, it is one part of an intricate structure called *Father and Son*, a book, by the way, that Gosse (who was afflicted with biases about the genre) claimed was not an autobiography. The main development in the book portrays the ever-widening rift between father and son, as Edmund more and more eschews his father's values and beliefs. Gosse traces his emerging self, recognizing in fascinating stages that his father is not God, not infallible, perhaps not even sensible, certainly not flexible. The episode depicted in the passage I have quoted is entirely on course.

[10] *Father and Son* (New York, 1963), pp. 192-193.

It shows young Edmund discovering some of his innate power—
the power to choose and affirm reality as he sees it. He despairs as
he lies to his father about Divine intervention and he simultaneously experiences triumphant movement into a new condition of
life: independence from the ego-strictures of the past. The passage
records a definite step in Edmund's development toward the fully
developed sensibility of none other than the writer who is recreating the essence of his life. In writing his autobiography, Gosse
moves beyond memory; he has established an organizing principle
that cannot have been *in* the events themselves. The "point" of his
life becomes the point of his book, just as, simultaneously, writing
the book gives meaning to his life.

At the level of consciousness, Gosse says that he writes the book
in order to document two ways of life, his father's (a disappear-
ing species) and his own. But his book emanates from his being.
Gosse's material is organized by his depiction of what he believes to
be an unfettered mind. We are not given an impartial portrayal of
two lifestyles, however—if readers hope for impartiality they must
look elsewhere than in autobiography. What we have here is Edmund Gosse's single, unified, monochronic experience of himself
escaping from the shackles (however lovingly inflicted) of his
father's religion. Gosse shares his experience of himself as a boy.
"Documentation" of his father's viewpoint (except for a few ex-
cerpts from his letters) is based solely on Gosse's interpretation of
his father's experience. While Edmund emerges as complex in nature, the elder Gosse is never portrayed as having levels of consciousness. He is never the "subject" in this book. In short, it is all
Edmund Gosse: *his* life story, shaped to perfection so as to disclose
the truth about himself and his father from one angle of perception,
his own. His father is not coprotagonist; he is merely a character in
Edmund's story. Recollections, memories, his "autobiographical
consciousness" are enlisted in the service of capturing the quintes-
sence of what he wants to say now, in the present, about his life.
Gosse uses these and other aids (fictional techniques, occasional
documentation, knowledge of history, style) in order to achieve his
autobiographical goals. Memories are indispensable for autobiography, but they are not the thing itself.

Gosse is not writing fiction. The dominant rhetorical signals all
point to the factuality of the account: it is written in the first person,
and it is ostensibly about the author himself. At no point in the
book does the slightest rhetorical lapse occur suggesting any other

reading. The fuller context, of which this passage is a representative sample, reveals factuality by depicting the religious/social matrix of the Brethren, by establishing the identities of the principal characters in Gosse's life, and so on. The entire strategy of the book is to convince the reader of its fidelity to true-life facts.

In the quoted passage Gosse admits, "It will be justly said that my life was made up of very trifling things, since I have to confess that this incident of the Browns' invitation was one of its landmarks." Here Gosse is giving us two truths about his life. First, we are reminded that a real life is usually made up of trifling things. Second (and of course he doesn't mean this consciously), the autobiographer "makes up"—that is, creates—his life from the trifles he arranges into a dominant pattern. Trifles stay trifles unless they are shaped into design. Gosse is saying that it is because the event is small that it is remarkable. The implication here is that he will not stop to fictionalize. He will simply record his true memories based on trivial things. Then he goes on to tell a "story," pretending that the events happened in just this way. The point is that his life is presently experienced as having been made up of trifling events, one of which he concocts—"making it up"—so that we can share in the experience that is for him reality. Notice how his so-called trifle looms large: "Never before, in all these years of my vocation, had I felt my resistance take precisely this definite form." The passage is an example of one of the paradoxes of life: a truth embodying its opposite—largeness in smallness, smallness in largeness. This paradox helps to give the passage the translucence characteristic of the real world—a place where the improbable often takes precedence over the probable.

Gosse records minute details in a novelist's fashion. He provides visual metaphors, allows us to feel through tactile images, provides convincing dialogue, plays omniscient narrator. But we do not mistake the passage for fiction. Rather, we participate in making it reflect reality. Notice that we never truly lose sight of the fact that Gosse is speaking to us directly about what happened long ago. He is always *there*, telling his story. When I read what Gosse's father allegedly said to him, I am aware that Edmund knows that he cannot remember what his father actually said or thought. In contrast, when I read in *The Cherry Orchard* that Lopahin says, "The train's late! Two hours, at least," it does not normally occur to me that Chekhov had to remember these words. I know that he is pretending that he has nothing to do with them. He is not there. Part of my reading experience—a part as real for me as my acceptance of the illusion of Gosse's father's words—is my knowledge that Gosse does not fully remember his father's exact utterance, that Gosse is, in fact, pretending to remember so that the truth of the episode can flow to me. The truth is in the pretense and made visible by it. The author says to me, "My life was as this tale I am telling." Viewed in such a way, an autobiography is comparable to an extended, epic simile. In what Wolfgang Iser has called the "virtual dimen-sion"[11]—the space in which the re-creation of the illusion occurs, somewhere between the text itself and my imagination—I intuit what it was like for Gosse's father to be speaking to the young boy. In other words, I don't take what Gosse says literally. It is Lopahin whom I take literally.

The simple truth that autobiography is not fiction is not threatened by the fact that a swatch of autobiography out of con-text may have the appearance of fiction. Nor is this truth threatened by the fact that authors may occasionally design their works to fall between the two genres. Truman Capote's *In Cold Blood* and Nor-man Mailer's *Armies of the Night* experiment succcesfully with both fable and fact. These experiments do not turn three hundred years of autobiographical writing into second-rate fiction. They merely show that good books can be written by drawing heavily from both experience and from imagination. The unicorn does not in-validate the horse.

In claiming that autobiography is a genuine literary genre, critics have done a service to this genre that until recently had been re-ferred to as, in Stephen Shapiro's phrase, "the dark continent."[12] But many of us overreacted in our zealous desire to convince others that autobiography is as much an art as any other form of literature, and we must now remind ourselves that although autobiography is literature, it is literature with a difference. In autobiography, unlike fiction, we expect the work to embody, even in its illusion, the truth of the life of the writer. As critics we may speak academically of the "illusion" of truth in autobiography, but I suspect that even the most punctilious critic expects truth as well as illusion in auto-biography. When I read Strindberg's *The Father*, I know that the

[11] "The Reading Process: A Phenomenological Approach," *New Literary History* 3 (1972): 279-299.

[12] "The Dark Continent of Literature: Autobiography," *Comparative Literature Studies* 5 (1968): 421-454.

author wishes me to accept a particular kind of truth embodied in the conflict beween the fictional characters, Adolf and Laura. Strindberg does not ask me to assume that these people are "real," nor does he invite me to speculate about him as author, although I may find myself doing both. But he does want me to appropriate as true the *meaning* of their marital war. On the other hand, when I read the autobiography, *Memories, Dreams, Reflections*, I know that Carl Jung wants me to look through the illusion of the created "Carl Jung" to the real Carl Jung beneath. He invites the kind of speculation that he expects will fuse the created "Carl Jung" with the author who has selected the words in order to create the illusion. Jung wants the reader to see and accept as true what he says about himself. Readers of autobiography do feel that they get to the truth of a person, even if the autobiographer is an egregious liar like Hitler or remote from them in sensibility like Albert Schweitzer.

I have discussed two misconceptions regarding autobiography. Now I would like to focus on two distinct aspects of autobiography that contribute to its ability to speak the truth about one's life. First and by far the more often neglected is its creation of what I will call its "ratification." Second is its self-conscious pointing to its own assumptions and, related to its assumptions, its horizon of implications.

Language creates illusions that tell the truth. The process of language constantly makes the discovery of truth possible because all language is rooted in human *being* and culture, so that even lies are anchored in being and contain the possibility of their own revelation. Nothing gets to the truth as well as "cross examination": words against words until the truth stands revealed. I am not saying, of course, that every lie is transparent to a reader. But as lies are rooted in truth, the ability to find truth resides (as does the understanding of subtle literature) in an ability to keep oneself open to the possible ways of "taking" an utterance. If an autobiographer tells many lies, his words will eventually reveal him as one who means something other than what he says.

All autobiographers create the illusion of the past coming to life. ("You got a gift for recording," L'il Henry tells Piri Thomas in *Seven Long Times*. "I'm reading and I'm seeing pictures in your words. You got a real talent.") However convincing an autobiographical text may be, the past is always an illusion because it never really existed: it has always been an illusion created by the symbolizing activity of the mind. The past must be created afresh. When formalized in words, autobiographical creation is literary art.

It is making something from nothing or from something else. But as I have argued, it is not fiction. What defictionalizes autobiography is both the readers' powers of cocreation and the author's animation in the present of his or her past. The author, it may be said, is always present in autobiography. And while it is possible to invalidate the present, it is in fact the only time zone in which human beings experience the truth. The experience of "now" is always, whether validated or not. Thus, no critic calls the essays in *PMLA* or *College English* "fictional" (even though these essays are wrought in words in a linear dimension) because they capture the present thinking of their authors. In this sense, they may be wrong but they are not fabular. Autobiography forges present meaning into the marrow of one's remembered life.

Life has a way of not living up to one's expectations. Writing autobiography is one of the strategies human beings have developed to make life matter. The way in which the illusion of the past is presented is, finally, the meaning of the author's life: it is the "form" one's life takes, and it is the only meaning there can be for a subject. Naturally, and paradoxically, it can change as time moves on. The meaning can alter dramatically or subtly. (John N. Morris has written of "versions" of the self and James Olney has written of its "metaphors.")[13] The illusion of the past occupies the present, but the present is no illusion. The present allows life to matter. The illusions of the importance of past and future endow life with something akin to significance, which the autobiographer then weaves into an enduring artifact.

Writing an autobiography ratifies the form one has given to one's life. The ongoing activity of writing discloses the being's ratification of the ego's illusion of the past, thereby solidifying it. The acceptance of the illusion, occurring in the present where meaning is possible, is what makes an autobiography capable of telling the truth. The ego invents a past—"I had to leave home at age eleven"; the being, standing outside of time, ratifies the ego by saying "I see, accept, and freely 'choose' the assertion of my ego." Autobiography is a passage to truth because, like all genuine experience, it rises from a ground of being that transcends one's memories, petty lies, grand deceptions, and even one's desire to be honest. As the autobiographer's ego manipulates the images on the page (the per-

---

[13] John N. Morris, *Versions of the Self: Studies in English Autobiography from John Bunyan to John Stuart Mill* (New York, 1966); James Olney, *Metaphors of Self: The Meaning of Autobiography* (Princeton, 1972).

sona, the illusion of the past), he is simultaneously transmitting, in the tone and mood of the work, the ratification of this version of his life. By ratifying—standing apart from the illusion and choosing it as the past—the being is reflected on the page as containing or embracing the illusion, keeping it in perspective and thereby transcending it. The past may appear to rule the present; but in fact all genuine power resides in the moment of creativity.

I wish to make this point as straightforward as possible. The autobiographer remembers himself or herself as behaving in a certain manner as an adolescent, and thus gives form to the memory in the emerging autobiography. There is always the assertion ("I did thus and such") and the implied "choice" of the assertion ("My putting this assertion on the page is my acceptance of it, my willingness to own and share it"). The assertion is one of the possible truths of the past; the decision to accept and communicate it as that which happened is the ratification in the present. In ratifying the past, the autobiographer discloses the truth of his or her being in the present. Thus, personal history is put forth in a certain light. The past may be an illusion, but the light of now is never an illusion. What it illuminates, it makes real. *Now* is the only source of light. Anything it shines on may be clarified. The image of one's personal history in autobiography is simultaneously in time and timeless, like Yeat's golden nightingale or like the image of a boy with a horse in Lincoln Steffen's autobiography.

In many autobiographies the ratification is negative—the light of now shines on the illusion the ego puts forth and reveals it as false. In this case, the autobiographer has not chosen one of many truths. He or she has lied; ego has attempted to manipulate and distort, to *prevent* disclosure. The being does not choose or ratify what the ego is alleging it has done. One's being knows—*is*—the truth even when one's mind goes unconscious. In these autobiographies the reader experiences dis-ease with the autobiography. It seems as if the author is lying (not, please, writing fiction), although readers cannot always easily put their finger on the lie. (Lionel Charlton creates just such an impression, as do Cellini and Maugham.) My point is that even in these autobiographies the duality exists between mind and being, between the assertion and the ratification. The mind creates the illusion of cause and effect. The being ratifies the illusion by letting it stand for reality. But if the mind is dishonestly pretending a cause and effect relationship in order to control readers' reactions and judgments, the being knows that the personal history is fake and does not choose it. What the being does choose is what it always chooses: that which is happening. And the reality in these autobiographies is that they are lying and misrepresenting. Very often the autobiographical disclosure of the author's experience—naturally very subtle—is that what he or she is saying veers from what is "truly" remembered. Since the ego is in conflict with the truth, the reader very often gets that message. The author has created an illusion of an illusion.

In reading *Charlton*, for example, the reader often feels that Charlton must have sat at his desk, remembered an experience from the past, rejected it as too revealing, replaced it with an acceptable (however implausible) substitute, depicted it with full knowledge of its distortion. All of this is capable of being sensed from the pages of the book, which is permeated with negative ratification, a ratification of that which is not written. The tone is forever slipping away from the content, giving itself away. Charlton is beside himself. He cannot see that what he is principally disclosing is his own emotional fear and dishonesty.

It has become fashionable in critical circles to say that autobiographers cannot be trusted. In my experience most autobiographers are honest (that's the whole point of the genre), with occasional distortions, honest evasions, discrete pockets of noncommunication. An honest autobiography puts its illusion of the past forward in good faith, not suspecting that it is but one angle of perception. The good faith is the ratification that this particular creation speaks as well as could any creation for the author's present sense of where he or she has been and the meaning of it all.

The second point I wish to stress is the role of *assumptions* in autobiography. Even more than in the reading of fiction, we find ourselves as alert to what is not said as to what is said in autobiography: we find ourselves considering the assumptions underlying the autobiographical assertions. Of course fiction, and indeed all human activity, arises from a body of assumptions, but for the most part fiction does not pause to point them out. The illusion in fiction is that it is "complete" in and of itself. It simply pitches in and tells its tale. "About thirty years ago, Miss Maria Ward of Huntington, with only seven thousand pounds had the good luck to captivate Sir Thomas Bertram, of Mansfield Park, in the county of Northampton, and to be thereby raised to the rank of a baronet's lady, with all the comforts and consequences of a handsome house and large income." This opening sentence of Austen's novel places us immediately in the fictional world that may or may not be Austen's, although this is clearly not the issue. It does not take time to comment on what its author is attempting to do; it is too busy doing it. On the other hand, most autobiographies include introductory remarks, even if their only purpose is to proclaim, like Gandhi's, that the book is not an autobiography. ("But it is not my purpose to attempt a real autobiography," Gandhi says at the beginning of one of the great autobiographies of modern times.)[14] Such introductory comments are enough to hint that the underlying assumptions are of the essence in autobiography and that a reader would do well to watch the text for indications of the assumption from which the illusions of the past are carved.

What sort of assumptions do I mean? I mean assumptions held in the present about autobiography as well as assumptions concerning the relationship between literature and autobiography. Assumptions too about what constitutes style in literature and life. I also mean assumptions about the author's own values, moral code, ethics, and assumptions about culture, society, religion. Assumptions about life itself; about feelings—one's own and others'. Assumptions about one's body and soul. I am thinking, for instance, about Gibbon's unstated assumptions that a man—a subjectivity— can be studied and described in the same way one would go about studying an empire—an object. Or Twain's assumption that autobiography is not literature since it need not be pruned and shaped as other works are. Or George Fox's, or Vavasor Powell's, or Anna Trapnell's or Bunyan's assumption that there is but one Truth and that he or she is in possession of it. Or Rousseau's assumption that if he writes long enough, he will outstrip time, freeing himself of shame and anxiety. Through sensitivity to underlying assumptions, the reader of autobiography is constantly sensing the impact of the author's present historical moment and the present message of his culture. Some have gone too far, suggesting that the autobiographer cannot be trusted because he or she speaks in a recognizable cultural accent. Others fault the autobiographer for not speaking broadly enough. Henri Peyre quotes Albert Thibaudet's attack on autobiography. For Thibaudet, autobiography is the "most false" genre, since it puts "into one's work the only part of oneself which one knows, that which reaches consciousness."[15] I

---

[14] *An Autobiography*, trans. Mahadev Desai (Boston, 1957), p. xii.
[15] *Literature and Sincerity* (New Haven, 1963), p. 210.

would say that a whole body of unstated assumptions arising from the pressure of his culture grounds the statements of all autobiographers. These do not render the autobiographer either a depersonalized nonentity or a monster of self-consciousness. Rather, they act as a foil against which the autobiographer's uniqueness can be discerned.

The assumptions create a horizon in the autobiography. The explicit narrative is "here," and the assumptions, especially those just dimly implied, are "there." Of course, the nearby, known assumptions overlap with the distant ones. The reader assumes the author's awareness of the known assumptions. For example, we take for granted Gibbon's assumption that for his contemporaries he has become important, perhaps as important as the Roman empire. Yet at the same time the reader asks questions pertaining to the distant, implied horizon—those deeper assumptions underlying conscious knowledge of oneself and one's culture. Does Gibbon have any idea what the fact of six uncompleted drafts says about him? Beyond the known assumptions, the reader senses ontological quasars.

This is the area of a text that is difficult to describe without resorting to airy abstractions and metaphors, for when we discuss the horizon of assumptions in an autobiography we come full cycle— we leave the concreteness of the "verbal construct" altogether. We are referring to the borderland of experience where the author's and reader's unstated assumptions overlap. Any comment in an autobiography will be rooted in assumption, and some comments may point off to the horizon. Often the reader simply cannot know whether what he is reacting to is actually implied by the text or whether the text has triggered associations in the reader's own horizon. But it is this very overlapping of the autobiographer's and the reader's horizons that adds to the undeniable aura of truthfulness surrounding the text. In fact, it may be said that the reader projects truthfulness from his or her own body of assumptions or that he or she allows the text to manifest itself at the level of the truth.

What happens is that the reader finds that he has been speculating inconclusively but with deep pleasure about the "truth" of the autobiographer's life and perhaps, unavoidably, about his own. These moments occur when the text suddenly reveals meaning so deep as to seem to be lodged in metaphysical or ontological ground. I do not mean the "objective" meanings available only to scholars but the deepest personal meanings unknown even to the subject—meanings that give rise to the whole structure of the autobiographical creation. For me these profound moments body forth a sense of my sharing life—being—with the author, no matter how remote he or she may be from me in some ways. The autobiographer springs open a door and gives me a glance into his or her deepest reality, at the same time casting my mind into a state of reverie or speculation. The being of the author is felt to merge with my own. For a moment I plummet deep into my own veiled assumptions, feelings, and self-meaning. It is the experience of *Zugehörigkeit* ("belonging"), in which we recognize our subordination and obligation to shared truths (embodied by language) larger than ourselves. It is the moment Teresa of Avila experiences when she reads the garden scene in St. Augustine's *Confessions*: "When I began to read the *Confessions*, I thought I saw myself there described, and began to recommend myself greatly to this glorious Saint. When I came to his conversion, and read how he heard that voice in the garden, it seemed to me nothing less than that our Lord had uttered it for me: I felt so in my heart, I remained for some time lost in tears, in great inward affliction and distress."[16] At such a moment, St. Teresa's language merges with that of St. Augustine who seems to be speaking not only *to* her but *in* her, merging the particulars of his past with the particulars of hers and creating a moment of transcendence.

If we understand the existence of this horizon (the outermost unconscious assumptions forming the boundary of the gestalt of the text), we can deal with one of the familiar paradoxical questions about autobiography: How can the presentation of one's life be true when other people surrounding the author—loved ones, professional colleagues, enemies—see the autobiographer in an entirely different way? I see myself as contemplative; my enemy sees me as cold and uninterested. I see my friend as wild and abandoned; she experiences herself as natural and fun-loving. And so on. Does the multiplicity of "readings" of character lead only to total, subjective relativity? Perhaps, if multiple perceptions are listed in a free-floating, unrooted way, as *examples* of ways in which a person's character may be experienced by himself and by others. I may see myself as contemplative. Others may see me as contemplative, or aloof, or shy, or detached, or cold, or absent-minded, or intense.

---

[16] *Confessions*, trans. J. M. Cohen (Middlesex, 1957), p. 58.

What looks like free-floating, subjective data when catalogued as a list will appear as something more solid when understood to be grounded in different personal and cultural assumptions and fixed within horizons. The "same" data can be truly and fully explained in many ways since their meaning will only surface in the perceptions of various subjects. It may be true that my own experience of myself is that I am contemplative, while it may be equally true that when I am being *contemplative for myself* I do not see my friend standing there. In his horizon—in which I emerge as a friend, someone for him to interact with and to validate his existence, his own sense of reality—he finds that I do not see him and rightly judges me to be, at that moment, "indifferent" to his needs and perhaps even "rude." I appear in his horizon as a nonvalidating entity; yet he does not appear in my horizon at all. He feels I am doing something cruel to him; within my own horizon, I am alone, thinking about the cosmos. Both explanations of the objective data (for example, he and I are standing in the same room, we have been friendly in the past, I am looking toward the wall, he is looking toward me) would be perfectly true because the data take on meaning only in the contexts of subjective experience. These seemingly contradictory truths can, of course, change. They are not fixed. My friend can reorient himself in a new horizon; he can leave. Or he can seek to alter mine. He can call my name, using his voice to shove the *fact* of his being into my horizon. Then, finding my friend within my horizon, I will cease to experience myself as contemplative, as the new horizon, involving a significant other, demands a different sense of self. (I will only realize that I have been contemplative when I cease to be so and create the symbols representing my immediate past.)

The autobiographer who speaks the truth about him or herself may produce a book that would most assuredly strike a close relative or an enemy as distorted or even false. Yet, if he is courageously open to the synthesizing process of meaning-making, the autobiographer will have produced a valid, honest, and perfectly true revelation of his life, couched in and defined by his horizons. The truth of the author's *life* will doubtlessly undergo erosion or alteration if he lives on for many years, but the truth of the *book* cannot change if it has vividly and honestly illuminated the past as experienced in a moment of now. If the autobiographer dies soon after the completion of the book (this of course often happens as autobiographies tend to be written by elderly people), then in their conterminousness the book and the life reveal the same truth. All artistic autobiographies tell the truth when they are, in Emerson's phrase, "captivating books": when an autobiographer knows "how to choose among what he calls his experiences that which is really his experience, and how to record truth truly."[17]

The interpenetration and crisscrossing of data in an autobiography is not only disconcerting to readers and acquaintances but to the author as well. Indeed, the autobiographer is likely to be fairly troubled since he or she is involved in the process of attempting to "fix" the life. The more one senses that the images of the mind (including all components of one's personal past) are in a constant flux, the more one's sense of reality may be threatened. The people with the most rigid and brittle sense of the factualness of their world are those who admit little or no contradictory evidence. For them the events of their lives are "objective." They would, for instance, be able to make little sense of William Earle's assertions that "the creature that can affirm nothing wholly or deny it either, while existentially confused if not paralyzed, is metaphysically sound; in the last analysis he expresses more vividly than anything natural the perceptual paradox between a transcendental ego and the existing ambiguities we are."[18] For people bent on protecting their corner as if it were the universe itself, it never occurs that objectivity itself "represents a tentative, constructed, and fairly limited area of being."[19]

On the one hand, we have the absolute sane certainty of a St. Augustine, or a Marcus Aurelius, or a Montaigne (certain of his awareness of uncertainty); on the other hand, we have the absolute insane certainty of a William Cowper. In the middle of the spectrum we see Rousseau, struggling to believe the very words he writes, but finding them pulling him toward conflicting interpretations of his own past experiences. Rousseau's *Confessions* is a masterpiece of the genre because it allows these conflicting truths to manifest themselves, creating a complex unity. Dishonest autobiographers impose a false unity or design where they fear the complexity of their own natures, doubt their own assumptions and hence their own reality. They falsely interpret events and omit others altogether in such a way as to create a false version of reality,

[17] *The Journals and Miscellaneous Notebooks of Ralph Waldo Emerson*, ed. A. W. Plumstead and Harrison Hayford (Cambridge, Mass., 1969), 8: 418.

[18] Earle, *The Autobiographical Consciousness*, p. 212.

[19] Ibid.

but as this dishonesty is always unratified, experienced readers detect it.

Augustine and Cowper, Rousseau and Montaigne—all of these writers truly disclose their sense of their own reality in their self-portraits. Because their (and our) reality is largely rooted in the shared assumptions of our culture, the written autobiography becomes a formal mode of maintaining the reality of reality. The autobiographer discloses the truth and at the same time fixes it by making it, paradoxically, more real, truer. One's "life" exists only in one's faith that what one assumes to be real actually is real. The autobiographer assembles words *now* in order to demonstrate that a life was lived, that it had a particular meaning, and that it was capable of making an impact on others. The results are, in Whitman's phrase, "full of life now."

The *content* of an autobiography is not alone sufficient to create truth. What actually transforms content into truth of life is the *context* that contains the content. By the context I mean the writer's intention to tell the truth; the ratification through the actual choices he makes word by word, as well as in his tone, style, and organization; the assumptions that permeate the book, giving rise to content while overlapping the reader's own sense of lived experience in the world. I would argue that it is the reader's willingness to experience and cocreate this context that allows autobiography to speak the truth.

The Style of Autobiography

Jean Starobinski

Translated by Seymour Chatman

A biography of a person written by himself: this definition of autobiography establishes the intrinsic character of the enterprise and
thus the general (and generic) conditions of autobiographical writing. But this is not merely the definition of a literary genre: in their
essentials, these conditions ensure that the identity of the narrator
and the hero of the narration will be revealed in the work. Further,
they require that the work be a narrative and not merely a description. Biography is not portrait; or if it is a kind of portrait, it adds
time and movement. The narrative must cover a temporal sequence
sufficiently extensive to allow the emergence of the contour of life.
Within these conditions, autobiography may be limited to a page or
extended through many volumes. It is also free to "contaminate"
the record of the life with events that could only have been wit-
nessed from a distance. The autobiographer then doubles as a
writer of memoirs (this is the case of Chateaubriand); he is free also
to date precisely various stages of the revisions of the text, and at
the moment of composition to look back upon his situation. The
intimate journal may intrude upon autobiography, and an autobiographer may from time to time become a "diarist" (this,
again, is the case with Chateaubriand). Thus, the conditions of autobiography furnish only a large framework within which a great
variety of particular styles may occur. So it is essential to avoid
speaking of an autobiographical "style" or even an autobiographical "form," because there is no such generic style or form. Here,
even more than elsewhere, style is the act of an individual. It is useful, nevertheless, to insist on the fact that style will only assert itself

under the conditions that we have just mentioned. It can be defined as the fashion in which each autobiographer satisfies the conditions of the genre. These conditions are of an ethical and "relational" order and require only the truthful narration of a life, leaving to the writer the right to determine his own particular modality, rhythm, span, etc. In a narrative in which the narrator takes his own past as theme, the individual mark of style assumes particular importance, since to the explicit self-reference of the narration itself the style adds the implicit self-referential value of a particular mode of speaking.

Style is currently associated with the act of writing. It is seen as resulting from the margin of liberty offered to the "author"[1] after he has satisfied the requirements of language and literary convention and of the use he has put them to. The self-referential value of style thus refers back to the moment of writing, to the contemporary "me." But this contemporary self-reference may appear as an obstacle to the accurate grasp and transcription of past events. Critics of Rousseau and Chateaubriand have often thought that the perfection of their styles—whatever the reality of the depicted facts—rendered suspect the content of the narrative, setting up a screen between the truth of the narrated past and the present of the narrative situation. Every original aspect of style implies a redundancy that may disturb the message itself.[2] But, obviously, the past can never be evoked except with respect to a present: the "reality" of by-gone days is only such to the consciousness which, today, gathering up their present image, cannot avoid imposing upon them its own form, its style. Every autobiography—even when it limits itself to pure narrative—is a self-interpretation. Style here assumes the dual function of establishing the relation between the "author" and his own past; but also, in its orientation toward the future, of revealing the author to his future readers.

The misunderstanding of this subject is in large measure the result of conventional ideas about the nature and function of style. According to the view that sees style as a "form" added to a "content," it is logical to regard qualities of style in autobiography with suspicion. ("Too beautiful to be true" becomes a principle of systematic objection.) This objection finds support in the ease with which a narrator may slip into fiction, a hazard that we ourselves

---

[1] I employ this term to designate an autobiographer independently of his quality as writer.

[2] Cf. Gilles-G. Granger, *Essai d'une philosophie du style* (Paris, 1968), pp. 7-8.

are surely aware of from our own experiences in recounting past events. Not only (in this view) can the autobiographer lie, but the "autobiographical form" can cloak the freest fictive invention: "pseudo-memoirs" and "pseudo-biographies" exploit the possibilities of narrating purely imaginary tales in the first person. In these cases, the *I* of the narrative, "existentially" speaking, is assumed by a nonentity; it is an *I* without referent, an *I* that refers only to an arbitrary image. However, the *I* of such a text cannot be distinguished from the *I* of a "sincere" autobiographical narrative. It is easy to conclude, under this traditional conception of style, that, in autobiography or confession, despite the vow of sincerity, the "content" of the narrative can be lost, can disappear into fiction, without anything preventing its transition from one plane to another, without there even being a sure sign of that transition. Style, as an original quality, accentuating as it does the importance of the present in the act of writing, seems to serve the conventions of narrative, rather than the realities of reminiscence. It is more than an obstacle or a screen, it becomes a principle of deformation and falsification.

But if one rejects this definition of style as "form" (or dress, or ornament) superadded to a "content" in favor of one of style as deviation (*écart*), the originality in the autobiographical style—far from being suspect—offers us a system of revealing indices, of symptomatic traits. The redundancy of style is individualizing: it singles out. Hasn't the notion of stylistic deviation been elaborated precisely with a view to coming nearer to the psychic uniqueness of writers?[3] Thus the celebrated aphorism of Buffon has been rediscovered (in a slightly altered sense), and the style of autobiography now appears to bear a minimal veracity in its contemporaneousness with the life of the author. No matter how doubtful the facts related, the text will at least present an "authentic" image of the man who "held the pen."

That brings us to some observations concerning more general implications of the theory of style. Style as "form superadded to content" will be judged above all on its inevitable infidelity to a past reality: "content" is taken to be anterior to "form," and past history, the theme of the narrative, must necessarily occupy this anterior position. Style as deviation, however, seems rather to exist in

[3] I refer, obviously, to the conception of stylistics implicit in the first period of the work of Leo Spitzer. Cf. *Linguistics and Literary History* (New York, 1962), pp. 11-14.

a relation of fidelity to a contemporary reality. In this case, the very
notion of style really obeys a system of organic metaphors, according to which expression proceeds from experience, without any
discontinuity, as the flower is pushed open by the flow of sap
through the stem. Conversely, the notion of "form superadded to
content" implies—from its inception—discontinuity, the very opposite of organic growth, thus a mechanical operation, the intervening application of an instrument to a material of another sort. It
is the image of the *stylus* with a sharp point that tends thus to pre-
vail over that of the *hand* moved by the writer's inner spirit.
(Doubtless it is necessary to develop an idea of style that envisages
both the stylus and the hand—the direction of the stylus *by* the
hand.)

In a study devoted to "Temporal Relations in the French Verb,"
Emile Benveniste distinguishes *historic* statement (*l'énonciation his-
torique*), a "narrative of past events," from *discourse* (*discours*), a
"statement presupposing a speaker and an auditor; and in the first-
named, an intention of influencing the second in some way."[4]
While the narrative of past facts in historic statement uses the *Passé
simple* as its "typical form" in current French (which Benveniste
calls "aorist"), discourse prefers to use the *Passé composé*. A glance
at recent autobiographies (Michel Leiris, Jean-Paul Sartre) shows
us, however, that the characteristics of discourse (statement tied to
a narrator named "I") may coexist with those of history (use of the
aorist). Is this an archaism? Or better, aren't we dealing in autobiography with a mixed entity, which we can call *discourse-history*?
This is surely a hypothesis that needs examination. The traditional
form of autobiography occupies a position between two extremes:
narrative in the third person[5] and pure monologue. We are very
familiar with third-person narrative; it is the form of the *Commentaries* of Caesar or of the second part of the *Mémoires* of La
Rochefoucauld, namely, narrative that is not distinguished from
history by its form. One must learn from external information that
the narrator and the hero are one and the same person. In general,
such a process is expressly a depiction of a series of important
events in which the editor puts himself into the scene as one of the
principal actors. The effacing of the narrator (who thereby assumes

---

[4] Emile Benveniste, *Problèmes de linguistique générale* (Paris, 1966), p. 242. See also,
Harald Weinrich, *Tempus. Besprochene und erzählte Welt* (Stuttgart, 1964).

[5] "In the narrative, if the narrator doesn't intervene, the third person is not opposed to any other, it is truly an absence of person." Ibid., p. 242.

the impersonal role of historian), the objective presentation of the protagonist in the third person, works to the benefit of the event, and only secondarily reflects back upon the personality of the protagonist the glitter of actions in which he has been involved. Though seemingly a modest form, autobiographical narrative in the third person accumulates and makes compatible events glorifying the hero who refuses to speak in his own name. Here the interests of the personality are committed to a "he," thus effecting a solidification by objectivity. This is quite the opposite of pure monologue, where the accent is on the "me" and not on the event. In extreme forms of monologue (not in the domain of autobiography but in that of lyrical fiction), the event is nothing other than the unwinding of the monologue itself, independently of any related "fact" that in the process becomes unimportant. We see the intervention of a process that is the opposite of that just described for third-person narrative: the exclusive affirmation of "I" favors the interests of an apparently vanished "he." The impersonal event becomes a secret parasite on the "I" of the monologue, fading and depersonalizing it. One need only examine the writings of Samuel Beckett to discover how the constantly repeated "first person" comes to be the equivalent of a "nonperson."

Autobiography is certainly not a genre with rigorous rules. It only requires that certain possible conditions be realized, conditions that are mainly ideological (or cultural): that the personal experience be important, that it offer an opportunity for a sincere relation with someone else.[6] These presuppositions establish the legitimacy of "I" and authorize the subject of the discourse to take his past existence as theme. Moreover, the "I" is confirmed in the function of permanent subject by the presence of its correlative "you," giving clear motivation to the discourse. I am thinking here of the *Confessions* of St. Augustine: the author speaks to God but with the intention of edifying his readers. God is the direct addressee of the discourse; the rest of mankind, on the contrary, is named in the third person as indirect beneficiary of the effusion that it has been allowed to witness. Thus the autobiographical discourse takes form by creating, almost simultaneously, two addressees, one summoned directly, the other assumed obliquely as witness. Is this a useless luxury? Shall we assume the invocation of God to be only

[6] On the role of autobiography in the history of culture, see Georg Misch, *Geschichte der Autobiographie*, 4 vols. (Bern and Frankfurt-am-Main, 1949-1969). See also Roy Pascal, *Design and Truth in Autobiography* (Cambridge, Mass., 1960).

an artifice of rhetoric? Not at all. God certainly doesn't need to receive the story of Augustine's life, since He is omniscient and sees
the events of eternity at a single glance. God receives the narrator's
prayer and thanksgiving. He is thanked for the intervention of His
Grace in the narrator's destiny. He is the present interlocutor only
because He has been the master of the narrator's previous fate: He
has put him to the test, He has rescued him from error, and He is
revealed to him ever more imperiously. By so openly making God
his interlocutor, Augustine commits himself to absolute veracity:
How could he falsify or dissimulate anything before One who can
see into his innermost marrow? Here is a content guaranteed by the
highest bail. The confession, because of the addressee that it presumes, avoids the risk of falsehood run by ordinary narratives. But
what is the function of the secondary addressee, the human auditor
who is only obliquely invoked? He comes—by his supposed presence—to legitimize the very "discursiveness" of the confession.
The confession is not for God, but for the human reader who needs
a narrative, a laying out of the events in their enchained succession.
The double address of the discourse—to God and to the human
auditor—makes the truth discursive and the discourse true. Thus
may be united, in a certain fashion, the instantaneousness of the
confession offered to God and the sequential nature of the explana-
tory narrative offered to the human intelligence. And thereby are re-
conciled the edifying motivation and the transcendent finality of
the confession: words addressed to God will convert or comfort
other men.

Let me add this remark: one would hardly have sufficient motive
to write an autobiography had not some radical change occurred in
his life—conversion, entry into a new life, the operation of Grace.
If such a change had not affected the life of the narrator, he could
merely depict himself once and for all, and new developments
would be treated as external (historical) events; we would then be
in the presence of the conditions of what Benveniste has named *history*, and a narrator in the first person would hardly continue to be
necessary. It is the internal transformation of the individual—and
the exemplary character of this transformation—that furnishes a
subject for a narrative discourse in which "I" is both subject and
object.

Thus we discover an interesting fact: it is because the past "I" is
different from the present "I" that the latter may really be confirmed in all his prerogatives. The narrator describes not only what

happened to him at a different time in his life but above all how he became—out of what he was—what he presently is. Here the discursive character of the narrative is justified anew, not by the addressee but by the content: it becomes necessary to retrace the genesis of the present situation, the antecedents of the moment from which the present "discourse" stems. The chain of experiences traces a path (though a sinuous one) that ends in the present state of recapitulatory knowledge.

The deviation, which establishes the autobiographical reflection, is thus double: it is at once a deviation of time and of identity. At the level of language, however, the only intruding mark is that of time. The personal mark (the first person, the "I") remains constant. But it is an ambiguous constancy, since the narrator was different from what he is today. Still, how can he keep from being recognized in the other that he was? How can he refuse to assume the other's faults? The narrative-confession, asserting the difference of identity, repudiates past errors, but does not, for all that, decline a responsibility assumed forever by the subject. Pronominal constancy is the index of this permanent responsibility, since the "first person" embodies both the present reflection and the multiplicity of past states. The changes of identity are marked by verbal and attributive elements: they are perhaps still more subtly expressed in the contamination of the discourse by traits proper to history, that is, by the treatment of the first person as a quasi-third person, authorizing recourse to the historical aorist. The aorist changes the effect of the first person. Let us remember too that the famous "rule of twenty-four hours"[7] was still generally respected in the eighteenth century, and that the evocation of past and dated events could not avoid recourse to the *passé simple* (except by using here and there the "historical" present). But it is the statements themselves, and their own *tone*, that make perfectly explicit the distance at which the narrator holds his faults, his errors, his tribulations. The figures of traditional rhetoric (and more particularly those that Fontanier defines as "figures of expression by opposition":[8] preterition, irony, etc.) contribute something too, giving to the autobiographical style its particular color.

I shall take Rousseau as an example.

[7] There is an excellent discussion of this problem in Weinrich, *Tempus*, pp. 247-253.

[8] Pierre Fontanier, *Les figures du discours*, introduction by Gérard Genette (Paris, 1968), pp. 143 ff.

The presence of the imagined addressee strikes us even in the preamble to the *Confessions*: "Qui que vous soyez que ma destinée ou ma confiance ont fait l'arbitre du sort de ce cahier. . . ."[9] Still more clearly, we find in the third paragraph of the first book, the double addressee (God, mankind) whose Augustinian prototype we have earlier tried to make precise:

> Que la trompette du jugement dernier sonne quand elle voudra; je viendrai ce livre à la main me présenter devant le souverain juge. . . . J'ai dévoilé mon intérieur tel que tu l'as vu toi-même. Être éternel, rassemble autour de moi l'innombrable foule de mes semblables: qu'ils écoutent mes confessions, qu'ils gémissent de mes iniquités, qu'ils rougissent de mes misères. (*Oeuvres complètes*, I, 7)[10]

To guarantee the veracity of his utterances, Rousseau, like Augustine, requires the presence of a divine gaze. But he requires it only at the outset, and then once and for all. Within the body of the book there is scarcely a single invocation or apostrophe to God. We note the diffuse presence of the reader (with whom Rousseau sometimes engages in fictive dialogue), a putative witness who is reduced most often to an indefinite *on*:[11] "It will be thought that . . ." (*on pensera que . . .*), "One will say that . . ." (*On dira que . . .*). Rousseau constantly assigns to this imagined interlocutor the objections of good sense and social convention. He also attributes to the interlocutor the suspicion that he feels surrounds himself. He strives to convince him of the absolute truth of his narrative, as of the abiding innocence of his intentions. The fact that his relation to God is looser than that of Augustine or Teresa d'Avila cannot help affecting the veracity of his statements. The preliminary invocation, one senses, is not sufficient: truthfulness must exist each moment, but Rousseau does not ask God to be a constant witness.

[9] Jean-Jacques Rousseau, *Oeuvres complètes* (Paris, 1959), I, 3: "Whoever you may be whom my destiny or my confidence has made the arbiter of the fate of this notebook. . . ." The translation is by Seymour Chatman.

[10] "Let the last trump sound when it will, I shall come forward with this work in my hand, to present myself before my Sovereign Judge. . . . I have bared my secret soul as Thou thyself hast seen it, Eternal Being! So let the numberless legion of my fellow men gather round me, and hear my confessions. Let them groan at my depravities, and blush for my misdeeds." From *The Confessions of Jean-Jacques Rousseau*, trans. J. M. Cohen (Baltimore, 1953), p. 7.

[11] Cf. Jacques Voisine, "Le dialogue avec le lecteur dans *Les confessions*," in *Jean-Jacques Rousseau et son oeuvre: Commémoration et colloque de Paris* (Paris, 1964), pp. 23-32.

In Rousseau's work the private emotions and conscience inherit some of the functions assigned to God in traditional theological discourse. As a consequence, the veracity of the narrative must be demonstrated with reference to intimate feeling, to the strict contemporaneity of emotion communicated in the writing. Pathos replaces the traditional address to a transcendent being as the sign of reliable expression. Thus it is not surprising to see Rousseau take from Montaigne and the Latin epistolary writers the *quicquid in buccam venit*, and to attribute to it, this time, a quasi-ontological value: the spontaneity of the writing, copied closely (in principle) from the actual spontaneous sentiment (which is given as if it were an old, relived emotion), assures the authenticity of the narration. So style, as Rousseau himself says, takes on an importance that is not limited to the introduction of language alone, to the technical search for effects alone: it becomes "self-referential," it undertakes to refer back to the "internal" truth within the author. In recalling old feelings, Rousseau wants to make the present narration strictly dependent on the "impressions" of the past:

> Il faudroit, pour ce que j'ai à dire, inventer un langage aussi nouveau que mon projet: car quel ton, quel style prendre pour débrouiller ce chaos immense de sentiments si divers, si contradictoires, souvent si vils et quelquefois si sublimes dont je fus sans cesse agité? Je prends donc mon parti sur le style comme sur les choses. Je ne m'attacherai point à le rendre uniforme; j'aurai toujours celui qui me viendra, j'en changerai selon mon humeur sans scrupule, je dirai chaque chose comme je la sens, comme je la vois, sans recherche, sans gêne, sans m'embarrasser de la bigarrure. En me livrant au souvenir de l'impression reçue et au sentiment présent je peindrai doublement l'état de mon âme, savoir au moment où l'événement m'est arrivé et au moment où je l'ai écrit: mon style inégal et naturel, tantôt rapide et tantôt diffus, tantôt sage et tantôt fou, tantôt grave et tantôt gai fera lui-même partie de mon histoire. (*Oeuvres complètes*, I, 1153)[12]

[12] "For what I have to say I need to invent a language which is as new as my project: for what tone, what style can I assume to unravel the immense chaos of sentiments, so diverse, so contradictory, often so vile and sometimes so sublime, which have agitated me without respite? . . . Thus I have decided to do the same with my style as with my content. I shall not apply myself to rendering it uniform; I shall always put down what comes to me, I shall change it according to my humor without scruple, I shall say each thing as I feel it, as I see it, without study, without diffi-

Among the diversity of styles cited by Rousseau, two particularly significant "tonalities" strike us in reading the *Confessions*: the elegiac and the picaresque.

The elegiac tone (as it is used, for example, in the celebrated lines that open the Sixth Book) expresses the feeling of lost happiness. Living in a time of affliction and menacing shadows, the writer takes refuge in the memory of the happy hours of his youth. The sojourn at Les Charmettes becomes the object of a fond regret: Rousseau is carried off by imagination, he tastes again vanished pleasures. Thus, by his imagination and at will, he fixes in writing a moment of his life in which he longs to hide. He is certain that such happiness will never come to him again:

> Mon imagination, qui dans ma jeunesse allait toujours en avant et maintenant rétrograde, compense par ces doux souvenirs l'espoir que j'ai pour jamais perdu. Je ne vois plus rien dans l'avenir qui me tente: les seuls retours du passé peuvent me flatter, et ces retours si vifs et si vrais dans l'époque dont je parle me font souvent vivre heureux malgré mes malheurs. (*Oeuvres complètes*, I, 226)[13]

The qualitative accent visibly favors the past, to the detriment of the present. The present in which these memories are set down is a time of disgrace; the old era that Rousseau is trying to recapture in writing is a lost paradise.

On the other hand, in narrative of the picaresque type it is the past that is "deficient": a time of weaknesses, errors, wandering, humiliations, expedients. Traditionally, the picaresque narrative is attributed to a character who has arrived at a certain stage of ease and "respectability" and who retraces, through an adventurous past, his humble beginnings at the fringes of society. *Then* he did

---

culty, without burdening myself about the resulting mixture. In giving myself up to the memory of the received impression and the present feeling, I shall doubly paint the state of my soul, namely at the moment when the event happened to me and the moment when I wrote it: my uneven and natural style, sometimes rapid and sometimes diffuse, sometimes wise and sometimes mad, sometimes grave and sometimes gay, will itself form part of my story." The translation is by Seymour Chatman.

[13] "My imagination, which in my youth always looked forward but now looks back, compensates me with these sweet memories for the hope I have lost for ever. I no longer see anything in the future to attract me; only a return into the past can please me, and these vivid and precise returns into the period of which I am speaking often give me moments of happiness in spite of my misfortunes." The translation is by J. M. Cohen.

not know the world, he was a stranger, he got by as best he could, more often for the worse than for the better, encountering on the way all the abuse, all the oppressive power, all the insolence of those above him. For the picaresque narrator, the present is the time of well-merited repose, of seeing oneself finally a winner, of finding a place in the social order. He can laugh at his former self, that obscure and needy wretch who could only respond in hang-dog fashion to the world's vanities. He can speak of his past with irony, condescension, pity, amusement. This narrative tone often requires the imaginary presence of an addressee, a confidante who is made an indulgent and amused accomplice by the playfulness with which the most outrageous behavior is recounted. For example, the Lazarillo de Tormès, the prototype of the picaresque hero, is offered to the reader as a character named simply *vuestra merced*, and, pleasantly inverting the Augustinian confession, presents himself with the vow "not to be holier than my neighbors"— "confesando yo no ser mas sancto que mis vecinos." Lazarillo's desire to begin at the beginning ("por el principio") is not without relevance to the method of Jean-Jacques' *Confessions*, for Lazarillo also wants to give a complete picture of his person ("por que se tenga entera noticia de mi persona").[14]

As a matter of fact, not only are purely picaresque episodes very numerous in the first six books of the *Confessions*, but it is not unusual to find elegiac episodes intimately mixed with picaresque, the change occurring back and forth with great rapidity. Shouldn't we recognize, here, in this full re-creation of lived experience, the equivalent of an important aspect of Rousseau's "system," a replica of his philosophy of history? According to that philosophy, man originally possessed happiness and joy: in comparison with that first felicity, the present is a time of degradation and corruption. But man was originally a brute deprived of "light," his reason still asleep; compared to that initial obscurity, the present is a time of lucid reflection and enlarged consciousness. The past, then, is at once the object of nostalgia and the object of irony; the present is at once a state of (moral) degradation and (intellectual) superiority.[15]

[14] *La vie de Lazarillo de Tormès*, introduction by Marcel Bataillon (Paris, 1958), Prologue, p. 88.

[15] I refer principally to *Discours sur l'origine de l'inégalité*. Cf. Preface and critical commentary in Rousseau, *Oeuvres complètes*, III.

Some Principles of Autobiography

William L. Howarth

Critics of autobiography still preside over an unfederated domain, so each feels compelled to begin with a new definition of the genre. We have an ample number of precedents, ranging from hostility to encomia, most of them centering on the relative value of history and art, fiction and fact. Others, tracing the growth of autobiography since the Middle Ages, call it a history of the human mind, reflecting man's rise from dogma to greater individuality. But these views all pack the same evolutionary bias: that recent lives are necessarily more complex, and their stories more challenging; that the content of a life shapes the form of its story, and not the other way around. Of paramount importance to most critics is the autobiographer's ideology or profession, which supposedly influenced the events and values of his book. So the critics customarily divide authors into separate categories and—working like so many vocational counselors—grade them according to religious denomination or social class. As a result, we learn that a "simple" faith produces a simple narrative, that a soldier writes as a soldier, a poet always as a poet.[1]

While this definition of autobiography may be useful for social historians, it is hardly a suitable basis for critical evaluation. Some readers have resisted the occupational mode of defining autobiography, preferring a broader and more inclusive scheme of classification. A partial disclaimer appears in Roy Pascal's influential book *Design and Truth in Autobiography*, which argues convincingly that autobiography is a unique literary form, offering its close readers a complex set of interpretive problems. But Pascal's sensi-

[1] For two examples of this approach, see Paul Delany, *British Autobiography in the Seventeenth Century* (London, 1969), pp. 1-5, and Daniel B. Shea, Jr., *Spiritual Autobiography in Early America* (Princeton, 1968), pp. ix-xi.

"Some Principles of Autobiography" by William L. Howarth originally appeared in *New Literary History* 5 (1974): 363-381. Copyright © 1974 by The Johns Hopkins University Press. Reprinted by permission.

tive analysis of the genre is marred by rather insistent value judgments. The "true" autobiography, in his opinion, tells us not merely of remembered deeds and thoughts but is for both author and reader "a spiritual experiment, a voyage of discovery." After this declaration we might well expect a hierarchical ranking of autobiographers, grouped according to the range of their great-circle sailing. Instead, Pascal follows the conventional route of typing by profession or calling: science (Darwin, Freud), politics (Hitler, Trotsky, Gandhi), while admitting that each story differs according to its author's "specific achievement." To date, only Francis Hart has disclaimed this evaluative view, charging that it imposes rigid and exclusive notions of propriety. More than one type of autobiography exists, Hart believes, and the task of critics is to help identify those variants. His "anatomy" of intentions is an admirable start in this direction, a trend I certainly hope to promote.[2]

As a contribution, I will propose a simple analogy: an *autobiography* is a *self-portrait*. Each of those italicized words suggests a double entity, expressed as a series of reciprocal transactions. The *self* thinks and acts; it knows that it exists alone and with others. A *portrait* is space and time, illusion and reality, painter and model—each element places a demand, yields a concession. A *self-portrait* is even more uniquely transactional. No longer distinctly separate, the artist-model must alternately pose and paint. He *composes* the composition, in both senses of that verb; his costume and setting form the picture and also depict its form. In a mirror he studies reversed images, familiar to himself but not to others. A single mirror restricts him to full or three-quarter faces; he may not paint his profile, because he cannot see it. The image resists visual analysis; as he moves to paint a hand, the hand must also move. The image is also complete, and entirely superficial; yet he must begin with the invisible, with lines more raw than bone or flesh, building volume and tone, sketch and underpaint, into a finished replica of himself. So he works from memory as well as sight, in two levels of time, on two planes of space, while reaching for those other dimensions, depth and the future. The process is alternately reductive and expansive; it imparts to a single picture the force of universal implications.

Autobiography is a literary version of this curious artifact. Lan-

<hr>

[2] Roy Pascal, *Design and Truth in Autobiography* (Cambridge, Mass., 1960), pp. 54, 132; Francis R. Hart, "Notes for an Anatomy of Modern Autobiography," *New Literary History* 1 (1970): 485-511.

guage and paint are clearly dissimilar materials, requiring different forms of selection or arrangement, but in autobiography vision and memory remain the essential controls, time and space the central problems, reduction and expansion the desired goals. An autobiography is equally a work of art and life, for no one writes such a book until he has lived out the requisite years. During his life he remains uncertain of cause and effect, rarely sensing the full shape or continuity of experiences. But in writing his story he artfully defines, restricts, or shapes that life into a self-portrait—one far different from his original model, resembling life but actually composed and framed as an artful invention. Autobiography is thus hardly "factual," "unimaginative," or even "nonfictional," for it welcomes all the devices of skilled narration and observes few of the restrictions—accuracy, impartiality, inclusiveness—imposed upon other forms of historical literature. So a reader can legitimately study autobiography as he does other literary genres, by identifying its structural elements and observing their complex relations. As a first step in determining autobiographical principles, we need to identify those elements.

ELEMENTS OF AUTOBIOGRAPHY

Coleridge tells us that most writing begins with a prime decision, an "initiative" that affects the author's entire process of composition, telling him what to write, when to edit, and how to unify the remainder. The decision to write one's autobiography is at least a strategic beginning, whether part of a master plan or born of frustration and personal anxiety. Northrop Frye, working back from Coleridge to Aristotle, identifies three elements that subsequently guide a writer's progress: *mythos*, *ethos*, and *dianoia*, or action, character, and theme.[3] In a single narrative these elements form a sequence of contexts and relationships, passing through alternate phases of dominance or dormancy. For my present purposes, the terms require both translation and modification: *character* and *theme* replace *ethos* and *dianoia*, while *technique* represents *mythos*, the author's action. In the case of autobiography, how he acts *upon* the narrative often overshadows how he acts *in* it.

Standing foremost in an autobiographer's strategy is the element

[3] Northrop Frye, *Anatomy of Criticism* (Princeton, 1957), pp. 52-73. Subsequent references are by page number.

of *character*, the image or self-portrait his book presents. Various factors determine that character: his sense of self, of place, of history, of his motives for writing. We must carefully distinguish this character from the author himself, since it performs as a double persona: telling the story as a narrator, enacting it as a protagonist. Although these two figures are the same person, artist and model, we may still distinguish their essential points of separation. They share the same name, but not the same time and space. A narrator always knows more than his protagonist, yet he remains faithful to the latter's ignorance for the sake of credible suspense. Eventually the reverse images have to merge; as past approaches present, the protagonist's deeds should begin to match his narrator's thoughts.

A second factor in autobiographical strategy is the element of *technique*, which embraces those plastic devices—style, imagery, structure—that build a self-portrait from its inside out. These technical components have not received the attention they deserve, with the exception of some promising work on style. But Pascal's assertion that style varies according to the autobiographical "personality" or "calling" (p. 79) has been challenged by Jean Starobinski, who holds that autobiographers determine style only insofar as it "satisfies the conditions of the genre."[4] Style, then, is not subservient to content, but is a formal device significant in its own right. Even the simplest stylistic choices, of tense or person, are directly meaningful, since they lead to larger effects, like those of metaphor and tone.

The final strategic element is *theme*, those ideas and beliefs that give an autobiography its meaning, or at least make it a consistent replica of the writer. Theme may arise from the author's general philosophy, religious faith, or political and cultural attitudes. His theme is personal but also representative of an era, just as other literary works may illustrate the history of ideas. In fact, autobiography has an especially inclusive thematic base, since its writers constantly grapple with issues—love, memory, death—that appeal to a broad reading public. We might attribute these themes to historical causes, noting changes in the interplay of authors and readers across the centuries. But this path can lead to rather broad generalizations; a simpler practice is noting how each autobiographer orchestrates his theme—in various guises and contexts—to

---

[4] Jean Starobinski, "The Style of Autobiography," *Literary Style: A Symposium*, ed. Seymour Chatman (New York, 1971), pp. 285-294.

give himself, his story, and his reader a stronger sense of intellectual unity. In its broadest sense, the theme of autobiography is *life*,
since the story cannot legitimately end in death—the hand must
pose while forever in motion. An autobiographer needs some other
form of narrative resolution, linking his personal ambitions with
those of a reader. As we shall see, thematic conclusions are the
clearest indication of differences in autobiographical strategy.

These three elements—character, technique, theme—operate as
continuous complements in autobiography, but they are best examined in sequence. Each of them relates to an isolated aspect of composition: the writer (character), the work (technique), and the
reader (theme); yet all three form a single chain of relationships
progressing from motive, to method, to meaning. By analyzing
these elements in sequence we can trace an outline of the autobiographer's strategy, distinguishing his achievement from other works
while affirming his place in a literary tradition. This method of
analysis should expand and diversify our notion of the genre; it also
challenges the practice of ranking works according to "truth,"
propriety, content, or aesthetic merit. For too long critics have held
that autobiography is "unique," that is, unprecedented but also
monolithic in form. I hope to encourage a new response, one that
finds more variety among the works and more similarity to established literary genres. If we can see that autobiographers do not always share the same principles, then we should no longer have to
read them with a single set of values.

AUTOBIOGRAPHY AS ORATORY

One means of recognizing some different principles of autobiography is to examine its pictorial equivalent, the self-portrait. We
can begin with two Renaissance paintings, both details from larger
frescoes: the self-portraits of Raphael and Michelangelo (figures 1
and 2).[5] At first glance, these pictures seem quite dissimilar.
Raphael is graceful and melancholy, his face blank except for two
large and tranquil eyes. Michelangelo appears as a flayed skin,
grotesquely tortured, his face melting into virtual anonymity. Yet

[5] For information on the paintings depicted here, I am indebted to two valuable
studies: Ludwig Goldscheider, *Five Hundred Self-Portraits from Antique Times to the
Present Day* . . . , trans. J. B. Shaw (Vienna, 1937), and Manuel Gasser, *Self-Portraits
from the Fifteenth Century to the Present Day*, trans. A. Malcolm (New York, 1963).
For photographic assistance, I thank Mr. Harold D. Connelly, Department of Art
and Archaeology, Princeton University.

both artists portray an idealized self, epitomizing a stage in their artistic careers: Raphael, dead at thirty-seven, paints the unblemished purity of Youth; while Michelangelo, who reached eighty-nine, depicts the inevitable corruption of Age. Both also subordinate themselves to larger, martyred figures: Raphael to Sodoma, a painter ruined by his own notoriety; Michelangelo to St. Bartholomew, resurrected but still the unknown Apostle. Raphael comments here on the destruction of Sodoma's fresco, directly above his own; Michelangelo wearily concludes his long struggle with the Sistine Chapel. Their portraits are sermons on a common theme, an artist's fame and fortune, that has an appropriate place within their larger allegories of Athens and Purgatory.

The paintings typify a class of self-portraits, those that preach an ideology, and they also resemble a group of autobiographers who share analogous *oratorical* aims. St. Augustine is the primary exemplar of this type of autobiography. And Augustine has many followers through the centuries: my representative choices, in this essay, are John Bunyan, Edward Gibbon, Henry Adams, and Malcolm X—all men who share a common devotion to doctrine, whether in religion, history, or politics.

Previous critics have recognized an "Augustinian" mode of autobiography, but they identify its features and practitioners with rather limited criteria. Many assume that all religious lives are in this category, separated by doctrinal barriers, but essentially "success stories" that teach the lesson of grace. Others adopt more formal positions, alternately calling the mode "dogmatic," "expository," and "epic."[6] Frye suggests a different approach in his explanation of the "high mimetic" mode, whose hero defines his superiority through the power of preaching or public oratory (pp. 58-59). Since its purpose is didactic, his story is allegorical, seeking to represent in a single life an idealized pattern of human behavior. The allegory often has messianic overtones, replete with suffering and martyrdom, as the orator leads his people to their rightful home. Doctrine alone does not give him this authority; to lead he must master oratory, the art of being heard.

Our five autobiographers represent this strategy, regardless of

[6] See Georges Gusdorf, "Conditions et limites de l'autobiographie," *Formen der Selbstdarstellung: Analekten zu einer Geschichte des literarischen Selbstportraits*, ed. Günther Reichenkron and Erich Haase (Berlin, 1956), pp. 18-23; Wayne Shumaker, *English Autobiography: Its Emergence, Materials, and Forms* (Berkeley and Los Angeles, 1954), pp. 142-157; and Robert F. Sayre, *The Examined Self: Benjamin Franklin, Henry Adams, Henry James* (Princeton, 1964), pp. 196-201.

1. Raphael and Sodoma, detail from *The School of Athens* (1509–1511). Rome, Vatican.

2. Michelangelo, detail from *The Last Judgment* (ca. 1540): St. Bartholomew and his flayed skin. Rome, Sistine Chapel.

their beliefs or aims. The common manifestation of a strong and principled character determines the persona's two didactic roles: as narrator, he teaches his prime lesson; as protagonist, he relives and learns from his days of sin or error. The narrator usually sympathizes with his protagonist, but only from a patronizing distance. Augustine certainly cannot relish his early acceptance of the Manichaean heresy:

> And because this strange form of piety of mine led me to believe that a good God had never created any evil nature, I came to the conclusion that there were two masses in opposition to each other, both infinite, but the evil one more contracted and the good one more expansive. And from this pestilent beginning other sacrilegious notions followed naturally.[7]

And Gibbon cannot graciously acknowledge his youthful conversion to the Church of Rome:

> To my actual feelings it seems incredible that I could ever believe that I believed in transubstantiation. But the conqueror oppressed me with the sacramental words, *"Hoc est corpus meum,"* and dashed against each other the figurative half-meanings of the Protestant sects. Every objection was resolved into omnipotence, and after repeating at St. Mary's the Athanasian Creed, I humbly acquiesced in the mystery of the Real Presence.[8]

In both passages the past has surrendered to present exegesis: Augustine finds his ideas "strange," "pestilent," "sacrilegious"; Gibbon mockingly attributes his "incredible" behavior to the forces of oppression and acquiescence. Both analyses clearly derive from a recent perspective, where theologian and historian dominate the narrative voice.

Such a strong, positive sense of character in autobiographers arises from a common motive: to carve public monuments out of their private lives. This didactic purpose, which explains Adams's choice of "Education" as a metaphor for his life, affects readers and authors alike. Each man writes for his own sake, to confirm the validity of his thesis, and also for the conversion of others. But he does not always respond to a "calling": if Augustine and Bunyan

---

[7] *The Confessions of St. Augustine*, trans. Rex Warner (New York, 1963), p. 105.

[8] *The Autobiography of Edward Gibbon*, ed. Dero A. Saunders (New York, 1961), p. 84.

exult in the triumph of God's unity, Gibbon and Adams resignedly accept the victory of universal decay. Malcolm X, caught between the forces of religion and history, ponders their alternatives and never quite chooses either way: "And if I can die having brought any light, having exposed any meaningful truth that will help to destroy the racist cancer that is malignant in the body of America—then, all of the credit is due to Allah. Only the mistakes have been mine."[9]

Inevitably, readers will ask if such a character is "true." Certainly, he is not "true to life," since he tells a censored account, epitomizing himself, like Raphael and Michelangelo, admitting no facts that fail to support his central thesis: Gibbon excludes his childhood, Bunyan and Adams omit their marriages. This censorship may savor of insincerity, but it also serves an orator's purposes as he converts the surviving details into meaningful allegory. Malcolm X writes exhaustively on the art of designing a perfect "conk"—a straightened hairdo that represents his bankrupt racial pride. The details are not literal history but figural narration. They give us selected aspects of a larger allegory, representing the Afro-American "experience" through the manipulative power of art.

Since art is his métier, the oratorical autobiographer closely attends to matters of literary technique. He is a master rhetorician, thoroughly versed in the arts of persuasion or argument and capable of any logical maneuver that serves his purpose. His rhetoric may be traditional, like Augustine's, proverbial, as is Bunyan's, or ornamental, like Gibbon's; in each case the style *is* the man, exactly reflecting his self-control. His most familiar devices are parallelism (especially in long series of subordinate clauses), amplification, and refrain; all convey his strength and coherence as an orator. An impressive example is in Adams's opening pages, where rhetoric becomes a landscape of his own mind:

> Winter and summer, cold and heat, town and country, force and freedom, marked two modes of life and thought, balanced like lobes of the brain. Town was winter confinement, school, rule, discipline; straight, gloomy streets, piled with six feet of snow in the middle; frosts that made the snow sing under wheels or runners; thaws when the streets became dangerous to cross; society of uncles, aunts, and cousins who expected

[9] *The Autobiography of Malcolm X*, ed. Alex Haley (New York, 1966), p. 382.

children to behave themselves, and who were not always gratified; above all else, winter represented the desire to escape and go free. Town was restraint, law, unity. Country, only seven miles away, was liberty, diversity, outlawry, the endless delight of mere sense impressions given by nature for nothing, and breathed by boys without knowing it.[10]

The style common to oratorical autobiography also affects its narrative mode and structure. Just as the painters subordinate themselves to others, so does each writer pose as an apologist, ready to defend his faith in a system larger than himself that explains earthly cause and effect. Gibbon and Adams, the two great skeptics, may seem unsuited to this description until we recognize their absolute *faith* in iconoclasm. As narrators, they all dismember their protagonists, who stand outside the unity of true belief: Adams calls his protagonist a "manikin," for whom his narrator, a "tailor," makes suits of clothing; narrator Malcolm identifies his protagonist with a succession of nicknames—"Mascot," "Home-boy," "Detroit Red," "Satan." But the two figures have to merge as narrative time passes. When living and writing begin to overlap, the tailor must become his own manikin, just as "Satan" becomes "El Haaj" (one who has seen Mecca). So the narrative structure joins text and preacher by simplifying time sequences, compressing some years and expanding others. Augustine's first four books cover twenty-eight years, the time of pagan confusion; the next five books treat only *four* years, climaxing his conversion; and the last four books abandon chronology for a celebration of the Christian life. Gibbon and Adams follow similar patterns, speeding hastily past early years, slowing down to focus on turning points (*The Decline and Fall*, the Columbia Exposition), then lapsing into topical discussion of current views. The early years seem to be an introit chanted while approaching a sanctuary; the final years are a doxology sung in praise of self-certainty.

The character and technique of an oratorical autobiography make its theme obviously apparent. The theme is *vocation*, the special summons that guided an entire life's work and now its story. Work made the story, story remakes the work: they justify each other by reducing all complexities to a single substance. Even Adams, who wanted to depict multiplicity, wrote instead a rigidly unified book. Unity is the orators' common theme, and it springs from a com-

[10] *The Education of Henry Adams*, ed. Ernest Samuels (Boston, 1973), pp. 7-8.

mon source: their belief in a superior force—God, History, Nature—that controls their entire careers, from remembered beginning to anticipated end. At the close of their books, all speak openly of death—with peace or foreboding, but in the same mood of stoic resignation.

To readers like Pascal, Augustine and his fellow writers seem least successful as autobiographers—"too exactly continuous and logical" in their rationalized versions of life. For James Olney, this mode is "autobiography simplex," a narrative—whether by Fox, Darwin, or Mill—dominated by a single metaphor, which its author understands and depicts in only a partial manner.[11] I cannot deny their strict narrative control or their limited preoccupations, but these qualities hardly seem defects, since I expect no more or less from other careful rhetoricians. Viewed more positively, each orator seems a pastoral figure, closely attentive to his listening flock, speaking aloud for the benefit of others. His own fame is important, but its object is to exemplify the ways of fortune. The reader is Augustine's principal auditor, despite his frequent invocations of God. What passes for private confession, for ideological harangue, may actually arise from deeper and far less selfish sources.

AUTOBIOGRAPHY AS DRAMA

We encounter a second autobiographical strategy via two unusual self-portraits by Parmigianino and Hogarth (figures 3 and 4). Parmigianino drew this peculiar image while observing himself in a convex mirror. Distorted to the normal eye (another convex lens), the picture has a natural appearance when viewed in a concave glass. Quite a visual riddle—when absurdity meets absurdity, the result is perfect sense! We learn little about Parmigianino from this picture, except that he was a playful young man. Perhaps he comments here on our notion of reality, certainly a public question, or maybe that Sphinx-like pose and enigmatic smile mask a private riddle. At any rate, he suggests both possibilities without openly taking sides. Instead of preaching an obvious sermon, he vividly impersonates, or dramatizes, several irreverent notions. Hogarth moves in a similar direction, avoiding direct comment for mocking

[11] Pascal, *Design and Truth*, p. 15; James Olney, *Metaphors of Self: The Meaning of Autobiography* (Princeton, 1972), pp. 39-41.

3. Parmigianino, *Self-portrait* (ca. 1523). Vienna, Kunsthistorisches Museum.

surrealism. In this whimsical self-portrait, also framed to suggest a mirror, he places himself beside his dog, whose face comically echoes its master's coarse, plebeian countenance. A few props complete this theatrical tableau: English culture (Shakespeare, Milton, Swift) resting by a palette inscribed "Line of Beauty and Grace," his droll title—and formal plan—for the entire composition.

The two painters resemble a class of autobiographers, equally original and devious, who share their *dramatic* principles. None of these writers has a thesis about his development; he assumes that he was and is essentially the same person, so his book depicts the past as a series of spontaneously ordered events. As an author he is unpretentious and impertinent, viewing life as a staged performance

4. Hogarth, *Self-portrait with a dog* (1745). London, Tate Gallery.

that he may attend, applaud, or attack, just as he pleases. Benvenuto Cellini exemplifies this strategy, in the company of James
Boswell, Benjamin Franklin, Sean O'Casey, and William Carlos
Williams. These are representative examples only; certainly Montaigne, Pepys, Casanova, and Mark Twain would also qualify. Re-

gardless of background or interests, all share a common preference for histrionics over dialectics, for acting instead of exhorting.

Critics have long accepted Cellini's importance as an autobiographical type, but mostly for historical reasons. To one he represents the triumph of "Renaissance individualism," unmatched in English autobiography before 1700 (praise that neglects Lord Herbert of Cherbury), but most assume that only soldiers, diplomats, and vagabonds fit this category, regardless of their literary talent. On more aesthetic grounds, others have called this mode "picaresque," "active," and "mixed,"[12] stressing that characters, scenes, and events dominate the narrative, not ideas. Again, Frye provides alternative criteria in his "low mimetic" mode, where characters entertain their readers with sensational adventures and boastful exploits (pp. 34-38). These swaggering heroes aggressively seek audiences, since society offers them the surest means of self-fulfillment. They are concrete, conventional types from whom two "narratives of probability" arise: realistic fiction and comic drama.

Our representative autobiographers exhibit strong traces of this theatrical character. Instead of dogma, they cherish idiosyncracy—not merely as a lesson to others but also as a performance of their innate skills. Yet performers are never self-sufficient; they must always obey the dictates of audiences, whose responses justify their craft. Each autobiographer thus functions in a double capacity, as artist and public servant: Cellini is a sculptor and soldier; Boswell, a writer and lawyer; Franklin, a satirist and statesman; O'Casey, a playwright and politician; Williams, a poet and doctor. Each balances the demands of self and society, moving easily between isolation and involvement, recalling his life for both private pleasure and public purpose. Apparently he understands the paradox of dramatic action, that an "actor" like Hamlet—or Parmigianino—can hold up the mirror to reality, faking a role to learn the truth. The dramatic autobiographer plays so many roles, from naif to schemer, that his exact identity is often a mystery. Franklin does speak smugly of his early success, but then ironically mocks his own fatuity:

> In reality, there is, perhaps, no one of our natural passions so
> hard to subdue as *pride*. Disguise it, struggle with it, beat it

[12] Delany, *British Autobiography*, pp. 168-169; Henri Peyre, *Literature and Sincerity* (New Haven, 1963), p. 205; Georges Gusdorf, *La découverte de soi* (Paris, 1948), Chapter 2; Shumaker, *English Autobiography*, pp. 158-177.

down, stifle it, mortify it as much as one pleases, it is still alive, and will every now and then peep out and show itself; you will see it, perhaps, often in this history; for even if I could conceive that I had completely overcome it, I should probably be proud of my humility.[13]

In his *London Journal* Boswell also hides behind masks, most of them confirming the buffoonish naiveté of their maker. But we know that he wrote the *Journal* carefully, inventing roles both for narrative appeal and as apprentice versions of his biographical personae, the simple toady and his Great Bear.

A puzzling mixture of fakery and truth, the dramatic autobiographer is equally divided between personal and cultural motives. Cellini opens his book with a bold annunciation:

It is true enough that men who have worked hard and shown a touch of genius have already proved their worth to the world. They have shown that they are capable men, and they are famous, and perhaps that should be sufficient. Still, I must do as I find others do, and so I intend to tell the story of my life with a certain amount of pride. There are many kinds of conceit, but the chief one is concern to let people know what a very ancient and gifted family one descends from.[14]

Yet for all his swagger, Cellini is no simple egotist—always his "ancient and gifted family" receives its proper due. He thanks those who helped him, admits his failures, and even praises superior artists like Michelangelo. He also insists on analogies between himself and the century, noting that both arrived in 1500 and thereafter shared a mutual history, including plagues, wars, and popes. Even Cellini's personality—robust yet sensitive, violent and gifted—emulates that paradoxical era; in every respect he is "The Renaissance Florentine," archetypal emissary of an entire culture. The other writers also have these historical dimensions: Franklin and Boswell represent "frontier" cultures, America and Scotland; O'Casey suggests that his unhappy childhood was also the tragedy of Ireland. Yet unlike the orators, this strategy derives its power from an apparent unconsciousness. The performers remain "in character" at all times; like Hogarth, they keep a stack of Great

---

[13] *Benjamin Franklin's Autobiography*, ed. Dixon Wechter (New York, 1965), p. 94.

[14] *The Autobiography of Benvenuto Cellini* (Baltimore, 1966), p. 15.

Books on hand but spare us any lame recitals—a concession to the audience that always wins applause.

This concoction of private and public motives certainly complicates the autobiographers' claims to "truth." They are all shameless liars and impersonators, slipping into disguises whenever, like Boswell, they need to walk some midnight Strand. But they dissemble obviously, with that disarming candor that is honest about its own deceit. The dramatic autobiographer also writes inclusively, compiling details to create a literal—not allegorical—version of life. At times these details help us to sense the truth, even when the writer cannot. In a famous passage, Cellini describes an allegedly supernatural event: "From the time I had my vision till now, a light—a brilliant splendour—has rested above my head, and has been clearly seen by those very few men I have wanted to show it to. It can be seen above my shadow, in the morning, for two hours after the sun has risen; it can be seen much better when the grass is wet with that soft dew; and it can also be seen in the evening, at sunset."[15] As J. A. Symonds first observed, Cellini's account is so detailed—down to time, place, and atmosphere—that modern readers can recognize his halo to be an optical illusion.[16] In effect, we correct his convexity with a concave glass, and so the uncensored story remains true to both Cellini's role and his audience's sensibilities—like a good piece of stage business, it is art and nature conjoined.

An easy balance between extremes also characterizes the dramatic autobiographer's literary technique. His style contrives not to prove but to portray a colloquial, conversational, and apparently spontaneous mind. This idiom is hardly accidental, since it accurately conveys a variety of effects. With a master like O'Casey, language produces whole characters, scenes, and cultures:

> —Be God, said the man with the wide watery mouth and the moustache drooping over it like a weeping willow, as he turned his head to speak to all in general, be God, they haven't spared any expense to turn Dublin into a glittherin' an' a shinin' show!
> —It's a shinin' sight to the eye that wants to see it so, said

[15] Ibid., p. 231.

[16] *The Life of Benvenuto Cellini*, trans. J. A. Symonds (New York, 1889), pp. xxii–xxv.

the conductor, with a bite in his voice; but to the Irish eye that sees thrue, it's but a grand gatherin' o' candles, lit to look sthrong, an' make merry over the corpse of our country.[17]

Of course, O'Casey wrote plays for a living, but the others also understand the principles of dramaturgy. They fabricate dialogue, shift scenery, arrange for lights and music—Boswell even writes scripts for his characters, complete with line tags and actor's cues. Their narrative devices are equally theatrical: Cellini modestly permits the Pope to marvel at his talent (choric response); Franklin highlights his wisdom by conversing with fools (analogous action). Boswell excels at recalling the significant conversation, O'Casey works entirely in that medium, and even Dr. Williams stages some effective scenes—in one, he delivers a three-hundred-pound woman of twins!

As in drama, the function of this narrative mode is to stress spectacle, the visible and pictorial aspects of life. Action, not exposition, becomes the author's principal tool, so his persona usually blurs its narrator and protagonist roles into one. Hogarth reminds us of this device, with a "Line of Beauty and Grace" abruptly linking him to his dog. That unity also supports the autobiographer's narrative structure, which follows certain dramatic principles. One is that circumstances will change, but not characters. Boswell and Franklin both depict their personal growth from naiveté to maturity, yet each life unfolds like a well-made play, according to the unities of time, place, and action. The important fact is each author's consistency—within those multiple impersonations, his irony, virtue, or artistry remain essentially intact, guiding him to an appropriate destiny. Thus Cellini tells his story as a succession of projects—from a tiny silver piece to the great bronze of Perseus—which consistently dramatize his growing talent.

On the back of his Perseus, Cellini wrought a secret self-image, which to most eyes seems only part of the statue's design (figure 5). Cellini's exact purpose remains obscure; we know only that he and Perseus continue to avoid Medusa's enchanting gaze.[18] We should take this emblem as a warning, and move cautiously while assessing the dramatic autobiographer's themes. His life lacks the voca-

---

[17] Sean O'Casey, *I Knock at the Door* (New York, 1964), pp. 275-276.

[18] For discussion, see *Tutta L'Opera del Cellini* (Milan, 1955), p. 44 and plates 46-49.

5. Two views of the *Perseus* (1554): *left*, Cellini's self-portrait; *right*, the full group. Florence, Museo Nazionale.

tional consistency of an orator's; with his multiple talents he is equally disposed to art or public life. So he does *both*, making jewels and defending forts, writing poems and removing tonsils.

If everything in life serves the artist, then he will value his native soil as highly as his personal talent. The dramatic autobiographer always pays special tribute to his earthly locale, whether Florence, Dublin, or Paterson. But he never bows to superior forces; for he is superior who acts his part well, at a given time and place upon the stage of life. His commitment is solely to life, so he never speaks of death at the close of his book. A play cannot end with its final curtain; in another performance it will always come to life again.

To many readers, Cellini and company only half succeed as autobiographers. Pascal acknowledges their charm and vigor, but characterizes their lack of reflection as "superficial." Lord Richard Butler admires the emphasis on action, yet notes that too much leads to simple memoirs, or "allobiography." David Levin responds well to Franklin's subtle irony, but—fearing less careful readers—finds the book "limited in pedagogical method."[19] But we must recognize that Franklin and the others are not teachers—they are actors, operating in the apparent reality of theatrical illusion. To understand their meaning, readers can turn only to these visible works, which hold the clues that may unlock their authors' intricate and often profound riddles.

AUTOBIOGRAPHY AS POETRY

Two famous artists, Rembrandt and Van Gogh, introduce us to a third autobiographical strategy. In his lifetime Rembrandt painted over a hundred self-portraits, seventy of them full studies. Viewed as a whole, they form a serial image, like frames in a strip of movie film. In these three examples (figures 6–8), Rembrandt's self-estimate alters as he ages—first vain (1631), then fanciful (1650), finally somber (1661)—and viewers may share in the movement of his discoveries. Van Gogh also painted numerous self-portraits, many as a form of therapy. In these two symbolic studies of his psyche (figures 9 and 10), one oriental, the other rustic, every detail—pose, frame, color, line—is a clue to his shifting, troubled

---

[19] Pascal, *Design and Truth*, p. 28; Lord Richard Butler, *The Difficult Art of Autobiography* (Oxford, 1968), p. 19; David Levin, *In Defense of Historical Literature: Essays on American History, Autobiography, Drama, and Fiction* (New York, 1967), pp. 70-75.

6. Rembrandt, *Self-portrait* (1631). Amsterdam, Rijksmuseum.

investigation. With both artists the important element is uncertainty—they ask themselves no consistent questions, find no
clear answers, and so continue to revise their self-portraits. Unable
to take an overview, they create a series of tentative pictures, each
more inconclusive than the last. The artists have neither preached
nor performed; theirs is the *poetic* act of continuing self-study.

Poetic autobiographers can also draw only tentative, experimental self-portraits. They share equally strong doubts, especially
about their current state of mind. Uncertain of the present, they
study the past for some explanation of their later difficulties. They

7. Rembrandt, *Self-portrait* (1650). Washington, D.C., National Gallery of Art.

are a moody, unpredictable lot, strongly critical of themselves and others, committed only to the right to change their ideas. Jean-Jacques Rousseau is the premier example of this strategy; his later followers include Henry Thoreau, Walt Whitman, William Butler Yeats, and James Agee. Again, these names are only representative—Goethe, Wordsworth, and Henry James could also be added. All are post-Romantic writers, tacitly sharing in that era's symbolist definition of "poetry" (the expression of fleeting, ineffable sensations), and many are American—perhaps, as Robert Sayre

8. Rembrandt, *Self-portrait as the Apostle Paul* (1661). Amsterdam, Rijksmuseum.

has suggested, because identity is an acutely puzzling problem on these shores.[20]

Critics have acknowledge Rousseau's distinctive form of autobiography, but again for limited purposes. He is praised for his ob-

[20] Sayre, *The Examined Self*, pp. 38-42. See also W. C. Spengemann and L. R. Lundquist, "Autobiography and the American Myth," *American Quarterly* 17 (1965): 501-519. An excellent survey of this subject, with bibliography, is Albert E. Stone, "Autobiography and American Culture," *American Studies: An International Newsletter* 11 (1972): 22-36.

9. Van Gogh, Self-portrait, *à mon ami Paul Gauguin* (1888). Cambridge, Mass., Fogg Art Museum.

sessive and contradictory self-consciousness, more bluntly labeled as "incredible paranoia." Readers less interested in neurosis have called similar autobiographies "critical," "narrative," and "elegiac,"[21] taking as respective models anthropology, fiction, and

[21] Peyre, *Literature and Sincerity*, pp. 86-97; Stephen A. Shapiro, "The Dark Continent of Literature: Autobiography," *Comparative Literature Studies* 5 (1968): 432; Gusdorf, *La découverte de soi*, Chapter 3; Shumaker, *English Autobiography*, pp. 185-213; Sayre, *The Examined Self*, pp. 202-208.

10. Van Gogh, *Self-portrait* (1888). Detroit, Institute of Arts.

poetry. Frye enlarges the final option by defining an "ironic" mode (pp. 324–325), where the author, not fully understanding himself, turns from his audience, suppresses moral judgments, and refuses to say what he means—or mean what he says. From his conceal-ment, a paradox emerges: he writes solely for himself, in the *lyric* genre, but the hero of his book is its reader, who alone can master its final form.

Our poetic autobiographers all seem equally paradoxical: they are "difficult" men, given to intellectual brooding and sharp critical dissent, searching always for private discoveries, uncertain of the proper course to follow. Indeed, they alter course frequently, beginning with motives that fail to pan out: Rousseau and Yeats seek their "true" pasts, Thoreau explains everything in terms of money, Whitman and Agee doom their books to failure. Eventually, these motives change—a fact that strongly influences their autobiographical character. When a writer does not fully understand his purpose, he can only portray himself as a serial image; his reader has to provide the missing continuity. Keats tells us that the poetical character has no ego, only negative capability, the power to be "in uncertainties, Mysteries, doubts, without any irritable reaching after fact and reason." In poetic autobiography this power operates at cross purposes with the genre, denying its traditional function of self-esteem but supplying a new measure of anxiety and dislocation that, ironically, post-Romantic readers find especially gratifying.

Given their authorial uncertainty, we must puzzle over how well these accounts record "the truth." Certainly, they seem not very true to the conventional aims of poetry—pleasure and instruction. Yet for each man, "truth" is a major preoccupation: Rousseau searches obsessively for his own "true self," Thoreau wants to "drive life into a corner," Agee vainly hopes to capture "a portion of unimagined existence." Consequently, their stories are all-inclusive in scope, rich with profuse detail. A slender book like Yeats's *Reveries* actually seems larger than Augustine's *Confessions*, for Yeats discusses art, politics, science, and religion, while Augustine treats mostly religion. If a poetic autobiographer lacks conviction, he at least permits us to witness his continuing experiments, successful or not.

This deemphasis on control creates problems as we consider matters of literary technique. Symbolist poetry is not an ideal model for prose narratives, but we can hardly deny that Whitman and Yeats narrate under the influence of their poetry. Their technical devices seem less artificial than Augustine's because they work for seemingly uncontrived effects, appropriate to an immediate context. Thoreau's description of "the scenery of Walden," for example, gradually becomes a complex, carefully wrought analogy for the human personality, yet never once does he violate the pond's physical reality: "It is earth's eye; looking into which the beholder measures the depth of his own nature."[22] Meaning is not imposed upon facts, it emerges from them—slowly, organically, as the ideas and images seem to find each other.

Since each of these autobiographers actually wrote verse, we have some justification for finding "poetic" devices in their prose. Sustained analysis of sample passages would undoubtedly reveal experiments with diction, rhythm, or imagery comparable to those in *Leaves of Grass* or *The Tower*. Certainly, their language fits Coleridge's definition of poetry, "the best words in the best order," and his injunction that the purpose of poetic language is primarily aesthetic, not didactic. If not metrical, the language *is* rhythmical; it abounds with figures of speech and suggests meanings without explaining them to death. Agee is the most "poetical" prose stylist of them all, as his passage on the retiring Gudger family may indicate:

> . . . and George's grouched, sleepy voice, and hers to him, no words audible; and the shuffling; and a twisting in beds, and grumbling of weak springs; and the whimpering sinking, and expired; and the sound of breathing, strong, not sleeping, now, slowed, now, long, long, drawn off as lightest lithest edge of bow, thinner, thinner, a thread, a filament; nothing; and once more that silence wherein more deep than starlight this home is foundered.[23]

Working here as a poetic neologist, Agee has found and shaped words that recapture his experiences and give them an entirely new significance, both to himself and to readers. His failure to control this sorcery eventually becomes Agee's tragic theme; but the style still fascinates readers and compels them to share in his agony.

These broad resources directly influence the narrative manner and form of a poetic autobiography. The narrators are less argumentative and entertaining than other types; one of their special passions is description—the ice at Walden, an Alabama cabin—arranged in long and intensely imagined catalogues. The persona remains fairly stable during these passages, separating into narrator-protagonist roles only in the story's final stages, as changes in attitude become more apparent. But finding structure in these stories remains a major difficulty, since even their authors usually

[22] *Walden*, ed. J. Lyndon Shanley (Princeton, 1971), p. 186.
[23] James Agee, *Let Us Now Praise Famous Men* (New York, 1969), pp. 55-56.

cannot see any overall patterns. So the reader shares the journey and charts its direction, noting any changes of course that may suggest progress. Rousseau writes with power and conviction of his youth, then stumbles into frantic delusions about his public career. Whitman moves in the opposite direction, from a hasty "synopsis" of early life to "authentic glints, specimen days" of his life as America's outsetting bard.

Yeats offers the best example of unpremeditated structure. He begins his *Reveries* assuming that childhood was an unhappy time, largely because of his father—a curious man, half disciplinarian and half iconoclast. So Yeats admires most his grandfather, a mysterious and seemingly all-powerful figure who dominated the entire family. But in the course of writing *Reveries*, Yeats comes to see his father anew, recognizing him as a source of ideas and tastes. Even the poet's aesthetic—freedom within order—mirrors his father's contradictory character. Exactly halfway through his narrative, Yeats pauses for a reestimate: "Looking backwards, it seems to me that I saw his mind in fragments, which had always hidden connections I only now begin to discover." That discovery made, the grandfather gradually loses his magical powers until, in the book's final scene, he dies pathetically, amid servants quarreling over his personal effects. Youth and its fantasies die with him, or so the narrator believes. But Yeats gives his story a final puzzling twist:

> For some months now I have lived with my own youth and childhood, not always writing indeed but thinking of it almost every day, and I am sorrowful and disturbed. It is not that I have accomplished too few of my plans, for I am not ambitious; but when I think of all the books I have read, and of the wise words I have heard spoken, and of the anxiety I have given to parents and grandparents, and of the hopes that I have had, all life weighed in the scales of my own life seems to me a preparation for something that never happens.[24]

Yeats defines here, as best he can, an enigmatic theme that haunts all of the poetic autobiographers. He compares "all life" (a weight) with "my own life" (a scales) and finds a disparity between them. His figure implies the need for suspension and balance, but instead he finds an essential inequity, "a preparation for something that

---

[24] *Reveries Over Childhood and Youth* in *The Autobiography of William Butler Yeats* (New York, 1965), p. 71.

never happens." The passage suggests an important paradox—that part and whole, self and others, must merge even though diametrically opposed. The other writers repeat this discovery, beginning with selfish and partial motives, ending with a need for others in order to be whole. Most sense this need clearly; but Rousseau is confused by his changes since youth, and so insists that readers will misinterpret him: "If anyone knows anything contrary to what I have here recorded, though he prove it a thousand times, his knowledge is a lie and an imposture."[25] Forever bound to his own idea of a "true self," Rousseau cannot see the pattern as it actually appears to readers.

An important difference among the three autobiographical strategies emerges from this discussion: Augustine and Cellini write books that either prove or depict a similar unity, but only Rousseau and his followers can reveal it *currente*. To them, vocation is not just a "calling" or public duty, but the creative act that autobiography itself demands. Writing a book becomes their means of fulfillment, for it assures them that the controlling force in life is neither God nor man alone but the imagination, where both of those powers are constantly potential. So each book remains as inconclusive as Rembrandt's self-portraits, without a definite end, expressing more than simple thoughts of life and death. Only the process of *becoming* is essential; if the book reveals that process, it endures, like a poem, forever.

Most readers feel that the poetic strategy is autobiography's finest effort, the "voyage of discovery" that Pascal values so highly. He finds in Rousseau the beginning of a new era in literary history, in which authors turn from genre traditions to themselves as centers of meaning and form. But that view exaggerates the extent to which autobiographical poets actually *understand* their meaning and form. Their principal virtue is freedom from traditional aesthetics, from the limits of argument and convention affecting most other autobiographers. The price of this liberty is a reader's eternal vigilance, since he must assume certain authorial obligations—an exciting transaction, surely, but not a little presumptive and even self-indulgent. For no matter how closely we peer into their self-portraits, we can never see beyond the autobiographers' mirrored reflections. As Yeats discovered, beneath their

[25] *The Confessions of Jean-Jacques Rousseau*, trans. J. M. Cohen (Baltimore, 1960), p. 605.

masks of benign serenity writers labor always in cold and despairing isolation: "I braved Taylor again and again as one might a savage animal as a test of courage, but always found him worse than my expectation. I would say, quoting Mill, 'Oratory is heard, poetry is overheard.' And he would answer, his voice full of contempt, that there was always an audience; and yet, in his moments of lofty speech, he himself was alone no matter what the crowd."[26]

[26] Yeats, *Reveries*, p. 65.

Confessions and Autobiography

Stephen Spender

The dictionary definition of the word *Autobiography* is: "the story of one's life written by himself." This starts a train of thought in my mind. "One's life written by himself"—just as if himself were A, B, or C, or some other writing his biography. Of course, the dictionary is right, but there is a world of difference in that "himself." Brown's Life written by Brown is—to my mind—a different proposition from Brown's Life written by Jones or Smith. At all events, it is a different proposition in the mind of Brown when he takes up his pen, remembering himself: though, in fact, he may well decide to pretend that he is Smith, writing his life as though he were another person. He may say: "What is significant about me in the minds of others is that which Jones or Smith would write as my biography. So let me pretend that I am Jones or Smith, and enter into a neighbor's-eye-view of myself." Yet in saying this, isn't Brown taking a tremendous step? In deciding to write his own biography as though he were Jones or Smith, isn't he excluding a whole world that is himself as he appears not to Jones or Smith but to himself?

Perhaps I overdramatize the affair: generals, statesmen, and big-game hunters—to take some random examples—may really appear to themselves exactly as they appear to other people. To themselves they are historic forces giving orders on battlefields, making speeches in Parliament, or moving through forests armed with guns like sticks, which they point at lions, tigers, and elephants. If there is anything left over from all this that is themselves, it is either unpublishable or else a charming proof to others of their humanity. For in the case of public personalities, humanity seems to begin where eccentricity appears, when they think or act in a way that is inconsistent with being generals, statesmen, or big-game hunters.

Yet unless one is to oneself entirely public, it seems that the problem of an autobiographer, when he considers the material of his own past, is that he is confronted not by one life—which he sees from the outside—but by two. One of these lives is himself as others see him—his social or historic personality—the sum of his achievements, his appearances, his personal relationships. All these are real to him as, say, his own image in a mirror. But there is also himself known only to himself, himself seen from the inside of his own existence. This inside self has a history that may have no significance in any objective "history of his time." It is the history of himself observing the observer, not the history of himself observed by others.

We are seen from the outside by our neighbors; but we remain always at the back of our eyes and our senses, situated in our bodies, like a driver in the front seat of a car seeing the other cars coming towards him. A single person, instead of being a tiny little automaton in a vast concourse of traffic that is the whole of humanity, is one consciousness within one machine confronting all the other traffic. From this point of view, being born into the world is like being a rocket shot onto the moon. And who knows whether being projected onto the moon would actually be so very different from being born into the world? At first one would perhaps feel very strange. But soon, one would—in the manner of all men—take one's own presence on the moon for granted, just as one takes the world for granted and accepts oneself as one of the others.

To feel strange, to retain throughout life the sense of being a voyager on the earth come from another sphere to whom everything remains wonderful, horrifying, and new, is, I suppose, to be an artist. Artists—whether they are writers or painters—are people who continue throughout life to realize that every experience is a unique event in time and space, occurring for the first and last time.

It might seem then, that autobiography was the most stimulating of forms for a writer. For here he is dealing with his life in the raw at the point where it is also his art in the raw. He can describe, through the history of his meeting with the people and things outside him, those opposite beings whom from the back of himself he sees coming towards him, the very sensation of being alive and being alone.

Yet, just because a writer is so rawly and newly in contact with his material—even because in his writing he draws so much on this new experience of ever first-seen life—autobiography may be especially difficult for him. For in this work, the expression of such naked solitude may be just what he wishes to avoid. He uses his observation in order to relate one thing to another, not to state experiences that are unrelated. Until his subjective experiences have become objectified—have become of a kind that he can identify and project into life outside himself—they are no use to him for his art. The essence of art is that opposite is related to its opposite. The subject has to be made object, the chaotic the formal, the unique the generally shared experience. Thus, although for a writer his autobiography is the vast mine from which he smelts ore to put into his works, it is also his aim to convert this ore into forms that are outside the writer's own personal ones.

In literature the autobiographical is transformed. It is no longer the writer's own experience: it becomes everyone's. He is no longer writing about himself: he is writing about life. He creates it, not as an object that is already familiar and observed, as he is observed by others, but as a new and revealing object, growing out of and beyond observation. Thus characters in a novel are based on the novelist's observation of real people and of himself. Yet they would not be "living" if they were just reported. They are also invented—that is new—characters, living in the scene of life that is his novel, independent of the material of real observation from which they came.

Thus autobiography does set the autobiographer a very special problem. The theme of his book is himself. Yet if he treats this theme as though he were another person writing about himself, then he evades the basic truth of autobiography which is: "I am alone in the universe." There may of course be many good reasons for refusing this truth. It may not be the writer's purpose to deal with it at all. He may be writing about himself because he is a part of history and his own best historian. Perhaps he thinks that the contribution he has made to politics or thought in his time should be recorded and that, being closest to it, he is the best person to record it. Thus we have in our time, by Albert Schweitzer, Freud, and Croce, excellent examples of objective, depersonalized autobiography. Then also there are reminiscences, like Sir Osbert Sitwell's volumes that are revealing of his family but tell us little about what it feels like to be in Sir Osbert's skin.

All this is perfectly justified. One does not have to defend it. Indeed, what one has to defend is the autobiographers who write about the intimate experience of being themselves. They are indiscreet, they are too interested in themselves, they write about things that are not important to others, they are egomaniacs. The nature of the inner human personality is such that if they tell what it is like to be themselves, they are immoralists, exhibitionists, pornographers. The inner voice of self-awareness is no respecter of human institutions, betrays other people, and reveals oneself as base. Maine de Biran—about whose *Intimate Journal* Mr. Aldous Huxley has written—expressed a doubt that the portrayer of the intimate self also feels. After discussing all his weaknesses, he reflects that perhaps the worst crime is all this interest in oneself.

Self-revelation of the inner life is perhaps a dirty business. Nevertheless, even in its ugliest forms we cannot afford altogether to despise anyone who—for whatever reasons—is the humblest and ugliest servant of truth. Human beings are instruments crawling about the surface of the earth, registering their reactions to one another and to things. Some of them are very crude instruments, others exact and sensitive. A human instrument is most exact about objective things when it is most detached from them. The effort to create form and objectivity in literature is detachment: and whoever writes of that which is most close to him—himself—is unlikely to achieve detachment.

Nevertheless in a day of pseudoscience when sociologists and psychologists are forever measuring the behavior of their neighbors, there is a justification for the autobiography that reminds us how lacking in objectivity human beings who set themselves up as observing instruments really are. The self-revelation of the experience of the self is a measuring of the human instrument by itself. The observer is self-observed.

The instrument, whether it is Rousseau in his *Confessions*, Restif de la Bretonne in his extraordinary outpouring *Monsieur Nicholas*, or Mr. Henry Miller in our own day, records without apparent regard for what, to all appearances, is objectively and historically most interesting, that in himself which is significant to himself. His purpose is to tell the exact truth about the person whom he knows most intimately—himself. His only criterion is naked truth: and usually his truth is naked without being altogether true.

The autobiographies of such self-confessors show pictures of themselves that if they had not been self-portrayed would certainly be unsuspected by their neighbors who only see from the outside the philosopher Rousseau, the journeyman printer Restif, the robust yet neighborly Mr. Henry Miller. Yet their books, although contesting defiantly the historical view of oneself, by oneself or by anyone else, have yet become a part of history—in Rousseau's case even a revolutionary part.

The sum of such works certainly makes one suspect the truth— even the historic truth—of official biography. If all men really have a point of view that looks from inwards outwards, then the true history of the world would be perhaps a sum of autobiographies, and not a sum of those biographies that are written by a man looking at another man from the outside. This is not quite true, because there is an objective life of society that in our public actions drives us along, disregards our subjective nature, and makes a philosopher, a printer, a writer, where the autobiographer says "this unique and unknown I." Yet Rousseau and the others make us suspicious of historians who offer as explanations for the crimes called history motives that are nearly always external, impersonal ones. Explanations so familiar that when we stumble on personal motives—such as Henry VIII's matrimonial reasons for precipitating the Reformation—we are rather at a loss, because they seem by their nature unhistoric. Perhaps they would seem less so if we knew more about the personal motives of other men in Henry VIII's time.

Restif de la Bretonne's *Monsieur Nicholas* is the autobiography of a journeyman printer who was born in Burgundy in the year 1734. His autobiography claims to be an entirely truthful account of more than sixty years of his life. It is in great part an account of the sexual exploits of a kind of plebeian Casanova. It purports to be written with the motive of revealing the exact truth about one human heart. Of course it has other motives: one is boasting; another is to make out that Restif was, under all his looseness, a pious moralist exhorting his readers to lead virtuous married lives. Yet despite his nauseating hypocrisy, Restif's plodding determination to describe the life he has known as seen from the very bottom of society and in terms of his own lowest experiences, does give an amazingly truthful picture of the eighteenth-century French lower classes. Hundreds of people are seen living miserably and trying to wrest a little forbidden pleasure out of life. Finally the effect is like seeing the inside of something—the inside, say, of a sofa, or a lined coat or a periwig. Restif's unctuous piety also serves a purpose—it is the gilt on the gingerbread, the outside point of view to which everyone pays lip service. Without it we would hardly recognize the back-to-front society Restif is describing. As a whole the book throws a rather salutary doubt on the history books' other side of the medal. Is not history—in the minds of most contemporaries—really something like the Lord Mayor's Show, which takes place in an important part of a town whose inhabitants are occupied in thinking about the furtive pleasures they may enjoy in cellars, garrets, and dark corners?

Restif de la Bretonne pretends, as I have said, that the purpose of his book is to preach a moral lesson. This brings us to another point about confession. All confessions are from subject to object, from the individual to the community or creed. Even the most shamelessly revealed inner life pleads its cause before the moral system of an outer, objective life. One of the things that the most abysmal confessions prove is the incapacity of even the most outcast creature to be alone. Indeed, the essence of the confession is that the one who feels outcast pleads with humanity to relate his isolation to its wholeness. He pleads to be forgiven, condoned, even condemned, so long as he is brought back into the wholeness of people and of things.

There could be no better example of this secret motive of the human heart than the opening pages of Rousseau's *Confessions*. Rousseau, it will be remembered, starts off by saying that he is about to undertake an enterprise that no one has ever undertaken before: namely to tell the whole truth about himself. In an extraordinary passage (which deserves to be illustrated by Mr. James Thurber) he then conjures up a picture of himself standing before the throne of the Almighty on the Day of Judgment, with his Confessions in his hand and reading them to the whole of assembled humanity. At the end of the reading (which must have taken up a good deal of eternity) Rousseau imagines himself challenging all his fellow beings to assert whether any of them dare say that after all he was a better man than this Rousseau, with all his sins and vices. God, who plays a rather passive role in Rousseau's heaven, is expected to call anyone who claims to have been a better man than Rousseau a liar.

Now what is the significance of this? Surely that the secret motive of Rousseau in undertaking that which he claims had never been attempted before was not to prove that he is different from other men but to prove that they are like himself. His *Confessions* are an attempt to force the hands of God and humanity, to confess that all are equally bad. Whether or not Rousseau was justified in claiming all men as his moral, or immoral, equals, there is something base in the attempt to make all life condone him, and I can understand the resentment that his name has always aroused. Society may be bad, but it should not be a conspiracy of guilty beings all loudly claiming that they are as bad as one another. Better than this the secrecy of the confessional, in which each person reveals his shame, without challenging the appearances that make up the decent hypocrisy of society.

And of course Rousseau does not tell the truth. There is a lie concealed within his very method. For to say to oneself: "If I tell the worst about myself I shall only reveal that I am no worse than other men" is dishonest. First, some men are better than others. Second, by the worst one means worst, and it is degrading to comfort oneself by attempting to prove that others are as bad as one's own worst. Third, there is the real possibility that Rousseau really might be worse than other people: there is the possibility of real moral solitude, and this is precisely what Rousseau cannot face. Perhaps the worst is the refusal to face this. Everyone is a liar about certain things. There are crimes to which we confess because they secretly flatter our sense of our own strength. But no one confesses to meanness, cowardice, vanity, pettiness: or at least not unless he is assured that his crime, instead of excluding him from humanity, brings him back into the moral fold.

Confession must always be to a confessor. The measuring rod of the human instrument is morality. And the human soul can only be measured adequately if there is an adequate confessor. Saint Augustine in his confessions bares his soul before a God who judges by a more accurate measuring rod than Rousseau's democracy. For what Rousseau is really confessing to is the spirit of democracy, and the nature and spirit of his confession measures that egalitarian confessor. He sees the virtues and vices as a kind of parliamentary system of the government of human morals, and he has a vague faith that the virtues and vices will somehow cancel one another out, leaving everyone equally good and equally bad with everyone else. The confessor, he claims, is also as good and bad as himself. Even God is implicated.

Thus confessional autobiography may be the record of a transformation of errors by values; or it may be a search for values, or even an attempt to justify the writer by an appeal to the lack of them. Saint Augustine's faults, even in the act of confessing them, are transformed by their avowal and become a witnessing of the power of God to save him. Rousseau reveals not only his own faults but also the pathetic fallacies of his belief that he is acquitted from faults by sharing them with other human hearts.

When we look at modern literature, we see that it is swamped with the material of confessional autobiography, though very few intimate revelations are written. This material is diverted into novels like Proust's or D. H. Lawrence's, or a book like T. E. Lawrence's *Seven Pillars of Wisdom*, which is in part crypto-confessional autobiography. When one considers the fashion for psychoanalysis, and how intimate confessions of thousands of people have flooded the statistics of sociologists like Dr. Kinsey, one suspects that ours is an age where many people feel a need to confess the tensions of their inner lives. Yet few autobiographies of a man's two lives are written. Instead we get books like Siegfried Sassoon's memoirs where a self-portrait verges on fiction, and novels where fiction is really autobiography. Why is this? I think it is because the inner life is regarded by most people as so dangerous that it cannot be revealed openly and directly. An antidote that can be applied at the very moment of revelation needs to be applied to this material. The antidote was once the Church. Today it is the vast machinery of psychological analysis and explanation.

So it is understandable that most people who write their autobiographies write the life of someone by himself and not the life of someone by his two selves. There certainly should not be many truthful self-revelations. All the same, when an André Gide or a Henry Miller comes along and says "I am I, and not a hero of fiction. I have thought unspeakable thoughts and done unthinkable things," he is measuring the capacity of human beings to tell the truth about themselves, and indirectly, by virtue of what he reveals, he is commenting on the values of the age in which he lives.

Recovering Literature's
Lost Ground
Through Autobiography

James M. Cox

My text is *The Autobiography of Thomas Jefferson*. It is hardly fair to contend that devoting attention to it is to recover lost ground for literature since there is scarcely any evidence that Jefferson's account of his life was ever held as literary ground. Literary critics and scholars of course ignore it. Historians and biographers accord it little more than perfunctory glances. The historian almost fatally sees the subjective element in all autobiography since he is perforce wearing his objective historical lenses. And the biographer, in self-defense, has to discount autobiographical reality in order to pursue the enterprise of biography at all. Yet despite its neglect, Jefferson's *Autobiography* will provide evidence of lost literary ground.

Even to assert that Jefferson's *Autobiography* is my text raises a problem, since that was not the original title of Jefferson's text. The narrative, first published in 1830 by Jefferson's grandson and literary executor, was entitled simply *Memoir*. Jefferson himself refers to his matter as memoranda. But in its modern reprintings (in the Putnam Capricorn paperback edited by Dumas Malone and in the Modern Library *Life and Selected Writings of Thomas Jefferson* edited by Adrienne Koch and William Peden) it is confidently presented as *The Autobiography of Thomas Jefferson* without so much as an editorial by-your-leave. This initial fact confirms what students of autobiography quickly learn—that is, the term autobiography is of relatively recent usage, its earliest recorded appearance having occurred at the end of the eighteenth century. Indeed, it was not until the middle of the nineteenth century that it began to be widely used as a

"Recovering Literature's Lost Ground Through Autobiography" by James M. Cox originally appeared as "Jefferson's *Autobiography*: Recovering Literature's Lost Ground" in *The Southern Review* 14, no. 4 (1978): 633-652. Copyright © 1978 by James M. Cox. Reprinted by permission of the author.

substitute for *memoir* and *confession*. Now the term is so dominant that it is used retroactively to include as well as to entitle books from the present all the way back into the ancient world. Thus Franklin and Vico, who wrote accounts or memoirs of their lives, appear before us with autobiographies. In addition to its triumph over time, autobiography is imperially employed in space by those who would apply it to novels, poems, essays, or even prefaces. Thus we now read that Henry James's prefaces to his New York Edition are really his autobiography; or that Freud's *Interpretation of Dreams* is his autobiography—and all this despite the fact that both men wrote narrative accounts of their own lives.

The historical emergence and domination of the term is one thing; the present critical emphasis on the subject is quite another. A collection of essays on autobiography would have been impossible as recently as a dozen years ago for the simple reason that the essays themselves did not exist; but they exist now in sufficient profusion that an editor can make a discriminating selection. This contemporary interest is a result of many factors: the relative "exhaustion" or critical exploitation of the traditional generic fields of drama, poetry, and fiction; the "political" possibilities of escaping from the seemingly aesthetic or closed dimension of imaginative literature into the historical and referential possibilities of autobiography; the theoretical potentialities afforded by the problematic reference that autobiography inevitably evokes; and, I think, the growing sense or fear that the "self" upon which the imperial extension of the term *autobiography* was predicated may in fact be nothing more than a fiction that contemporary critical theory will at last expose. Language will at last be recognized as writing the self; we will give up the ego and search for ourselves in that shifty pronominal shifter—the "I" of discourse.

My choice of Jefferson's autobiography as an exemplary text is indirectly related to all these possibilities, yet my reasons for choosing it are direct and different. First of all, it is a memoir, and, since I think that much criticism avoids the memoir, it is in a category of autobiography that needs attention. The memoir is, after all, pointed toward history and fact whereas literary criticism invariably seeks after creativity and imagination. There is a distinct tiresomeness about the ease with which literary critics assure themselves that "mere" fact has little to do with the art of autobiography. The truth or falsity of autobiography is thereby subordinated to the creativity, the design, the "inner" truth of the

narrative. The more we can say—and I have said it—that the autobiographer is creating and not inertly remembering his past life in
the present, the more we can claim for autobiography a presence all
but identical to the fictions and closed forms of "imaginative" literature both generated and mastered by New Critical literary theory.

What this procedure has meant in practice is a contraction of the
imaginative orbit. Teachers, students, and critics of literature have
more and more retreated from the world of fact, leaving it to the
historian or the political scientist. If there is too much fact or idea in
a piece of writing, it is under threat of abandonment. Look at how
Ruskin, Mill, Carlyle, and Newman have faded from the field of
undergraduate and even graduate study. The novel has all but
routed the essay from the period course. Indeed, I think—or
hope—that the present interest in autobiography is in part a hunger-
ing for a literature of content. Yet even here, the rampant "imaginative" tendency is evident. Thus autobiographies devoted to the
emotional consciousness of the writer have been much more subject to investigation than the memoir, particularly the memoir of
well-known public figures. More literary attention has been paid to
Frank Conroy's *Stop-time* than to Grant's *Memoirs*. After ?",
Grant's book is really "about" the Civil War, and Grant himsel .s
an "historical" figure. The same is true of Jefferson and his book. A
chief reason that I have chosen Jefferson's book is that it is almost
defiantly in the tradition of the memoir and therefore resistant to
the aspect of mind that literary students have come to call the imagination.

The issue of choosing Jefferson's text goes beyond the matter of
memoir; it goes to Jefferson himself and the relation of Jefferson to
the study of American literature. All teachers and students of the
subject know that lack of pure literary content (if pure literature has
content!) is the norm and not the exception in the colonial and fed-
eral periods. There are few novels, no dramas to speak of, and precious little poetry prior to 1820. There are instead a host of sermons, diaries, personal and captivity narratives, histories, and
political pamphlets. Yet in this very area abounding in what we are
now pleased to call nonfiction prose (the very designation tells us
just how utterly fiction has come to dominate literary study), it is
the Puritans who hold the field. Why is this true? Why is Jefferson,
for example, so essentially neglected? I imagine that Jefferson is a
central figure for historians and political scientists—as central, let us
say, as Hawthorne, Melville, or Whitman are to American litera-

ture. Whatever the case, he certainly is not central in any department of English. Jonathan Edwards receives much more literary attention than Jefferson; he even gets prominent presentation in an anthology called *Major Writers of America* edited by a galaxy of the most distinguished American literary scholars. Any teacher of American literature knows that the Puritans so dominate the study of early American literature that by the time the weary student gets through them in a course there is time only to be profoundly relieved with *The Autobiography of Benjamin Franklin*. Even Franklin is likely to be abused by any teacher who has worked himself into a state of sufficient high seriousness to endure the Puritans.

The Puritan ascension could be attributed to three causes: Harvard, Yale, and Perry Miller. Though that answer is hardly as facetious as it may sound, it is nonetheless inadequate. There is the Civil War, which consolidated, secularized, and even regionalized the original Puritan impulses into a dominant sway of American imperialism only now in the process of disintegrating. Then too there is probably a subliminal academic sympathy with the long, losing, embattled intellectualism of the Puritans; it may be an obscure donnish trade-off in which American literary scholars let the historians have Jefferson in exchange for Edwards, the grandfather of Aaron Burr; certainly it betrays the willingness of literary scholarship to link itself to morality more readily than to politics. Whatever the cause of Jefferson's slight hold on the literary mind, there is no possible way to justify Edwards as a superior writer or thinker. *Notes on Virginia* is in every way a more significant book for American literature than Edwards's *On the Freedom of the Will*—a text which, if we are to give things away, might well be surrendered to the philosophers or theologians. All this is not to demean Edwards; it is to disclose the absurd logic that has somehow placed him ahead of Jefferson. Think of the students in American literature who have been subjected to Edwards's dreary "Personal Narrative" yet retain profound ignorance of Jefferson's memoir.

The point remains, however, that Jefferson did write an autobiography; and Jefferson, whatever else he was, was a writer—probably the most powerful writer America has produced. Despite the complaints an instructor of English might make about his tendency toward weak passive constructions, there is probably no more powerful statement written by an American than "all men are created equal." How wise Robert Frost was to have his sensitive speaker in "The Black Cottage" observe that that Jeffersonian sentence "will trouble us a thousand years." It is the most volatile text that we know or have. And although no one really believes it to be true, who could wish that it had not been written? And written into the very conception of the country?

In all probability, Jefferson shouldn't have written an autobiography; certainly his own ideas about the past constituted a strong counterthrust to whatever requests came from without or whatever impulses came from within to furnish the world his autobiography. He had spent a great part of his life trying to overthrow the past; he had even maintained throughout most of his long life that every generation had a right to its own revolt. Something of that counterthrust is evident in Jefferson's contention for privacy in the first paragraph of the autobiography: "At the age of 77, I begin to make some memoranda, and state some recollections of dates and facts concerning myself, for my own more ready reference, and for the information of my family."[1]

Beyond this blunt assertion of age, we know very little about the writing of the book, and Jefferson's biographers provide practically no information beyond Jefferson's initial declaration. He began it 6 January 1821, when he was struggling to get his last great project, the University of Virginia, into being; when the Missouri Compromise cast its dark shadow on his country's future; when he felt his own powers increasingly at the mercy of the benevolent nature his reason had imagined; and when he could see how the American revolutionary impulse had set in motion a movement eventuating in the tyranny of Napoleon and the subsequent massive conservative balance of power in the wake of Waterloo. In this connection, it seems strange that Dumas Malone, in his relatively extensive introduction to the *Autobiography*, has not a word to say about the writing of the book—which likely means that he will have no more to say when he concludes his massive biography. And Erik Erikson, who devoted a small book to the issue of discerning Jefferson's identity, never discusses the autobiography.

To be sure, Jefferson himself is somewhat casual in his relationship to the book. He did not "finish" it—it covers the years from his birth in 1743 until his return from France in 1790 to join Washington's administration—but here it is important to realize that

---

[1] "Autobiography of Thomas Jefferson," in *The Life and Selected Writings of Thomas Jefferson*, ed. Adrienne Koch and William Peden (New York, 1944), p. 3. Page references for the "Autobiography" will hereafter be given in the text.

first-person autobiographies cannot really be finished except with the death of the author. Jefferson is aware of the problem and keeps before himself principles of procedure sufficiently tentative to free him from the necessity of completing his project and to liberate him into the possibility of quitting his book when he wants to. Midway in his text he finds himself involved with the problem of education and announces his intention of returning to the subject "towards the close of my story, if I should have life and resolution enough to reach that term; for I am already tired of talking about myself" (p. 51). Presumably Jefferson had life enough left, but he evidently lacked the resolution. Or perhaps the resolution was directed toward completing the building and opening of the University of Virginia rather than getting to the point in his narrative where he could return to the subject of education. In any event, he never recurs to the subject, but stops his autobiography with his visit to Benjamin Franklin upon returning to America.

Between Jefferson's beginning and ending, he does not pursue or cover his personal life; instead he sedulously avoids it. He offers all but nothing about his parents, having only this to say of his mother and his mother's family: "They trace their pedigree far back in England and Scotland, to which let everyone ascribe the faith and merit he chooses" (p. 3). Though the irony here could be construed as savage, it is more likely bland. As for his father, Jefferson estimates his worth in a few measured words of praise. Nothing at all about his brother and six sisters—other than that they exist in number, not in name. And only the barest mention of his marriage to the widow Martha Skelton, daughter of John Wayles, which doubled Jefferson's property; later on, there is the fact of her death, which ended ten years of what he calls "unchecquered happiness" (p. 53). As if this were not lack enough, there is hardly a word in the book about Monticello, the passion of Jefferson's life. Small wonder that the book exists as a dead text to students of literature—dead for those ignorant of it, and dead no doubt to those who, looking for the "life" of autobiography, would see only its absence in this book. Above all, it is dead to biographers who, complacently settled in the assurance that their narratives will give us the life of Jefferson (even as those same narratives pursue him to his death), see the memoir as little more than a fund of inert facts.

This deadness in the book is actually the resistance of Jefferson's text to those who believe that personality is life. In Jefferson's hands, the memoir is not so much dead as it is a death mask—a still life molded from the outer lineaments of the face with which Jefferson faced the world. Lacking the color of a portrait, the death mask follows the lines of form rather than image. It is cold; it is hard; it is resistant; it is there. Of course, the notion of memoir as death mask is no more than a metaphor that might carry us away. Like almost every autobiography, Jefferson's is in words, and we have to do the best we can with them. The question looms: In view of Jefferson's omission of his personal life, what is his written life?

His life is, first of all, his writing. It is, as he writes in that already quoted first sentence, his beginning to make memoranda and to state recollections of dates and facts concerning his life. The acts of writing and beginning and stating are the verbs that signal both the structure and style of the book. Beginnings are more important than endings; statements are more important than narration; recollections are more important than memory; dates and facts are more important than emotion and consciousness. But it is not his present beginning to write that interests Jefferson, except insofar as that act is wedded to his past writing—and wedded in such a way as to make the past writing a present fact.

That is why Jefferson all but dispenses with his early life in a swift movement toward the key event of his life, his authorship of the Declaration of Independence.[2] To make the fact present, Jefferson gives his text of the Declaration, prefacing it with these remarks:

> As the sentiments of men are known not only by what they receive, but what they reject also, I will state the form of the Declaration as originally reported. The parts struck out by Congress shall be distinguished by a black line drawn under them; and those inserted by them shall be placed in the margin, or in a concurrent column. (p. 21)

The presence of what Jefferson contends is his original text seems to me a remarkable fact in his autobiography. (Admittedly, such a fact may not offer the thrill to a student of literature available in *Moby*

---

[2] In *Inventing America: Jefferson's Declaration of Independence* (New York, 1978), pp. 167-168, Garry Wills makes the excellent point that the fire which destroyed Jefferson's home at Shadwell on 1 February 1770 also destroyed scholarly access to the world that had made Jefferson. I would add that, since it destroyed almost all that Jefferson had written, it destroyed Jefferson's own access to that world of his past. Wills makes a valiant effort to reconstruct Jefferson's lost world, but Jefferson left it out of his life.

Dick or *Huckleberry Finn*.) Yet one should not have to be a specialist in history or autobiography to find that text and that fact interesting. Not only is there the substantive meaning in the additions to and deletions from Jefferson's original (for example, the deletion of Jefferson's attribution of slavery to George III and also of his renunciation of *all* British kings forever; and the addition of reliance "upon the protection of divine providence" in the last paragraph of the document); there is the enormous significance of Jefferson's fact. Whatever Jefferson is eliminating from his written account of his life—his personality, his inner feelings, his private relations—he is stating, affirming, and maintaining his original authorship of the Declaration. If, as author, he had to subject himself to the revision and censorship of a deliberative body, he is nonetheless—rather, all the more—the writer contending at the end of his life for his original text.

Much as we might want to look between the lines for Jefferson's concealed personality, it is of first importance to see that Jefferson sees his life in this book as what he had written for his country and the world. He had, after all, practically written the world for his countrymen to live in. Though it is possible to feel only the deadness of both that fact and the original text, it is equally possible to see them as possessing the energy of Jefferson's revolutionary individuality controlled by his political equilibrium. To see the original text paralleling the adopted text is to see how profoundly Jefferson had converted himself into political energy and how completely he sees that political and historical text as his life. Jefferson does not have to say anything about himself—and perhaps *cannot* reveal himself—because he originally translated himself into a text that began the history and life of a people. It is just this text that becomes the opaque effacement of the private self we continually yearn for in autobiography; yet it is worth remembering that this pronouncedly self-evident text—so publicly and so inertly part of our consciousness—guarantees our privacy even as it perpetually declares our public existence as a nation. Surely it is fitting that such an author as Jefferson—and there is only one such author—would understandably obscure the private self from public eyes, as if his Declaration, which converted the private "I" into the public "we," were the impenetrable façade at once creating and sealing off private space behind its monumental prose.

To be sure, in his autobiography Jefferson converts himself back into the "I" of autobiographical discourse. Yet the reader who has sensed the dimensions of Jefferson's Declaration can gain energy from as well as give it to the external and resistant structure of Jefferson's memoir. Believing that any inference about Jefferson's inner life not based on generous interest in the solid surface of his written life will be hollow indeed, I want to pursue the body of Jefferson's narrative as if it were the foundation of his being. However much I may fail to penetrate the mask of Jefferson, I will at least have given something of an introduction to the contents and organization of the book. Such a pursuit may leave us in a position to infer an inner space.

Jefferson follows his assertion of himself as author of the Declaration with an account of the two great debates that occurred during the framing of the Articles of Confederation: the debate on Article XI as to whether slaves should be counted as population in determining national taxation; and the debate on Article XVII on whether the Confederated States should have equal votes or votes in proportion to their population in deciding questions. Jefferson never discloses his views on the two issues but meticulously and scrupulously summarizes the arguments of the speakers on both sides, finally indicating how the states voted. These central questions on taxation and representation, dull though they may seem in Jefferson's summary, were the perennial questions of America. They had risen to unite the colonies in division from England; they threatened to divide the United States throughout the period of confederation and constitution; and they were to haunt the nation until 1865. In writing about them in 1821 in the immediate wake of the Missouri Compromise, Jefferson was touching at the storm center of his country. Yet he never once alludes to the ominous history and significance that these questions had for the past, present, and future of his country; he vouches instead for the authenticity of his meticulous report on the basis of his having taken it from notes written *at the time* of the debates. Thus his past writing is again claimed as the foundation of his present text at the same moment that the status of history is conferred upon the spoken opinions of more than forty years between the experience and the book. It is vital to see this process if we are to understand that Jefferson is not relying on facts but continuing to make facts. We may say that any reader can ascribe to these facts "the faith and merit he chooses." In Jefferson's text, they are reported with the stillness and detachment of statements—as if, in the world announced by the Declaration, the colonies had indeed become *states* and could speak for themselves.

Conventions, Congress, Declaration, statement, states: the world of government. It is to this world that Jefferson both gave and dedicated so much of his life—with, it must be remembered, tremendous reluctance and resistance—and to which he gives practically all of it in his autobiography. Though by no means modest in relating his contributions, neither is he vain. Instead he states, or reports, his contribution to the making of government just as he reported bills to the Virginia Legislature, to which he went after the Articles of Confederation were framed. Those bills—to establish courts of justice, to abolish laws of entail, to suspend importation of slaves, and to establish religious freedom—Jefferson considers the cornerstones of "a system by which every fibre would be eradicated of ancient or future aristocracy; and a foundation laid for a government truly republican" (p. 51). The vision here is implicitly architectural, one in which democratic structure will replace aristocratic texture.

This whole portion of the autobiography recounting Jefferson's authorship of the Declaration and his work in the Virginia legislature constitutes Jefferson's contribution to the establishment of representative government; in style it reflects his own self-government—his own inner system of checks and balances. The decision to avoid declaiming or defending himself, the determination to stay in his public rather than in his personal life, and the refusal to moralize his actions are all suppressions of self in order to make a life of representation and not a representative life. It is just here that Jefferson's autobiography differs so widely from Franklin's, which is a wonderfully representative life. Franklin makes public his relatively obscure early life and shows how he succeeded in governing himself; Jefferson tends much more toward seeing his life as a result of the history he has made by writing.

From his account of "laying the foundations of a government truly republican," Jefferson moves to his contributions to that government as it entered the world of existing governments. He notes his development of a standard of currency based on the decimal system, his work in the Congress to help ratify the Treaty of Paris, his career as Minister Plenipotentiary in Paris as a successor to Franklin. Before embarking on this extensive sequence of material, he insistently indicates his decision not to recount his life as Governor of Virginia:

> Being now, as it were, identified with the Commonwealth itself, to write my own history, during the two years of my administration, would be to write the public history of that portion of the revolution within this State. This has been done by others, and particularly by Mr. Girardin, who wrote his Continuation of Burke's History of Virginia, while at Milton, in this neighborhood, had free access to all my papers while composing it, and has given as faithful an account as I could myself. (pp. 52-53)

This quotation makes clear that Jefferson sees his life as a history of himself; it also reiterates how deeply Jefferson identifies history with written documents. At the same time, it makes a clear distinction between a person's own history and his public life. As governor or president, Jefferson would apparently see his life as identical with the state or nation and therefore as available to a historian as to himself, provided the historian had "free access" to the papers of his subject.

Yet the placid clarity of the quote deserves scrutiny. After all, Jefferson's "own" history is itself largely public. What after all, is the Declaration of Independence if not a totally public "life" of Jefferson? The very question begins to yield its answer. The Declaration is, as Jefferson sees it, his own text, and in this autobiography he can control that text even though he could not totally control it in the Congress. He can, even as he relates the history, lay claim to his authorship. As governor of Virginia he was much more the "property" of the state. Of course it would be possible—I think too possible—to point out that his career as governor was not so successful as his work in Philadelphia and in France. A better connection is Jefferson's design for his tomb, which he made during the same period that he wrote his autobiography. He directed in no uncertain terms that three, and only three, of his acts would constitute his memorial: "Author of the Declaration of American Independence, and of the Statute of Virginia for religious freedom & Father of the University of Virginia."

Author and father! these are the terms Jefferson kept somehow and somewhere for himself. To have authored those texts and to have fathered that structure were claims Jefferson felt strong

enough to be engraved on his stone. These were acts that had some
priority over the history Jefferson was a part of. Yet the moment he
is past those acts of authorship, Jefferson is at the threshold of being
·merely part of the history his very authorship has made possible.
At just this moment in his text Jefferson is betraying some of the
pressure his act of autobiography is beginning to put on him. Moving into areas of his life where the equilibrium between his own history and the history he has lived through is being broken, he is at
the threshold of being a prisoner of his own text. His very life had
been similarly threatened, for he was forever at the threshold of
being the prisoner of the free country he had "written." No wonder he felt a certain freedom in France, where he was, after all, out
of the country he had written.

Even so, Jefferson's account of his diplomatic years involves him
in difficulties. Going to France may have seemed preferable to remaining governor of Virginia at the time Jefferson made the decision; and it might have seemed a preferable memory when Jefferson
wrote his life. But it was by no means an escape. The first thing to
see, however, is the disposition of Jefferson's narrative. As a diplomat, he is commissioned to negotiate treaties that will ensure
commercial equity and protection for the new country that he was
originally delegated to author; as a writer, he is publishing *Notes on
Virginia* in Paris. He thus represents both his state and country to
and in the Old World. More important, the author of a country
that has literally intruded itself into the sequence of history is observing the disequilibrium caused by this new historical force in the
society of nations. Jefferson writes at length of the betrayal of the
Dutch Republic into English hands by the Prince of Orange. Any
reader with a moderate sensitivity to history will see that Jefferson's
intention is to show how quickly and successfully counterrevo-
lutionary forces (inevitably embodied by England, which had, in
Jefferson's view, driven the American colonies to revolution) as-
saulted the forms of republican government.

At the same time Jefferson watches the irresistible tide of repub-
licanism emerge in and sweep through France. He not only occupies a box seat in what he earlier calls the theatre of revolution as
it shifts to France but he is himself something of a center of attraction in the unfolding drama, for the republican intellectuals in
France come to him for advice on how to proceed. Experienced in
revolution, Jefferson was a shrewdly practical counsellor as well as
a diplomat who had to maintain a poised balance between his sym-

pathies and his responsibilities. Balanced though he might be between his beliefs and his diplomacy, he was a passionately partisan
republican and remained one right up to the time he wrote the autobiography. Nevertheless, at the time he was in France, he was
caught in a swiftly moving chain of events that got rapidly out of
control; but probably more important, at the time of writing, Jefferson faced the course of history that had intervened between 1789
and 1821. Thus, if he was caught in the chain of events in 1789, in
1821 he was confronted by the very narrative of history. Significantly enough, Jefferson's exposition of issues begins to be transformed into a narrative of events as he recounts the beginning of
the French Revolution. Author as legislator is replaced by author as
observer.

Although Jefferson recounts those momentous events with great
authority, he clearly and inescapably knows that he is in a new relation to his narrative. Indeed, he knows much better than would
many a literary critic. This is what he observes as he emerges from
his extended account of events in France:

> Here I discontinue my relation of the French Revolution. The
> minuteness with which I have so far given its details, is dispro-
> portioned to the general scale of my narrative. But I have
> thought it justified by the interest which the whole world must
> take in this Revolution. As yet, we are but in the first chapter
> of its history. The appeal to the rights of man, which had been
> made in the United States, was taken up by France, first of the
> European nations. From her, the spirit has spread over those of
> the South. The tyrants of the North have allied indeed against
> it; but it is irresistible. Their opposition will only multiply its
> millions of human victims; their own satellites will catch it,
> and the condition of man through the civilized world, will be
> finally and greatly ameliorated. This is a wonderful instance of
> great events from small causes. So inscrutable is the arrange-
> ment of causes and consequences in this world, that a two-
> penny duty on tea, unjustly imposed in a sequestered part of it,
> changes the condition of all its inhabitants. I have been more
> minute in relating the early transactions of this regeneration,
> because I was in circumstances peculiarly favorable for a
> knowledge of the truth. Possessing the confidence and inti-
> macy of the leading Patriots, and more than all, of the Marquis
> Fayette, their head and Atlas, who had no secrets from me, I

learned with correctness the views and proceedings of that party; while my intercourse with the diplomatic missionaries of Europe at Paris, all of them with the court, and eager in prying into its councils and proceedings, gave me a knowledge of these also. My information was always, and immediately committed to writing, in letters to Mr. Jay, and often to my friends, and a recurrence to these letters now insures me against errors of memory. (pp. 109-110)[3]

I quote Jefferson at length here because the passage shows his sure consciousness of what he is about. He sees his narrative, true architect that he was, in terms of scale and proportion; he knows that the history in which he participated is utterly central and utterly continuous; he knows that he took part in its beginning and thus knows without having to insist that his written life has a priority all its own; he is sure of the truth of his account not only because he was a privileged observer with access to both sides but because he committed his experience immediately to writing. That is why he has no doubt of the cause and substance of his writing being the history of the future and why he sees history itself as a book with chapters—as if all our lives were in the process of becoming a text. Steady and measured though Jefferson's rhetoric is in such a passage, the events being recounted are violent. More important, the book of history that Jefferson envisions is also violent. Though he believes that the condition of man will be ameliorated, he just as clearly states that the process will be as violent as it is relentless.

The assurance and the detachment of Jefferson's narrative breathe a confidence that is at the heart of the stillness and purity of his life of himself. Describing the discussion with the leading patriots who came to his quarters to confer upon the revolutionary course of action to pursue, Jefferson remarks:

> The discussions began at the hour of four, and were continued till ten o'clock in the evening; during which time, I was a silent witness to a coolness and candor of argument, unusual in the conflicts of political opinion; to a logical reasoning, and chaste eloquence, disfigured by no gaudy tinsel of rhetoric or decla-

---

[3] A point worth noting in this passage is Jefferson's emphasis on the tyrants of the North and the revolutionaries of the South. This division has particular resonance for the world that Jefferson was envisioning in 1821.

mation, and truly worthy of being placed in parallel with the
finest dialogues of antiquity, as handed to us by Xenophon, by
Plato and Cicero. (pp. 108-109)

This passage, by implication surely a direct slash at the rhetoric of
Edmund Burke, shows Jefferson's own aspiration—a style cool,
chaste, logical, free from ornamental texture, which will take its
place with the monumental writing of the classical age in which history has been distilled back to the texts that ultimately constituted it
in the beginning.

Does this mean that the time that has transpired since Jefferson
committed himself to his initial text has no meaning? Of course
not. The time between becomes something of a spacial perspective
in that it is all but silent, yet remarkably present in its silence. Thus
intervening years do not provide a bridge of introspection, regret,
nostalgia, or correction over which an erring, reconstructive, or
reflective memory can pass as a rhetorical force. Neither time nor
perspective are bifurcated in Jefferson's narrative. The present from
which he writes is not a point from which to review the past so
much as it is a point of vantage from which to stabilize it, to reinforce it as the fixed source and foundation of the present. Memory
itself is, in Jefferson's eyes, inevitably erring; reflection is self-
justifying. These are the faculties which, in an autobiography, generate the emotional, confessional, and defensive self that Jefferson
neither wants nor believes his written life to be. He wants instead to
have written his life into history at the outset, and he is clearly confident that he has so written it. That is why the text of the Declaration is so early and so completely present in the *Autobiography*.

The distinction between Jefferson's "own" self and history has its
primary basis in the difference between Jefferson's text and that
which the Congress adopted. And the chief difference resulting
from congressional modification of Jefferson's text, as Jefferson sees
history, is the presence of slavery in the United States. Although
Jefferson does not openly lament congressional action, it is clear
from his autobiography that he is determined to disclose that slavery is a flaw in the structure of the builder, not in the design of the
architect. Yet it is just as clear from Jefferson's references to slavery
that he is by no means smug about his own relation to the subject.
Every time he touches upon it his rhetoric betrays an urgency bor-
dering on fear. Judicious scrutiny of his original text of the Declara-

tion discloses this urgency and intensity in the accusations hurled at the King for having perpetrated the institution.[4] The fear is overtly expressed in Jefferson's remarkable discussion of the racial and social implications of slavery in Notes on Virginia. It could of course be argued that neither of these texts is quite the text of the *Autobiography*; that would be true for Notes on Virginia but precisely false for the Declaration, since it is Jefferson's original text of that document that absolutely *is* the text of his autobiography. And it is in that original text that we (as readers and as Americans) have the privilege of seeing for ourselves Jefferson's attempt to escape the issue of slavery by charging it to the King. The effort did not work then because the delegates could not agree on giving up slavery and so deleted that item as one of the King's crimes.

But there is another point in Jefferson's text at which he comes to grips with the issue of slavery. Just before concluding his account of the bills he "reported" to the Virginia legislature—those bills that would form the foundation for a government "truly republican"—Jefferson remarks the failure of his bill to stop importation of slaves to pass the legislature. His observations deserve quoting at length:

> The bill on the subject of slaves, was a mere digest of the existing laws respecting them, without any intimation of a plan for a future and general emancipation. It was thought better that this should be kept back, and attempted only by way of amendment, whenever the bill should be brought on. The principles of the amendment, however, were agreed on, that is to say, the freedom of all born after a certain day, and deportation at a proper age. But it was found that the public mind would not yet bear the proposition, nor will it bear it even at this day. Yet the day is not distant when it must bear and adopt it, or worse will follow. Nothing is more certainly written in the book of fate, than that these people are to be free; nor is it less certain that the two races, equally free, cannot live in the same government. Nature, habit, opinion have drawn indelible lines of distinction between them. It is still in our power to direct the process of emancipation and deportation, peaceably, and in such slow degree, as that the evil will wear off insensi-

[4] Wills makes the striking observation that Jefferson is actually charging the King with *freeing* the slaves and encouraging them to turn against their masters. See *Inventing America*, p. 72.

bly, and their place be, *pari passu*, filled up by free white labor-
ers. If, on the contrary, it is left to force itself on, human nature must shudder at the prospect held up. We should in vain
look for an example in the Spanish deportation or deletion of
the Moors. This precedent would fall far short of our case. (p.
51)

That paragraph immediately follows Jefferson's indication that he is
tired of talking about himself and may not have "life and resolution" to return to the subject of education "towards the close" of
his story.

Like Jefferson's inclusion of the original text of the Declaration,
the passage seems to me one of the great presences in his autobiography. It is immediately vital for any reader. American history and
American identity are so intricately related to it that it would be sad
indeed to think that it is "history" rather than "literature." It is
writing by the author of the Declaration of Independence and it has
to be faced. It would be easy to explain it away, just as it would be
easy to fulminate about Jefferson's bigotry, just as it would also be
easy to say that we live in a liberated time and must remember that
Jefferson didn't have all the advantages we have. None of these responses strikes me with anything like the force of the very presence
of that paragraph. Far better to face the historical truth of the
statement than to moralize or psychologize the issue. Very few
modern readers would find emancipation and deportation an adequate answer to the question of American slavery. They would,
however, have to acknowledge that it was an answer that was
never tried. Instead, there was emancipation by force and with a
violence fully equal to Jefferson's prophetic fears.

To recognize so much is by no means to claim that emancipation
by force should not have been tried. It is to see instead that Jefferson
was fully recognizing the violent history that the Declaration of Independence had inaugurated and was himself realizing the inevita-
bility and the irresistibility of the force that had been unleashed. He
himself is hoping that something can be done. When he says that he
does not believe that the two races can live in the same government, we have to know that we are still contending that they can;
that contention is nothing less than the violent course of our history. And if we are not *certain* that the two races can live "in the
same government," we are nonetheless committed to the proposition that they can. It took a Lincoln to articulate that proposition on

a bloody battlefield; it has taken more than a hundred years of political turmoil, breach of law, violation of civil rights, and adamantine
Supreme Court rulings to sustain the proposition. That hundred
years is not merely shameful, as some would have it; rather, it is
violently powerful and is inseparable from a powerful and dominant central government that has become a major world power
with a foreign policy by no means unrelated to the antislavery
moral force Lincoln's Emancipation Proclamation incorporated
into the identity of the government. It has been a foreign policy
backed by fire and violence sufficient to give us pause at last. Few
would want the pause to be momentous enough to cripple our contention and our hope that the two races can live together peacefully;
yet surely we want it to be intense enough to give us present consciousness of Jefferson's text.

If we are students of that text and if we have consciousness to
give, then the text becomes something more than dead. We can see
that freedom and deportation is a conflict for Jefferson strong
enough to bind him in paradox. Thus his unforgettable observation
that "nothing is more certainly written in the book of fate than that
these people are to be free" is violently balanced by a counterweight, equally certain, to the effect that the two races cannot live
together and remain equally free. Jefferson almost always seeks balance, but not balance as antithesis so much as balance as equilibrium. The balance that he enunciates here is all but a paralyzing sta-
bility, causing him to appeal for resolution of an unreconcilable
conflict. The measure of the weakness of that appeal is located in
the forbidding future prospect—a prospect so fearful that it will
force human nature to "shudder." That verb, though muted in Jefferson's essentially temperate cadences, deserves all the weight the
most sensitive reader can give it, for Jefferson eschews violent,
florid, and hyperbolic rhetoric. His language is that of declaration,
not proclamation.

Yet this very passage, coming as it does at the end of his cool
account of his achievements in the Virginia legislature, shows a fear
of the future. And it shows that fear at precisely the moment Jefferson is at the threshold of entering his account of his years in
France—the violent narrative that he envisions as contributing to
the first chapter of the new history of freedom. Before the reader
can know what Jefferson will recount, Jefferson is already envisioning a future in which freedom is written in a book of fate. In other
words, before Jefferson can reach that point in his past where a nar-

rative of violent events overcame his deliberative exposition, he has, in his exquisitely restrained manner, revealed momentous anxiety about the future.

This anxiety, once perceived, is richly in the text, not beneath it. A student of literature or psychology might wish to convert it too quickly into terms of personality. I am not averse to seeing it in such terms, provided there is a determined effort to see the text first in terms of history. To have felt the life of Jefferson's history—his memoir—is to be at the threshold of surmising a mythic Jefferson, which is to say a symbolic reading of the life of the author of our country. I want to trace such a myth in its most tentative outlines—not only because such a reading is tentative but because autobiography as memoir holds itself in relation to history as well as to personality. It is to the text of his country, after all, that Jefferson gave himself; and that country which Jefferson continued to serve and in which he lived becomes in turn the book of history to which he alludes. Even so, there is a symbolic narrative to be inferred from Jefferson's form.

If Jefferson gives little attention to his parents and even to his wife, it should be remembered that his texts, this one included, are hard on parent figures. The Declaration itself, after its great steady assertions, becomes a whole series of assaults upon the King—and upon all kings. The bill for religious freedom decentralizes, defuses, and diffuses the energy of God. And Jefferson's other bills were to abolish primogeniture and entail. These monumental decisions, which are inseparable from writing this country into being, enter the stream of history and eventuate in the killing of the king and queen in France. Though he left France before they were executed, their deaths and the subsequent tyranny of Napoleon are glaring facts in the space between Jefferson's present text and that past text he is stabilizing. Was the original structure wrong to have brought such violence?

As he moves forward to the portion of his narrative in which his own ideas become a force in history, the clarity, serenity, and security of his perspective are all but brought to judgment. The anxiety, first manifestly evident in his remarks on slavery and the book of fate, is implicitly active in the form of narrative itself. Deliberation is superseded by sequence; history as text becomes history as chapter; fear of the future leads into anxiety about the past; rhetoric of declaration is brought to the threshold of becoming rhetoric of defense.

Faced with the regicide at the end of his account of the beginning of the French Revolution, Jefferson once again finds himself appealing—but appealing or wishing that an event had not happened, not that it will not happen. Separated from the King by an ocean, Jefferson and his countrymen had been spared the necessity of killing George III; they declared their country separate from the mother country, as indeed it geographically was. Yet their revolution had set in motion the much more violent French Revolution. Wishing that a constitution had been formed on the lines of limited monarchy, leaving the King "to do all the good of his station, and so limited, as to restrain him from its abuse," Jefferson sees the King as a well-intentioned yet weak victim of a vicious and violent queen:

> But he had a Queen of absolute sway over his weak mind and timid virtue, and of a character the reverse of his in all points. This angel, as gaudily painted in the rhapsodies of Burke, with some smartness of fancy, but no sound sense, was proud, disdainful of restraint, indignant at all obstacles to her will, eager in the pursuit of pleasure, and firm enough to hold to her desires, or perish in their wreck. (p. 104)

Thus does Jefferson essentially absolve the King and accuse the "wife" and "mother" of dragging the weak "father" to the guillotine. And so ends Jefferson's history—the text that he initially wrote has become the book of history in which he lived. He sees how violent that history will be; he has seen how violent it has been. Yet even here Jefferson refuses to desert the principle of revolution:

> The deed which closed the mortal course of these sovereigns, I shall neither approve nor condemn. I am not prepared to say, that the first magistrate of a nation cannot commit treason against his country, or is unamenable to its punishment; nor yet, that where there is no written law, no regulated tribunal, there is not a law in our hearts, and a power in our hands, given for righteous employment in maintaining right, and redressing wrong. (p. 105)

Spiritually, or rather familially, Jefferson is willing to sacrifice or guillotine both mother and father in order to hold the principle of revolution. That means that he returns to his country from France a parricide—or a self-made orphan—rather than a self-made man.

But hold! Jefferson's text is neither history nor revelation of personality. It is memoir. As students of literature, we might want it to reveal Jefferson's ego; as students of history, we might want it to provide a myth of the American self. But it is autobiography as memoir, which means that it will relate itself to the external world of the author in history, not to the inner world of self-reflection. Thus, if I have surmised a Jeffersonian myth of the "Author of the Country" as self-made orphan when he leaves France, it is a wonderful fact of Jefferson's memoir that it ends in Philadelphia— where the Declaration had been written—with Jefferson's visit to Benjamin Franklin, the original self-made man who lies on his deathbed. What is the exchange between them? What indeed but Jefferson's narrative to an anxious Franklin about the momentous events in France; and what indeed from Franklin but, upon Jefferson's inquiry about Franklin's progress on the history of his own life, the gift of a manuscript portion of that life and the double request by the dying Franklin that Jefferson keep it. Jefferson writes that he returned the manuscript to William Temple Franklin after Franklin's death. But he concludes his autobiography fearing that Franklin's grandson has somehow failed to publish it. He even suspects that he has suppressed it, since it established views "so atrocious in the British government." And Jefferson concludes his autobiography with a question and a suspicion:

> But could the grandson of Dr. Franklin be, in such degree, an accomplice in the parricide of the memory of his immortal grandfather? The suspension for more than twenty years of the general publication, bequeathed and confided to him, produced, for awhile, hard suspicions against him; and if, at last, all are not published, a part of these suspicions may remain with some. (p. 114)

Here, at the culmination of Jefferson's text, is a reemergence and even an intensification of anxiety—but revealed this time not toward future or past so much as to the text of autobiography itself. It is certainly worth knowing that four years before Jefferson wrote his memoir William Temple Franklin had actually published the portion of his grandfather's memoirs to which Jefferson alludes. That portion was no small fragment of Franklin's life but a crucial and extended account of his negotiations in London in 1774-1775. In A. H. Smyth's edition of Franklin's works, the narrative account, addressed to Franklin's son, comes to eighty long printed pages.[5] Jefferson, usually meticulous in such matters, had ample time and opportunity as well as every reason to check his suspicion rather than doing what he did, which was to end his memoir with his recollection of the contents of the "lost" manuscript. Perhaps even more revealing, Jefferson himself had written a letter to William Duane in 1810 giving a significantly different though essentially parallel account of his visit with Franklin. Julian Boyd, in an extended and informative editorial note,[6] gives what must be forever the definitive account of the transaction. As Boyd sees things, Jefferson is in error about William Temple Franklin because of his suspicion that the young man was in British pay, but he is remarkably accurate in his memory of what was in the document.

A common-sense account of this ending might well see it as Jefferson retiring from the effort to check every statement against past letters and other archival evidence. I think such a possibility not unlikely. At the same time, to see Jefferson yielding to his long held suspicion allows us the indulgence of a symbolic reading of the ending. If Jefferson returned from France (in the text of his memoir) a self-made orphan, he finds his true and strong father in the self-made Franklin, the oldest of the founding fathers. In giving Jefferson the manuscript he had originally written to his illegitimate son, Franklin bequeaths his text to his "legitimate" son in order to insure it from possible carelessness or abuse by the illegitimate grandson (Franklin, true to his revolutionary identity, founded a firm line of illegitimacy!). Jefferson, who had no sons, sees in his own failure to protect his bequest a betrayal of his patrimony as well as the possibility of parricide by the grandson—and not only Franklin's parricide by William Temple Franklin but his own by his grandson. This seems to me an extraordinarily apt ending of the life of a true revolutionary, the Author of our Country, who believed all his life that there should be a revolution every twenty years. Such a belief would have been weak indeed had it lacked the power to generate such a fear.

Similarly, such a symbolic reading of Jefferson would be weakly literary if it failed to recognize that Jefferson's conclusion to his own memoirs actually serves to destabilize the definitive text of Franklin's *Autobiography*, that wonderful first book of American

[5] *The Writings of Benjamin Franklin*, collected and edited by Albert Henry Smyth, 10 vols. (New York and London, 1905-1907), 6: 318-398.
[6] *The Papers of Thomas Jefferson*, ed. Julian P. Boyd (Princeton, 1971), 18: 87-97.

literature. Anyone who reads Franklin's account of his negotiations with the British will see how much that text belongs with any edition of Franklin's *Autobiography*. Carl Van Doren, almost alone among editors of Franklin's autobiographical writings, saw how essentially a part of the *Autobiography* it was. Written on shipboard as Franklin returned from England in 1775, it is by an author who, having recognized the adamantine hostility of the British government to its American colonies, is himself committed to hot-hearted revolution. No wonder the old man gave it to Jefferson upon *his* return from Europe to assume the duties of Secretary of State in Washington's cabinet; no wonder Jefferson could have felt that, in having it, he had a part of his "father's" life as original as his own original text of the Declaration. And, having let it slip through his fingers, no wonder he trembled at the loss of a *text*, this author who was so truly an Author. Though he may have been wrong in his suspicion of William Temple Franklin, he was right in his memory of that text being a part of "the history of his own life," which Franklin on his deathbed was preparing for the world.

If we reclaim that text from the obscure burial it suffers in the Franklin papers, we will see Franklin's account of himself at the moment he departs from England to become a revolutionary American. He is the true expatriate that Jefferson, almost alone of all the revolutionaries, believed all Americans to be. Seeing so much, a student of American autobiography might begin to experience the full capacity of the Author of our Country to destabilize everything fixed before him.

Autobiography and
the Making of America

Robert F. Sayre

That autobiography is a wide-spread and characteristic form of American expression now seems to be well recognized. In the last ten or fifteen years a number of books and articles have been published on the subject, more are in the works, and many universities now have courses on it or on some aspect of it.[1] Students and teachers of autobiography are even accused of riding a bandwagon or of turning to this "new" field now that there is supposedly nothing left to write about poetry and the novel. But the wonder is that literary scholars have taken so long to acknowledge something that is not only currently interesting but historically rich and culturally revealing.

Forms of autobiography inevitably showed up in the earliest exploration narratives and travellers' tales that described and promoted the new land. A somewhat more personal kind of autobiography appeared in colonial chronicles and settlers' narratives such as William Bradford's *Of Plymouth Plantation* and John Winthrop's *Journal*. In the eighteenth century, before Americans had written any plays, novels, or much poetry of distinction, a number of them wrote uniquely interesting diaries and autobiographies: the diaries of Samuel Sewall and William Byrd, the *Journal* of Sarah Kemble Knight, the *Personal Narrative* of Jonathan Edwards, the *Journal* of John Woolman, and Crèvecoeur's *Letters from an American Farmer*.

---

[1] For two review-essays on American autobiography, see Albert E. Stone, "Autobiography and American Culture," *American Studies: An International Newsletter* 11 (1972): 22-36, and Robert F. Sayre, "The Proper Study—Autobiographies in American Studies," *American Quarterly* 29 (1977): 241-262.

Today, this Puritan and colonial "personal literature" has far more appeal (although we may not be very objective observers) than any of the sermons, pamphlets, and political tracts that were still the more numerous kinds of expression. We may prize this literature more today than twenty years ago mainly because contemporary American writers as varied as Norman Mailer, Lillian Hellman, Malcolm X, Maxine Kingston, and Vladimir Nabokov have gradually made us extrasensitive to all autobiography. This same sensitivity now reinforces our recognition that some American literary classics are autobiographies—Franklin's, Thoreau's *Walden, The Education of Henry Adams*—and that a great many more are autobiographical. Autobiography may be the preeminent kind of American expression. Commencing before the Revolution and continuing into our own time, America and autobiography have been peculiarly linked.

As Americans ought to know well, however, quantity and concentration do not necessarily produce quality. Whatever praises the literary nationalist might like to sing, American writers have been no more capable of great autobiography than have writers of other nations. There is no American egotist to come near to Cellini—not even his great admirer Mark Twain. There is no American Rousseau, and most readers would find Thomas Wolfe a pale substitute for Proust. There is no great American autobiographer who depicts the intellect and spirit like Mill or Newman, no self-analyst like Jung, and no chroniclers of Puritan familial oppression like Edmund Gosse and Samuel Butler. And I have a feeling that the reason is the very identification of autobiography *in* America *with* America. An American seems to have needed to be an American first and then an autobiographer, and this places some limits on his or her achievement (a point that I will discuss in more detail later).

In any case, autobiography in America is somehow both a part of our daily vernacular and our earliest heritage, reaching back to the Puritan diaries and the seventeenth- and eighteenth-century travel narratives, the Indian captivity narratives and the "biographies" and "autobiographies" of notable Indian chiefs, the countless success stories of businessmen and celebrities, the protest stories of exslaves and victims, the tales of pioneering and the "Americanization" of immigrants, the deceitful apologies of scoundrels and rogues, the utterly artificial "True Confessions" in magazines of romance and pornography, the formulae of high-school yearbooks, photograph albums, curricula vitae, and *Who's Who*. Autobiography in America is not only a genre with significant origins and distinguished classics, it is also an industry, a sometimes handmade, sometimes machinemade common commodity, like "grubby" clothes and three-piece suits, old family mansions and pickup trucks with campers. And like clothes, cars, and houses it is a necessity, or almost a necessity, that we have to have—for work and for entertainment—in order to say who we are and where we've been. "Slowly the history of each one comes out of each one," said Gertrude Stein. "Sometime then there will be a history of every one." And she went on, in a more acerbic tone, "Every one is always busy with it, no one of them then ever want to know it that every one looks like some one else and they see it mostly every one dislikes to hear it."[2]

Therefore, the study of autobiography in America clearly cannot be confined to studies of masterpieces any more than the study of domestic architecture can be confined to the work of Louis Sullivan and Frank Lloyd Wright. Besides these masters, there were hundreds more architects outside of Chicago who were also designing for the successful middle and upper class; and for every architect, there were hundreds of carpenters and contractors, working from mail-order catalogues, design books, or just custom and requests. They built the homes that the masses of Americans have lived in —which Sullivan and Wright railed against and tried to improve. Such masters, however, usually had the power to express their ideals and principles more articulately than the common man so that in brief studies such as this we depend on them. But I make the comparison to architecture because of the tendency in so much American writing (which Richard Poirier has noticed) to think of style and self-expression as a house, "a world elsewhere." The "American book"—be it novel, poem, or autobiography—builds an ideal house (like Thoreau's), a house of fiction (like James's) that is an improvement on the shabby, imitative, or mundane houses in which we are born. The autobiography is, or can be, that second house into which we are reborn, carried by our own creative power. We make it ourselves, then remake it—make it new.

The comparison to architecture (rather than to clothes, the more traditional metaphor for autobiography) is also apt because of the effect the lives and works of Americans have had on the American

[2] Gertrude Stein, "The Gradual Making of the Making of Americans," in *Lectures in America* (Boston, 1957), pp. 139, 141.

landscape. The "building" of civilization in the United States has been like the construction of a vast enclosure over the continent, an actual fulfillment of the visionary domes of Buckminster Fuller. But this "structure" is not simply a roof or canopy; it is plowed lands and excavations for railroads and highways, underground networks of pipes, cables and tunnels, the digging out of mines and the raising of factories and mills, the coeval building of thousands of authorities, traditions, and institutions. The image of this activity appears now in television commercials for savings and loan associations, which may have adapted it from WPA documentaries of the 1930s that extolled land reclamation and hydroelectric power; and such films should remind us that autobiography is certainly not the only or necessarily the best record of all this enormous human activity. The amassed diversity and prodigious energy of modern America should not be seen exclusively through the window of autobiography anymore than through the steel doorway of a bank vault. The permanent records of America are ultimately safe and complete only in the sticks and stones, the memory and texture of the civilization itself. But the achievement of autobiography is that it has been the special form in which some of the builders have compiled their own records of their work—and their unifying work, their own character. Therefore, American autobiography is different from the autobiographies of other nations simply in the degree to which Americans are and are not different. America has had its backwoodsman; Canada its *coureur de bois*. Americans are immigrants; so are South Africans and Australians. Germany, England, and other nations have also had inventors, founders of industrial fortunes, labor leaders, reformers, and so on. But American autobiographers have generally connected their own lives to the national life or to national ideas. As Scott Fitzgerald wrote in the 1930s, America is not a land or a people.

> France was a land, England was a people, but America, having about it still that quality of the idea, was harder to utter—it was the graves at Shiloh and the tired, drawn, nervous faces of its great men, and the country boys dying in the Argonne for a phrase that was empty before their bodies withered. It was a willingness of the heart.[3]

---

[3] F. Scott Fitzgerald, *The Crack-Up*, ed. Edmund Wilson (New York, 1956), p. 197.

We may not agree with Fitzgerald that "willingness of the heart" is
the idea, but we can agree with his broader perception. From the
times of Columbus, Cortez, and John Smith, America has been an
idea, or many ideas.

The importance of this perception to American autobiography is
great. Autobiography is not the most intellectual of genres (sometimes it seems quite the opposite), but ideas play a crucial role in it.
"Nearly always," as Northrop Frye has said, "some theoretical and
intellectual interest in religion, politics, or art plays a leading role in
the confession. It is his success in integrating his mind on such subjects that makes the author of a confession feel that his life is worth
writing about."[4] Ever since its origins in religious confessions, autobiography has afforded the author the opportunity to show how
his life has been the fulfillment of ideas. The autobiographical hero
is the representative of the ideas that he has lived by and seen succeed or, in some cases, fail. The autobiographer is not only a
"who," he is also a "what"—what he lived for, what he believed in
and worked for. Louis Sullivan called his story *The Autobiography of
an Idea*. Adams made the point another way when he substituted
"Education" for "Autobiography." And Lincoln Steffens, who
was probably influenced by Adams, wanted to call his autobiography *A Life of Unlearning*.

In this study I would like to pursue the connection between autobiography and these ideas about America—to see what some of
the ideas have been, how they have organized the lives that Americans have lived and the stories they have written, and how they
have progressed and changed. For Americans to have built this
"House" of civilization and autobiography in a mere two or three
hundred years is an impressive feat. We may be critical of it, but we
still have to wonder at the extent of the work and the unity of purpose that in spite of constant conflict and disagreement finally went
into it. A study of some of the major autobiographies may help us
to see what the unifying purposes and methods were.

Fitzgerald's association of America and ideas tells us much about
his own autobiographical writing. In the 1920s his stories and
novels described his own yearnings and actions as if they were
those of his whole generation. As he said later in 1931, the Jazz Age
"bore him up, flattered him and gave him more money than he had

---

[4] Northrop Frye, *The Anatomy of Criticism* (Princeton, 1957), p. 308.

dreamed of, simply for telling people that he felt as they did." But having been a hero and then having been ditched, he began to ponder hard on the hero's relation to America. The same nation that had lifted him up, making him rich and famous, had put him down, leaving him great debts and small markets. Worse yet, he was a scapegoat on whom Americans of the 1930s beat out their shame for their own earlier extravagance and irresponsibility. Adulation had turned to scorn. So it was not the "land" or the "people" who had changed; it was the idea or ideas of America. His own description of the idea, "a willingness of heart," seems almost chosen to endure these shifts in political and economic weather: it could apply equally well to a twenties millionaire like Gatsby or a thirties Hollywood producer like Monroe Stahr. But primarily it applied to Fitzgerald. If he could satisfy himself that a President like Lincoln and the soldiers of Shiloh and the Argonne had it too, that seemingly objectified his heroic idea.

In a general way, however, he was still doing something to which he had guiltily confessed in the "Crack-Up" essays. There, in the midst of describing his loss of vitality, his discouragement, and his overdrawn resources, he reported his alarming discovery that for twenty years he had no conscience of his own and had been living by or off the virtues of other men. He proceeded to list five of them. In intellectual matters his conscience was Edmund Wilson. For his ideas of "the good life," he borrowed from another friend. In literary style, he did not imitate his friend (obviously Hemingway), "because my own style . . . was formed before he published anything, but there was an awful pull toward him when I was on a spot." A fourth man was his silent adviser in "my relations with other people," which seemed better than using Emily Post's "systematized vulgarity"—but which was still borrowing. His "political conscience," the fifth, had been almost dead for ten years, but when it revived he took it from a lively younger man. Then, with the list made he realized that "there was not an 'I' any more—not a basis on which I could organize my self-respect." He was without a "self . . . like a little boy left alone in a big house."[5]

To most readers this has seemed like a shocking exposure of the barrenness of American values. In none of these most important areas did Fitzgerald have the example of parents or a secure cultural tradition. Religion was no help. The books and instruction he had

[5] Fitzgerald, *The Crack-Up*, p. 79.

received in college were no help. His "self" was just a boyish selection of the attributes of five friends, each of whom looked superior in one respect.

From this it is easy to see that the "individuality" that supposedly lies behind autobiography and that Americans patriotically endorse may be a sham. Is it a nation of individuals, as the publicists proclaim, or a nation of conformists, each scrambling to imitate somebody else? But in America individuality and conformity are less opposites than complements. As Tocqueville observed in *Democracy in America*, the same revolutions that set men free to make up their own minds, "to seek the reason of things for oneself, and in oneself alone," also set free the energies of public opinion, which "does not persuade others to its beliefs, but it imposes them and makes them permeate the thinking of everyone."[6] But valuable as it is, Tocqueville's analysis failed to perceive the subtler ways in which this dialectic of individuality and conformity has worked in America. Tocqueville somehow could not see beyond an image of solitary, beleaguered individualists (like Descartes, Voltaire, or the American village atheist) surrounded by howling censors and excited journalists. Fitzgerald's confession does not imply that he took his conscience from public opinion but from five comparatively distinguished and accomplished friends. His selection of these five, out of all the possibilities, shows Fitzgerald *acting* as an individual, being independent of both the mob and the pressures of tradition and authority. At the same time, it is a sign of what makes him so charmingly like all the rest of us. He is the undergraduate who wants to be as bright as A, as good in sports as B, a class president like C, as good looking as D, and so on. Or he is the adult who wants X's interesting job, Y's fine house, and the community respect of Z. The bad word for this, of course, is envy, and we should not deny its bad effects. But the good word for it is emulation, the ambition to improve one's self by equalling or surpassing an esteemed rival.

Significantly, John Adams was the original American authority on the "instinct of emulation," as he called it. For Adams this was an instinct second only to self-preservation as a force in human life, and he carefully studied its application to politics and education and its role in American government. Unfortunately, his essays on the

---

[6] Alexis de Tocqueville, *Democracy in America*, ed. Phillips Bradley (New York, 1960), 2: 3, 11.

subject were part of an extensive critique of the French Revolution, done as translations and commentaries on an Italian historian, Enrico Caterino Davila, who had written on the sixteenth-century civil wars in France. The later essays were also interpreted by Adams's enemies as advocating monarchy, so he quit the project. The combination of this almost unbelievable muddle of intentions and its allegedly treasonous position has kept the essays, the *Discourses on Davila*, from ever being known to more than a few dedicated political scientists and Adams admirers. But they are brilliant speculations on a difficult subject that is also embarrassing to discuss frankly.

The essays' relevance in terms of American autobiography stems from Adams's conviction that the revolutionary abandonment of inherited titles and aristocratic rank makes everyone compete all the more fiercely for the *"distinction"* that can only be received from other people—"to be observed, considered, esteemed, praised, beloved, and admired by his fellows," for these kinds of attention are many, and so are the forms that emulation takes.

> When it aims at power, as a means of distinction, it is *Ambition*. When it is in a situation to [be apprehensive] that another, who is now inferior, will become superior, it is denominated *Jealousy*. When it is in a state of mortification, at the superiority of another, and desires to bring him down to our level, or to depress him below us, it is properly called *Envy*. When it deceives a man into a belief of false professions of esteem or admiration, or into a false opinion of his importance in the judgment of the world, it is *Vanity*.[7]

Only a few men seek distinction from their benevolence, and even in them this urge is weaker than the temptations to vice and riches, which are the much easier ways of winning attention. Yet worse than poverty and as painful "as the gout or stone" is neglect. The poor man suffers most because *"he is only not seen."*[8]

Thus a man seeks to make himself known not only from a desire for praise but from a dreadful fear of being despised and obscure. Where Adams is not so clear or so passionate is on the difference between imitation and emulation. The clearest differentiation he

---

[7] John Adams, *Discourses on Davila*, in *The Works of John Adams*, ed. Charles Francis Adams (Boston, 1851), 6: 233-234.

[8] Ibid., p. 239.

makes is in the sentence beginning, "Emulation, which is imitation and something more—a desire not only to equal or resemble, but to excel. . . ."[9] He seems to place them on a continuum, in which imitation is doing as well as someone else, emulation doing better. One does not try to excel by being altogether different or by choosing a different course. Fame is attained by following someone already accomplished and then becoming more accomplished. Indeed, this is implicit in Adams's selection of the word "emulation" as his name for this great instinct—not "fame," "ambition," "vanity," "pride," or one of the other terms in the usual moral vocabulary. One of those terms would have also prejudged the desire as impure. On the other hand, "emulation" is entirely neutral; its moral value is not in itself but in how it is used or in *who* is imitated and excelled. For the vice-president of the United States writing in 1790, the way to "distinction" was in imitating other worthy men and trying to excel them!

The emulation that Adams personally practiced, however, was primarily that of classical or European models. He and his friend and rival Jefferson (whose ideas about an "aristocracy of merit" were basically similar) formed their rhetoric—their *gravitas*—in public duty, and their architecture from the most advanced improvements of the ancients. So, significantly, neither of them were autobiographers in the modern sense. Adams's Puritan inheritance made him exquisitely self-critical and meticulous in his diaries and records of private and public affairs. Jefferson's sense of history made him very scrupulous in compiling a final record of his work. But they had not imitated the manners of the men around them (certainly not in the almost chameleon manner of Fitzgerald), and therefore they could not have experienced the same sense of being like their contemporaries. Their lives could only be important in terms of their actions; they had not lived in order to resemble or feel like other men. Neither did they expect others to imitate them. Close imitation of one's own life might be expected only of sons, but even sons would, like other educated men, also model their lives on the classical orators, magistrates, and generals. Plutarch had served them; he would serve later generations too.

When emulation is of one's own contemporaries, the making of the self becomes much different. Our first response is to imagine that the self vanishes altogether, as in Poe's short story, "The Man

[9] Ibid., p. 267.

of the Crowd." The narrator of that story is so intrigued by an old man he has seen on the London streets that he follows him all night long. Eventually, he becomes so obsessed by the man's aimlessness that he pictures him as an image of modern vacuity, "the genius of great crime," the man who "refuses to be alone." One possible meaning of the story is that in becoming the man's ever-present shadow the narrator has become equally criminal: all the abuse he heaps on this chosen double applies to himself as well. And similar parables appear in many of the nineteenth-century stories involving a *doppelgänger*. The imitator becomes like the model in vice as well as virtue. The model knows no more than the imitator. Or the model had modeled *himself* on yet another person—possibly the original imitator. On the other hand, because the narrator in such stories is both the pursuer and the speaker, he is different from the man he pursues. The self may be an enigma—as hard to fathom as any other self or being whom one tries to study—but the power to describe that enigma is an expression of life. Furthermore, unlike Poe's obsessed narrator, one does not have to fasten oneself like a shadow or leech to *one* other individual (or nonindividual). One can, like Fitzgerald, discriminate carefully and still choose five worthy models. Finally, whether we like it or not, the dynamics of modern society force these imitations on us. If we are to be different from our fathers and also different from the white marble gods they found in Plutarch or the grizzly patriarchs they chose from the Bible, then we must imitate contemporaries. We don't all want to live in our fathers' houses, even in a restored Mt. Vernon or Monticello. If we choose replicas of these monuments, we want the most modern plumbing and air-conditioning. So we take it as a matter of faith that every generation must have its innovators and also its critics, revisers, publicists, restorers, and copiers. To have a conscience that is not one's own seems like an abominable way to live; but then, when one makes that discovery or simply must go against it, one can the more easily tear it up and go to hell. And start all over.

At this juncture I would like to review some of the observations I have made so far. American autobiographers, I have noted, are mainly different from others according to the ways in which America has been different. America is an idea. Her autobiographers are like American houses, with many imported imitations of foreign styles—the English Puritan, the Palladian Historical, the

Mercantile Journalistic, to suggest a few—and mixtures of these styles with new forms and experiences. They are also related to the House, American civilization, and the ideas that have been erected so rapidly over the building site of approximately 3,000 by 1,500 miles. Just as important, they have been instruments in building the House, for they have helped to create the national character and to define the methods and purposes of the builders. Autobiography has been a way for the builder to pass on his work and his lessons to later generations, to "my posterity," as Benjamin Franklin called it. Autobiographers are both the emulators and the emulated. All of this has made autobiography very significant in America, perhaps essential, but as we shall shortly see, it has also encouraged certain kinds of expression at the expense of others. The House has its limits.

Franklin's large role in these developments should by now be fairly clear. The version of his life that he called his *Memoirs* was as necessary to the making of America as his other domestic improvements like the lightning rod and the "Pennsylvanian Fire-Place." And just as he never patented these inventions but allowed anyone to imitate them, he had no objections to anyone's imitating his worthy life. He wanted it and expected it. Unlike Jefferson, Washington, Adams, and most of the other leaders of the Revolution, he had not emulated great classical or European models, not in public affairs, literature, or architecture. As he tells us in the *Autobiography*, his models had been plain writers like Defoe and Bunyan, improved by a little Addisonian grace. In his domestic arrangements Franklin began as very utilitarian, and in public virtues and service he esteemed contemporaries of rank whom he had observed: Cotton Mather, Bradford (a successful printer), and various colonial leaders. He is so stereotyped as "self-made" that this point needs emphasis. One of the themes of the *Autobiography* is Franklin's selection of his "consciences," as Fitzgerald might have called them. These "consciences" constituted both the ideas he would live by and also some few of the distinguished men in different fields whom he imitated and from whom as a young man he sometimes hoped to gain favor. Franklin's countertheme is the bad behavior of some lazy men and braggarts who are not to be imitated, several of whom go "down to Barbadoes," out of the way in the West Indies. Between is the support Franklin exchanged with other plain young tradesmen such as the members of his Junto. As unknown leather-apron men, they recommended business to one another and, thanks to the "Standing Queries" that Franklin drew up for discussion at each meeting, they kept each other abreast of new ideas, new business opportunities, and new community projects. The pattern for success used by Franklin and his friends was not virtue and industry alone; it was also to *trade* with each other in ideas as well as business and to gather around them everybody and everything that could be valuably promoted. The Junto seems to have been part junta—a group of intriguers—but mostly a combination of business/service club and intellectual society. Appropriately, organizations of both kinds are historically descended from it.

A major intention of the *Autobiography* is to reveal this pattern and to promote it for imitation elsewhere in America. In 1771 when Franklin commenced writing, he might have told many other stories such as the story of the scientific experiments that had won him international fame. But as James M. Cox has recently pointed out, the timing was significant. In May 1771 he had written to the Massachusetts Committee of Correspondence (Thomas Cushing, James Otis, and Samuel Adams) virtually predicting the American rebellion and its outcome.[10] It is natural to believe that in August 1771, when he began writing the *Autobiography*, these and many other differences between England and America were still on his mind. Although he liked England and was enjoying the hospitality of an English Bishop, that man, Jonathan Shipley, "almost alone among the bishops upheld the rights of the American colonists and of the British dissenters."[11] Although it had counterparts in England, Franklin's tradesman's story was more common in America. To Americans it was, or would become, a version of national epic—and one that they must seek to repeat without shame. Up until he wrote (as, indeed, for long after), most successful tradesmen were still ashamed to admit humble origins and aped the upper classes. John Adams, for example, thought that the man "from obscure beginnings" had to bear "a load of sordid obloquy and envy."[12] But Franklin could speak plainly about his success, and he could also seek imitators. His audience was not to be his contemporaries but the generations of Americans to come. Thus the open-

[10] James M. Cox, "Autobiography and America," *Virginia Quarterly Review* 47 (1971): 261. The full text of the letter is in *The Papers of Benjamin Franklin*, ed. William B. Willcox (New Haven, 1974), 18: 102-104.

[11] Carl Van Doren, *Benjamin Franklin* (New York, 1945), p. 413.

[12] Adams, *Discourses*, p. 237.

ing part of the *Autobiography* is addressed to his "Dear Son"—not the actual one, who was over forty years old and governor of New Jersey, but the apprentices and tradesmen, the legions of American "sons" who might someday read him when they were just starting their businesses. When he returned to the *Autobiography* in 1784, he included the letters from the two friends, one English and the other American, that explicitly urged him to continue. His life would be an example to youth, an advertisement for America, a book "worth all Plutarch's Lives put together."

The limits of Franklin's *Autobiography* as *biography* nearly all stem from the shaping of the hero to this didactic national purpose. Because the portrait of the young Franklin is so convincing and because the man writing takes such evident pleasure in him, despite his "errata," it is hard to believe that the young Franklin was not pretty much as described—a precociously bright, ambitious lad who for a time wasted himself in satire, disputatiousness and occasional rowdiness and who then knuckled down to work hard, to thrive, and to help others (except, of course, his competitors). But those who know the rest of his writing still know the distortion. The young man in the *Autobiography* is patently a boy's Franklin (full of malice towards little boys, Mark Twain pointedly said); the young Franklin's way with his girls and the adult Franklin's way with girls, women, and other men is scarcely mentioned. His love of learning, travel, and leisure enters mostly as the reward of early industry. His cultivated eighteenth-century playfulness and his cunning opportunism are enough present, however, to make us wonder whether he is not, at times, satirizing himself so as to let readers know that *he* regrets the omissions, the limits of his own self-portrait. For writing as an American, his limits were the utilitarian, mercantile culture he wished to symbolize. Once it had its fire companies and insurance plans, clean streets and street lamps, schools, hospitals, libraries, militia, and all the rest of Ben Franklin's improvements, the hero might relax a little—stop behaving like a Robinson Crusoe tirelessly lugging things in from the wrecked ship (England) in order to improve every part of his domain (America). But this different hero would have to await the civilization of the land.

In contrast to Franklin in 1771 and after, Walt Whitman in 1855 was a nobody. His career as schoolteacher, newspaperman, hack writer, and carpenter seems to have been modest to a fault; it was in no way distinguished. In fact, Whitman might make an interesting study in the misery of the unknown, uncelebrated, ignored man John Adams described—the man who is not seen. To my knowledge, he never spoke of himself as a "nobody," but the word has such emotive force in nineteenth-century American writing that I think it fits.[13] Moreover, his pathetically maniacal lecture notes from the 1850s suggest how desperately he *wanted* to be known.

> The idea of strong live addresses directly to the people, adm. 10¢, North and South, East and West—at Washington,—at the different State Capitols—Jefferson (Mo.)—Richmond (Va.)—Albany—Washington &c—promulging the grand ideas of American ensemble liberty, concentrativeness, individuality, spirituality &c &c.
> Keep steadily understood, with respect to the effects and fascinations of *Elocution* . . . that although the Lectures may be printed and sold at the end of every performance, nothing can make up for that *irresistible attraction and robust living* treat of the vocalization of the lecture, by me,—which must defy all competition with the printed and read repetition of the Lectures.[14]

Perhaps the delusions of grandeur that are so obvious here were equally obvious to the first readers of *Leaves of Grass*—one of the reasons they found it so embarrassing and offensive or just ridiculous. Whitman's brag was like that of a stump orator who had no reputation, no qualifications, a mad message, and no shame.

Yet previous reputation was not always the easy inducement to writing autobiography that it is now, nor lack of it a great barrier. Puritan and Quaker conversion narratives were written by earlier unknowns who felt that God's grace was more than sufficient subject, and in certain ways Whitman bears a striking resemblance to these writers. As the "sinner" was once out of the sight of God, so the "nobody" was/is out of the sight of friends, admirers, the praise of other people. And the corollary of this is that for Whitman, America and nature and the emulation of other men replace God as the impelling agents and issues for writing. As Daniel Shea has

---

[13] Consider the title of the autobiographical fragment by Louisa Catherine Adams (wife of John Quincy Adams) begun in 1840, "The Adventures of a Nobody," and Emily Dickinson's poem, "I'm Nobody, Who Are You?" Consider, too, that these are both works of unrecognized, sensitive women!

[14] Clifton Joseph Furness, ed., *Walt Whitman's Workshop* (Cambridge, Mass., 1928), p. 33.

noticed,[15] there are intriguing connections between the beginning of John Woolman's *Journal*—

> I have often felt a motion of love to leave some hints in writing of my experience of the goodness of God, and now, in the thirty-sixth year of my age, I begin this work.

—and the lines Whitman added to "Song of Myself," which stressed not a divine "motion of love" and "goodness of God" but his American origins and energy and hope.

> My tongue, every atom of my blood, form'd from this soil, this air,
> Born here of parents born here from parents the same, and their parents the same,
> I, now thirty-seven years old in perfect health begin,
> Hoping to cease not till death.
>
> [Ll.6-9]

In a word, Whitman had not experienced the "goodness of God" but the goodness of America. It was what had formed him, so that when he began to celebrate his "self," he celebrated his country. But as well as being his place of birth and nurture, America was an idea and ideal that he strove to embody. America as a land expressed his spiritual and physical muscle. It was new, unknown, wild, and untamed. He was youthful, also unknown, rowdy, and "barbaric." And since these traits were mostly identified with the West and the frontier, he identified himself with the West, too, even though he lived on the streets of Brooklyn and Manhattan. As a nation, America stood for the revolutionary ideas of life, liberty, and the pursuit of happiness. He, as a citizen, would represent these values in "a simple separate person," one who treated all men and women equally, who resisted "anything better than my own diversity," who had this "deathless attachment to freedom," and yet uttered "the word Democratic," the word "En-Masse." The paradoxes of America—as out of many, one; as new and yet ancient—were to be his personal paradoxes as well. He would share in all the success and suffering of the nation as a whole. He would emulate America, and he would become the ideal common man (also a paradox) whom other Americans could imitate, remember, and one day celebrate.

[15] Daniel B. Shea, Jr., *Spiritual Autobiography in Early America* (Princeton, 1968), p. 255.

The ironies of these identifications are familiar enough not to need elaboration here. When Whitman set out on his ambitious program of writing the autobiography of America and becoming the eponymous voice of the American people, he initially shrieked in registers he could not sustain. By the late 1850s he was a victim of shames and self-doubts he had not anticipated.

Oppress'd with myself that I have dared to open my mouth,
Aware now that amid all that blab whose echoes recoil upon me I
   have not once had the least idea who or what I am,
But that before all my arrogant poems the real Me stands yet
   untouch'd, untold, altogether unreach'd, . . .
                                   ["As I Ebb'd . . . ," ll. 26-28]

The further irony is that even as he wrote out of this anguish in poems of the "Sea-Drift" series, he never told his readers—or even left evidence to his biographers—about the precise causes of it. Was it the death of some lover? If so, was the lover male or female? Was he battling over his homosexuality? Was he undergoing some more general crisis of middle age? Despite all of his earlier imperatives to be "undisguised and naked," here he became peculiarly vague, guarded, and secretive. Later, he was almost equally indirect and evasive in talking about the origins of *Leaves of Grass* and the "long foreground" to it that Emerson had wondered about. In his more factual autobiography, *Specimen Days* (which celebrated Whitman the man and not just an idea), he continued expressing all his care for America and his poems but simultaneously withdrew into his public persona as "the good gray poet." That title, given to him by his public relations man William O'Connor, was like a big heavy overcoat in which he could stroll about, digging notes out of the pockets and expressing various aspects of himself—some important, some utterly trivial—but in which he could also wrap himself in continued mystery.

When we speak of the Whitman tradition in American poetry we are still wrestling with this mystery. Does he stand for a Western populism as do Sandburg and Lindsay, an affirmative embrace of native themes like Hart Crane, an identification with common objects and experience like Williams, or the post-Christian poetics of Stevens? As Ginsberg asked, "Walt Whitman, which way does your beard point tonight?" Still, most of these poets have followed him in identifying themselves with ideas. They mainly differ in what they construe his and their ideas of America to be. American poetry is autobiographical because the ideas need embodiment in a person, and the most available person is not Columbus, or Hiawatha, or John Brown but the poet who represents these and all other heroes.[16]

Yet as wide as the range is between Franklin the successful tradesman and Whitman the anonymous poet, the two of them by no means encompass all of American autobiography or all of the varieties of American autobiographical heroics. Although they have had many followers, there are still several other individuals and types that must be considered. How has the idea of America served and been served by the autobiographers who have not been a part of American success and have not been able to praise its life, liberty, and pursuit of happiness? Where, if at all, have they seen their lives as representative and therefore (in Franklin's phrase) "fit to be imitated"? What of upperclass, disaffected men like Henry Adams, Henry James, and Robert Lowell, on the one hand, and of black and radical autobiographers like Frederick Douglass and Malcolm X, on the other?

We can clearly see that Henry Adams was thoroughly aware of his difference from these Franklinian and Whitmanian traditions. As the grandson of presidents and an heir to family wealth and power, he could hardly present himself as a typical American. As he says in the opening sentence of the *Education*, he was born in the shadow of Boston State House and "on the summit of Beacon Hill" (or near it). From that moment on, however, the meaning of this distinguished and privileged inheritance becomes a continuing issue, and in the next sentence he suggests that being a Boston, Unitarian Adams is comparable to being a circumcised Jerusalem "Cohen," the identity of both being fixed by ancient tradition and therefore "heavily handicapped in the races of the coming century." Such a comparison (outlandish in every sense of the word) is more than a nasty expression of Adams's anti-Semitism. The stereotypical Jew, while being the racial opposite of the Boston gentile is also a product of ancient patriarchy, indeed, the very one on which the Puritan patriarchy in some ways modeled itself. And in the economic and ancestral "races" of the twentieth century, the

[16] In this discussion of Whitman and the tradition of the poet's identification of himself with America, I have drawn generally from the dissertation by Lowell E. Folsom, "America, The Metaphor: Place as Person as Poem as Poet" (University of Rochester, 1976).

"Adamses" of old New England heritage and the "Cohens" of Poland and Russia would eventually find themselves running together. To do so, both would have to unburden themselves of long-accustomed tradition, and one of the questions of the Darwinian battle for survival would be, Which would adapt more readily to the new conditions of America—the "free fight," the "education" of the century?

Adams's comparisons and contrasts with Jewish immigrants remind us of the immense immigration to America during the 1890s and the early 1900s that alarmed so many of the "old" Americans of Adams's caste and lineage. Could these "hordes" be assimilated and would they learn American ways or would they "overwhelm" the country? One answer was in Jacob Riis's *The Making of an American*, one of the most popular autobiographies of the period. The scrappy but good-natured Danish immigrant Riis, who had personally worked with New York immigrants and had succeeded in journalism and reform (where Adams had previously failed), was a reassuring illustration of how America could absorb its immigrant flood if each generation helped the next and if they all improved the cities and neighborhoods in which they lived. Further testimony to immigrant drive and successful assimilation came from other autobiographies of the period like Edward Bok's and S. S. McClure's. Jane Addams's *Twenty Years at Hull House* (1910) looked at the problem from the other side—that of the daughter of an old established family—but it showed how such a woman could find herself by working with immigrants and how America could increase its richness by appropriating their diversity.

Adams, as we know, "stood alone." He pictured himself as having nothing to do with the ideas of America as they were represented by these immigrants, whether in working with them and learning from them or, God forbid, having them emulate him. And yet one of his professed purposes in the *Education* was "to fit young men, in universities or elsewhere, to be men of the world." An "education" is hardly worth describing if it does not have some instructive value, and in some ways *The Education* is an even more didactic book than Franklin's. But a good deal of the time it teaches by negatives. The irony directed at "Adams," the boy in his father's study, the traveller in Europe and "private secretary" in London, the ineffectual writer of history and "pilgrim of world's fairs," is supposedly intended to warn younger men of the errors of this simple and trusting acceptance of tradition, this dilettantism, or this high-minded pursuit of reason and order. Adams the author shows the "faults of the patchwork" worn by Adams the character. According to the author, a true American would get a sensible education in mathematics and foreign languages from a public school, would not live in Europe, would become a scientist or engineer, and would be expedient rather than idealistic in his private and public life. He would learn from the efficiency of the Dynamo; he would ignore the Virgin. As every reasonably perceptive reader knows, however, these implied recommendations are also negatives, or they are asserted in tones of such mixed affirmation and despair that the reader must at once examine them more closely. Does Adams really mean this? Is America and the modern world really so dull, pragmatic, and amoral? Is this the world that I, the reader, want to live in? If it is the world I live in, is not Adams's own world of elegant insinuations, great historical vision, and broad knowledge and vital curiosity not a better one?

The result, paradoxically, is that Adams draws us into at least a part of the world from which wealth, caste, and tradition initially excluded us. On cruder levels, we envy him. He gives us enough of a picture of the bygone pleasures and securities of that "eighteenth-century" world of his grandfather that we want to see and know more. We—or the modern scholars and editors who act for us—rush to annotate him and to assemble information about his famous friends and acquaintances, his house designed by H. H. Richardson, his clever wife, his travels, the books he read, and so on. Or, if this bores us and eventually seems futile, we may realize that Adams is better emulated than envied. He is a standard of excellence. His critique of modern society is one that we learn from. Even as he presents disintegration, he represents a great spiritual and intellectual integrity. And by having demolished so much of the provincial America of his own inheritance and the blind, grasping materialistic America in which he lived, he has helped us to imagine the broad, synthesizing visions that he claimed were impossible. If he does not make us "men of the world," he makes us wish that we were like these men.

Other privileged Americans like Henry James, Edith Wharton, and Robert Lowell did not write such ambitious autobiographies as did Adams. Nevertheless, they were like him in also rejecting the confined though comfortable societies in which they grew up. As authors they almost had to, and we should remember all the uncles and cousins they describe who went on living in their tight New

York or Boston upper class, collecting rents, managing trusts, and so forth. As a group autobiographers are people who have been different from their family, friends, and the people around them. They also offend or risk offending one of the basic pieties of close-knit bourgeois society, privacy, which is deemed so essential to keeping the secrets of family business and to hiding scandal. But what partially sustained these writers in their rebellions against these customs—and what they implicitly appealed to in their readers' psyches—was a sense that an American life should not be confining, that it ought to be adventurous, open, and free. The higher ideal of America thus helped to liberate them from the actual America in which they were raised. Henry James quoted with approval his father's letter to Emerson explaining that the children would be taken to Europe, "to absorb French and German and get such a sensuous education as they can't get here." His father's actual words had been "get a better sensuous education than they are likely to get here," but James wanted to make the point more emphatic. And even though he hardly proposed his own unusual life as a model, James did often think of it as having made Europe and this European liberation more available to other Americans.

The theme of upperclass flight to Europe is a sort of refined variation on the ever-recurring theme in black autobiography of flight from slavery, flight from the South to the North, and flight, also, from America abroad. Both testify to that fundamental, continuing contradiction in America between the idea of freedom and human fulfillment and the reality of oppression, conformity, and mean narrowness of spirit. They are the countermeasures to the success stories and the assimilated immigrants' proud tales of "Americanization." Indeed, the smugness and boastful patriotism of these dominant types is part of the oppression encountered by the others. Their complacency affirms America as it is, making the condition of the oppressed all the harder to change.

Therefore, in black autobiography one constantly finds refutations of the white ideas of America, of both the white concepts of white character and the white concepts of black. Frederick Douglass's words about slave singing are a good example:

I have often been utterly astonished, since I came to the north, to find persons who could speak of the singing, among slaves, as evidence of their contentment and happiness. It is impossible to conceive of a greater mistake. Slaves sing most when they are most unhappy.[17]

The prevalence of these kinds of corrections of white error and complacency also indicates that Douglass and other escaped slaves were writing for a white audience. That was the audience that needed to be illuminated. But since the white audience had never been slaves (at least, in the physical sense), the author obviously did not expect it to imitate him. Rather, the black man hoped to deliver the white man from political ignorance to knowledge, and therefore Douglass's goal was to teach and persuade rather than to acquire white imitators. His original experience did not represent an American ideal but an American shame that had to be changed.

Yet in another sense Douglass and other outstanding black authors *have* represented an American ideal. One of the special features of his *Narrative* is that it does not tell the story of his flight itself, as that might compromise those who helped him and only help masters in preventing other escapes. With this suspenseful part of the story missing, Douglass seems to have been the more concerned with detailing the stages of his resolution to escape. The long sequence of episodes in his learning how to read and write, his growing independence from his masters, his criticism of other slaves, and his blood-chilling fight with Covey the slavebreaker make a much more profound story than a narrative of escape could ever be. It is similar to religious conversion narratives, with the emergence of his own concept of himself as a free-man-to-be supplanting the stages of grace and salvation. Moreover, in this story the acquisition of a hard-won, secret, and subversive education is perhaps most important, for it is education that is finally the equalizer of white and black and the object that the Southern masters had guarded most closely. With an education, Douglass can not only "write my own pass" to be off the plantation (in itself a significant symbol), he can also become an articulate hero, one who can use the power of language and persuasion to tell his own story and use it in the liberation of other men and women.

Douglass's story is repeated in so many black autobiographies—Richard Wright's, James Baldwin's, Malcolm X's—that it is truly archetypal. It also shows why autobiography has been the major kind of literature for blacks and most other oppressed Amer-

[17] Frederick Douglass, *Narrative of the Life of . . .* (Garden City, N.Y., 1963), p. 15.

icans. The person who can write his own story can rise from the status of the unknown and inarticulate and can thus relate that story *to* others and to the stories *of* others. The assumed accuracy and authenticity of autobiography—its historicity—give it greater authority than the fictions of novels or the theater, especially since the fictions are more likely to have been written by whites or people who have not had these experiences themselves. In writing his or her story, the autobiographer becomes the known individual that most Americans would like to be. Or to return to the earlier figure of speech, the autobiographical hero enters the House of America.

What I have attempted to do in this essay is to demonstrate the relationship between ideas of America and a number of different or even contradictory kinds of American autobiography. As I look back at them, I find that they make something roughly approximating a kind of American mandala or a horizontal wheel with four points—a compass rose of four significant American directions. In the East is Benjamin Franklin, looking further east to his English origins and to model English writers like Defoe and Bunyan but also looking to the West and other directions to the new American who will one day imitate him. In his *Autobiography*, his life was a kind of instrument to be studied and adopted by other men who wished to become prosperous and useful. In the South—which is not just a geographic direction but a different condition—is Douglass, who used his life as an instrument of persuasion. In coming from slavery and oppression, he and other black or once excluded people told a story that would change the national character or renew it by making it responsive to conditions it had previously ignored. Properly or not, to Douglass and other former victims, the axis of America did not lie East and West between tradition and opportunity but between oppression and freedom. And the freedom needed renewal and redefinition as much as the oppression needed to be escaped.

For Whitman, the mythically wild and unknown West was America, an inspiration to the poet to identify himself with it and "promulge" its meanings. A noisy mystic, he is the antithesis of the practical, famous Franklin. His "autobiography" does not tell *how to*, it says *start to*, then becomes the nation and man. Finally, is Adams, representing that northern elevation that looks back on harsh simplicity but that also looks in the other directions for its own escape and toward new opportunity. Wealth, caste, and the excellence of ancestors is a burden, but it is also a critical standard and a source of independence.

As I attempted this summary, I was also aware that for reasons of economy this essay has given too much attention to famous autobiographies. The men and women of the frontier, the nineteenth-century ministers and missionaries who frequently wrote their life stories, the rogues and school teachers and business leaders are missing. So are the memoirs of military leaders and statesmen, some of which also have the inward-looking dimension of autobiography. But there may be a final lesson in this. Neither the memoir of the public person nor the private experience of the uncelebrated person represents the ideas of America in the way that these more famous autobiographies do, for the memoir of the public person is apt to promote ideas to the exclusion of private life and the private experience of the uncelebrated individual chronicles private experience without consciously identifying it with national ideas. The former is perhaps too much a citizen; the latter takes his citizenship more or less for granted. Thus neither has been so valuable to other Americans as the autobiographers to whom citizenship, in the broadest sense, is a major issue in their total development. Whether we like them or not, Franklin, Whitman, Douglass and Henry Adams, John Adams and Scott Fitzgerald have been leading architects of American character. They have built the Houses in which many of the rest of us have lived. But all of them address, primarily, men, or men and boys. Henry Adams's total suppression of Clover Hooper's story—whatever the reason—now looks less like an idiosyncracy and more like a reversion to American type. To tell the rest of the story—of what went on *in* the House—will be a challenge for the years ahead.

Black Autobiography:
Life as the Death Weapon

Roger Rosenblatt

This life we live is a strange dream, and I don't believe at all any account men give of it.—H. D. Thoreau

You might see somebody get cut or killed. I could go out in the street for an afternoon, and I would see so much that, when I came in the house, I'd be talking and talking for what seemed like hours. Dad would say, "Boy, why don't you stop that lyin'? You know you didn't see all that. You know you didn't see nobody do that." But I knew I had.—Claude Brown

Whatever else it may be, autobiography is the least reliable of genres—one person in relation to one world of that person's manufacture, which is that person in macrocosm, explained and made beautiful by that same person in the distance, playing god to the whole unholy trinity. Nevertheless, the three are lonely; they do not trust themselves any more than they trust each other, and with reason, as each is persistently reminded of his capacity to cheat and distort by the enterprise in which all are engaged. There is in the subject, the loneliness of the oppressed; in the object, the loneliness of the oppressor; in the artist, the loneliness of the overseer, of infinite manipulation. None feels genuine kinship with anything outside its own limitations. This is why all autobiography is minority autobiography.

Perspectives notwithstanding, however, there still is such a thing as objective reality, which is where black autobiography, a minority within a minority, takes its power. The question of whether black autobiography exists as a genre can be answered in the same terms as the more frequent question concerning whether black fiction exists as a genre; it exists as a special form of literature because there are discernible patterns within black autobiographies that tie them together and because the outer world apprehended by black autobiographies is consistent and unique, if dreadful. Black fiction is often so close to black autobiography in plot and theme that a study of the latter almost calls the existence of the former into question. The response of a reader to both genres—could this really be so?—is equally astonished and rhetorical.

Yet not all black autobiography is the rehearsal of horrors. Like fiction, black autobiography has changed both with the times and temperaments it conveyed. For the past hundred years it has fallen into roughly the same categories as the fiction. We have accommodationist autobiographies such as James D. Corrothers's *In Spite of the Handicap* and William Pickens's *Bursting Bonds*; autobiographical versions of the stories of the "talented tenth": Marshall W. ("Major") Taylor's *The Fastest Bicycle Rider in the World* and Mary Church Terrell's *A Colored Woman in a White World*; autobiographies of the Harlem Renaissance: Zora Neale Hurston's *Dust Tracks on the Road*, William Stanley Braithwaite's *The House Under Arcturus*, Langston Hughes's *The Big Sea*, and Claude McKay's *A Long Way from Home*; and we have the literature of direct protest and social comment: W.E.B. DuBois's *Dusk of Dawn*, Angelo Herndon's *Let Me Live*, Richard Wright's *Black Boy*, and the contemporary autobiographies of Malcolm X, Eldridge Cleaver, Chester Himes, and Angela Davis. The material is various but the polemics are similar.

"Polemics" means the art of disputation, technically the use of argument to refute errors of religious doctrine. There is argument in black autobiography, but no single orthodoxy. The rights of Zora Neale Hurston are not the rights of William Stanley Braithwaite; the achievement of Malcolm X is not the achievement of Langston Hughes. Conceptions of right and achievement, as well as of failure, are as different in this literature as the minds that held them. Yet there are two elements in black autobiography that are constant, whether we are watching Major Taylor on a bicycle track or Malcolm X in prison. They are the expressed desire to live as one would choose, as far as possible; and the tacit or explicit criticism of external national conditions that, also as far as possible, work to ensure that one's freedom of choice is delimited or nonexistent. These are the "arguments" of the genre. They also represent the two points where black autobiography and black fiction become inseparable and explain each other.

Both black fiction and black autobiography occur mainly in the period of modern literature. Except for slave narratives, we have very few works in either genre that go back before 1890, and the great majority of material was written after 1920. Ordinarily, we know what to expect of such material: a high degree of subjectivity, of protest against established social norms and assumptions; perhaps most prominent, an elaborately conceived and abstract sense of victimization on the part of the central character. Despite its technical modernity, neither black fiction nor black autobiography gives us these things. There is social protest, of course; but it does not rely on an abstract "victim" for its medium. When the central character is black, the abuses are authentic. No black American author has ever felt the need to invent a nightmare to make his point.

This element of historic authenticity has brought both genres closer to the precincts of classical tragedy than any other modern literature, with the possible exception of Ireland's at the turn of the century. The ability of an author to count on violence, unfairness, poverty, a quashing of aspiration, denial of beauty, ridicule, often death itself, is as close to a reliance on divine inevitabilities as a modern writer can come. Blackness itself therefore becomes a variation of fate, the condition that prescribes and predetermines a life. Fictional and autobiographical heroes who go up against fate are likewise contending with their own blackness, and they have just as much chance of succeeding as a person who wishes to get out of his own skin. This contest gives both genres their power and form.

The situation is, of course, essentially crazy. Why should either an actual or fictional hero be able to depend on his destruction as a given? It is very nice to congratulate Bob Jones of Chester Himes's *If He Hollers Let Him Go* on his proximity to classical tragedy, a proximity manifest in Jones's having been demoted, betrayed, beaten up, deserted, framed, jailed, and forced to enter the army for no other reason than that he is black; yet we acknowledge that no white American in similar circumstances would share such honors. Minority autobiography and minority fiction deserve their minority status not because of comparative numbers but because of the presence of a special reality, one provided for the minority by the majority, within which each member of the minority tries to reach an understanding both of himself and the reality into which he has been placed. When these two understandings collide, as they always do, we begin to get a clear picture of how uniquely alone our heroes are, real or imagined.

Near the end of his autobiography, *Black Boy*, Wright tells a story of his working for white men in an optical factory in Memphis. His supervisors came to him one morning and told him that Harrison, another black man working in a rival optical company across the street, held a grudge against Wright. They said that Harrison was going to kill him. Harrison's supervisors had told him the same story about Wright. When Wright and Harrison met that noon, each tried to learn why the other was angry. When they discovered the hoax, they agreed to try to let the thing pass.

But their white supervisors would not have it. They kept goading both workers, and they armed the two of them with knives. Failing to antagonize them, they then urged Wright and Harrison to settle their nonexistent grudge in a bare-fist boxing match for five dollars each. Wright refused at first, but Harrison convinced him that this would be easy money, that they could pull punches and fool the white men. The white men were elated at the news, and offered to buy dinners for the combatants. Stripped to the waist, Wright and Harrison squared off on a Saturday afternoon in a basement before an all-white audience jeering and shouting obscenities. They punched lightly at first; then harder and harder. Eventually they had to be pulled apart, having beaten each other senseless.

With certain symbolic additions this anecdote is recreated at least twice in black fiction: in the "Box-Seat" chapter of Jean Toomer's *Cane* and in the battle-royal scene of Ellison's *Invisible Man*. In *Cane* we are shown two dwarfs pounding each other incessantly as part of a theatre performance for the amusement of a degenerate audience seeking to obliterate the savagery in themselves: one set of misfits hoisting their self-esteem by urging on the brutality of another set. In *Invisible Man*, our hero has been valedictorian of his high-school class, and has been told to appear before the local white men one evening in order to receive his rewards. His rewards consist of being blindfolded and shoved into an arena with other blindfolded black boys, all outfitted with boxing gloves for a desperate free-for-all. Afterward, the boys are tossed coins on an electrified carpet. As in the Wright-Harrison anecdote they are meant to destroy themselves for the entertainment of the white citizens who would gladly pay them handsomely for their self-destruction.

The point of this story, in fact and parable, is repeated regularly; a black man seeking recognition in the white world must be brutalized to the extent that when recognition comes, it will be to him as an animal. If he decides not to fit this pattern at the outset, he will be pushed by its designers until he becomes violent in protest. Should he become violent enough, he will be considered an animal and so satisfy his predetermination just as effectively. Either way he will be functioning according to external dictates that run counter to his will, and despite the fact that he is sane and reasonable, he will only be judged so by joining a world that is unreasonable and fundamentally mad.

Wright and Harrison would not speak to each other after their fight. They were ashamed of having been duped at the expense of each other, which was the expense of themselves and of all blacks so demeaned. Yet they had no reason to be ashamed. They had been goaded into a false and illogical act that somehow became logical and true. At the end of their fight, Wright and Harrison *did* hold a grudge against each other, just as their white supervisors had initially contended. The madness of the situation did not reside in the hysteria of the onlookers, nor even in the confusion of defeat and victory or of power and impotency on the parts of the boxers. It resided in the fact that a lie became the truth and that two people who had thought they had known what the truth was wound up living the lie.

The crime that the state wishes to pin on Bigger Thomas, Richard Wright's *Native Son*, is rape. By the time he is captured and jailed, Bigger has committed manslaughter on one girl, has decapitated her body; has bashed in the head of another girl and tossed her from a window; he has also committed burglary; yet the crime of which he is accused is rape, which in fact he did not do. De Quincey said that there is no telling what depths a man may reach having committed murder: he may drink; he may become lazy; eventually he even may not always tell the truth. In an upside-down hierarchy it is reasonable that Bigger be accused of rape rather than murder. Rape represents his self-assertion in the white world, a crime which that world would not abide.

So, in *The Autobiography of Malcolm X* Malcolm is astonished when his small band of burglars is finally caught. None of the authorities in Boston is interested in the burglaries per se but rather in the fact that the band consisted of two white women and three black men: "How, where, when, had I met them? Did we sleep together? Nobody wanted to know anything at all about the robberies. All they could see was that we had taken the white man's women." There is a mirror principle operating in all of black writing, one that shows black heroes functioning in continual opposition to the white lives about them. In a sense the literature itself is a mirror into which the characters are locked. Everything they think, feel, and do seems turned the wrong way, and even when it is not, there are those available to say that it is, and, like the white citizens of Memphis or Boston, who are able to prove it.

As crazy as all of this is, it is not only true to life, but it also *rings* equally true in autobiography and fiction. "What if history were a madman?" asks the Invisible Man. In terms of the general history of black and white American relations, the question seems gratuitous. The consistency of the madness accounts not only for the correspondences between black autobiography and fiction but for the remarkably consistent picture of white America drawn from the works of black writers. Whether we are reading the autobiographies of W.E.B. DuBois, Claude McKay, and Mary Church Terrell, or the fiction of Paul Laurence Dunbar, Ann Petry, William Melvin Kelley, or James Baldwin (*Another Country*), what we see before us is the same strange and colorless land, terrorized and confused, persistent in the hatred of its own.

Through such a place walk various autobiographical characters as classic heroes playing themselves in the theatre of the absurd. From the outset they are witnesses to two versions of reality that are in perpetual friction. One is the reality of their wishful thinking. It consists of a vast yet potentially solvable puzzle that they address as children and that they hope to conquer as grown-ups—*Yes I Can*, said Sammy Davis, Jr.—a world of reasonably constructed labyrinths, rewards, and punishments. The other is a madhouse, a hall of mirrors that, like the castle of Keats's "Eve of St. Agnes," continually shifts its shape and refutes the best efforts of these autobiographical characters not to conform but to be different and special. "I aspire to the craziness of all honest men," said LeRoi Jones. Autobiography as a genre should be the history of individual craziness, but in black autobiography the outer reality in which heroes move is so massive and absolute in its craziness that any one person's individual idiosyncrasies seem almost dull in their normality.

One of the most moving autobiographies of the twentieth century is the *Autobiography* of Edwin Muir, the British poet. It has the simple structure of all great autobiographies, and is thoroughly straightforward, particularly at moments of severe introspection. One of those moments occurred when Muir, a formal and self-contained man, underwent psychoanalysis for the first time.

Watching his various coats of self-protection peel off he quietly observes: "I saw that my lot was the human lot, that when I faced my own unvarnished likeness I was one among all men and women, all of whom had the same desires and thoughts, the same failures and frustrations, the same unacknowledged hatred of themselves and others, the same hidden shame and griefs."[1] More than an acknowledgment of personal self-discovery, this confession is a modern autobiographical device. Like most modern poetry it presumes psychological kinship with the reader, presumes not only that both confessed and confessor share the same post-Freudian world of experience but the same conception of experience as well: that life consists of self-deception, self-revelation, and self-absolution in roughly the same linear progression for all people. The presumption was accurate for Edwin Muir primarily because he was not only modern but white.

Angelo Herndon's autobiography, *Let Me Live*, operates on other assumptions. The Herndon case, as some may remember, was an international concern in the 1930s. The question shuttling between the Supreme Court and the courts of Georgia was whether Herndon, a young black Communist, would be sent to a chain gang for eighteen to twenty years on a trumped-up charge that in 1932 depended on the efficiency of the Antislave Insurrection Law of 1861. Unlike Muir, Herndon did not seek an understanding of reality through an interpretation of his dreams. This was not necessary. On 11 July 1932, Herndon was arrested and held in jail for eleven days for distributing Communist leaflets to the Atlanta unemployed. On 22 July, he was formally indicted for attempting to incite insurrection on 16 July, on which date he was in jail. That fact notwithstanding, or perhaps because of that fact, the two chief witnesses against Herndon were the assistant prosecutor and the chief jailor. "This was one of the worst vaudeville shows I had ever seen," said Herndon of his trial; "and yet the most interesting to me, for this particular vaudeville show happened to hold my life in the balance."[2]

The sense of circus or madhouse that controls much black autobiography inevitably controls the decisions of the main characters themselves. Recognizing an elusive and unpredictable situation, they adapt to it for survival, becoming masters of both physical and psychological disguise, in part to avoid their hunters. Malcolm X

---

[1] Edwin Muir, *An Autobiography* (London, 1954), p. 158.

[2] Angelo Herndon, *Let Me Live* (New York, 1937), p. 229.

moves from one mask to another in his autobiography. He is variously known as Malcolm, Malcolm Little, Homeboy, Detroit Red, a prison number, even Satan, until he reaches the identification of Brother, which to him is not a mask but himself. Conversely the Invisible Man finds his identity in Rinehart, the con man and quick-change artist whose being is nonbeing, who is all things to all people. Sonny of *Manchild in the Promised Land* wears the mask of the house nigger when it serves him, as does Bigger. In both black autobiography and black fiction the final discarding of masks is a character's primary goal because such an act is a demonstration of selfhood and freedom.

Yet in autobiography as a genre this discarding can never be complete. Even Malcolm as Brother Malcolm is Malcolm in costume, as Richard Wright is in the guise of adolescent in *Black Boy* and as Langston Hughes is in the guise of writer in *The Big Sea*. In autobiography one is not merely getting at the self but at reality as well, the one not existing outside its relation to the other. Malcolm's early libertinism was a way of investigating reality, a different but no less authentic way than his role as proselytizer for Allah. Every autobiographer, black or otherwise, must find a guise or voice with which to come to terms with himself and his world. If he is candid, he will admit to a number of voices and guises that he will adopt as his mind and world enlarge. "We wear the mask," said Dunbar, "and mouth with myriad subtleties."

Ideals of the true self and the true world nevertheless persist. Against these ideals all costumes and masks are arrayed. One senses a straining toward perfection in all autobiography—perfection of a kind that connects the individual with a cosmic pattern that, because it is perfect in itself, verifies that individual's own potential perfection. This pattern or system is not the world created by the individual in his autobiography; it is an ideal that must be read in interstices between subject and object within the autobiography, in the particular selections of the artist-self, and, just as often, in the guesswork that we apply to all books that move us. Nor is it a flexible perfection. There is for every autobiographer an absolute ideal. Falling short of it is perhaps what inspires the autobiography in the first place; but if we are to understand the lives detailed before us we must know this ideal as fully as we know the "realities" given us.

The ideals of black autobiography are the preposterously traditional ideals of reason and consistency. Despite and within the idiosyncrasies of individual authors, all seek a structure of life, of history, that is something other than viciously circular. On the threshing floor, John Grimes of Baldwin's *Go Tell It on the Mountain* hears a voice that tells him, "you got everything your daddy got." Since John's daddy, Gabriel, "got" a fearful and misshapen existence, John's future is not what one calls bright. On the morning of his father's funeral, Baldwin, just turned nineteen, was on the threshing floor of his mind:

> "But as for me and my house," my father had said, "we will serve the Lord." I wondered, as we drove him to his resting place, what this line had meant for him. I had heard him preach it many times. I had preached it once myself, proudly giving it an interpretation different from my father's. Now the whole thing came back to me, as though my father and I were on our way to Sunday school and I were memorizing the golden text: And if it seem evil unto you to serve the Lord, choose you this day whom you will serve; whether the gods which your fathers served that were on the other side of the flood, or the gods of the Amorites, in whose land ye dwell; but as for me and my house, we will serve the Lord. I suspected in these familiar lines a meaning which had never been there for me before. All of my father's texts and songs, which I had decided were meaningless, were arranged before me at his death like empty bottles, waiting to hold the meaning which life would give them for me. This was his legacy: nothing is ever escaped. That bleakly memorable morning I hated the unbelievable streets and the Negroes and whites who had, equally, made them that way. But I knew that it was folly, as my father would have said, this bitterness was folly. It was necessary to hold on to the things that mattered. The dead man mattered, the new life mattered; blackness and whiteness did not matter; to believe that they did was to acquiesce in one's own destruction. Hatred, which could destroy so much, never failed to destroy the man who hated and this was an immutable law.[3]

Baldwin's appeal at base is the appeal for sanity. When the appeal is not answered, as it usually is not, something curious, in the Lewis Carroll sense, happens to the heroes of black autobiography; they disappear. Just as Bob Jones vanishes into the anonymity of

[3] James Baldwin, *Notes of a Native Son* (New York, 1968), pp. 94-95.

the army at the end of *If He Hollers Let Him Go*; as James Weldon Johnson's Ex-Colored Man eliminates himself by passing for white; as the Invisible Man disappears literally, so do Richard Wright, Malcolm X, Eldridge Cleaver, and others disappear at the close of their narratives. Like Troilus, they ascend to one or another conception of heaven, ready for a new life, a life into which they have died. As artist and individual, they are refined out of existence at the end of that life—Cleaver calling upon his "Queen," his "Black Woman" to put on her crown and "build a New City on these ruins"; Malcolm acknowledging, almost celebrating, his impending death. When the masks and disguises have been used and laid aside, nothing remains but the future that because unknown can be thought utopian.

Every autobiography, black and white, is an extended suicide note; both announcement and vindication of the event. The life recorded is the life complete to a specific point, and is therefore as good as dead. In *Metaphors of Self*, James Olney has noted the similarity of the following autobiographical statements—Darwin: "I am not conscious of any change in my mind during the last thirty years"; Mill: "From this time . . . I have no further mental changes to tell of"; Newman: "From the time that I became a Catholic, of course I have no further history of my religious opinions to narrate." Each autobiographer tells us what a fictional character would not need to tell us—that no further growth will occur. Each has chosen a point in his life where he could see a pattern of the whole. Having seen it, he isolates it and lays it to rest through the act of autobiography itself.

One reason for this may be the desire to bring life as close to art as possible—not merely in order to give life a lovely shape, but because art is not criticized as harshly as life. The decision to write an autobiography is never as brave as it seems, particularly in an age where nothing self-conscious can be unforgivable. In modern autobiography, one enters an arena where the rules are clear. The life theoretically laid bare before us is in fact protected by that acknowledgment. Indeed, the only autobiographies we tear apart are those that appear to be hiding something.

But this is the lesser reason. One writes autobiography not because one seeks art or safety but out of a desire to see both a shape and an end to one's life, to seek the end of everything that has been in flux and process, and at the same time to understand it all. "Everything" is, after all, every thing—all orders and disorders known and felt by the "I." When that "I" has said stop, if only momentarily, to its apprehension of the world, it has likewise said stop to the world, stop to all things; it has called upon vast silence and infinite space. *Black Boy* concludes with the following lines:

> With ever watchful eyes and bearing scars, visible and invisible, I headed North, full of a hazy notion that life could be lived with dignity, that the personalities of others should not be violated, that men should be able to confront other men without fear or shame, and that if men were lucky in their living on earth they might win some redeeming meaning for their having struggled and suffered here beneath the stars.[4]

This is Wright after his own funeral, bound for glory. His autobiography, not unlike the earliest seventeenth-century English autobiographies, describes the progress of the soul through various regions of doubt and torment toward deliverance.

The difference between Wright's statement and Darwin's, which is the difference between modern black and white autobiography generally, lies in paradox. White autobiographers whose lives have progressed within a linear conception of history, that is, who have advanced in step with the advancement of their understanding of reality, find a stopping point and "end" their lives at it. But black autobiographers whose lives have progressed within a cyclical conception of history find no stopping point on the circle essentially different from any other point. "That's the end in the beginning and there's no encore," says Ellison. The result is that the black autobiographer in a sense spins off his circle and is carried by the centrifugal force of the life he has led to a state that anticipates grace. Despite the fact that he has been traveling in a circle, the black autobiographer, by the invention of the autobiography itself, has managed to get somewhere. Unlike his white counterpart, he dies but has a future.

That future, which is not solely his own but that of his people and national ideals, generally seems more important to him than the life that he has gone to such pains to record. In fact, he seems to care very little for his life, regarding it as the product of molting, as an aspect of the unattractive past. Every cosmology begins in self-knowledge. Since the "argument" of black autobiography is

---

[4] Richard Wright, *Black Boy: A Record of Childhood and Youth* (New York, 1966), p. 285.

against the existing universe of which the narrator was and is an essential if uncomfortable part, the "argument" of the work is extended against the self. Black autobiography annihilates the self because by so doing it takes the world with it.

At the beginning of *Black Boy*, after young Wright had set his house afire, he said, "I yearned to become invisible, to stop living."[5] That episode incidentally bears the same tension between accident and intent as Bigger Thomas's killing of Mary Dalton. Wright's wish to obliterate himself accompanies the act of nearly destroying his house, his own family; he willingly would see everything go at once. Yet invisibility can have substance. Much later, citing the inspiration that such writers as Dreiser and Lewis provided, Wright "felt touching [his] face a tinge of warmth from an unseen light."[6] His faith in that light, which is literature, is one of his reasons for writing *Black Boy*. The autobiography is an example of its own thesis, which places trust in the word and invests it with a life of its own.

"The thought of suicide," said cheerful Nietzsche, "is a great consolation: by means of it one gets successfully through many a bad night." For most black autobiographers the night has been bad and long. After a time they have declared it finished, risen to their particular bright and morning star, and created in their suicide notes a social document. Their works are briefs in their own defenses, briefs for salvation, since suicide is a sin. But they are also briefs against the nation, which has provided false religion and false gods. Polemics means the use of argument to refute errors of doctrine. These books both depend on and dispute the Word as it has been handed down.

This said, we are nevertheless reminded every time we read one of these works that the human mind is singular. The self in autobiography is alone, but so is the reader. The autobiographer wishes the reader to be alone and counts on it because whatever else may separate them from each other, their states of loneliness are mutually recognizable. For the black autobiographer this is a central connection; he is after all not a minority in relation to his lonely reader. They are equal in the exchange, equal because of the experience of the artifact. On this level—which is the one level where men may help each other—the artifact and the polemics are one.

[5] Ibid., p. 11.
[6] Ibid., p. 283.

Malcolm X and
the Limits of Autobiography

Paul John Eakin

When a complex and controversial figure writes a book that has achieved the distinction and popularity of *The Autobiography of Malcolm X*, it is inevitable that efforts will be made to place him and his work in the perspective of a literary tradition. Barrett John Mandel, for example, has identified in Malcolm X's story the paradigm of the traditional conversion narrative. His reading of Malcolm X's autobiography, and it is a characteristic one, assumes that the narrative expresses a completed self.[1] Further, Ross Miller has suggested that such an assumption is central to the expectations we bring to the reading of any autobiography: "The pose of the autobiographer as an experienced man is particularly effective because we expect to hear from someone who has a completed sense of his own life and is therefore in a position to tell what he has discovered."[2] Even Warner Berthoff, who has admirably defined Malcolm X's "extraordinary power to change and be changed" as "the distinctive rule of his life," seems to have been drawn to this sense of the completed self when he attempts to locate the *Autobiography* in a special and limited literary tradition, that of the political

[1] "The Didactic Achievement of Malcolm X's Autobiography," *Afro-American Studies* 2 (1972): 269-274. For other treatments of the *Autobiography* as a conversion narrative see Warner Berthoff, "Witness and Testament: Two Contemporary Classics," *New Literary History* 2 (1971): 318, 320, and Carol Ohmann, "*The Autobiography of Malcolm X*: A Revolutionary Use of the Franklin Tradition," *American Quarterly* 22 (1970): 131-149. Louis E. Lomax has identified Malcolm X as the St. Paul of the Black Muslim movement. See *Malcolm X: The Man and His Times*, ed. John Henrik Clarke (New York, 1969), p. xvii.

[2] "Autobiography as Fact and Fiction: Franklin, Adams, Malcolm X," *Centennial Review* 16 (1972): 231.

testament in which "some ruler or statesman sets down for the particular benefit of his people a summary of his own experience and wisdom."[3]

The rhetorical posture of Malcolm X in the last chapter would seem to confirm Berthoff's reading and to fulfill Miller's autobiographical expectations, for it is indeed that of the elder statesman summing up a completed life, a life that has, as it were, already ended:

> Anyway, now, each day I live as if I am already dead, and I tell you what I would like for you to do. When I *am* dead—I say it that way because from the things I *know*, I do not expect to live long enough to read this book in its finished form—I want you to just watch and see if I'm not right in what I say: that the white man, in his press, is going to identify me with "hate."[4]

If Malcolm X's anticipation of his imminent death confers on this final phase of autobiographical retrospection a posthumous authority, it is nevertheless an authority that he exercises here to defend himself against the fiction of the completed self that his interpreters—both black and white, in the event—were to use against him.[5] Each of his identities turned out to be provisional, and even this voice from the grave was the utterance not of an ultimate identity but merely of the last one in the series of roles that Malcolm X had variously assumed, lived out, and discarded.

Alex Haley's epilogue to the *Autobiography* reveals the fictive nature of this final testamentary stance that Berthoff regards as definitive. Here Haley, Malcolm X's collaborator in the *Autobiography*, reports that the apparent uncertainty and confusion of Malcolm X's views were widely discussed in Harlem during the last months of Malcolm X's life, while Malcolm X himself, four days before his death, said in an interview, "I'm man enough to tell you that I can't put my finger on exactly what my philosophy is now, but I'm flexible" (428). Moreover, the account of the composition of the *Autobiography* given by Haley in the epilogue makes it clear that the fiction of the autobiographer as a man with "a completed sense of his

---

[3] Berthoff, "Witness and Testament," pp. 319, 321.

[4] *The Autobiography of Malcolm X* (New York, 1973), p. 381. All subsequent references are to this edition and will appear in the text.

[5] For example, see Reverend Albert Cleage, "Myths About Malcolm X," in Clarke, *Malcolm X: The Man and His Times*, pp. 13-26.

own life" is especially misleading in the case of Malcolm X, for even Haley and the book that was taking shape in his hands were out of phase with the reality of Malcolm X's life and identity. Thus Haley acknowledges that he "never dreamed" of Malcolm X's break with Elijah Muhammad "until the actual rift became public" (405), although the break overturned the design that had guided Malcolm X's dictations of his life story to Haley up to that point. The disparity between the traditional autobiographical fiction of the completed self and the biographical fact of Malcolm X's ceaselessly evolving identity may lead us, as it did Malcolm X himself, to enlarge our understanding of the limits and the possibilities of autobiography.

The original dedication of the *Autobiography*, which Malcolm X gave to Haley before the dictations had even begun, places the work squarely in one of the most ancient traditions of the genre, that of the exemplary life:

> This book I dedicate to the Honorable Elijah Muhammad, who found me here in America in the muck and mire of the filthiest civilization and society on this earth, and pulled me out, cleaned me up, and stood me on my feet, and made me the man that I am today. (387)

This dedication (later cancelled) motivates more than half of the *Autobiography* in its final version. The book would be the story of a conversion, and Malcolm X's statement recapitulates in capsule form the essential pattern of such narratives: in the moment of conversion a new identity is discovered; further, this turning point sharply defines a two-part, before-after time scheme for the narrative; the movement of the self from "lost" to "found" constitutes the plot; and, finally, the very nature of the experience supplies an evangelical motive for autobiography.

What concerns us here, however, is not the much studied features of conversion and the ease with which they may be translated into the formal elements of autobiographical narrative but rather the natural and seemingly inevitable inference that the individual first discovers the shape of his life and then writes the life on the basis of this discovery. Some version of this temporal fiction, of course, lies behind most autobiography, and I would emphasize it as a corollary to Miller's definition of the completed self: the notion that living one's life precedes writing about it, that the life is in some sense complete and that the autobiographical process takes place afterward, somehow outside the realm of lapsing time in which the life proper necessarily unfolds. The evangelical bias of conversion narrative is especially interesting in this regard, for it supplies a predisposition for such an autobiographer to accept this supporting fiction as fact, since he believes that conversion works a definitive transition from shifting false beliefs to a fixed vision of the one truth. It is, accordingly, when a new discovery about the shape of one's life takes place during the writing of one's story that an autobiographer may be forced to recognize the presence and nature of the fictions on which his narrative is based. The experience of Malcolm X in his final period did foster such a recognition, and this knowledge and its consequences for autobiographical narrative may instruct us in the complex relation that necessarily obtains between living a life and writing about it. However, before we consider the *Autobiography* from the vantage point of the man who was becoming "El-Hajj Malik El-Shabazz" (Chapter 18), let us look at the *Autobiography* as it was originally conceived by the man whose first conversion in prison had transformed him from "Satan" (Chapter 10) to "Minister Malcolm X" (Chapter 13). This is, of course, the way we do look at the *Autobiography* when we begin to read it for the first time, especially if we are relatively unfamiliar with the life of Malcolm X.

The Malcolm X of these years was firmly in command of the shape of his life, tracing his sense of this shape to the pivotal and structuring illumination of conversion itself.[6] At this point his understanding of the design of his experience, especially his baffled fascination with the radical discontinuity between the old Adam and the new, closely parallels the state of St. Augustine, Jonathan Edwards, and many another sinner touched by gracious affections, so much so that the student of spiritual autobiography is likely to feel himself at home on familiar ground:

[6] Although Malcolm X's *Autobiography* resembles the traditional conversion narrative in many ways, there are important differences as well. For example, it is somewhat misleading to speak, as Mandel does, of Malcolm X's first conversion to the Muslim faith of Elijah Muhammad as the typical "false conversion" of spiritual autobiography. A "false conversion" is usually presented as false by the man who has since found the true faith. This is not Malcolm X's treatment, for in his case the "false conversion" is only partly false, and hence not to be wholly rejected (as the older Jonathan Edwards rejected the miserable seeking of his youth). Again, Mandel pushes these correspondences too far when he identifies the "tension" of the last pages of the *Autobiography* as an expression of the familiar postconversion fears of "back-sliding." Malcolm X knew that Elijah Muhammad had sentenced him to death. See Mandel, "The Didactic Achievement," pp. 272–273.

For evil to bend its knees, admitting its guilt, to implore the forgiveness of God, is the hardest thing in the world. . . . When finally I was able to make myself stay down—I didn't know what to say to Allah. . . . I still marvel at how swiftly my previous life's thinking pattern slid away from me, like snow off a roof. It is as though someone else I knew of had lived by hustling and crime. I would be startled to catch myself thinking in a remote way of my earlier self as another person. (170)

If we consider Malcolm X's account of his life up to the time of his break with Elijah Muhammad (in Chapter 16, appropriately entitled "Out"), what we have in fact is a story that falls rather neatly into two sections roughly equal in length, devoted respectively to his former life as a sinner (Chapters 3-9) and to his present life as one of Elijah Muhammad's ministers (Chapters 10-15). This two-part structure is punctuated by two decisive experiences: his repudiation of the white world of his youth in Mason, Michigan, and his conversion to Islam in prison at Norfolk, Massachusetts.

Malcolm X describes the "first major turning point of my life" (35) at the end of the second chapter—his realization that in white society he was not free "to become whatever *I* wanted to be" (37). The shock to the eighth-grade boy was profound, for despite his traumatic childhood memories of the destruction of his family by white society, Malcolm X had embraced the white success ethic by the time he was in junior high school: "I was trying so hard . . . to be white" (31). What follows, in Chapters 3 through 9, is Malcolm X's account of his life as a ghetto hustler—his first "career"—just as his role as a Black Muslim minister was to be his second. If Allah preserved him from the fate of an Alger hero or a Booker T. Washington, from a career as a "successful" shoeshine boy or a self-serving member of the "black bourgeoisie" (38), he was nevertheless destined to enact a kind of inverse parody of the white man's rise to success as he sank deeper and deeper into a life of crime.[7]

This is the portion of the *Autobiography* that has been singled out

[7] In "Malcolm X: Mission and Meaning," *Yale Review* 56 (1966), Robert Penn Warren reads Malcolm X as a success in the Alger tradition (pp. 161-162), and he notes that, setting aside the hatred of the Black Muslims for white society, their values of temperance and hard work resemble the virtues that have made the white middle class what it is (p. 165). In her "*The Autobiography of Malcolm X*: A Revolutionary Use of the Franklin Tradition," Ohmann stresses Malcolm X's story as a "parodic inversion" (p. 136) of the success story, and she adds that Malcolm X himself later recognized it as such (p. 137).

for its vividness by the commentators, with the result that the conversion experience and its aftermath in Chapters 10 through 15 have been somewhat eclipsed. It would be possible, of course, to see in the popularity of this section nothing more than the universal appeal of any evocation of low life and evil ways. In addition, this preference may reflect an instinctive attraction to a more personal mode of autobiography with plenty of concrete self-revelation instead of the more formal testimony of an exemplary life. Certainly Alex Haley responded strongly to this narrative, and so did Malcolm X, though he tried to restrain himself:

> Then it was during recalling the early Harlem days that Malcolm X really got carried away. One night, suddenly, wildly, he jumped up from his chair and, incredibly, the fearsome black demagogue was scat-singing and popping his fingers, "re-bop-de-bop-blap-blam—" and then grabbing a vertical pipe with one hand (as the girl partner) he went jubilantly lindy-hopping around, his coattail and the long legs and the big feet flying as they had in those Harlem days. And then almost as suddenly, Malcolm X caught himself and sat back down, and for the rest of that session he was decidedly grumpy. (391)

Haley captures here the characteristic drama of the autobiographical act that the juxtaposition of the self as it is and as it was inevitably generates. Malcolm X's commitment to his public role as "the fearsome black demagogue" conflicts with his evident pleasure in recapturing an earlier and distinctly personal identity, the historical conked and zooted lindy champ of the Roseland Ballroom in Roxbury, the hustling hipster of Small's Paradise in Harlem.

If the *Autobiography* had ended with the fourteenth or fifteenth chapter, what we would have, I suggest, is a narrative that could be defined as an extremely conventional example of autobiographical form distinguished chiefly by the immediacy and power of its imaginative recreation of the past.[8] It is true that this much of the

---

[8] To describe this first part of the *Autobiography* as conventional is by no means to deny the importance of Malcolm X's first conversion as a milestone in the rise of black self-consciousness in America. In the two recent studies of black American autobiography, however, this is not the guiding perspective. Sidonie A. Smith, in *Where I'm Bound: Patterns of Slavery and Freedom in Black American Autobiography* (Westport, Conn., 1974), reads the experience with the Nation of Islam as the third in a continuing series of disillusionments teaching Malcolm X that "his freedom

Autobiography would usefully illustrate the survival of the classic pattern of conversion narrative in the contemporary literature of spiritual autobiography, but this interest would necessarily be a limited one given Malcolm X's reticence about the drama of the experience of conversion itself. For Malcolm X the fact of conversion is decisive, life-shaping, identity-altering, but unlike the most celebrated spiritual autobiographers of the past he chooses not to dramatize the experience itself or to explore its psychological dynamics.[9]

It seems probable that when Malcolm X began his dictations to Haley in 1963 he anticipated that his narrative would end with an account of his transformation into the national spokesman of Elijah Muhammad's Nation of Islam (the material covered in Chapters 14 and 15 of Haley's text). This was not destined to be the end of the story, however, for the pace of Malcolm X's history, always lively, became tumultuous in 1963 and steadily accelerated until his assassination in 1965. In this last period Malcolm X was to experience two events that destroyed the very premises of the autobiography he had set out to write: the most well-known convert to the Black Muslim religion was first to break with Elijah Muhammad (Chapter 16, "Out") and then to make a pilgrimage to Mecca (Chapter 17), where he underwent a second conversion to what he now regarded as the true religion of Islam. The revelation that Elijah Muhammad was a false prophet shattered the world of Malcolm X and the shape of the life he had been living for twelve years:

> I was like someone who for twelve years had had an insepara-
> ble, beautiful marriage—and then suddenly one morning at
> breakfast the marriage partner had thrust across the table some
> divorce papers.
> I felt as though something in *nature* had failed, like the sun or

---

within the community is finally only a chimera" (pp. 96–97). In *Black Autobiography in America* (Amherst, 1974), on the other hand, Stephen Butterfield places Malcolm X's Black Muslim phase in the larger context of his development as a black revolutionary: "Malcolm X, pimp and drug pusher, convict, Muslim minister, Pan-Africanist, pilgrim to Mecca, lifting himself up to become one of the few men who could have been the Lenin of America before he was cut down by gunfire" (p. 184).

[9] Ohmann interprets the reticence of Malcolm X on the subjective nature of his conversion experience as a manifestation of his "distrust of the inner life, even an antipathy to it." See "*The Autobiography of Malcolm X*: A Revolutionary Use of the Franklin Tradition," pp. 134, 139–140.

the stars. It was that incredible a phenomenon to me—
something too stupendous to conceive. (304)

The autobiographical fiction of the completed self was exploded for
good, although Malcolm X, with a remarkable fidelity to the truth
of his past, was to preserve the fragments in the earlier chapters of
the *Autobiography*, as we have seen.

The illumination at Mecca made Malcolm X feel "like a complete human being" for the first time "in my thirty-nine years on
this earth" (365), and he assumed a new name to symbolize this
new sense of identity, El-Hajj Malik El-Shabazz. In the final chapters of the book (18 and 19) we see Malcolm X in the process of
discarding the "old 'hate' and 'violence' image" (423) of the mili-
tant preacher of Elijah Muhammad's Nation of Islam, but before he
created a design for the life of this new self he was brutally gunned
down on 21 February 1965. In fact, it is not at all certain that Malcolm X would have arrived at any single, definitive formulation for
the shape of his life even if he had continued to live. In the final
pages of the last chapter he observes:

No man is given but so much time to accomplish whatever is
his life's work. My life in particular never has stayed fixed in
one position for very long. You have seen how throughout
my life, I have often known unexpected drastic changes. (378)

With these words Malcolm X articulates a truth already latent but
ungrasped in the autobiographical narrative he originally set out to
write in his evangelical zeal: his life was not now and never had
been a life of the simpler pattern of the traditional conversion story.

Because this complex vision of his existence is clearly not that of
the early sections of the *Autobiography*, Alex Haley and Malcolm X
were forced to confront the consequences of this discontinuity in
perspective for the narrative, already a year old. It was Haley who
raised the issue when he learned, belatedly, of the rift between Malcolm X and Elijah Muhammad, for he had become worried that an
embittered Malcolm X might want to rewrite the book from his
new perspective, and this at a time when Haley regarded their collaboration as virtually complete ("by now I had the bulk of the
needed life story material in hand," 406). Malcolm X's initial response settled the matter temporarily: "I want the book to be the
way it was" (412). Haley's concern, however, was justified, for a
few months later, following Malcolm X's journey to Mecca, Haley

was "appalled" to find that Malcolm X had "red-inked" many of the places in the manuscript "where he had told of his almost father-and-son relationship with Elijah Muhammad." Haley describes this crisis of the autobiographical act as follows:

> Telephoning Malcolm X, I reminded him of his previous decision, and I stressed that if those chapters contained such telegraphing to readers of what would lie ahead, then the book would automatically be robbed of some of its building suspense and drama. Malcolm X said, gruffly, "Whose book is this?" I told him "yours, of course," and that I only made the objection in my position as a writer. He said that he would have to think about it. I was heart-sick at the prospect that he might want to re-edit the entire book into a polemic against Elijah Muhammad. But late that night, Malcolm X telephoned. "I'm sorry. You're right. I was upset about something. Forget what I wanted changed, let what you already had stand." I never again gave him chapters to review unless I was with him. Several times I would covertly watch him frown and wince as he read, but he never again asked for any change in what he had originally said. (414)

Malcolm X's refusal to change the narrative reflects, finally, his acceptance of change as the fundamental law of existence, and yet, curiously, by the very fidelity of this refusal, he secures for the remembered past and for the acts of memory devoted to it such measure of permanence as the forms of art afford.[10]

The exchange between the two men poses the perplexing issue of perspective in autobiography with an instructive clarity: To which of an autobiographer's selves should he or even can he be true? What are the strategies by which he may maintain a dual or plural

[10] In his essay "Modern Black Autobiography in the Tradition," Michael G. Cooke argues that rewriting is an "essential issue for autobiography" and one unaccountably neglected by students of the form. See *Romanticism: Vistas, Instances, Continuities*, ed. David Thorburn and Geoffrey Hartman (Ithaca, 1973), p. 259. Cooke concludes that "the distinctive feature of the *Autobiography* [*of Malcolm X*] is its naturalistic use of time, the willingness to let the past stand as it was, in its own season, even when later developments, of intellect or intuition or event, give it a different quality" (p. 274). In "Notes For an Anatomy of Modern Autobiography," Francis R. Hart writes that "the autobiographer has always had to consider how to manage, and whether to dramatize, the discontinuities inherent in autobiographical recreation [*sic*]," and he sees Malcolm X as facing this problem courageously and creatively. See *New Literary History* 1 (1970): 489, 501.

allegiance without compromise to his present vision of the truth? In fact, the restraint of the "telegraphing" does leave the climax intact,[11] and yet Malcolm X's decision not to revise the preceding narrative does not produce the kind of obvious discontinuity in authorial perspective that we might expect as a result. Haley's part in this is considerable, for his contribution to the ultimate shape of the *Autobiography* was more extensive and fundamental than his narrowly literary concerns with foreshadowing and suspense might seem to suggest. Despite his tactful protest that he was only a "writer," Haley himself had been instrumental in the playing out of the autobiographical drama between one Malcolm X, whose faith in Elijah Muhammad had supplied him with his initial rationale for an autobiography, and another, whose repudiation of Elijah Muhammad made the *Autobiography* the extraordinary human document it eventually became. If the outcome of this drama was formalized in Malcolm X's expulsion from the Nation of Islam, it was already in the wind by the time the dictations began in earnest in 1963. Alex Haley was one to read between the lines.

Haley recalls in the epilogue that at the very outset of the project he had been in fundamental disagreement with Malcolm X about the narrative he would help him write. He reports that Malcolm X wanted the focus to be on Elijah Muhammad and the Nation of Islam: "He would bristle when I tried to urge him that the proposed book was *his* life" (388). At this early stage of the collaboration Haley portrays two Malcolms: a loyal public Malcolm X describing a religious movement in which he casts himself in a distinctly subordinate and self-effacing role, and a subversive private Malcolm X scribbling a trenchant countercommentary in telegraphic red-ink ball point on any available scrap of paper. Determined to feature this second Malcolm X in the autobiography, Haley lured this suppressed identity out into the open by leaving white paper napkins next to Malcolm X's coffee cup to tap his closed communications with himself. Haley carefully retrieved this autobiographical fallout, and taking his cue from one of these napkin revelations

[11] Malcolm X specifically alludes to the impending crisis in Chapter 12, pp. 197-198, 210; in Chapter 14, pp. 264-265; and in Chapter 15, p. 287. For instances of an undercurrent of retrospective criticism of Elijah Muhammad, see Chapter 10, p. 168 (his false teaching); Chapter 11, pp. 187, 189 (his immorality); Chapter 14, p. 248 (his insecurity); p. 252 (his worth as a leader). These passages, reflecting as they do Malcolm X's altered vision of the man he had formerly worshiped, are presumably interpolations from a later phase of the dictations.

(interestingly about women), Haley "cast a bait" (389) with a question about Malcolm X's mother. Haley reports that with this textbook display of Freudian savvy he was able to land the narrative he was seeking:

> From this stream-of-consciousness reminiscing I finally got out of him the foundation for this book's beginning chapters, "Nightmare" and "Mascot." After that night, he never again hesitated to tell me even the most intimate details of his personal life, over the next two years. His talking about his mother triggered something. (390-391)

From the very earliest phase of the dictations, then, the autobiography began to take on a much more personal and private coloration than Malcolm X originally intended. What Elijah Muhammad accomplished, autobiographically speaking, when he "silenced" Malcolm X, was to legitimatize the private utterance of the napkins that had already found its way into the mainstream of a narrative initially conceived as an orthodox work of evangelical piety. After his separation from the Nation of Islam, Malcolm X comments that he began "to think for myself, . . . after twelve years of never thinking for as much as five minutes about myself" (306). Haley reports two napkin messages of this period that signal the consequences of Malcolm X's new sense of himself and his power for the nearly completed *Autobiography*:

> He scribbled one night, "You have not converted a man because you have silenced him. John Viscount Morley." And the same night, almost illegibly, "I was going downhill until he picked me up, but the more I think of it, we picked each other up." (406)[12]

Not only was Malcolm X rejecting the simple clarity of the original conversion narrative he had set out to tell but he was no longer disposed to sacrifice to the greater glory of Elijah Muhammad his own agency in the working out of his life story.

In the final chapters of the *Autobiography* and in the epilogue, as Malcolm X moves toward a new view of his story as a life of changes he expresses an impressive, highly self-conscious awareness of the problems of autobiographical narrative, and specifically

---

[12] The second of the two messages reformulates and repudiates the original dedication of the *Autobiography*.

of the complex relationship between living a life and writing an autobiography. All of his experience in the last packed months, weeks, and days of his life worked to destroy his earlier confident belief in the completed self, the completed life, and hence in the complete life story. Thus he writes to Haley in what is possibly his final statement about the *Autobiography*: "I just want to read it one more time because I don't expect to read it in finished form" (426). As Malcolm X saw it at the last, all autobiographies are by nature incomplete and they cannot, accordingly, have a definitive shape. As a life changes, so any sense of the shape of a life must change; the autobiographical process evolves because it is part of the life, and the identity of the autobiographical "I" changes and shifts. Pursuing the logic of such speculations, Malcolm X even wonders whether any autobiography can keep abreast of the unfolding of personal history: "How is it possible to write one's autobiography in a world so fast-changing as this?" (408). And so he observes to Haley, "I hope the book is proceeding rapidly, for events concerning my life happen so swiftly, much of what has already been written can easily be outdated from month to month. In life, nothing is permanent; not even life itself" (413-414).

At the end, then, Malcolm X came to reject the traditional autobiographical fiction that the life comes first, and then the writing of the life; that the life is in some sense complete and that the autobiographical process simply records the final achieved shape. This fiction is based upon a suspension of time,[13] as though the "life," the subject, could sit still long enough for the autobiographical "I," the photographer, to snap its picture. In fact, as Malcolm X was to learn, the "life" itself will not hold still; it changes, shifts position. And as for the autobiographical act, it requires much more than an instant of time to take the picture, to write the story. As the act of composition extends in time, so it enters the life-stream, and the fictive separation between life and life story, which is so convenient—even necessary—to the writing of autobiography, dissolves.

Malcolm X's final knowledge of the incompleteness of the self is what gives the last pages of the *Autobiography* together with the epilogue their remarkable power: the vision of a man whose swiftly unfolding career has outstripped the possibilities of the traditional

[13] See Cooke, "Modern Black Autobiography in the Tradition," pp. 259-260, on "the problem of the self and time" in autobiography.

autobiography he had meant to write. It is not in the least surprising that Malcolm X's sobering insights into the limitations of autobiography are accompanied by an increasingly insistent desire to disengage himself from the ambitions of the autobiographical process. Thus he speaks of the *Autobiography* to Haley time and again as though, having disabused himself of any illusion that the narrative could keep pace with his life, he had consigned the book to its fate, casting it adrift as hopelessly obsolete. Paradoxically, nowhere does the book succeed, persuade, more than in its confession of failure as autobiography. This is the fascination of *The Education of Henry Adams*, and Malcolm X, like Adams, leaves behind him the husks of played-out autobiographical paradigms. The indomitable reality of the self transcends and exhausts the received shapes for a life that are transmitted by the culture, and yet the very process of discarding in itself works to structure an apparently shapeless experience. Despite—or because of—the intractability of life to form, the fiction of the completed self, which lies at the core of the autobiographical enterprise, cannot be readily dispatched. From its ashes, phoenix-like, it reconstitutes itself in a new guise. Malcolm X's work, and Adams's as well, generate a sense that the uncompromising commitment to the truth of one's own nature, which requires the elimination of false identities and careers one by one, will yield at the last the pure ore of a final and irreducible selfhood. This is the ultimate autobiographical dream.

Michel Leiris: Mazemaker

Germaine Brée

One could consider Michel Leiris's[1] literary work, or even his work in its entirety, as a single autobiographic text. Interrupted at intervals, on occasion espousing different generic masks (poetry, novel, ethnographic studies, prefaces to various literary or artistic volumes), it comes to a halt rather than ends with each successive volume, only to start off again with the next. I shall refer here, however, only to that part of his work that belongs properly to the autobiographic mode in a more limited sense: to the volumes predicated upon a deliberate and sustained (though idiosyncratic) autobiographic project—to the four volumes grouped under the title *The Rule of the Game*, preceded by the prefatory *Manhood*. Leiris warns us that with *Frêle bruit* (Frail Sound, 1976) that project has drawn to a close. *Frêle bruit* is his "last word." At seventy-five he is playing his last cards as autobiographer. He has laid out like a deck

[1] Born in Paris in 1901, in a well-to-do upper-middle-class family, Leiris early joined the surrealist group, whose techniques and poetics inspired his first poems and a novel, *Aurora*, written in 1926-1927 but not published until 1946. A deep depression took him into psychoanalysis; as an antidote to the dangers of disintegration through the excesses of subjectivism, he became an ethnographer. He is now a curator at the anthropological Musée de l'Homme in Paris. His "autobiographic quest" began at the time of his break with the surrealist group in approximately 1929. *Manhood* (1939) and the four still untranslated volumes of *The Rule of the Game* (*Biffures*, 1948; *Fourbis*, 1955; *Fibrilles*, 1966; *Frêle bruit*, 1976) constitute (especially the last four) what I shall consider in this article as a particular form of "antiautobiographic autobiography." (*Biffures* are erasures, words struck out; if we indulge in word games—games Leiris likes to play—the word also suggests bifurcations, forks in the road; *Fourbis* suggests "odds and ends" but also things that are polished up; *Fibrilles* suggests threadlike fibers that might possibly be woven into something). Unless I quote from *Manhood*, all translations in this article are mine.

of cards the fragmentary passages that make up the volume: "dealing them out, displacing them, grouping them as one lays out cards
for a game of patience" (p. 7). The word Leiris uses here is *réussite*.
It designates both the game of patience he specifically evokes and an
act or project successfully brought to completion.

Leiris is not a man who uses words without weighing their implications. But if a *réussite* there is, for him it can be understood in
no ordinary sense of the word, whether in terms of Leiris's life as he
sees it, or in terms of a literary success:

> Failure everywhere: as a writer, because almost unable to go
> beyond the scrutiny of self he had only rarely acceded to
> poetry and, furthermore, knew that he was not made of the
> same timber as those whose fate is hanging, madness, or a
> definitive departure;[2] as a rebel, since he had never abandoned
> bourgeoise comfort,[3] and after stubborn revolutionary im-
> pulses, he had to admit that averse to violence as much as to
> sacrifice, he was not of the stuff of which militants are made;[4]
> as a lover, since his sentimental life had been of the most banal
> and his sensual ardour had soon cooled down; as a traveller,[5]
> since, confined to a single language, his mother tongue, he had
> perhaps been less apt than anyone else to feel at ease with
> people and things, even in his own clime. From his profession
> as ethnographer, he had, concretely, drawn very little: highly
> specialized work in the language of initiates in the Sudan and

[2] Allusions to the fate of such poets as Gérard de Nerval, who had periods of
madness and hanged himself; Rimbaud, who "left" France abandoning a literary
career; and Lautréamont, who died young. Leiris obviously had imagined himself in
the romantic role of the poet who drops out and dies, unable to live in a stultifying
society.

[3] Leiris married fairly early into the well-established Kahnweiler family (who
were well-known art dealers), and has always been deeply attached to his wife; these
facts destroy his wish to see himself as the convention-breaking rebel or the outcast
poet. "What led me to place demands upon myself [in the writing of *Manhood*], is
the fact that I am married, that I love my wife a great deal." See *Manhood: A Journey
from Childhood into the Fierce Order of Virility*, trans. Richard Howard (New York,
1963), p. 50.

[4] Since his surrealist days, Leiris has been a left-wing man; his latest political activity was to protest against the abject conditions of the immigrant workers in Paris.
Again, here he is measuring his actions against a mythology of ultimate political
martyrdom.

[5] Since his first journey to Africa as a member of a Dakar-Djibouti ethnographic
expedition (1931-1933), Leiris has travelled quite extensively. In addition to Africa,
he has also journeyed to Haiti, Martinique and Guadeloupe, to Cuba and to China.

on ritual possessions in Ethiopia; work on 'negro art' based on secondary sources and, without much significance, in spite of high-minded intentions, other works with an anti-racist bias; finally (and this was, he would think in his blackest hours, what was most worthy of mention) a few articles manifesting his will to put ethnography at the service, not of Western science, but of the peoples of the third world, a naive will, it is true, since those peoples are concerned with quite other things. (pp. 287-288)[6]

Leiris's sharply reductive balance sheet (which sets the sternly judgmental observer apart from the objectified "he," temporarily displacing the subjective "I") calls for some interpretation. For, if seen from outside with only its surface patterns visible, Leiris's long and respectable life could hardly be called a "failure." From the outset, he has lived in a privileged stratum of society, participating more fully than most in the sophisticated intellectual and artistic life of Paris. The roster of his friends from Raymond Roussel and Max Jacob, both of whom he knew as an adolescent, to André Masson, Sartre, Simone de Beauvoir, Camus, Picasso, and Giacometti among many others, could in itself have furnished abundant material for traditional memoirs. The list of his works and their variety are far from negligible; and he has consistently lived through the difficult years of his adult life (the years of the German occupation included) with more than average dignity. His reductive balance sheet, couched as it is in terms of the grandly romantic roles he failed to live up to, strikes one as being rather suspect. The mask does not entirely fit what one knows of the man. It reads like a set piece. And it is perhaps designed specifically to cast doubt upon itself, in the writer's eyes as well as in the readers'. Leiris's "simple confession," as he once called it, is indeed never a simple affair.

That the positive aspects of his existence are absent from the *bilan* is symptomatic, for they are just as absent, on the whole, from his entire autobiographic work. In *Manhood* and more sparsely and fragmentarily in the successive volumes, we catch sight of his childhood and adolescent world, later of the traveller and of his abortive love affairs, sometimes too of the poet involved in his word games and word associations. But only rarely do we get a

---

[6] For a bibliography of Michel Leiris's ethnographic works, see the special Leiris issue of *Sub-stance* 11-12 (1975): 147-155.

glimpse of his married life, of the social or professional man. Leiris gives us very little information on the outer, factual surfaces of his life. They obviously do not concern his project. But it is notable that in his survey of his failures, he does not mention the twelve hundred-odd pages of *Manhood* and *La règle du jeu*. Perhaps in his eyes these represent the *réussite* and the counterweight to those other lacks and "failures."

Until recently Leiris has received scant attention from either readers or critics.[7] Only the first section of his "immense monologue," *Manhood*, has reached what one might call a reading public. Consequently, and particularly in the English-speaking world, since it is the only volume available in English, *Manhood* has often been considered the exemplification of Leiris's use of the autobiographic medium. Nothing could be more misleading. As Leiris moves from volume to volume he approaches his material differently. The modification of the form that his investigation into his existence takes is not only central to this "autobiographical quest" but it is in fact its "raison d'être."

The card-game analogy, like many such in his text, is strictly to the point, for Leiris applies the research methods of the anthropologist to his own personal life. He has constituted an archive (an extensive one it would seem) of index files wherein he accumulated the data upon which he works—the record of dreams, of fantasies, encounters, love affairs, moods, word games, poems, observations, fragments of analysis. He has also kept a diary; and he refers to loose sheets of paper on which he notes more sustained thematic developments. As Leiris the ethnologist attempts to decode and interpret the miscellaneous data he collects, collating, classifying, associating, searching for some symbolic meaning beneath the surface phenomena, so Leiris the autobiographer proceeds with the materials of his life. His index cards are complex and achronological elements that may contain, as he points out, both the material of his investigation and his analysis of that material, involving him thereby in a kind of circularity.

---

[7] Although scattered articles have appeared since the mid-forties, with the exception of Maurice Nadeau's 1963 *Michel Leiris et la quadrature du cercle*, major critical studies did not begin focusing on Leiris's work until the seventies. Of these studies the best known are Philippe Lejeune's *Lire Leiris, autobiographie et langage* (Paris, 1975) and, in America, the chapter on Leiris in Jeffrey Meihlman's *A Structural Study of Autobiography: Proust, Leiris, Sartre, Lévi-Strauss* (Ithaca, 1974), which is a psychoanalytic (Lacanian) approach. Neither atttempts fully to span the work.

Removing himself from the immediacy of the present, he studies the data, sifts, shuffles, combines in order to see how to link for the purposes of presentation (in the two senses of the word) the heterogeneous material under scrutiny, with the hope that a pattern will appear. His is a traditional effort to find some meaning within—"below" the surface of passing events. This implies at least a hypothetical assumption that there is—or should be—something beyond mere appearances.

He works much as we work in our scholarly research, drawing from archives, laying out the same deck of cards over and over again but always proposing new combinations, new patterns of interpretations. Of necessity, however, Leiris must "invent" the cards he plays, for in the first place he needed to transfer the fragmentary data of his everyday experience to the written page before he could hope to search for an architectonics of the ensemble. He did not take his self-appointed task lightly. "If indeed one of the most 'sacred' goals a man can give himself is to acquire a knowledge of himself as accurate and intense as possible, it becomes clearly desirable that each, scrutinizing his memories with the maximum honesty, should examine whether he can detect some sign allowing him to discern what color the notions of the sacred takes on for him": so he defined his task at the time he was about to publish *Manhood*.[8]

From the outset Leiris was not content to equate autobiography with retrospective narrative, since it was his intent to use the autobiographic mode as a vehicle, not as an end. In the course of many years of practice he defined many times not only the nature and complexities of his task but also his will to proceed with the maximum honesty. It became a major—perhaps the major—theme of his writing. One fairly late definition seems to subsume most others: to pursue "the written formulation of that immense monologue that in a sense is given me, since all its substance is drawn from that which I have lived, but which in another sense obliges me to a constant effort of invention, since I must introduce an order in that indefinitely renewed substance, churn up its elements, adjust them, refine them until I manage in some measure to grasp their significance" (*Fibrilles*, p. 77). The card game turns into a game of Tarot.

Leiris distinguishes several components he must take into ac-

[8] "Le sacré dans la vie quotidienne" (The Sacred in Everyday Life) in "Pour un collège de sociologie," *Nouvelle revue Française* (1938), quoted in *Ecrivains d'aujourd'hui, 1940-1960*, ed. Bernard Pingaud (Paris, 1960), pp. 320-321.

count: that which has been or is being lived (indefinitely renewed); the continuous inner but apparently not as yet worded soundless monologue carried on with himself; the formulation in writing that imposes its invented order upon the fluid inner substance and monologue; and the decoding of the emergent pattern whereby that which was lived becomes readable. An osmosis takes place as existence is translated into writing, a phenomenon Mehlman accurately discerned when he defined Leiris's "autobiographic quest" as the attempt "to become alive (*bio*) to oneself (*auto*) in what the French call the elusive realm of *l'écriture (graphie*: writing)."[9] This is not an easy position to hold. It posits a series of tensions: first, between the indefinitely renewed stuff of existence with its accompanying inner discourse and the writing that seeks to arrest and circumscribe it; second, between the slow tempo of the act of writing and the tempo of the life meanwhile continuing to develop; third (and as a consequence), the discrepancy between the self in the mobile present and the always anachronistic work of self-presentation or re-presentation involved in the writing.

In the first instance, a "metadiscourse" underlies the effort of selection and organization required by the writing of a text. It puts the autobiographer's task in double jeopardy: the slippage into a tautological reduplication of its premises will disconnect it from the reality it was to reveal; it will then both replace and mask that reality it was meant to bring to the surface. In the second and third instances the complicated meshings of heterogenous time patterns that the autobiographic effort of self-display sets in motion compromise the hope of a self-discovery that would open up a perspective not only on the past but on the future. This Leiris set up as one of his goals: "Who is that I," he asks, "that self of mine around which everything is articulated?" Ethnographer that he is, he seeks in the materials of his life the central symbolic order that could give them significance.[10] In terms of that *hors-texte*—the reality beyond the text that is his life—the project "to establish one's portrait in

[9] Mehlman, *A Structural Study of Autobiography*, p. 14. Mehlman sees Leiris's attempt as showing the "impossibility" of creating oneself in writing, a point of view I shall discuss later.

[10] Leiris has not abandoned the surrealist aspirations toward a unifying "center," although he has abandoned the search. He hopes, as he has sometimes said, that the materials he has gathered will help someone else produce the decoding he has not achieved. Using another range of vocabulary, we might say that Leiris's text is an attempt to produce a *signifié* (a signification) from a plethora of signifiers, and that the attempt itself becomes in its turn a signifier calling for a new search for a *signifié*—a never-ending ever more abstract process.

writing will remain illusory if one proposes to portray in his interiority he who, at that moment, is holding the pen and not another whom one already knows only through memory when he projects himself upon the page." Then "the inevitable discrepancy" between the moment in which one writes and the moment one would describe may turn into a "crying dissonance." The "time of the book" and the "time of life" fail to coincide; another such gap opens between the time span of the writer writing and the time span during which he turns into the reader—and possibly the rectifier—of his text (*Fibrilles*, pp. 220-221).

In this labyrinthine situation the status of the text itself is open to question. The pathway that the act of writing was to "invent" twists and turns upon itself. Leiris's determination not to be caught in the trap of a rhetoric that would contaminate the authenticity of his investigation inevitably leads him to try new methodical prospections. From volume to volume and sometimes within a single volume, he has, he states, tried "one after the other various trails and tunnels" (*Fourbis*, p. 73). The image of the maze, although never fully explicated, surfaces here, each path opening up on another in a multiple itinerary that is interminable in the full sense of the word. The only way to terminate is to stop. No final resolution takes place. A Leiris-Daedalus refuses to be led to the center of the maze he has built to entrap himself, and he simultaneously seeks to escape it by acquiring the clear sense of its design. My analogy here is not altogether gratuitous; for the function of the maze in the first place seems to have been in great part to prevent anyone from reaching its center.

Leiris of course did not start out with the full sense of the problematics in which he had become involved. But the reader-critic (myself) may surmise that the *réussite* to which he alludes in the opening page of the last volume to date of his autobiographic quest is that he has eluded the temptation to answer his question. At one time it had been his intent to do so. A projected title, *Fibules* (the clasps holding together the Roman toga), notified the reader that Leiris was to assemble into a single garment the fragmentary materials provided by the preceding volumes. The project did not materialize. *Frêle bruit* is composed of fragments between which, in the layout of the pages themselves, interstices open up into a kind of void. Admittedly Leiris fears and loathes the fact and idea of death. The deferment of any resolution to his quest leaves open the question of the presence of that inner self; it implies that the center around which all else is articulated cannot be reached by language, belongs then perhaps to the enigmatic realm of "the sacred" to whose exploration he had dedicated himself at the outset. Failure to reach it would consequently be a manner of success. For as we are apprised on the back cover of *Frêle bruit*, Leiris's investigation has yielded him as self-knowledge only the sense of being motivated by a few rather generally shared inner drives: ". . . an aspiration to the marvelous, the will to commitment in the struggle against social inequity, the desire for a universality that led him to establish contacts with other civilizations. . . ." While possessed by "horror" of death, in that "horror" the "sacred" most surely still haunts Leiris's world; and, in counterpoint, even in his old age the elusive sense of an absent center maintains its status as a never circumscribed exigency of creativity. On every level and in this same fashion Leiris continually balances and keeps alive conflicting hypotheses.

One could roughly classify the successive volumes as follows: *Manhood*, the investigation of formative personal and cultural myths, rooted in a childhood world in which the marvelous and the sacred coincide. *Biffures* elucidates the associations embedded in both the poetic and the private use of a shared language with their charge of the "marvelous," his natural ambience or "clime" as poet. With *Fourbis*, in the context of the war and its aftermath, Leiris investigates his aspirations to overcome the horror of death by moving beyond the closed circle of his subjectivity toward the glamorous "other." The movement reveals his need of an ethic that would allow him to sustain the poetic life within the societal. *Fibrilles* is his book of voyage and return in space and across time, not the least of which is the account of Leiris's journey toward death in attempted suicide. Of *Frêle bruit*, one might conclude that in relation to *Manhood*, the book of his thirties, it is the book of old age, a kind of post-face to the rest, all passion spent. What is lost in this classification is the close interaction between experience, memory, and analysis that through the labor of writing and via the network of language binds each volume to the others in what Leiris speaks of as a form of symphonic orchestration and which I prefer to compare to a carefully built maze.[11] For while the maze leaves one in uncertainty as to which path inward one should take, it is

[11] In this respect, Leiris's work seems to me to have some affinity with the work of the British sculptor Michael Ayrton, who re-created the Cretan maze in a Connecticut estate and who uses it in his sculptures as a recurrent motif for the human brain. See his account of his enterprise in *Horizon*, Spring 1970, pp. 57-65.

also a maze that reshapes itself continually, within an inevitable circularity. This is more particularly true of the three central volumes, *Biffures*, *Fourbis*, and *Fibrilles*. In each of these works, what changes is the criterion adopted for the written ordering of the text. This turns the reader who attempts to define Leiris's procedures as autobiographer into a meta-meta-critic; the initial meta-critic is always Leiris himself. Seen in this perspective and as a whole, *The Rule of the Game* has the elusive contours of mobile sculptures projected in space by a play of light or of mirrors.

Manhood, the initial volume in the autobiographic project, offers an insight into the process whereby Leiris's material acquires a kind of plasticity. Furthermore, it was in the course of writing this book that Leiris evolved the famous analogy between the *tauromachia* and the practice of literature as he understood it,[12] deducing therefrom the poetic or "rule of the game" that he seeks to apply in the succeeding volumes. This is Leiris's first attempt at dealing with the problematics of the genre that on finishing *Manhood* he had thought he had solved: for *Manhood* was first conceived as a "meta-autobiography," a consciously structured narrative whose episodes revealed, as in Sartre's later *The Words*, an underlying, comprehensible pattern that determined the book's organic structure. Leiris's organizing pattern was, of course, quite different from Sartre's.

Manhood is constituted by a prologue carefully situated in time: "I have just reached the age of thirty-four" is the opening sentence, a statement that implies that the book it introduces is now finished and that it has led to an understanding of the man meticulously drawn in the prologue. The subtitle, "A journey from childhood to the fierce order of virility," suggests the well-worn analogy of life and journey, with its teleology and suggested theme of initiation into a symbolic cultural order. But a set of notes to the text (pp. 147-150) undercuts the very notion of a goal attained. "I will be thirty-five when these pages are published for the first time. Such a gap would justify a new book." Other notes suggest the same *glissement* or slippage in time and undermining of the underlying organization of the book. "Today, I would no longer explain this

---

[12] The first edition of *L'Age d'homme* (1939) did not contain this essay, which was included in the 1946 edition. In the first edition of *Manhood* (1963) it appears as a Postface, which it quite properly is; but in the 1968 edition it has become a Preface, an evolution that recalls Jacques Derrida's discussion of the nature of the preface in his *De la grammatologie*. The bulk of Leiris's text was written between 1931-1935, although some of the *fiches* or card files probably date back into the twenties.

in psychoanalytic terms." These remarks open gaps in the text that the Afterword (pp. 151-162)—later to become the Foreword—further emphasizes. For it presents two texts situated at a chronological distance from each other, thereby establishing a multiple perspective on the book "completed" in 1935. The first, written in 1939, rapidly evokes three dates, three shifting perspectives: 1922, the date at which "the author of *Manhood* reached the climacteric which inspired the title of his book"; then 1935, when the author "completed the book" at a time when he "no doubt supposed his existence had already sustained enough vicissitudes for him to pride himself on having attained the age of virility at last." There, it should be noted, the climactic date (1922) is outflanked within the text itself as the dates 1925 and 1929 emerge in the course of the writing. The overlapping of the "times" of memory, experience, and writing is already a feature of the text. Finally, the "collapse" of the organizing belief opens the way to a restructuring of the materials presented: "Now in 1939 . . . the author freely acknowledges that his true 'manhood' remains to be written." The successive perspectives detach the narrative structure from the materials and pose the question of the relation of the autobiographer not only to his materials but to what he does with them—the manner in which he presents and "re-presents" them—which leads to all the problems of self-display, self-revelation, narcissism, myth-making, and veracity endemic to the autobiographic mode. It was precisely these problems that Leiris later dramatized, with gentle irony, in the comparison of the autobiographer and the toreador. To this much discussed poetics, I shall return later.[13]

Of all the autobiographic volumes, *Manhood* comes closest to the traditional narrative model as analyzed by Philippe Lejeune: from a given point in time and in achievement (Leiris's access to "manhood"), the autobiographer retrospectively and in chronological sequence tells how he got there. And indeed *Manhood* goes back to the usual though fragmented scenes of childhood and moves on through a stormy adolescence in the post World War I years to 1929. The narrative is not linear in the sense that no apparent effort

[13] The themes of the *tauromachia* and the Minotaur were in the air at this time. Leiris belonged to the group of writers who wrote for the postsurrealist review, *Minotaur*. Among them was Bataille who made a major theme of the *tauromachia*; Picasso, a close friend of the Leirises, also made use of it. The *tauromachia* is of course connected via the relation of man and bull with the Minotaur and the labyrinth, one of the pervasive myths of the time.

has been made to link the fragments in a continuous discourse. Often introduced by quotations, the successive chapters appear as vertical juxtapositions, laid out side by side, a technique of montage and collage reproduced within each section. The book as a whole gives an impression of both enigmatic strangeness and yet unity. For the reader, *Manhood* is certainly the most intensively fascinating volume in Leiris's sometimes tedious autobiographic itinerary.

Leiris proceeds methodically and on two levels: the selection of his materials and his reading of them. To the first level—what we might call the selected deck of cards extracted from his archives— he has given us the key: "If I assemble all those facts borrowed from what was, when I was a child, my daily life," he wrote, after a brief listing of the main episodes recounted in the first chapter of *Manhood*, "I see taking shape little by little an image of what is, for me, the sacred . . . something which, in sum, I cannot conceive very well except as marked, one way or another, by the supernatural."[14] The terrain of his autobiographic quest was defined by the combination of the surrealist myth with the anthropological research of Mauss (one of Leiris's masters) into the origin and function of the sacred and the taboo in the life of collectivities. And at the time this was also a major preoccupation of Georges Bataille and Maurice Blanchot with whom Leiris was fairly closely connected. (A certain almost obsessional fascination for the sacred was a minor cultural phenomenon of the thirties.) Leiris's investigation was directed toward the exploration of what "sacralized" these episodes in his life, whether individual or cultural. His parents' addiction to opera had fostered his early, fascinated absorption in the theatrical representations of opera which, at this stage of his investigation, he saw as having shaped his sexual mythology and expectations, the inner theater of his latent erotic desires. Freudian psychoanalysis, which postulated that erotic desire with its escort of repression and symbolic transferences was the key to personal behavior, suggested the hypotheses that gave the episodes that Leiris had selected their unity and meaning. It turned his otherwise insignificant adventure into an erotic script, finally epitomized symbolically in two figures, Cranach's Judith and Lucretia. Leiris recognized that these figures had "perhaps" been charged by him with an arbitrary allegorical significance in which love, cruelty, and death

[14] Leiris, "Le sacré dans la vie quotidienne," p. 320.

dramatically combined. But by elucidating his own myths, Leiris hoped to be able to objectively examine the modalities of his sexual behavior as texts to be rationally decoded. He would thus presumably be able to confront reality, understand and control his erotic drives, and become at last an initiate in "the fierce order of virility," while giving the erotic drives aesthetic validity as had Cranach.

His revolt against the culture that had imposed upon him the fear and repression of these erotic drives explodes violently in *L'Afrique fantôme*. In *Manhood*, such emblems as Judith, Lucretia, Holofernes, and *The Raft of the Medusa* exteriorize and demythify Leiris's childhood sublimations. But the writing yields its own mythology, a personal language that Leiris will then bring under scrutiny. And indeed the next step Leiris took (in *Biffures*) was to explore the associations at work in his language, only to find that the verbal networks he thus established were mere fantasy. And so it would be with each new tentative at organizing his *fiches*.

This is where the allegory of the *tauromachia* takes on its multiple meanings. That in his role as autobiographer Leiris aspires to function with the bullfighter's qualities of skill in performance, courage, and mastery in self-exposure is the more evident of its connotations, and the strict ritual of the combat as the toreador confronts the unpredictable assault of brute violence is what seems most to attract him in the image. For the autobiographer, the chaotic assault of the adversary seems to embody the brute substance upon which he works. That some intimation of the quasi-physical struggle inherent in the act of writing should reveal at least the "shadow" of the bull's horn—that is, the threat of mutilation, wound, or death—seems to Leiris the guarantee that the writing meshes into a real *hors-texte* and is not functioning merely as yet another verbal, that is "mythic," construct.

Only much later in *Fibrilles* will Leiris spell out in detail a large list of the self-imposed rules of the game his bullfight image embodies, rules that sharply constrain the autobiographer's "performance" of the autobiographic act. Curiously the code developed is largely negative: not to lie, not to promise what you can't execute; not to use words lightly, not to get caught in a rhetoric. Leiris sought to compose a rhetoric, an ethic, and a tactics for the autobiographer that would be binding for both the societal man responsible to others for what he reveals of their lives and for the writer responsible for the use he makes of language. All the rules he formulates spell out the meaning he ascribes to the word "authenticity." Here Leiris becomes a kind of Boileau of autobiography, albeit only in regard to himself. In brief, in Leiris's codification the exigency of complete and objective truth is qualified by a rule of respect for others, including the reader: therefore the absence of any allusion—except fleetingly—to the most intimate relations in his life; thence too the absence of the sensational and shocking, at least in the linguistic texture of the discourse. To the "taboos of conduct" Leiris added the "taboos of writing": the elimination of jargon and gratuitous lyricism, the search for a strict adherence to the most accurate expression. As he considered it anew in *Fibrilles*, he realized much later that the formalistic code implicit in the allegory of the *tauromachia* was a mistake. He corrected it by an act of faith: "It is man that counts with the use he makes of language, eventually what he thinks about it and not language itself" (pp. 245-246). This reverses the attitude implicit in the allegory of the *tauromachia*, summarizing his thirty-year itinerary and situating him clearly among the literary humanists in the cultural topography of his time.

Biffures was the beginning of an adventure, a search for an answer to a question left unsolved by *Manhood* but insistently raised by *le vécu* of the years of war and German occupation: how to merge into a single system the writer's "poetic art" and an ethical code of *savoir-vivre*; in other words, how to conciliate the "magic adventures of language" with the "vital seriousness" of life. If, in the main, the first emphasis in Leiris's code was on the "conversion" of life into *writing*, the final emphasis seems to veer toward the opposite: writing leads back to the man, the seeker, caught in the uncertainties of his passage through language.

The reader who has followed Leiris, the "lost-promeneur who tries to make his way out by reconstructing his itinerary," may find the process tedious. But in effect Leiris has thoroughly dramatized and explored the quasi-insoluble conflicts at work in the very postulation that autobiography is a generic and definable literary category. In this sense, *The Rule of the Game* presents an exemplary act of "deconstruction." And Leiris knows this: he states that he has left us with the assembled materials for writing the autobiography rather than with the autobiography itself, thus suggesting that critic-readers will produce the unifying schemas that escaped him. Leiris's strategy as autobiographer, geared to his horror of annihilation in death, would then qualify the notion of failure, though it would not perhaps appear as a victory.

The Other Voice:
Autobiographies of Women Writers

Mary G. Mason

"Why hath this lady writ her own life?" The question posed by
Margaret Cavendish, Duchess of Newcastle, near the end of the
True Relation of My Birth, Breeding and Life (first published 1656) is
no doubt a rhetorical one, set up to be knocked down by the response that would follow. But for Margaret Cavendish it was also
a question that existed in a real realm of controversy outside of
the rhetorical mode, for looking forward it anticipated "carping
tongues" and "malicious censurers" who would ask it "scornfully"
after the *True Relation* had been published, and looking back it
echoed a question that Dame Julian of Norwich, the first English
woman to protest that she *would* speak out about herself, felt compelled to bring up nearly three centuries earlier: "But because I am a
woman, ought I therefore to believe that I should not tell you of the
goodness of God, when I saw at the same time that it is his will that
it be known?"[1] Behind Julian's account is God's desire that his
goodness in his dealings with her be known; behind the Duchess's
account there lies quite a different desire. In both instances, however, it is "because I am a woman" that the two writers feel it
necessary to defend—whether mildly or otherwise—their excursions into autobiographical writing.

[1] Julian of Norwich, *Showings*, trans. Edmund Colledge and James Walsh (New
York, 1978), Chapter 6 ("short text"), p. 135. This edition of the "Shewing of
God's Love" or the "Sixteen Revelations of Divine Love" includes both the "short
text," written shortly after Julian experienced the revelations, and the "long text,"
written some twenty years later; it supersedes all previous editions and will hereafter
be cited in the text.

"Why hath this lady writ her own life? since none cares to know whose daughter she was or whose wife she is, or how she was bred, or what fortunes she had, or how she lived, or what humour or disposition she was of." Having thus granted speech to the scurrilous tongues, the Duchess proceeds to give as good as she foresaw getting and in so doing reveals some highly pertinent facts about women's lives and the writing of women's lives that are applicable not only to the fourteenth through the seventeenth centuries but to our century as well.

> I answer that it is true, that 'tis to no purpose to the readers, but it is to the authoress, because I write it for my sake, not theirs. Neither did I intend this piece for to delight, but to divulge; not to please the fancy, but to tell the truth, lest afterages should mistake, in not knowing I was daughter to one Master Lucas of St. Johns, near Colchester, in Essex, second wife to the Lord Marquis of Newcastle; for my Lord having had two wives, I might easily have been mistaken, especially if I should die and my Lord marry again.[2]

That she was more or less willing to be defined by her relationship to her father and her husband/Lord is a matter of considerable moment in the life and the life-writing of the Duchess of Newcastle; that she undertook that life-writing "for my own sake," "to divulge," and "to tell the truth" so that posterity should not mistake her for the first Duchess, for a possible third Duchess, or for any other duchess at all is of very different but equal moment. And it is to be remarked too that in her response Margaret Cavendish succeeds in shifting the emphasis of the question from "why hath this *lady* writ her own life" to "why hath *this* lady writ her own life"—which transforms the issue from a sterile battle of the sexes into a creative exploration of particular past experience and unique present being.

Strict generic classification might refuse to consider either Julian's *Revelations* or Margaret Cavendish's *True Relation* to be autobiography on the grounds that there is relatively little self-dis-

---

[2] *A True Relation of My Birth, Breeding and Life*, appended to *The Life of William Cavendish, Duke of Newcastle*, ed. C. H. Firth, 2nd ed. (London, n.d.), p. 178. Citations in the text are to this edition of the *True Relation*. The "carping tongues" and "malicious censurers" are in an "epistle" on p. 154. *A True Relation* first appeared in 1656 as part of *Natures Pictures Drawn by Fancies Pencil to the Life* and was republished as an appendix to *The Life of William Cavendish* in 1667.

closure or narrative content in Julian's account of God's dealings with her and that the *True Relation* is compromised as "genuine" autobiography both by its brevity (some twenty-four pages) and by the circumstances of its composition and publication (originally shuffled together with a motley of sketches in verse and prose—*Natures Pictures drawn by Fancies Pencil*—it was left out of the 1671 edition of that collection). Nevertheless, these two early women writers established patterns of relationship and of self-identity that were to be followed by later women whose works were incontestably autobiographies; moreover they were joined by two other women, each of whom "writ her own life"—again one in the fourteenth/fifteenth and one in the seventeenth century—to fill out, as it were, a quaternity of possible patterns according to which women would compose their lives and their autobiographies in succeeding centuries. And though it is not generally recognized, one of these writers—Margery Kempe—produced (ca. 1432) what is actually the first full autobiography in English by anyone, male or female—*The Book of Margery Kempe*, "a schort tretys and a comfortabyl for synful wrecchys," in which she narrates her astonishing life as a demonstration of " þe hy & vnspecabyl mercy of ower souereyn Sauyowr Cryst Ihesu."[3]

The fourth of these early prototypes, Anne Bradstreet, wrote her very brief spiritual autobiography (only five pages long) about the same time that Margaret Cavendish published her *True Relation*, intending it not as surety of identity for posterity nor as a comforting treatise for "synful wrecchys" but as a legacy "to my dear children" who, she hoped, might "gain some spiritual advantage by my experience." Though she did not bring nearly as many children into the world as did Margery Kempe (eight to the earlier woman's fourteen), it is nevertheless highly characteristic that Anne Bradstreet should address her autobiographical exercise to her children and that their spiritual welfare should have been foremost in her thoughts.

In these four works—Julian's *Revelations* or *Showings, The Book of Margery Kempe*, Margaret Cavendish's *True Relation*, and Anne Bradstreet's spiritual account "To My Dear Children"—we can discover not only important beginnings in the history of women's autobiography in English as a distinct mode of interior disclosure

---

[3] *The Book of Margery Kempe*, ed. Sanford Brown Meech (London, 1940), p. 1. Citations in the text are to this edition of *The Book of Margery Kempe*.

but also something like a set of paradigms for life-writing by women right down to our time. And while there are some obvious disadvantages inherent in distinguishing literary works by gender, in the specific instance of autobiography, where a life is so intimately joined to the act of writing, one can achieve certain important insights into the possibilities and necessities of self-writing if one first isolates according to gender and then brings female and male autobiographical types back into proximity in order that they may throw light (at times by sheer contrast) on one another. Nowhere in women's autobiographies do we find the patterns established by the two prototypical male autobiographers, Augustine and Rousseau; and conversely male writers never take up the archetypal models of Julian, Margery Kempe, Margaret Cavendish, and Anne Bradstreet. The dramatic structure of conversion that we find in Augustine's *Confessions*, where the self is presented as the stage for a battle of opposing forces and where a climactic victory for one force—spirit defeating flesh—completes the drama of the self, simply does not accord with the deepest realities of women's experience and so is inappropriate as a model for women's life-writing. Likewise, the egoistic secular archetype that Rousseau handed down to his Romantic brethren in his *Confessions*, shifting the dramatic presentation to an unfolding self-discovery where characters and events are little more than aspects of the author's evolving consciousness, finds no echo in women's writing about their lives. On the contrary, judging by our four models, the self-discovery of female identity seems to acknowledge the real presence and recognition of another consciousness, and the disclosure of female self is linked to the identification of some "other." This recognition of another consciousness—and I emphasize recognition rather than deference—this grounding of identity through relation to the chosen other, seems (if we may judge by our four representative cases) to enable women to write openly about themselves.

Both Julian and Margery Kempe, writing in the mystical tradition of personal dialogue with a divine being who is Creator, Father, and Lover, discover and reveal themselves in discovering and revealing the Other. Speaking in the first person, with a singleness of vision that allows for no distractions or ambivalences, Julian establishes an identification with the suffering Christ on the cross that is absolute; yet, while such a total identification might seem to suggest a loss of self, the fact is that Julian is in no way obliterated as a person, for her account is shot through with evidence of a vivid, unique, and even radical consciousness. Margery Kempe, by way of contrast, speaks in the third person (she figures throughout her narrative as "*þ*is creatur") to a Christ who, when he is not her infant ("for *þ*u art to me a very modir," he once tells her, p. 91) is her manly bridegroom. Unlike Julian's single visioned *Revelations*, *The Book of Margery Kempe* displays a dual sense of vocation: the wife-mother, pilgrim-mystic roles, which were continuous throughout Margery Kempe's life, represent a rather more common pattern of women's perception of themselves as maintaining two equally demanding identities, worldly and otherworldly, both of which, however, are ultimately determined by their relation to the divine.

Like Julian's, Anne Bradstreet's brief retrospection is possessed of a singleness of focus, but because her spiritual autobiography comes out of the Puritan tradition and out of the early days of the New England colonies, its intense focus falls not on a personal figure but on a spiritual community. When we place Anne Bradstreet's prose autobiography alongside her autobiographical poetry, we can observe in both a unique harmonizing of the divine, the secular, and the personal, a unifying of a public and a private consciousness.

Margaret Cavendish, author of the first important secular autobiography by a woman, limns her own portrait in a double image, herself and her husband, the Duke of Newcastle. (Here, incidentally, the history of women's life-writing parallels the history of men's life-writing, secular autobiography being in both cases a latter-day development out of or away from religious self-examination.) The focus of the *True Relation* might better be called duo than dual, and while Margaret Cavendish does not exactly subordinate herself to her husband's image, she obviously identifies herself most sharply when she is identifying him too. The full-length biography of her husband was written some ten years after the Duchess produced her own short autobiography, and at about the same time that she was writing the life of her husband she also wrote a utopian fantasy, *The Blazing World*, in which she once again splits and reunifies the self-image, appearing both as Duchess of Newcastle and as Empress of the Blazing World—as both herself and another. As we shall see, this duo pattern is a fairly common one in women's autobiographies (indeed in Margaret Cavendish's time two other well-known women, Lucy Hutchinson and Lady Anne Fanshawe, wrote their memoirs and actually appended them to their husbands' biographies).

The Duchess of Newcastle was insistently and prolifically literary, which might seem to set her *True Relation* off from the three spiritual autobiographies; likewise, those three spiritual and didactic documents might not appear amenable to consideration as works of literature. However, as with Margaret Cavendish, the assertion of self in Julian, Margery Kempe, and Anne Bradstreet is accompanied by a strong sense of themselves as authors. Julian's literary intentions were obviously not primary, but even she shows consciousness of being an author, and the book she produced has gradually assumed its rightful place in the great lyrical-mystical tradition of English literature. Margery Kempe, though she was illiterate and was therefore obliged to dictate her story to others, nevertheless took her role as author very seriously indeed—so seriously that the composing and transcribing and the recomposing and retranscribing of her book became a major obsession. But in the end she found the satisfaction of that obsessive need to be both creative and curative: "And sche was many tyme seke whyl þis tretys was in writyng, and, as sone as sche wolde gon a-bowte þe writyng of þis tretys, sche was heil & hoole sodeynly in a maner" (p. 219). Like Julian, Margery Kempe made a contribution not only to the development of autobiography in English but to other literary modes as well: the eclectic structure of her *Book* draws on a number of literary conventions of the time—voyage and pilgrimage literature, lives of saints, fables—and in its strung-along plot of dramatized episodes, it moves toward fiction and the picaresque novel.

Margaret Cavendish leaves the reader in no doubt about her sense of a literary calling. In the *True Relation* she tells us that she was conscious of her vocation in childhood, and was even then "addicted . . . to write with the pen [rather] than to work with the needle" (p. 172). This longstanding addiction to "scribbling" (as she herself called it) eventually made the Duchess one of the first "literary ladies" of England: she published thirteen books in her lifetime, and as she makes very clear in the epistle prefatory to the *True Relation*, she will not have it that any hand other than her own was involved in the production of these volumes. Moreover, besides being a very early secular autobiography, her *Life* also foreshadowed later developments both in the novel of education and in social novels. Anne Bradstreet, though she was vastly different from Margaret Cavendish both as a woman and as an author, nevertheless echoes her contemporary in the prologue to "The Four Elements" when she declares her fondness for the "poet's pen," and writes that "I am obnoxious to each carping tongue / Who says my hand a needle better fits."[4] In its distilling of a spiritual story to its essence, the little autobiography that came from that pen can be seen as a paradigm of the Puritan "way of the soul," and of course Anne Bradstreet's contribution to the American poetic tradition requires no demonstration. It was important for each of the four autobiographic exemplars to consider herself in one way or another an author, or else her days would have been consigned to work with the needle, and her story, with its self-discovery and self-expression achieved through "other" reference, would have gone untold.

Although we know little about the facts of her life, since the *Revelations* are of spiritual truths and not factual details, Dame Julian of Norwich was probably from a well-bred family and educated at the convent of Carrow by Benedictine nuns, who would have taught her some reading and writing . . . and some needlework. The scholarly and literary allusions in her *Revelations* tell us that as a recluse she acquired much learning and a broad knowledge of classical spiritual writings. Julian received a religious vocation early in her life, and she prayed for an illness that would both confirm and deepen her vocation; that illness, the gift and sign of her grace, she experienced on 13 May 1373 during her thirty-first year. After surviving this crisis and confirmation of illness, she was granted a vision of Christ and the Crucifix that lasted for a period of five hours with fifteen "showings" or lessons of divine love, followed by a sixteenth "showing" one night later. On her recovery she became an anchoress, spending over twenty years of her life in an anchorage adjoining St. Julian's Church in Conesford, Norwich.[5] Apparently she recorded her experience soon after her illness with the

---

[4] *The Works of Anne Bradstreet*, ed. Jeanine Hensley (Cambridge, Mass., 1967), p. 16. All references to Anne Bradstreet's writing in the text will be to this edition. "Carping tongue(s)" is also, interestingly enough, Margaret Cavendish's phrase in much the same context.

[5] A comprehensive source for biographical materials on Julian is to be found in a group of commemorative essays edited by Frank Dale Sayer, *Julian and Her Norwich* (Celebration Committee, 1973).

help of a scribe (this is the version that has been known to us for some time as *A Shewing of God's Love*), but in 1393, after twenty more years of meditation and revelation, she set down a fuller account of her experience in the version commonly known as *Sixteen Revelations of Divine Love*.[6]

A Shewing of God's Love, which I take to be the better text for consideration as an autobiography, has nothing of the climactic structure of a conversion story (being thus set off from the Augustinian masculine model) but concentrates instead on the illumination of one moment—the vision of Christ and the Crucifix— gradually understood by way of the sixteen revelations following it. Although the account shares the traditional movement of the "ascent toward God" of mystical writings, it is primarily a narrative that is told on the one hand with amazing detachment and objectivity but on the other hand with an intense personal identification with the figures of God and Christ who dialogue with Julian directly and answer the questions troubling her. There are three distinct autobiographical sections to Julian's narrative: the first, a description of herself before the illness; the second, a description of the illness; and the last (five hours after the "shewings"), an account of her reaction to her recovery. Always aware of the possibility of self-delusion, Julian took care to record the physical changes and effects of her illness with a dry precision approaching clinical detachment. The reactions of others present are noted: her mother, for example, Julian says, "held up her hand in front of my face to close my eyes, for she thought that I was already dead or had that moment died" (p. 142). Her narrative also recalls the physical sensations that she experienced with approaching death—"After that I felt as if the upper part of my body were beginning to die. My hands fell down on either side, and I was so weak that my head lolled to one side" (p. 128). Later a series of moods follows as a state of deathly resignation gives way to joy and awe at the miracle of the vision and recovery, followed in turn, after the showings, by a period of doubt and despair—"And I was as barren and dry as if the consolation which I had received before were trifling" (p. 162)—but this too is eventually resolved into the final mood that she describes as one of "rest and peace."

This personal narrative of illness, vision, and recovery employs a

[6] Both versions, labelled respectively the "short text" and the "long text," are to be found, very conveniently, in the Colledge/Walsh edition of 1978 (see note 1).

traditional "homely" imagery[7] that, in addition to serving the ends of narrative, is also possessed of a poetic resonance vastly expanding the significance of Julian's story and, especially in moments of epiphany, charging it with dramatic intensity. Following her initial vision of Christ, the first "shewing" reveals Julian's special place in God's love and in the plan of his creation.

> And in this he showed me something small, no bigger than a hazelnut, lying in the palm of my hand, and I perceived that it was as round as any ball. I looked at it and thought: What can this be? And I was given this general answer: It is everything which is made. I was amazed that it could last, for I thought it was so little that it could suddenly fall into nothing. And I was answered in my understanding: It lasts and always will, because God loves it. (P. 130)

Identifying not only with the insignificance and frailty of the hazelnut but also with its particularity and durability as part of God's creation, Julian sees in herself something of the mystery and grace of the Virgin Mary, who is "a simple, humble maiden, young in years" but who for all her humility and insignificance will become, as the Queen of heaven, "greater, more worthy and more fulfilled, than everything else which God has created and which is inferior to her" (p. 131). The hazelnut, symbol of the strength of the meek and insignificant, becomes a guiding metaphor for this narrative of a woman—Julian or the Virgin—who is in herself less than the least but in God's love greater than the greatest.[8]

The most intense moment of Julian's narrative follows this poetic disclosure when, after a vision of Christ's "blessed face . . . caked with dry blood" (p. 136), there is a sudden revelation of the unity and harmony of all things contained in the smallness of a hazelnut: "And after this I saw God in a point,[9] that is, in my understanding, and by this vision I saw that he is present in all things. . . . I marvelled at this vision with a gentle fear, and I thought: What is sin?" (p. 137). This sense of unity—the medieval view that God is a circle

---

[7] On the use of traditional imagery, cf. Karl Stone, *Middle English Prose Style: Margery Kempe and Julian of Norwich* (The Hague, 1970).

[8] For the concept of a guiding metaphor, see James Olney, *Metaphors of Self: The Meaning of Autobiography* (Princeton, 1972).

[9] This is the literal reading; the phrase is rendered "in an instant of time" in the Colledge/Walsh edition.

whose center is everywhere and whose circumference is no-where—is at the very heart of all religious perception, and it informs as well the entire tradition of revelatory English lyric poetry from the Anglo-Saxon "Dream of the Rood" right down to the latter-day Romantic model that transfers the role of the religious mystic to the poet. The fact that in Julian it is rather the other way around—that is to say, the role of the poet is assumed by the religious mystic—does nothing to alter the essential similarity. Although she still had moments of doubt and despair to pass through before returning to the serenity of achieved understanding, the ultimate impression that Julian leaves her reader with is the sense of peace that comes with her unitary vision: "And so our good Lord answered to all the questions and doubts which I could raise, saying most comfortingly in this fashion: I will make all things well. . . . you will see that yourself, that all things will be well" (p. 151).

As commentators have lately pointed out, there are certain revolutionary elements in Julian's work that we are in a peculiar position to appreciate perhaps only as a result of recent events—elements that in some ways make her achievement seem closer to our time than to the fourteenth century. When coupled with the profoundly traditional nature of Julian's mystical writing, however, the real effect of this "modernness" is to give to her individual achievement the feeling of timelessness that invests any archetype or archetypal work. During the twenty years of meditation and study between the first and second versions of her experience, Julian gradually arrived at an understanding of the nature of God that, because it was determined by her understanding as a woman, seems startlingly contemporary to the reader today. Through use of what might be called feminine imagery in the closing chapters of the second version of her book, Julian develops a concept of the feminine principle of the Godhead that attributes the feminine to the Third Person of the Trinity, the Holy Spirit. This was indeed an ancient theological concept, but it was probably unknown to Julian in the fourteenth century, and it is almost completely lost to us in the twentieth century. Although she uses some maternal imagery that was conventional in her day—the imagery, for instance, of Christ's love for mankind as a mother's for her child—Julian is doing something strikingly original and going far beyond the conventional or the received when she says, "God almighty is our loving Father, and God all wisdom is our loving Mother, with the love and goodness of the Holy Spirit, which is all one God, one Lord" (p. 293), or again when she declares simply, "as truly as God is our Father, so truly is God our Mother" (p. 296). This restores the feminine Sophia to her rightful place of honor and glory. She is not only Mother, Daughter, and Bride of the Deity but an equal One with the other Two of the Trinity: "And so I saw that God rejoices that he is our Father, and God rejoices that he is our Mother, and God rejoices that he is our true spouse, and that our soul is his beloved wife" (p. 279). Of course God is Father, but He is Mother too, and this—though Julian sensed it and expressed it clearly enough—is what was forgotten for so long. In reformulating this little-known concept, Julian adds to her earlier conclusion that "All things will be well" a new understanding of just *how* things will be well.[10] "All will be well and all will be well, and every kind of thing will be well" (p. 225) when we recognize the diverse unity and plenitude of God's creation, when we perceive the breadth and variety of human consciousness, realized here in Julian herself, and when we acknowledge the needful balance of man and woman in the understanding of God's nature. Embracing another in mystical revelation thus does not obliterate Julian's consciousness as a person or as a woman nor does it lead to any poverty of personality; on the contrary, it intensifies and deepens her uniquely feminine understanding of the importance, indeed the needfulness, of both man and woman in God's creation as in His/Her being.

If Julian figures among women autobiographers as the recluse who chooses a life of contemplative withdrawal, Margery Kempe offers us a portrait of the pilgrim engaging in the world continuously, actively, even aggressively. Although *The Book of Margery Kempe* has considerably less stylistic merit than Julian's *Showings*, it nevertheless represents an important, alternate mode of self-conception and self-narration of a life possessed of a dual vocation. In 1413, when Margery Kempe went to Julian (by that time a well-known anchoress) for spiritual counsel, she was a woman forty years old and twenty years married but now sworn to live chaste with her spouse. She had borne fourteen children, had tried her hand at home-brewing and a milling business, and had experienced

---

[10] A recent study of this aspect of Julian's teaching points out that although she does not attribute motherhood to the Holy Spirit specifically, her description of what the Holy Spirit *does* fits in with the hypothesis that this person of the Godhead might properly be called God the Mother. See Sister Mary Paul, *All Shall Be Well: Julian of Norwich and the Compassion of God* (Oxford, 1976).

a spiritual conversion that gave her a very special religious vocation (rather unnerving in some of its manifestations) that was to mark her out as most eccentric in manner, hence suspect to many she encountered, and that created the dilemma of conflicting roles that eventually defined her life. Although they could hardly have been more dissimilar as personalities, the two women seem to have gotten on well enough together, as we can gather from Margery Kempe's account of the meeting. Presumably Julian found some comforting words to offer about the authenticity of Kempe's vocation; she may also have advised the younger woman to record her experiences in writing (as the Norwich White Friar, Master Allan, had already suggested she do), so that the uniqueness and peculiarity of those experiences should not be lost to the world.

Kempe's special brand of religious enthusiasm, although generally recognized as authentic by church divines somewhat removed from direct contact with it, led local English officials to a suspicion of Lollardry—to a suspicion, that is, that she was one of those followers of John Wycliffe who went about the English countryside preaching against the establishment of church and state. The religious vocation she enjoyed and others suffered was expressed in extreme emotionalism; in particular, she was possessed of the "gift of tears," a spiritual boon that manifested itself in hysterical weeping and in copious whoops and shouting (this latter gift of shouting was given to Kempe in Jerusalem while on her pilgrimage to the Holy Land)—all a consequence of a compelling identification with the Passion. Her demonstrations of faith were all extreme and bizarre: in church, for instance, she insisted on praying while lying prostrate in front of the altar, a position, as one commentator has noted drily, "inconvenient to parishioners"; and she was uniformly aggressive in her advice to cleric and lay person alike whether on civic or spiritual matters. While such characteristics are not unusual in saints' lives, they were nevertheless disturbing to the simple countrymen around her, who had little experience of the ways of saints. They were also often disturbing to her fellow pilgrims, who had not been granted all the gifts that afflicted Margery Kempe.

Kempe's third-person ("þis creatur") narrative proceeds more or less chronologically (the chronology is sometimes a bit shaky because she dictated from memory to two different amanuenses on two separate occasions) through a series of dramatized scenes and episodes, interspersed with revelatory conversations between herself and Christ, who appears to the creature "in lyknesse of a man,

most semly, most bewtyuows, & most amyable" (p. 8). Kempe's
exercise of the traditional third person is a minor stroke of genius,
for it confers some sense of objective reality on scenes that might
otherwise have little enough of the realistic about them—for example, her vision of her mystical marriage to the Godhead in Rome in
the company of Mary, the Twelve Apostles, Saint Katherine, Saint
Margaret, and numerous others of the saintly fold. Another kind of
episode also benefits from the quasi-objectivity of the third-person
perspective: these are the "court scenes" depicting interviews with
clerics and officials. Although they are thoroughly traditional and
evoke similar episodes in the lives of (for example) Catherine of
Siena and St. Thomas More, they were nevertheless drawn directly
from Kempe's own experience. Her account of one such episode, in
which the Archbishop of York hinted at heresies and accused her of
Lollardry, reads thus: "Sche [the creature], answeryng *p*erto,
seyde, 'I preche not, ser, I come in no pulpytt. I vse but comow-
nycacyon & good wordys, & *p*at wil I do whil I leue'" (p. 126).
Exasperated by Margery's persistence, her fearlessness, and her
superiority in disputation, the Archbishop finally responded with a
lament that was itself almost archetypal. Driven beyond the limits
of his tolerance, he asked, "Wher schal I haue a man *p*at myth ledyn
*p*is woman fro me?" The Archbishop was doubtless not the first
(nor would he be the last) figure of the establishment whose immediate heart's desire was to find a man—stable, reliable, and un-
gifted in religious ways—that might lead this woman away from
him.

In one of her revelations, God informs his "dowtyr" Margery, "I
haue ordeynd *p*e to be a merowr amongys hem [the people of the
world] for to han gret sorwe *p*at *p*ei xulde takyn exampil by *p*e" (p.
186). Indeed Kempe's *Book* does mirror her as a religious model of
sorrowing human compassion, but it also mirrors—and from a
specifically feminine point of view—the entire medieval world in
which her remarkable presence moved and had its being. More
than five hundred years later, we as readers are introduced to
townspeople, pilgrims, foreigners, Englishmen abroad, clerics
both hostile and friendly, magistrates, nobility, the poor and sick
whom Kempe served. And in closer focus her *Book* brings to life a
whole array of individual characters: the divine figures of God,
Christ, Mary, and a host of saints; Margery Kempe's family, husband, son, and daughter-in-law; a number of spiritual confessors,
among them Master Allan, who was responsible for encouraging

her religious enthusiasm; figures of historical or social prominence such as Philip Repington, Bishop of Lincoln, Thomas Arundel, Archbishop of Canterbury, the Duke of Bedford, the Mayor of Leicester; and finally a number of individualized commoners such as the lascivious steward who tried to rape Kempe at Leicester and the protecting jailer who saved her, or the broken-backed Richard who loaned her money in Rome. This is the very stuff of the novel, a form yet to be born, and Kempe's progress through it seems modeled on the structure of picaresque fiction but before the model itself existed.

The "fiction" of Margery Kempe's *Book* is framed by the author's story of personal conversion, and while it follows a stylized, conventional pattern—a first conversion after sickness, a period of penance and temptation ending in a second conversion or illumination, a five-year period of initiation culminating in a mystical marriage in Rome—it also bears Kempe's individual and individualizing imprint, whether it be in her particularized portrait of her husband, who was more supportive than other husbands faced with a "holy" wife, or in her fear of being deluded and her consequent meticulous concern for accuracy. As Hope Emily Allen says in her prefatory note to *The Book of Margery Kempe*, "I have found no equivalent production anywhere," and she goes on to say that she finds Margery Kempe's originality in this, the first full-length autobiography in English, similar to the originality of "other creators of literary types" (p. lvii).

The ultimate frame for both her conversion tale and her picaresque progress is the story of the book's composition given in the proem. In creating her book she was creating her proper image, in creating her text she was recreating her exemplary life—hence Kempe's obsession with getting it right. According to the account in the proem, Margery Kempe had been urged early in her life to write down her experiences, but she refused, perhaps fearing the difficulties other women had encountered when they claimed personal revelation. Then, when she felt the time was right, she became frustrated by the inadequacy of her scribe (an Englishman who had lived in the Lowlands and whose language and pen were both poor), so she set out after a better scribe in the person of a priest—"a prest whech þis creatur had gret affeccyon to" (p. 4)— who, however, at first demonstrated a mighty reluctance to transcribe the story of "þis creatur" inclined to hysteria. Nevertheless, having exhausted the full range of excuses available to him, the reluctant priest finally surrendered to Kempe's insistence, and having gone so far as to agree to be her amanuensis he went the rest of the way to become her staunchest supporter.

Various miraculous events associated with the priest's transcription of Kempe's story are recounted in the proem by way of "authenticating" the sanctity of that story and one wonders if the priest was not perhaps responsible for introducing this traditional device of hagiographic literature. Be that as it may, however, the chief manipulator of *The Book of Margery Kempe* is Margery Kempe herself as we may perceive clearly in the originality of the book's form and in the individuality of the voice that speaks through it. Whether she was primarily trying to promote herself as a saint or merely felt that her story was interesting enough to be told, Kempe was doing what every autobiographer does—tracing a perceived pattern in her life story, thus realizing for her readers a portrait of the individual that she was. Margery Kempe was a determined woman, in no way more than in this very determination to get her story told and to get it told right, which always involved the delicate balance of those dual elements that composed her tale as they composed her personality: wife and pilgrim, mother and mystic, superior debater but equally superior weeper, earthly bride of John Kempe and mystical bride of Jesus Christ, mother not only of fourteen children but "very modir" of her Savior as well. Hers was a woman's story well worth the telling, and tell it she would and did.

Margaret Cavendish, otherwise a very different woman from Margery Kempe, could hardly be said to have been less determined about telling her story than her predecessor in literary self-portraiture; nor was the woman Virginia Woolf called "the hare-brained, fantastical Margaret of Newcastle" (*A Room of One's Own*) much behind the tear-gifted mystic/pilgrim of Lynn in the ways of eccentricity. But turn eccentricity to another light and it becomes indistinguishable from the great Western ideal of individualism, and as any reader can testify, the most notable quality of the Duchess of Newcastle's writing is the sense of a strong individual, a sharply distinctive personality overwhelmingly present in every line. "For I think it no crime," the Duchess says, "to wish myself the exactest of Nature's works, my thread of life the longest, my chain of destiny the strongest . . . also to do my endeavour, so far as honor and honesty doth allow of, to be the highest on Fortune's wheel and to hold the wheel from turning, if I can" (p. 176). And the Duchess set about making herself if not "the exactest" at least one of the most singular of Nature's works, outfitting herself in such a bizarre manner that crowds gathered round to amuse themselves with the sight of her whenever she ventured forth in her coach. But such attention was not unwelcome to the Duchess, for as she said of the strange garments that caught the world's eye, "I am so vain (if it be vanity) as to endeavour to be worshipped, rather than not to be regarded" (p. 177). The crowds that came to laugh may not have stayed to worship, as the Duchess fondly imagined, but merely in regarding her they already fulfilled a large part of her desire.

Yet, for all her singularity, for all her strong individuality and distinctiveness of personality, for all her fantasticalness, Margaret Cavendish required a substitute figure or other—an alter ego really—with and through whom she might identify herself. This need particularly makes itself felt in the telling of her life story. Margaret Cavendish found in the Duke of Newcastle both her husband and her Lord, but remarkably enough she succeeds in making this of him without ever dimming the bright light of her own personality. "And though I desire to appear to the best advantage, whilst I live in the view of the world," she writes, immediately after the passage on the prodigality in her dress that took the world's fancy, "yet I could most willingly exclude myself, so as never to see the face of any creature but my Lord as long as I live, inclosing myself like an anchorite, wearing a frieze gown, tied with a cord about my waist" (pp. 177-178). Julian also did this—that was her life story, though her Lord was quite a different one—and while we may doubt that the Duchess would have been as successful as she imagines in imitation of Julian, we shall never know for certain because neither the Duke nor her life ever demanded that she essay the existence of an anchoress. Receiving her revelations and showings, Julian relates to a superior figure: she looks *up* to Christ and the Crucifix. On the other hand, in her biography of her husband and in her *True Relation*, Margaret Cavendish's gaze is directed neither up nor down but dead level: he is the warrior of an epic, but his wife is beside him—in all ways equal to him—as a poet. Your deeds, she says to the Duke in an epistle prefatory to his biography, "have been of war and fighting, mine of contemplating and writing" (p. xxxviii). And it is very revealing that in *The Blazing World* the Duchess all but drops the Duke from the picture—but doing so she finds it necessary to come up with another alter ego, the Empress of the Blazing World herself, who is not only empress but philosopher, warrior, and goddess, a more than sufficient replacement for the discarded husband and Lord and a satisfactory stand-in for the Duchess's own imagined self.

A True Relation of My Birth, Breeding and Life, written when the young Margaret Cavendish was in exile with her husband in Antwerp (they waited out the period of the Commonwealth abroad), is a very loosely structured narrative that tends to rattle on, but it is not chaotic or irrational as some critics have claimed. The first of the two main parts to the narrative composes an exterior portrait of the sitter, describing her "birth, breeding and actions"; the second gives "something of my humour, particular practice and disposition"—it composes an interior portrait, including the sitter's temperament and her moral character. The fitting conclusion to this narrative is the Duchess's "apology" for writing her own life, which argues, as we have noted, that she has a right to tell her story, a right to be ambitious and to try to control her fate, and above all a right to make her identity known as Margaret Lucas Cavendish, all three of the nominal elements being of equal significance in the identity.

This assertiveness at the end brings us a considerable distance from the hesitancy of the girl at the beginning, for although the narrative seems to proceed aimlessly, the truth is that all the details are made to contribute to the portrait of an emerging young woman. Margaret Lucas, daughter, sister, and lady-in-waiting (and more or less submissive in all three roles) becomes Margaret Cavendish, Marchioness, wife of a Marquis in exile (her husband was made a Duke after their return to England), and a woman on her way to becoming a confident and prolific author in half a dozen different modes. The story she tells is of a comfortable and pleasant adolescence interrupted by fate in the form of the "unnatural wars" that came "like a whirlwind" destroying the Lucas family who had been "feasting each other like Job's children" (p. 160); exiled from her home by fortune, she found her husband, he too a victim of fate, and because he respected her as a person and gave her his affection with an "unalterable decree of his promise," she honored and loved him—though "it was not amorous love," she explains, for "I never was infected therewith, it is a disease, or a passion, or both, I only know by relation, not by experience" (p. 162). He who "was her only tutor" became likewise her Lord, and at this point in her life Margaret Cavendish could do little but accept her "self" as a mere shadow of the Duke. According to the young woman composing her portrait in a double image, even in writing he was greatly her superior, for he wrote "what wit dictates to him," while she could lay claim to nothing more than "scribbling." Her expressed fear was that in her "scribbling" her pen could not keep up with her "fancies," and indeed she had some reason to fear, for the syntax of individual sentences frequently gives way altogether before the heated rush of all the swarming, ill-assorted, and half-formed thoughts besetting her brain.[11] Even so, and already at this young age, she was not without literary ambition nor untouched by "that last infirmity of noble mind"—on the contrary, she writes that "I fear my ambition inclines to vain-glory, for I am very ambitious; yet 'tis neither for beauty, wit, titles, wealth, or power, but as they are steps to raise me to Fame's tower, which is to live by remembrance in after-ages" (p. 177). This passage is followed shortly by the Duchess's claim that she could easily renounce the world for her Lord, and the *True Relation* then concludes with her own very strong uxorial self-identification, humble as yet as an author but confidently assertive as a Marchioness.

The *Life of William Cavendish*, written almost twenty years after the *True Relation* and ostensibly to glorify her husband as a loyal subject and successful general, is clearly not the work of a novice but the work of a writer who is certain that she has arrived both as author and as woman and who conveys that certainty in her relationship to her subject and in the assurance of her manner. While the Duchess no doubt sincerely wished to promote her husband's career with her book, she was equally intent on answering her own

[11] Cf. the following passage coming at the end of the epistle that stands before *A True Relation* where the Duchess characteristically combines undaunted self-confidence with touching frankness about her limitations: "I desire all my readers and acquaintance to believe, though my words run stumbling out of my mouth, and my pen draws roughly on my paper, yet my thoughts move regular in my brain. . . . For I must tell my readers, that nature, which is the best and curiousest worker, hath paved my brain smoother than custom hath oiled my tongue, or variety hath polished my senses, or art hath beaten the paper whereon I write" (p. 154). Cf. the Duchess's anger at the reason for the limitations of women's knowledge and skill, which she credits to their lack of education. In a famous epistle, written in 1655 to the universities of Oxford and Cambridge explaining her views on the neglect and "despisements" of "the masculine sex to the female," she writes, "So we [women] are become like worms that only live in the dull earth of ignorance, winding ourselves sometimes out by the help of some refreshing rain of good education, which seldom is given us." See *Philosophical and Physical Opinions* (London, 1663).

critics and skeptics and on establishing herself in fame right alongside her Duke. "But the great God, That hath hitherto blessed both your Grace and me," she says to the Duke in a prefatory address, "will, I question not, preserve both our fames to after ages, for which, we shall be bound most humbly to acknowledge His great mercy" (p. xxxviii)—and also, no doubt, His great justice, for separate and equal "fames to after ages" for the Duke and Duchess was no more than the simple due of each of them. Alterity but equality—this might be the motto of *The Life of William Cavendish*, for it nicely describes the marital relationship the biography defines and also the identity that the Duchess herself achieves in both the biography and the earlier autobiography.

Social convention and the responsibility of her rank would scarcely permit the Duchess to write an autobiography as long as her husband's biography or as long as she might have felt she deserved, but she got around those inconveniences of social decorum and etiquette by composing an extended fantasy self-portrait in *The Blazing World*. In this work she manages to appropriate to herself, through identification with the Empress, those various roles of author, warrior, scholar, and leader earlier assigned to the Duke. The heroine of this story escapes abduction and rape to become the empress of a hidden kingdom where she presides over a symposium of learned men, becomes founder of a church specially designed for women, and leads a successful military campaign. In the latter role of warrior-goddess she appears "in her garments of light, like an angel or some Deity." At the suggestion of her wise men—and very wise they prove to be, too—the Empress summons up the soul of the Duchess of Newcastle to act as her scribe, and the two of them strike it off very well indeed as the Duchess becomes the Empress's Platonic other self and her fondest companion. The two of them share a number of adventures, including an aerial flight to London and to Welbeck where the Duke, who is practising horsemanship and fencing, proves gallant and charming but not really up to the problem posed by the two Platonically united women. In the end, with the Duke pretty much forgotten, the Duchess is so enamored of the order and peace and harmony of the realm over which the Empress presides that she feels she must have one herself and so sets about creating a world of her own, equally well-ordered, harmonious, and delightful.

What Margaret Cavendish is about in *The Blazing World* is made clear in the prologue, in which she tries to come to terms with that ambition that had frustrated her as a woman but had given her a vocation as a writer:

> Though I cannot be Henry the Fifth, or Charles the Second, yet I endeavour to be Margaret the First; and although I have neither power, time nor occasion to conquer the world as Alexander and Caesar did; yet rather than not to be Mistress of one, since Fortune and the Fates would give me none, I have made a World of my own; for which no body, I hope will blame me, since it is in every one's power to do the like.

This fantasy world, created by the Duchess to replace the real world that she had "neither power, time nor occasion to conquer," has about it much of the "female gothic" (as Ellen Moers describes the mode) wherein imaginary heroines have all the adventures and fulfillments denied their creators in life.[12] As she implies in "Some Few Notes of the Authoress" tacked on at the end of her biography of the Duke, Margaret Cavendish was not willing to be "a spectator rather than an actor," but since the world offered her no stage on which she might act, she had to imagine into existence another world, a blazing world and "a Peaceable World" as she calls it,[13] of which, more than spectator or actor, she was the Empress and ultimately the "onlie begetter." Her husband might be an epic warrior, the world might refuse to permit Margaret Cavendish such ambition, but in the end she creates or recreates even her husband and his epic deeds and through creation of him and his world she also creates herself and her own world—or World, to give it the upper-case grandeur she herself confers on it. The focus and the image of Margaret Cavendish's self-creation and self-projection would perhaps have been double in any time—other women have chosen to split or double their self-images in a similar way in later centuries—but they were more certain to be so in the seventeenth century, which may in part account for one's feeling that the Duchess of Newcastle is the real archetype of the double-focus writer: that is, she was the one who established the pattern according to which many subsequent women would imagine their lives and literary careers and would structure their autobiographies.

---

[12] Ellen Moers, *Literary Women: The Great Writers* (New York, 1976), pp. 122-140.

[13] *The Description of the New World Called the Blazing World* (London, 1666), p. 14.

Anne Bradstreet, born in Cavalier England some ten years before Margaret Cavendish, ended her life in the far-off American colonies, and upon her first coming to that strange land she felt almost as much an exile from her true home as Margaret Lucas had felt when forced to leave England for the Continent. "After a short time," Anne Bradstreet tells her children in the little account of her spiritual life, "I changed my condition and was married, and came into this country, where I found a new world and new manners, at which my heart rose" (p. 241). In contrast to the Duchess of Newcastle, however, who determined "to be the highest on Fortune's wheel and to hold the wheel from turning, if I can," Anne Bradstreet soon subdued her heart and her will to what she saw as God's providence and accepted the complex fate of being an American and a member of the Puritan community as her destiny, for she never supposed it was in her power to turn Fortune's wheel as she chose or to prevent its turning if she would: "But after I was convinced that it was the way of God, I submitted to it and joined to the church at Boston." Although this did not put an end to all of her sorrows, she felt that all tribulation, like all good fortune, was from the hand of God, who "never suffered me long to sit loose from Him, but by one affliction or other hath made me look home, and search what was amiss" (pp. 241-242). After the fully secularized *True Relation* of the Duchess of Newcastle, Anne Bradstreet's brief and eloquent account represents a return to the tradition of religious autobiography but with this great difference: the author realizes her own deepest self-image not through identification with Christ as the crucified savior nor with Christ as the resurrected bridegroom but through identification with an entire spiritual community as a collective other. This is to be profoundly in the world and of it, but a world newly transformed, and transformed through and through, by the power of providential destiny so that its people are become God's Chosen People. If it was exile, then, to leave England for the colonies, it was exile to something closely approximating the Promised Land.

Addressing her life story "To My Dear Children," Anne Bradstreet draws circles of identity around herself—the inner circle of her immediate family through whom she achieves her most intimate identity; the intermediate circle of the Puritan communities of Cambridge, Ipswich, and Andover; and the outer circle of the Massachusetts Bay Colony—which returns us, in a sense, to the inner circle, for her father, Thomas Dudley, was governor of the colony and her husband, Simon Bradstreet, was both an important leader in the community and a representative of the colony to the mother country (and later, after his wife's death, he too became governor of the colony). This reconciliation—indeed merger—of an individual and a collective consciousness doubtless came naturally to Anne Bradstreet not only because of her family's involvement in community and colony governance but also because of her thoroughly traditional, Renaissance understanding of cosmic order. According to this understanding, the world in which we play out our moral destinies is the center of a divine plan harmonized by a series of natural, civil, theological, and human correspondences—in effect, "the great chain of being" of poets and philosophers of the sixteenth and seventeenth centuries. Anne Bradstreet's quaternity of poems about natural and human quaternities (dedicated, significantly, to her father)—"The Four Elements," "Of the Four Humours," "Of the Four Ages," "The Four Seasons"—demonstrate well enough her natural, unquestioning acceptance of these divine/human/natural correspondences establishing cosmic order all up and down the chain. For such a cosmos God is the provider and His the providence that determines every event of greatest or least apparent significance, and in that cosmos God can at any time choose to intervene, selecting some group of people—a family, a community, a colony—to be his Chosen People elected to execute His divine plan in a new world.

Anne Bradstreet's identification with the secular and religious community of the Massachusetts Bay Colony was made a very personal one first through her father and then through her husband. Her much loved and admired—in fact, almost worshipped—father represented for her not only a parent but also a governor, magistrate, and spiritual model: in a very real sense, he *was* the community for her, and as he embodied her public and private consciousness, the colony came to be her extended family. In the elegy written on her father's death in 1653 ("To the Memory of My Dear and Ever Honoured Father Thomas Dudley, Esq."), she says that his God shall be "God of me and mine" (p. 202), and in the conclusion of the poem she imagines his spiritual destiny and her own as one, foreseeing their ultimate reunion in heaven:

> Where we with joy each other's face shall see,
> And parted more by death shall never be.

With Simon Bradstreet, the second masculine embodiment of her secular and divine community, Anne Bradstreet enjoyed a relationship that was equally intimate and powerful though of course different in kind from the relationship with her father. "If ever two were one, then surely we," she declares in the first line of the poem "To My Dear and Loving Husband" (p. 225), and this two-in-oneness, this virtual sharing of a single individual consciousness, seems an exact expression of her singular good fortune in discovering her private passion perfectly at one with her public duty: both were figured for her in her husband, and with him she developed a private community of eight children who came to represent a most intimate collective consciousness in her life. In her poem "In Reference to her Children" (p. 232), she tells the personal history of her sons and daughters—"eight birds hatched in one nest"—most of whom have grown up and left the family community. Her tender but unsentimental acceptance of their departure, which leaves her free to further develop her own gifts, shows her sure sense of her own identity even as her private community dissolves.

The task of writing her spiritual autobiography (apparently undertaken at the suggestion of her son Simon) was the fulfillment of a sacred duty to her family, both immediate and extended, who, in the early stages of infancy and colony, might "gain some spiritual advantage" from her experience, her example, and her encouragement. "I will begin," she says, "with God's dealing with me from my childhood to this day" (p. 240). She then divides her life into four periods: childhood development of conscience; a youthful period of folly; a conversion after smallpox; and a final acceptance of her spiritual destiny after arrival in the new world. The events recorded from her life are very few, and they were all selected because they bear ultimate reference to her experience in community—community of family, community of Puritans, community of God. Included are her first "correction" by God when he "smote" her with small pox, her marriage, her arrival in New England and her joining of the church or "community," the long-awaited arrival of her first child, and finally, an event of the future, the hope that each of her children would come to a new spiritual birth ("I now travail in birth again of you till Christ be formed in you," p. 241).

Looking back over her spiritual progress, Anne Bradstreet acknowledges the efficacious "chastening" administered by God through sickness, weakness, and weariness, and she confesses to spiritual doubts—not, however, doubts about the existence of God that is revealed "in the wondrous works that I see, the vast frame of the heaven and earth" (p. 243) but doubts about the exclusive rightness of the Puritan way. "Why may not the Popish religion be the right [one]?"—this is a question, she says, that "hath sometimes stuck with me" (p. 244), and a startling question it is for a Puritan to admit to in her spiritual record; but it bears witness to her scrupulous honesty and even more to her generous embrace of a wider spiritual reality and more various spiritual possibilities than the confining doctrine of her community would allow for. Even so, Anne Bradstreet says, she overcame her doubts, rejected the Popish religion for its "vain fooleries . . . , lying miracles and cruel persecutions of the saints," and in effect submitted her more tolerant religious conscience to the straiter and stricter conscience of the community.

Having come through all afflictions and overcome all doubts, Bradstreet concludes her spiritual record with a prayer to the God she has chosen and who has chosen her: "Now to the King, immortal, eternal, and invisible, the only wise God, be honour, and glory for ever and ever, Amen." Or at least one supposes this would be the conclusion—after all, where can you go from "Amen"?—but in fact there is yet to come a brief personal address to her children, the beginning and end of Anne Bradstreet's life story: "This was written in much sickness and weakness, and is very weakly and imperfectly done, but if you can pick any benefit out of it, it is the mark which I aimed at" (p. 245). This brings us back to the beginning and to that most intimate, inner circle of identity that was Anne Bradstreet's family, for her spiritual autobiography commences with the address to "My dear children" immediately following a little dedicatory poem:

> This book by any yet unread,
> I leave for you when I am dead,
> That being gone, here you may find
> What was your living mother's mind.
> Make use of what I leave in love,
> And God shall bless you from above.

What is surprising about Bradstreet's story is that a woman born and educated in Cavalier England and given the natural gifts and inclination to be a poet could confine herself to such an exacting Puritan community and still create the mature and distinct poetry of her later life. For Anne Bradstreet, it was the merging of her private consciousness with her collective consciousness that enabled her to be free to achieve her own unique identity as a poet. Her autobiography illustrates this merging and unifying process from the inner circle of her husband, family, and community to the outer circle of God's providential creation. Her poetry witnesses her individual voice.

Julian's intensity of focus on a single divine figure and a corresponding intensity of being realized through relationship to that figure; Margery Kempe's dual vocation in this world and in another and her dual focus on these two separate, secular/religious worlds; Margaret Cavendish's pairing of her image with another, equal image and her doubling of the self-image whether in husband or in fantasy creation; and Anne Bradstreet's harmonious merger and identification with a collective consciousness and a corporate other—these are the four great originals, the lived and recorded patterns of relationship to others that allowed these women, each in her own characteristic way, to discover and delineate a self and to tell the story of that self even as it was being uncovered and coming into existence. Later women, while participating to a degree in one or another of these early archetypes, naturally varied the patterns of their *Lives* as the various experiences of their lives required them to do—mixing two or three patterns, discovering new possibilities in the originals, striking out new patterns of their own. One element, however, that seems more or less constant in women's life-writing—and this is not the case in men's life-writing—is the sort of evolution and delineation of an identity by way of alterity that we have traced in the four paradigms. Relation to another autonomous being (Margaret Cavendish), relation to one single, transcendent other (Julian), relation to two others (Margery Kempe), relation to a multiple collectivity, a many-in-one (Anne Bradstreet)—these are four distinct possibilities, and while there are no doubt more, the number of possibilities is certainly not infinite.

The pattern most frequently adopted (and adapted) by later women has unquestionably been the solution recorded in the life and writing of Margaret Cavendish—the pairing of one's own image with another, equal image. A modern parallel to the Duchess's story is to be found in the two-volume autobiography of Beatrice Webb, who was another woman with a strong sense of identity. Her first volume, *My Apprenticeship*, is dedicated to Sidney Webb, Beatrice Webb's marital other; the second volume, *The Partnership*, opens with a chapter entitled "The Other," which, unsurprisingly, is a minibiography of her husband/partner. Likewise,

Elizabeth Barrett (Browning as she was to become), who as a young girl wrote brief autobiographical accounts that reveal—as with the Duchess of Newcastle—an early vocation as a writer,[14] tells the story in her autobiographical *Sonnets from the Portuguese* of her identification with Robert Browning, her husband, a poet less known than she was when they married. In the present century, Simone de Beauvoir's public/private relationship to Jean-Paul Sartre has often been at the center of the self-defining efforts of her autobiographical volumes without at all diminishing the strong sense of her identity. In recent American autobiography, Lillian Hellman reveals most about herself in her trilogy when she creates portraits of other people in her life, and though she depicts more than one other, these others come as it were in succession rather than collectively. A variant on this pattern of alterity-equality is to be found in stories where the other is neither a partner nor an equal, neither a spouse nor a creation of the writer but is instead an over-whelming model or ideal that has to be confronted in order that the author's identity be realized—such is the relationship, for example, of H.D. (Hilda Doolittle) to Freud in her autobiographical *Tribute to Freud* where the author figures as analysand rather than wife. Margaret Cavendish's second way of doubling the self-image not in biography/autobiography but in fantasy (*The Blazing World*) has found favor with women novelists who have either projected that image so that they might enjoy in fiction what they never could in life (*Jane Eyre*, for example, to which Charlotte Brontë, inciden-tally, gave the subtitle "autobiography" only a few years after that word had first been used by an author as title for a book) or have projected male images (father, brothers, lovers, husbands, clergy-men) so that they might resolve feelings of hostility or unwilling compliance in themselves toward such masculine figures.[15]

Although it is unusual to find the singleness of Julian's mystical vision in later writers, there is something of this in Emily Brontë's

---

[14] "Two Autobiographical Essays by Elizabeth Barrett," in *Browning Institute Studies*, ed. William S. Peterson (New York, 1974), 2: 119-134. The first essay, "My Own Character," was written when Elizabeth Barrett was twelve (1818): the sec-ond, "Glimpses into My Life and Literary Character," when she was fourteen (1820). That these two essays should have been published in *Browning Institute Studies* is not without a certain poignant significance.

[15] Cf. Elaine Showalter, *A Literature of Their Own: British Women Novelists from Brontë to Lessing* (Princeton, 1977), especially pp. 133-152.

"Imagination" or "sterner power," as she calls the divine presence in one of her poems, and Heathcliff, Brontë's fictional other, is virtually a demonic version of Julian's personal God. Christina Rosetti, one of the few important literary women of the nineteenth century to write autobiography undisguised (*Time Flies: A Reading Diary*, which doubles as an Anglican devotional text), conveys both in religious verse and in love poetry a feeling of single-mindedness reminiscent of Julian's. In our time, Simone Weil, radical activist and religious contemplative, has displayed a Julianesque intensity and scrupulosity in numerous essays devoted to autobiographical self-examination; with her vision focused both on this world and a world beyond, she also continues the attempt of Margery Kempe to discover herself in worlds usually opposed but here joined by the being of the autobiographer. For echoes of Margery's accounts of peregrinations and pilgrimages in this world, we should look to the writing of women travellers—the narratives of Harriet Martineau, for example, and the itineraries with commentaries by Anna Brassey (*A Voyage in the Sunbeam*, 1880), Lady Duff Gordon (*Letters from Egypt*, 1865), and Lady Anne Blunt (*A Pilgrimage to Nejd*, 1881), the granddaughter of Lord Byron, who set off on horseback with her husband, Wilfred Scawen Blunt, into the interior of Arabia (and there discovered and translated some important Arabic poetry, published as *The Seven Golden Odes*) but later left Blunt to continue her pilgrimage as her own writer and her own woman.

Few subsequent women writers have found themselves in a personal/public community like Anne Bradstreet's—or indeed in a family like hers—and when considerable strain is not evident in the attempt to harmonize private vision with communal duties, it is most often because the attempt has not been made in such a total, inclusive context as was Bradstreet's (*The Autobiography of Saint Thérèse of Lisieux*, 1911, gives testimony from nineteenth-century France of the heroism it took for a young woman to preserve a sense of self that balanced the opposed claims of a religious community with those of a possessive family). Angela Davis may think of identifying with "the people" in her *Autobiography*, but that group is more a political abstraction than a living reality; and she must relate to a personal other (George Jackson is clearly more to her than an emblem of a black revolutionary hero) through letters written to him in prison. Although Dorothy Day's *The Long Lone-*

liness bears witness to a harmony of public and private life, she has chosen not to become a writer but to record her story through her life as she lives it.

The four models discussed here by no means exhaust the possibilities. For some women writers, it is not a man, or men, or a community but a woman, or women, who provide the other of identity: Margaret Mead, though thrice married, is most self-revealing in *Blackberry Winter* when she writes about her daughter and about her own role as daughter; in *Memories of a Catholic Girlhood*, a portrait of the adolescent Mary McCarthy emerges from daguerrotypes of the grandmother, the aunt, and the deceased mother; and Nikki Giovanni's *Gemini* outlines a similar pattern with the grandmother, the mother, and a friend (Claudia) all helping the author define herself as a black woman poet. On the other hand, there is a kind of unattached "otherness" about Gertrude Stein's *Autobiography of Alice B. Toklas* and *Everybody's Autobiography* or about Isak Dinesen's *Out of Africa*. And, as one might well expect, there have been failures and negative results consequent upon attempts at self-identification through relation to another: between *Snapshots of a Daughter-in-Law* (1963) and *Diving into the Wreck* (1973) Adrienne Rich saw the failure inherent in a conventional identification with her husband (this she attempts in *Snapshots*) and abandoned it in the later volume as a way of arriving at a valid image of herself. Ellen Moers has noted the revealing similarity in the titles of Sylvia Plath's *The Bell Jar*, Anaïs Nin's *Under a Glass Bell*, and Violette Leduc's *L'Asphyxie*, translated as *In The Prison of Her Skin*,[16] all of them suggesting psychological enclosure, imprisonment, and suffocation. And the autobiography of imprisonment, represented in women's writings from Charlotte Perkins Gilman's autobiography to the story of Sylvia Plath, shows the grim tale of a woman's claustrophobia when she cannot get out of the prison of the self or of her nightmare when she is kept from coming into her own self through the proximate existence of another or others.

"Why hath this lady writ her own life?" Dame Julian had reasons that the Duchess of Newcastle could scarcely know, and Margery Kempe's motives were not at all Anne Bradstreet's. Yet, for all the surface dissimilarities, for all the diversity of motive and manner among the four, there is something that ties these life stories to-

---

[16] Moers, *Literary Women*, p. 297.

gether and draws them into proximity with autobiographical excursions by later women writers while simultaneously setting them apart from autobiographies written by men in any place and any time. It is inconceivable that a man should have—*could* have—written a book like *The Book of Margery Kempe* or the *Showings* of Julian of Norwich (although the mystic comes closest to expressing the human spirit without the confinement of gender), unimaginable that Simon Bradstreet could have produced such an address as his wife's "To My Dear Children" or that William Cavendish would have been capable of writing *A True Relation* bearing any resemblance at all to Margaret Lucas Cavendish's *True Relation*. It will be well to recall here a point made earlier: that the real question should bear the emphasis, "why hath *this* lady writ her own life"—and together with that question should go its corollary, "*How* hath this lady writ her own life?" Enough has been said to show that four different women have told four different stories in four different ways and yet have told this essential story—essential to each of them as an individual, essential to women in general, and essential to the history of autobiography—so that we recognize them each and all as distinctively, radically the story of a woman. And this should help us to the conclusion that since the history of autobiography is largely a history of the Western obsession with self and at the same time the felt desire to somehow escape that obsession, our four models, who record and dramatize self-realization and self-transcendence through the recognition of another, represent an important addition to that history. Along with later women who followed, varied, or diverged from the original patterns in writing out their lives, these four pioneers have had a special role to play in the development of the genre of autobiography.

Some Versions of Memory/
Some Versions of Bios:
The Ontology of Autobiography

***

James Olney

The practice of autobiography is almost as various as its practitioners, and this truth is yet truer—it becomes nearly absolute—when
the primary commitment of the practitioners in question is literary
rather than, say, political, scientific, or historical. When the autobiographer thinks of himself or herself as a writer and would put
down "writer" (or "poet," "novelist," or "playwright") when
asked for a profession, the tendency is to produce autobiography in
various guises and disguises in every work and then—this being the
other side of the coin—to seek a unique form in a work properly
called "an autobiography" (or any other name pointing to the same
thing) that may reflect and express the life and the vision of this individual writer alone. As I am going to consider autobiographies
by several men of letters, these preliminary observations seem to
me necessary, for it may well be that the case would be different if
the autobiographies had been written by physicians, or educators,
or statesmen.

There are a couple of indices (perhaps there are more, but I shall
only deal with two) to which we can look for some understanding
of the species of any particular autobiography in progress. The indices that I have in mind are "memory" and "*bios*." I will investi-
gate these two critical indices as follows: I will first present some

***

A part of James Olney's "Some Versions of Memory/Some Versions of *Bios*: The
Ontology of Autobiography" originally appeared in his "W. B. Yeats's Daimonic
Memory," *Sewanee Review* 85 (1977). Copyright © 1977 by the University of the
South. Reprinted by permission of the journal.

observations and speculations about what I am going to call the ontology of autobiography—that is, the special order of reality that an autobiography can make claim to; I will then try to sort out the various, subtle, and shifting interrelationships between the life imitated or recounted in an autobiography and the faculty of memory (or nonmemory) that captures or recaptures, constitutes or reconstitutes that life; my next step will be to show how a particular concept of the *bios* informing autobiography and a particular use or disavowal of memory together determine the specific ontology of a given autobiography; and finally I want to illustrate all of these theoretical points with references to the autobiographies of Richard Wright, Paul Valéry, and W. B. Yeats. I hope that this simple list of names, comprising three writers as different from one another as they could well be, will suggest the impossibility of making any prescriptive definition for autobiography or placing any generic limitations on it at all.

Bios, which lies at the literal and figurative center of autobiography (between *autos* at the beginning and *graphē* at the end), is a Greek word meaning "life," and it provides the root for a whole series of words in English—biology, biometer, bioscope, etc. A Greek dictionary will define the word more exactly as "the course of life: lifetime." But this immediately raises some interesting and difficult questions for the theoretician of autobiography, more particularly for the ontologist of autobiography. If *bios* is "the course of life, a lifetime," and if it is already spent and past, then how is it going to be made present again, how is it ever going to be recaptured, how is that which is no longer living going to be restored to life? When "is" has been transformed into "was," when the unique moment of the present slips into the huge abyss of the past, if it remains in any sense real at all, then it must be within a new and entirely different order of reality from that informing the present: one kind of reality attaches to the present; quite a different kind of reality (if indeed any) attaches to the past. In his essay included in this volume, Barrett Mandel gives provocative expression to this notion when he says, "the past . . . never really existed: it has always been an illusion created by the symbolizing activity of the mind." When does the past exist? When has it ever existed? Did the past exist yesterday? last week? a year or ten years ago? Certainly it did not: not *as* the past. "The past never existed . . ."—just so.

Heraclitus gave classic expression to the autobiographer's dilemma thus: "Heraclitus somewhere says that all things flow and nothing remains still, and comparing existing things to the flowing of a river, he says that you would not step twice into the same stream" (Plato, *Cratylus*, 402a). Right there, in clearer language and more dramatic metaphor, is what phenomenologists and pro-tophenomenologists have been telling us for approximately the past one-hundred years. Let me look a little more closely at Hera-clitus's expression of the phenomenological bind. He compares "existing things to the flowing of a river": now the phrase trans-lated "existing things" is *ta onta* and *onta* (whence we derive the word "ontology") is the neuter plural present participle formed from *einai*—"to be." Hence, *ta onta* signifies "those things that are," or "those things that exist" (ontology is thus a theory of the nature of being or existence), and it is *ta onta* that Heraclitus com-pares to the flowing of a river. Further we should observe that as a present participle denoting a continuing action or a continuing state, *ta onta* points not to a finished condition but to an ongoing *process*—the process of being, the process of existing. (In English the present participle of "to be," according to its two different senses, would render "those things that are being" or "those things that are existing.")

Moreover—and this turns us in a new direction—a Greek dic-tionary will reveal that *ta onta* means not only "the things which actually exist," it also means "the present, opposed to the past and future." Thus the past and future, besides not being present, do not exist, have never existed as such—as past and future—nor will they ever exist: they are not included in *ta onta*. By its linguistic defini-tion, Heraclitus's *onta* denies the existence of any stable, unchang-ing, timeless reality—such a superior reality as Plato always claimed for his Ideas and felt that he could find in the *estin* ("is"—the present tense of "to be" rather than the present participle: as it were, a timeless present) of Parmenides.

Taking the two faces of the definition together, one could say that *ta onta* means all things existing in a concrete, dense moment of time that is the phenomenological, time-bound present. Heraclitus compares this state to the incessant, irresistible flowing of a stream, and you will never, as he says, enter that stream, that same unique density of experience, time, and consciousness, twice. However, is it not the autobiographer's claim or hope that through the act of writing he can bring his *bios* to be included among *ta onta*—that he can make his *bios* or his life one of those things that actually exist in and as the present? This is his claim or hope; but if I might borrow the rhythm of my expression from W. B. Yeats, I should say that so long as *bios* is understood as the course of a lifetime and nothing else, this will be more hope than claim, more illusion than hope.

It would, however, be possible (though ancient Greek gives little authority for this) and, I believe, profitable to understand *bios* in a number of other senses. When, in English, we say that an old man (or an old dog) still has plenty of life left in him, we do not mean plenty of "lifetime"; when we say, "You live your life, I'll live mine," we do not mean "You live your course of life"; when in the King James Version, Jesus says, "I am the resurrection and the life," we would hardly be justified in understanding him to mean, "I am the resurrection and the course of a life"; when Socrates says, "The unexamined life (*anexetastos bios*) is not worth living," he does not have in mind the three score years and ten that we take as the average lifetime of the individual. And this is also the case with other uses of the word "life" where it does not signify an historical matter, the course of a certain number of years, but instead means spirit, or vital principle, or the act of consciousness, or transcendent reality, or a certain mode of living, a certain set of personality and character—what John Henry Newman called "the idea of moral unity" displayed in a particular life as lived. I suggest that one could understand the life around which autobiography forms itself in a number of other ways besides the perfectly legitimate one of "individual history and narrative": we can understand it as the vital impulse—the impulse of life—that is transformed by being lived through the unique medium of the individual and the individual's special, peculiar psychic configuration; we can understand it as consciousness, pure and simple, consciousness referring to no objects outside itself, to no events, and to no other lives; we can understand it as participation in an absolute existence far transcending the shifting, changing unrealities of mundane life; we can understand it as the moral tenor of the individual's being. Life in all these latter senses does not stretch back across time but extends down to the roots of individual being; it is atemporal, committed to a vertical thrust from consciousness down into the unconscious rather than to a horizontal thrust from the present into the past.

What, then, would be the implications for an ontology of autobiography that would follow from adopting any of these radically different senses of the central term *bios*? If *bios* is the historical course of a life, then at any given present moment of that life it is necessarily true that all things have flowed and that nothing remains: "is" has been transformed into "was" and has thereby been drained of all vitality, of all reality, of all life; "what was" no longer composes a part of *ta onta*, the present, the sum of things that are now existing or that are now being. If, on the other hand, *bios* is taken as the vital principle or the unique spark—life as transformed by being lived through this one-of-a-kind medium—then there is nothing but "is": there is no "was" in the picture and there is clearly no relation between "is" and "was". We are left with a present no doubt formed by the past but utterly sundered from it. "If all time is eternally present," T. S. Eliot says, "All time is unredeemable." And to redeem the time is one of the autobiographer's prime motives, perhaps *the* prime motive—perhaps, indeed, the only real motive of the autobiographer. (But as there is *bios* and there is *bios* and as there is memory and there is memory, so also there is redemption and there is redemption, as I shall point out later.)

There are a number of ways that the autobiographer can free himself of this bind that makes all time either perpetually past or perpetually present and in either case apparently unredeemable. I am going to outline three strategies by which the autobiographer can resolve the dilemma of *bios*—one a strategy that employs memory in a fairly ordinary but nevertheless creative sense (Richard Wright); another that abandons memory altogether (Paul Valéry); and a third that transforms it out of all recognition (W. B. Yeats). Let me begin with the way of memory. If *bios* in the sense of "lifetime" is seen not simply as a span of years—set, complete, and finished: a simple case of "was"—but as a *process* ever moving towards the ineluctable present of "is" and if memory can be taken as a backward projection of "is" that gathers up into its own creative image all that "was becoming," then the autobiography of memory, having become a vital and intensely creative mode, attains to a certain philosophical dignity. The key is to view *bios* as a process the whole of which the autobiographer is in a position to see, recall, and compose; and it is up to the autobiographer to cut it where he will so that the process will be complete and unified. Moreover, because that process is viewed retrospectively by the autobiographer it will be seen as a teleological process, as moving towards a specific goal, a specific end. I might clarify what I wish to say by putting it another way: if *bios* is a process, then it possesses a certain shape, and we might say that memory is the forever hidden thread describing this shape. The thread necessarily remains hidden, unconscious, unknown to the individual until the time when it rises to consciousness *after the fact* to present itself to him as recollections that he can then trace back—a kind of Ariadne's thread—to discover the shape that was all the time gradually and unconsciously forming itself.

What I propose is that the term *bios* simultaneously incorporates the two foregoing senses: it is both the course of a life seen as a process rather than a stable entity and the unique psychic configuration that is this life and no other. In Platonic terms, I propose that we understand a world of becoming that is moving perpetually towards the world of being that is this phenomenological, eternal present (*ta onta*); or, in reverse perspective, that we should understand memory as a faculty of the present and an exact reflection of present being that also recapitulates and reverses the entire process by which present being has come to be what it is. As Plato does time and again, I would wed Heraclitus's moment-to-moment world of becoming to Parmenides' timeless world of being, and I would then say that memory can be imagined as the narrative course of the past becoming present and that it can be imagined also as the reflective, retrospective gathering up of that past-in-becoming into this present-as-being.

What all the successive moments that stretch out as the past have been in process of becoming is, of course, the present, and the present is thus the end, the goal, or the *telos* of the past. Looking forward from the past to the present (or from the present to the future, as one may prefer), could we not say that Heraclitus's stream is not only time and the passage of time but that looking backward from the present to the past, it is also memory? Time carries us away from all of our earlier states of being; memory recalls those earlier states—but it does so only as a function of present consciousness: we can recall what we were only from the complex perspective of what we are, which means that we may very well be recalling something that we never were at all. In the act of remembering the past in the present, the autobiographer imagines into existence another person, another world, and surely it is *not* the same, in any real sense, as that past world that does not, under any circumstances, nor however much we may wish it, now exist. "This," in T. S. Eliot's phrase, "is the use of memory," and the autobiographic strategy I have just described is what I take to be the strategy of Richard Wright's *Black Boy*.

Although it is no doubt the most complex resolution of the autobiographer's dilemma, this is not the only possible strategy: there are other ways of attacking the problem, each of which involves its own special sense of *bios* as well as its own special idea of the use of memory in the making of an autobiography. There is a kind of thinker and writer for whom *carpe diem* is a necessary temperamental injunction and who, concentrating everything in passing moments of awareness, seizes the moment very intensely indeed and fixes on it with everything he is. We do not always (in fact, do not often) consider the work of such a writer to be autobiography, yet if we accept that a legitimate definition of life—*real* life—can be "consciousness" with its now and now and now immediacy, then we will be the less disinclined to call his work "autobiography," even if, within the confines and categories of literary genre, it is classified as lyric poetry.

When I say that "consciousness" might be accepted as a legitimate synonym for the *bios* of one kind of autobiography, I have in mind consciousness in itself, pure and untouched by either time or history. To take one example, Henry James would not qualify as an autobiographer of pure consciousness because his subject is the evolution of consciousness and his autobiography is therefore a matter of time, of history (albeit personal), of narrative, and of memory; and likewise R. G. Collingwood takes the development of his thought as the *bios* of his autobiography and so traces back through memory the history and narrative of his mental evolution. In the pure act of consciousness, on the other hand, there is no before and after, no summary present that recapitulates the past and projects itself into the future; there is only consciousness itself, bright, shining, ticking, sufficient unto itself, conscious but of nothing in particular and with no necessary content—conscious, perhaps, only of being conscious. Should there be an autobiographer who holds to this sense of *bios* (and there is, or was, in Valéry), then memory will have no place at all in the making of his autobiography, which will be a purely formal affair, without historical, biographical, or narrative content—indeed, without *any* necessary content—and insofar as it adheres to an imitation of *la conscience pure* and thus succeeds in attaining to the state of *l'autobiographie pure*, it will sing the same exquisite, senseless song as *la poésie pure*: the inexplicable and lovely music of consciousness that, if it means anything at all, means only itself. I will shortly offer textual demonstration.

"In a higher world it is otherwise," Newman once remarked, "but here below to live is to change, and to be perfect is to have changed often." If an autobiographer is concerned with life as lived "here below" in a world of men, movement, and events, he will necessarily have recourse to memory to trace all those changes through which his life has passed and that have been its defining quality. But what if the life he would write is not as one lived "here below" but is as the life lived in that "higher world"? What if he looks to essences rather than to accidents and to what an individual is in idea rather than to what he or she is in fact? Then, as Newman says, "it is otherwise": there will be not so much change as restoration of a perfected state; not so much memory tracing back through successive states as instantaneous recollection of what was in the beginning; not so much the historical past-of-becoming moving forever into a present-as-being as a simple transcendence of all historical process. The *bios* of that "higher world" is unmoving, unchanging, full, and timeless: it participates not in the shifting, shadowy illusions of an existence in time but in the clear, absolute reality of Plato's eternal world of forms.

I would not be understood to mean, however, that any autobiographer can look straight at eternity and tell us what it is—even Socrates or Diotima would fail in the attempt; and when Jesus says, "I am the resurrection and the life," he does not tell us precisely what that life *is* that he is. Living "here below" as he does and therefore looking on life "here below" as he must, the autobiographer of the "higher world" seeks to discern the *Bios* behind the *bios*—the archetypes that lie immediately behind types and, at a greater remove, behind individuals. Such a *Bios* in which paradigms and archetypes disport themselves in freedom and delight will ultimately yield itself not to memory—at least not to memory in the ordinary sense of that word and faculty—but only to anamnesis as Plato describes it: the recollection or intuition from within this life of forms viewed and known perfectly in eternity between this life and an earlier one. There are not many autobiographers of the higher world of forms, paradigms, and archetypes, but I think I can offer one fair instance of the autobiographer as anamnesiologist: W. B. Yeats.

Richard Wright is a powerful example of the autobiographer of memory—a creative memory that shapes and reshapes the historic past in the image of the present, making that past as necessary to this present as this present is the inevitable outcome of that past. "Memories," Erik Erikson has said, "are an intrinsic part of the actuality in which they emerge," and that actuality of which memories are an intrinsic part and in which memories emerge is nothing other than *ta onta*, the sum of those things that really exist now, a seamless fabric woven of perception, consciousness, memories, and the surrounding universe—in other words the entire phenomenal present, both interior and exterior: that which Heraclitus likens to the flowing of a river. Memories and present reality bear a continuing, reciprocal relationship, influencing and determining one another ceaselessly: memories are shaped by the present moment and by the specific psychic impress of the remembering individual, just as the present moment is shaped by memories. The "now" of consciousness is as it is because of the interrelationship between events (or history) and memories of events (or reaching back in present consciousness to earlier formative experiences). Following his observation that memories "are an intrinsic part of the actuality in which they emerge," Erikson goes on to say that "at best, memories connect meaningfully what happened once and what is happening now," and I suggest that in our investigation of Wright we would do well to attend carefully to the word "meaningfully."

Wright composed *Black Boy* (and, at the same time, as a part of the same manuscript, what is now known as *American Hunger*, which is an interesting but unsuccessful continuation from *Black Boy*) in 1943, some fifteen years after leaving the South, some six years after leaving Chicago for New York, and about three years after publication of *Native Son*. *Black Boy* begins with the protagonist, "I," at four years of age setting fire to the house, fleeing in fright and panic, and, for punishment, being beaten until he was unconscious and suffering fearful hallucinations; and the book concludes with "I" fifteen years older in age and countless years older in experience of the ways of the American South, "aboard a northward bound train" headed from Memphis to Chicago. As we can determine from Richard Wright's biography, the terminal dates of *Black Boy* would have been 1912 and 1927, a span of fifteen years, a time long enough (especially when lived by a black boy in Mississippi and Tennessee) to be taken for the *bios* of autobiography, "the course of life: lifetime."

Having referred to Wright's biography, however, let me hasten to say that although his dates coincide with the dates of the "I" of *Black Boy*, Richard Wright is not the same person as the hero of that book, not the same as "I" or "Richard" or the "black boy," not by several light years. "Black Boy" (and now I mean the central figure of the book) is the creation, or re-creation if you will, of someone who is himself *not* "black boy"; of someone, in fact, who is infinitely far removed from that identity. This is what I meant when I said that in trying to remember the past in the present the autobiographer imagines another person, another world into existence— Richard Wright imagines into existence the person of "black boy" and the world that is the world of the book called *Black Boy*. "Black boy" himself imagines nothing into existence; he is a creature of events and circumstances, creator of nothing, a figure helplessly impelled forward on Heraclitus's river of time. On the other hand, by means of an encompassing and creative memory, Richard Wright imagines it all, and he is as much the creator of the figure that he calls "Richard" as he is of the figure that, in *Native Son*, he calls "Bigger."

Now what is that person like, what is that world like, that Wright imagines into existence? What, in other words, are those memories like that Wright draws on to create his "black boy" as person and as book? The first scene, when "Richard" sets fire to the house, provides a paradigm for the entire book: there is first fear, then panic and flight, and finally violence, and though elsewhere the violence comes before the fear, panic, and flight, these are the constant elements from the first page to the last. This gives us to understand that such was the sum of "black boy's" experiences growing up in the South—fear, panic, flight, violence; violence, fear, panic, flight—and that the only escape was the one that "black boy's" creator himself found: "in full flight," as he calls it, "aboard a northward bound train." (That Wright found little better in the North is beside the point: this is the narrative of "black boy," and when he gets aboard that train it signifies the end of that identity, the death of "black boy"—and, as we know, also the eventual birth of Richard Wright. Just as Frederick Douglass left behind his slave identity and his name when he escaped to the North, so in his departure for Chicago Richard Wright leaves behind his black boy identity and the various names and labels the South had affixed to him.)

The narrative of "black boy's" Southern existence begins with his setting fire to the curtains and then the house. Here is how Richard Wright recalls and describes the experience of "Richard" from a remove of some thirty years: "The fire soared to the ceiling and I trembled with fright. Soon a sheet of yellow lit the room. I was terrified; I wanted to scream but was afraid. . . . Soon my mother would smell that smoke and see the fire and come and beat me. . . . I would run away and never come back. I ran out of the kitchen and into the back yard." He crawls under the house. "Presently footsteps pounded on the floor above me. Then I heard screams. . . . I was stiff with terror. . . . The screams came louder. . . . I yearned to become invisible, to stop living. The commotion above me increased and I began to cry." Eventually his father finds "Richard" and drags him out, but "the instant his hand left me I jumped to my feet and broke into a wild run, trying to elude the people who surrounded me, heading for the street." He is caught again, and finally his mother whips him (and this, we should remember, was a four-year old boy):

> I was lashed so hard and long that I lost consciousness. I was beaten out of my senses and later I found myself in bed, screaming, determined to run away. . . . I was lost in a fog of fear. . . . Whenever I tried to sleep I would see huge wobbly white bags, like the full udders of cows, suspended from the ceiling above me. Later, as I grew worse, I could see the bags in the daytime with my eyes open and I was gripped by the fear that they were going to fall and drench me with some horrible liquid. Day and night I begged my mother and father to take the bags away, pointing to them, shaking with terror because no one saw them but me. Exhaustion would make me drift toward sleep and then I would scream until I was wide awake again; I was afraid to sleep. Time finally bore me away from the dangerous bags and I got well. But for a long time I was chastened whenever I remembered that my mother had come close to killing me.[1]

I don't know how many people have had a childhood like the one re-created in *Black Boy*, but the basic components of this first scene are repeated so many times in the book that we must see violence, fear, panic, and flight as the definitive, shaping facts of the "black boy's" life and of Wright's memories of that life. Later the boy works out what he calls a hypothetical statement about God and human suffering to counter a companion who was urging religion on him, and, as the author says, it was "a statement that stemmed from my knowledge of life as I had lived, seen, felt, and suffered it in terms of dread, fear, hunger, terror, and loneliness" (p. 127).

---

[1] Richard Wright, *Black Boy* (New York, 1966), pp. 11-13. Hereafter references to this edition of *Black Boy* will be given in the text.

We must ask ourselves, then, is all of this narrative of violence, fear, and flight the making of Richard Wright's vision or an expression of it? Or are they not complements and corollaries of one another, opposite sides of one coin, a history going forward to create Richard Wright, Richard Wright's memory going backward to re-create the "black boy"? This, I suggest, is *bios* as the course of black boy's life, his lifetime, and it is also *bios* as Richard Wright's achieved vision, his understanding, his unique psychic configuration. To put it another way, the *bios* of *Black Boy* is Richard Wright's past life, his past experience, his existence as "Richard" or as "black boy"—hence the strong narrative element. It is also Wright's present life, his achieved vision, his existence as a writer and thinker—hence the important element of commentary. And these two *bioi*, these two lives are not the same, not by any means; but they *are* significantly joined by what we call memory.

Throughout *Black Boy*, Richard Wright is in search of meaning for his experience, and given the strategy that he follows as autobiographer, the way that he can hope to attain to meaning is through exercise of a memory that lifts events transpiring in time out of the Heraclitean stream and into a realm of order where events bear to one another a relationship of significance rather than of chronology. The achieved condition, the achieved vision of the present can do this for all of the events occurring in the past and composing in their totality the historic *bios* of the individual. At one point in *Black Boy* Wright says that his "mother's suffering grew into a symbol in my mind," and he speaks of "the fear" and "the dread," "the meaningless pain and the endless suffering" that "conditioned my relation to events that had not yet happened, determined my attitude to situations and circumstances I had yet to face" (p. 111). That Wright is here looking both forward and backward along the line of *bios* and the thread of memory—forward from past events to present consciousness and backward from present consciousness to past events—becomes obvious when we reflect that his mental state as he writes has been "conditioned" by just those events of which he is writing. He goes on to say that these repeated experiences of suffering, fear, and dread—the basic conditioning elements of his youth—were "to make me keep forever on the move," forever in flight, "as though to escape a nameless fate seeking to overtake me" (p. 112). Fear and suffering, incessant flight, and a nameless fate—what do they add up to for the man remembering it all? They add up, Wright says, to "a notion as to what life meant that no education could ever alter, a conviction that the meaning of living came only when one was struggling to wring a meaning out of meaningless suffering."

These three elements of fear, flight, and fate are also, of course, the structural dominants of *Native Son*: Book One is entitled "Fear"; Book Two, "Flight"; Book Three, "Fate." As those emotional facts conditioned Wright's life, imposed a structure on his *bios*, and determined his vision, so he turned that achieved vision and structure back to give shape and direction to his novel and his autobiography and to impute a meaning to his experience that could be there only by this reflexive return on the past. The vision possessed by Richard Wright—or the vision that possessed Richard Wright—in the early forties was as responsible for the character of "Richard" as for the character of "Bigger," for the structure of *Black Boy* as for the structure of *Native Son*, for the "meaning of living" wrung from experience in the autobiography as for the protoexistentialist note on which the novel concludes.

Perhaps this will be made clearer if, returning to the two senses of *bios*, I remark that if we define it only as the vital principle, then we should have to say that the first two books of *Native Son* are autobiography, for in them we find a full imitation of the vision to which Wright had attained. However, if we hold both definitions simultaneously, then of course *Native Son* is not an autobiography because in the making of it memory does not reach back into an historical, personal past, back down the Heraclitean stream, to retrace a lifetime, the course of life. Only *Black Boy* does that. On the other hand, *Black Boy* would itself be at least a partial failure were it not composed simultaneously of narration and commentary, past experience and present vision, and a fusion of the two in the double "I" of the book—"I" as "Richard," the "black boy" of fifteen, twenty, and thirty years earlier; and "I" as "Richard Wright," a mature man, an urban intellectual, an accomplished writer brooding over his life and its meaning. This double-referent "I" delivers up a twofold *bios*—here and now, there and then, both the perpetual present and the historic past—and it is the tenuous yet tensile thread of memory that joins the two "I"s, that holds together the two *bioi*, and that successfully redeems the time of (and for) Richard Wright.

There is a very common, largely implicit assumption (and for the most part doubtless a justifiable assumption) that autobiography is easy reading and that it presents no problems of understanding for the good reason that it attempts no elaborate feats of meaning and it plumbs none of the obscure depths in which modern poetry and contemporary fiction have their being. Besides, say the critics who support this view of the matter, autobiography is what it seems to be and says what it means, unlike poetry or fiction or whatever else that is *not* what it seems to be and is forever saying what it does *not* mean. No one, so goes the assumption, need worry about knowing exactly what is going on in an autobiography. Well and good.

Then comes Paul Valéry, who was always fastidious in choosing his words exactly, saying (and more than once, both to himself in his *Cahiers* and to others in correspondence: so we cannot comfort ourselves with the impertinent assumption that he misspoke) that his longest and most obscure poem (*La Jeune Parque*)—and therefore one of the most obscure poems of this century—is "an autobiography" and that the Narcissus theme (on which three or four other difficult, fascinating poems are based) is his "poetic autobiography." As if this were not exasperation enough for the good souls who want their autobiographies simple and comprehensible, Valéry once said of "Le cimetière marin" (which he never called an autobiography), "As for the content of the poem, it is made up of memories of my native city. It is almost the only one of my poems into which I put something of my own life." For generic sensibilities, that is wanton aggravation: a poem into which he put nothing of his life is "an autobiography," and "almost the only one of my poems into which I put something of my own life" is *not* an autobiography; or, to put it in other words, a poem that draws on memory to reconstruct something from the poet's personal past is *not* an autobiography, while a poem that disdains memory altogether and has in it nothing of the poet's personal history *is* an autobiography. This is enough to make many readers throw up their hands and simply abandon Valéry as a bad case and an unprofitable one in any discussion of autobiography; but I think those many readers would be wrong, and I urge not joining them in haste.

Interestingly enough, students of Valéry are not dismayed by this sort of thing. So far as they are concerned, it provides grist for the same intellectual and emotional mill as the poems: Valerians are put to the test to understand how *La Jeune Parque* can be an autobiography just as they are put to the test to understand the intent of *La Jeune Parque* itself. (For the poem was not originally conceived as an autobiography of any kind: it was first intended as a final addition to a volume of early poems that André Gide wanted to republish; then it was intended as an "exercise" to occupy the poet's mind during wartime; and only in the outcome, as Valéry wrote to Gide, did it come to be—and to be seen as—his autobiography.) In contrast to students of the poet, students of autobiography are likely to dismiss Valéry's repeated claims as so much obscure carrying-on—just like his poetry.

I am well aware of the severe attitude almost certain to be adopted by many critics of the autobiographical mode when one introduces the heresy of calling a lyric poem an autobiography, for I have already had experience of that attitude when I claimed that T. S. Eliot's *Four Quartets* could well be considered an autobiography. (In passing, I should remark that the notion that *Four Quartets* can be taken for an autobiography does not disturb students of Eliot, however much it may dismay students of autobiography. The latter, I gather, feel the security of generic definitions giving way under them, and they apparently become queasy as they sense the waves of chaos and ancient night—against which the barriers of genre have provided some protection—threatening to overwhelm us all.) I now think that *La Jeune Parque* offers a more extreme and therefore a better case than even *Four Quartets* for the argument that a lyric poem can perfectly well be an autobiography and that the view of poetry that informs all of Valéry's work provides a more elegant theoretical ground for a consideration of poetry, autobiography, and creativity in general than anything we can find in Eliot. What we can find in Valéry's theory and practice, however, in no way invalidates the argument that *Four Quartets* is "an autobiography"; quite the contrary—it serves to confirm and strengthen that argument at every point.

Here an immensely important distinction must be drawn between the noun "autobiography" and the adjective "autobiographical." I maintain that just as it is possible to have a work that is "autobiographical" without its being "an autobiography" so also—nor am I being wantonly paradoxical—it is possible to have a work that is "an autobiography" without its being "autobiographical." Everyone will acknowledge that Lawrence's *Sons and Lovers*, for example, or Joyce's *Portrait of the Artist* is "autobiographical"; no one, however, myself included, will want to say that either of the books is "an autobiography." And so also with a first-person "autobiographical" novel like *David Copperfield*. Dickens's "I" is to a certain but very limited extent self-referential; and I imagine that it might be possible to determine the extent to which the "I" is self-referential in any given passage of the novel by determining the emotional pressure or the emotional dislocation that informs (or deforms) the passage in question. But here the bind gets tighter and the argument more prickly, for I believe that most readers would agree that the "I" that surfaces at infrequent intervals in *Four Quartets* is also to a certain—but again very limited—extent self-referential:

> So here I am, in the middle way, having had twenty years—
> Twenty years largely wasted, the years of *l'entre deux guerres*—
> Trying to learn to use words, and every attempt
> Is a wholly new start. . . .

Of course the "I" here has reference to Eliot and his personal experience, but it also has a much larger and more general reference, as we can see in the fact that elsewhere in the poem Eliot freely uses the first-person *plural*, the second-person, and even the third-person to contain and express much the same sort of experience:

> We shall not cease from exploration
> And the end of all our exploring
> Will be to arrive where we started
> And know the place for the first time.

> You are not here to verify,
> Instruct yourself, or inform curiosity
> Or carry report. You are here to kneel
> Where prayer has been valid.

> Ash on an old man's sleeve
> Is all the ash the burnt roses leave.[2]

All of these first-, second-, and third-person, singular and plural self-references aside, however, what I wish to say is that Eliot's poem is an autobiography not because of self-referential pronouns but in spite of them. The self-referential pronouns (very limitedly self-referential, I should emphasize once more) give a very slightly autobiographical character to Eliot's poem as, to a much greater ex-

---

[2] That the entirely anonymous "old man" here refers to Eliot and that the ash on his sleeve refers to Eliot's experience as a fire-watcher from the roof of Faber and Faber during World War II we can learn in *Affectionately*, *T. S. Eliot* (London, 1969) by William Turner Levy and Victor Scherle.

tent, they do to Dickens's novel. But what makes the poem "an autobiography" (in contrast to an "autobiographical" poem) is not a matter of content but of form: it is through the formal device of "recapitulation and recall" that Eliot succeeds in realizing his *bios* as poet and spiritual explorer. For the rest of the argument as it pertains to Eliot I refer the reader to Chapter 5 of *Metaphors of Self* and turn now to the argument, in a more extreme form, as it turns on *La Jeune Parque*.

Unlike *Four Quartets* and also unlike "Le cimetière marin," *La Jeune Parque* is not in the least degree "autobiographical"; its "I" is not even slightly self-referential. And while *Four Quartets* announces, "This is the use of memory," Valéry's poem discovers no use at all for memory and, in a comment on *La Jeune Parque*, the poet disavowed the least desire to exercise memory or in any way to recall the past. So what is the *bios* of this poem that he called his autobiography? It is nothing other than pure, atemporal consciousness or awareness or active sensibility—or better yet, it is consciousness of consciousness, the awareness of being conscious and of exercising consciousness. Would it be right for us to say that consciousness *cannot* provide the *bios* of autobiography? The question no doubt answers itself, at least so far as Valéry and his poem/ autobiography are concerned. *La Jeune Parque*, Valéry wrote to a correspondent, is a "poem born of a contradiction. It is a meditation with all the breaks, the resumptions, and the surprises of any meditation. But it is a meditation in which the meditator as well as the object of meditation is *conscious consciousness*."[3] This turns consciousness, and thus the Valerian *bios*, in on itself but not back on its history (which is what we get in Henry James's autobiographical volumes, where we are presented with the evolution of a consciousness), for there is in *La Jeune Parque* no return to the past but only a more and more intense awareness of conscious existence— "*la conscience consciente*"—in the present. As in the marvellous phrase describing the universe in Yeats's *Vision* ("a great egg that turns inside-out perpetually without breaking its shell"), Valerian consciousness turns inside-out perpetually but keeps its inner-outer shell wonderfully intact; it begets on itself its own likeness, its own

---

[3] "Ce poème est l'enfant d'une contradiction. C'est une rêverie qui peut avoir toutes les ruptures, les reprises et les surprises d'une rêverie. Mais c'est une rêverie dont le personnage en même temps que l'objet est la *conscience consciente*." From a letter of 1922 to Aimé Lafont published in the Pléiade *Oeuvres*, ed. Jean Hytier, 2 vols. (Paris, 1957), 1: 1636.

perfected image, and that likeness, that image, is the poem called *La Jeune Parque*. But one crucial fact must be observed: because consciousness is a phenomenon that is determined not in terms of content but only in terms of form, so *La Jeune Parque* must be a *formal* mirroring or a *formal* imitation of its subject/object rather than a narrative recounting of historical contents such as we can find in (for example) Wordsworth's *Prelude*.

The speaker or the "I" of *La Jeune Parque* (which translates as "The Young Fate"—that is, one of the three Fates, the three *Moirai* or the three *Parcae*, of classical mythology) is a woman (just as *conscience*, "consciousness," is in French a feminine noun) which immediately violates all gender expectations in an autobiography by a male. Furthermore, the "I" is apparently a composite of several mythic figures (Psyche, Eve, Helen, Pandora, Aphrodite, the Fates)—again a violation of all the expectations that genre-observing critics would insist upon—who wakes up at night and, in a manner of speaking, thinks; or perhaps we should do better to say not that she thinks but that she engages in a borderline revery, half-sleeping, half-waking (something akin to Molly Bloom's soliloquy in the last chapter of *Ulysses*, except that there is no discernible personal or historic reference for what passes through the Parque's revery as there is for the contents of Molly Bloom's revery). This intricately woven web of revery, itself the product and image of the complex articulation of consciousness rising out of and sinking back into the unconscious—a web with "neither beginning nor end but only nodal points" (*Oeuvres*, 1:1636)—Valéry wished to render in the form of "a monologue," a "recitative" or operatic solo for female voice (*Oeuvres*, 1:1629). This is *La Jeune Parque*, the entire poem. Moreover, what the Young Fate says or sings or weeps (however we are to describe her performance of the recitative) has no narrative continuity about it and no ideational content at all; in particular, it certainly has no personal, historical content from the poet's past and none of the ideas that Valéry loved to pursue privately but that he thought altogether unsuited to verse. ("My ideas," Valéry once wrote, repeating Diderot, "are my whores." What Valéry sleeps with in his poetry—or more precisely what he wakes to in *La Jeune Parque*—is not a whore nor an idea but a rhythm, the rhythm of emergent consciousness; and that rhythm, Valéry said, controlled him and his poem rather than, as with his whores and his ideas, the other way around.)

When told that this rather eerie solo for contralto voice is Va-

léry's autobiography, many readers of *La Jeune Parque* will doubtless react as Joyce's father did when he first saw Brancusi's "Portrait of James Joyce" (a portrait that consists of a spiral convolution
with three ruler-straight lines of varying length, one below the spiral, the other two on one side of it: the "Portrait" is reproduced in
Richard Ellmann's biography of Joyce). "Jim has changed more
than I thought," John Joyce is reported to have said of his son's portrait. The content of Valéry's poem (if we can speak of content at
all) bears about the same relationship to the events of his life as
Brancusi's lines do to any good photograph of Joyce. Yet a perceptive reader of *Ulysses* or *Finnegans Wake* will understand how Brancusi could call his spiral and lines a "Portrait" just as a perceptive
reader of Valéry, as Valéry himself said, would discern his autobiography in the form of *La Jeune Parque*. "Anyone who knows how
to read me," Valéry wrote in a letter of 1917, the year *La Jeune Parque* was first published (it was four years in the making), "will read
an autobiography in the form. The *content* matters little—it is made
up of commonplaces. True thought is incompatible with poetry."[4]
This, of course, is the doctrine of *la poésie pure*, and as practised in
La Jeune Parque, where consciousness stands in for *bios* and where
strict formal observances "constitute the true object," it produces
what one might call "*l'autobiographie pure*."

As nature to a vacuum, so the art of Valéry to impurity: his art
simply abhors all that is impure—and few things, as one could
demonstrate from a hundred conventional autobiographers, are
more impure than memory. Memory distorts and it transforms; it
causes some people pain and others happiness, or it brings both
pain and happiness at the same time; it apologizes and it justifies, it
accuses and it excuses; it fails to recall anything and then recalls
much more than was ever there—indeed, memory does virtually
everything but what it is supposed to do: that is, to look back on a
past event and to see that event as it really was. This being so, the
man who understands *bios* as "the historic course of a lifetime" and
who naively imagines that memory is a sufficient faculty for recovering that lifetime as it really was might write an interesting autobiography, but it will not be what he supposes it to be. As with
every autobiographer who tries to recapture his personal history,
such a writer will re-create the past in the image of the present, but

---

[4] "Qui saura me lire lira une autobiographie, dans la forme. Le *fond* importe peu.
Lieux communs. La vraie pensée n'est pas adaptable au vers" (*Oeuvres*, 1: 1631-
1632).

because of his naive faith in memory as an unfailing tie to a real past, he will not perceive that this is what he does. Valéry was very far from being a naif, however, and in *La Jeune Parque* he neatly sidesteps the entire difficulty involved in trying to recall the past by redefining *bios* so as to resituate it in a timeless present and thus deny memory any place at all in his autobiography.

"While the *historical* element of a self generally plays the principal role," Valéry wrote of *La Jeune Parque* in a notebook entry, "I preferred here, and elsewhere, its feeling of an eternal present,"[5] and this distinguishes very nicely his own performance in autobiography from that of others including, for example, Richard Wright. What Valéry calls the self's "feeling of an eternal present" is a more immediate reality, surely, than any part of the past that memory can recall even when it does so with the least degree of impurity it can manage. And one of the most notable features of *La Jeune Parque* is just this immediacy—the immediacy of an emergent, nocturnal consciousness, unable to distinguish clearly who, where, and what it or anything else is. The "recitative," faithful to a consciousness waking in the night, proceeds by a series of questions that are as clear and pure in form as they are obscure and confused in content. In other words, they render with great fidelity the feeling of a psyche, half-sleeping and half-waking, emerging from unconsciousness in the small dark hours of the night:

> Qui pleure là, sinon le vent simple, à cette heure
> Seule, avec diamants extrêmes? . . . Mais qui pleure,
> Si proche de moi-même au moment de pleurer?
>
> Cette main, sur mes traits qu'elle rêve effleurer,
> Distraitement docile à quelque fin profonde,
> Attend de ma faiblesse une larme qui fonde,
> Et que de mes destins lentement divisé,
> Le plus pur en silence éclaire un cœur brisé.[6]

---

[5] Jackson Mathews, ed., *The Collected Works of Paul Valéry*, vol. 1: *Poems* (Princeton, 1971). Vol. 1 also includes "On Poets and Poetry," selected and translated from the Notebooks, and this passage comes from that section, p. 424. It occurs in the *Cahiers* (Paris, 1957-1961) 18: 533.

> [6] Who is that weeping, if not simply the wind,
> At this sole hour, with ultimate diamonds? . . . But who
> Weeps, so close to myself on the brink of tears?
>
> This hand of mine, dreaming it strokes my features,
> Absently submissive to some deep-hidden end,

Who weeps there? It is Psyche awaking in the night—"*la conscience consciente*" in confused revery over her (its) own being, consciousness struggling vaguely to raise herself (itself) out of the unconsciousness of sleep.[7]

And naturally this is all enacted and rendered in the present—eternally in the present—for one pole of the self's existence is "its feeling of an eternal present." Proust might busy himself forever "à la recherche du temps perdu," (and so might nine-tenths of the autobiographers of the world—stout champions all of memory as a creative and recreative faculty), but Valéry was of a very different mind.[8] "Whatever I have done soon ceases to be a part of me," he says in "Memoirs of a Poem"—that poem being *La Jeune Parque*. "Those recollections which lead me to relive the past are painful: and the best of them are unbearable. I certainly would not busy myself by trying to recover time past!"[9] Nor does he need to worry about thus busying himself in his autobiography, for its time is the eternal present, its *bios* is an ever renewed and eternally emergent

---

> Waits for a tear to melt out of my weakness
> And, gradually dividing from my other destinies,
> For the purest to enlighten a broken heart in silence.

(Translated by David Paul, *Collected Works*, 1: 69)

[7] Cf. the poem to this fascinating passage on "waking up" from Valéry's *Cahiers*:
Waking up. There is no phenomenon more exciting to me than waking.

Nothing *tends* to give a more extraordinary idea of . . . *everything*, than this autogenesis. This beginning of what was—which also has its beginning. *What is*—and this is nothing but shock, stupor, contrast.

Here, a state of equidifference takes place as if . . . there were a moment (among the most unstable) during which no one is yet the *person one is*, and *could again become another!* A different memory could develop. Whence the fantastic. The external individual remaining, and the whole psyche substituted.

Emphases and ellipses are in the text. (See the *Collected Works*, vol 15: *Moi*, pp. 17-18.) In precisely the same way that *La Jeune Parque* is Valéry's autobiography, so are the voluminous *Cahiers* (as Valéry in fact remarked). It is significant that Valéry worked on the *Cahiers* in the early morning hours upon waking and they, like the poem, record the new beginning of emergent consciousness.

[8] It is true that in vol. 15 of the *Collected Works* there appears a previously unpublished piece called "Autobiography," but it is surely one of the least revealing, least forthcoming documents ever to bear that title, and one of the least original as well. It reads very much as if Valéry were thumbing his nose at the conventional expectations of conventional readers ("You want content? Here it is.") for example, when, after a laconic listing of dates and events, it concludes with "Etcetera. . . ." So much for *that* kind of autobiography.

[9] "Memoirs of a Poem," in the *Collected Works*, vol. 7: *The Art of Poetry*, p. 104.

consciousness, and the focus of its creative effort is not on past events nor on the past as seen in the present but on language itself and the forms of poetry assumed and created by language. "LITERATURE. What is 'form' for anyone else is 'content' for me," Valéry wrote in his notebooks, and in another entry referring to *La Jeune Parque*, he remarked, "The FORM of this song is an *autobiography*."[10] For a writer like Valéry (and we must not forget that he was always a writer, essentially and temperamentally a writer, even in the years of silence preceding *La Jeune Parque*), language was the major event of life. Other events were external and insignificant, and none could compare with words in their importance, in the shaping effect they had on Valéry's life. Moreover, according to his own description, words and rhythms *happened* to Valéry like any other event, only they happened, as it were, from within, and the self of his autobiography, therefore, is created by language and its forms, not the other way around. And referring to his poem/autobiography, Valéry said, "I started out from the language itself" (*Oeuvres*, 1:1632).

The monologue of *La Jeune Parque* is composed of the most brilliant (and, at the same time, obscure), frequently bizarre, unattached images cast in the strictest, most severe, and apparently inevitable mold of French verse—Alexandrines that are never enjambed, that always observe exact placing of the caesura, and that sound like nothing so much as Racine without sense. (In a notebook entry on the making of *La Jeune Parque*, Valéry quoted the Racinian line—"Le jour n'est pas plus pur que le fond de mon cœur"—that seems a perfect expression of the spirit of the Parque's monologue: the line from *Phèdre* sounds like it could well be a line of the Valerian song.) There is an astonishing, unremitting, uncompromised and uncompromising purity of diction and syntax in the Young Fate's solo. And of course Valéry was right: there are very properly no ideas here; sounds, images, and verse movement are the poem's sole "content." "I had a devil of a time with the *words*," Valéry wrote to a correspondent. "I made more than a hundred drafts. The transitions cost me infinite trouble."[11] These transitions, over which Valéry worked so long and so hard, correspond to the modulations of the singing voice, and as they occur in

[10] The first quotation is from *The Art of Poetry*, p. 183; the second is quoted by Octave Nadal in *La Jeune Parque* (Paris, 1957), p. 165.

[11] "J'ai eu un mal du diable avec les *mots*. J'ai fait plus de cent *brouillons*. Les transitions m'ont coûté une peine infinie" (*Oeuvres*, 1: 1636).

the poem they are nothing less than formal imitations, or formal representations, of mental synapses—the synapses of conscious awareness.

When he had completed this *"rude exercice,"* as Valéry called it (an exercise pursued with single-minded intensity throughout the four years of World War I) he discovered, as he wrote to André Gide, "a certain sense of autobiography (intellectual autobiography, to be sure)" about the finished poem.[12] It came to seem an autobiography of psyche (or Psyche) during the war years, and for Valéry it was an Horatian monument more lasting than bronze that he created to redeem that desolate time and to do honor to the language through which psyche came to consciousness. "See then that ye walk circumspectly, not as fools, but as wise, Redeeming the time, because the days are evil." Valéry might as well have been obeying the Pauline injunction, as it was not past time but present time—the present time of the evil war years and, in the poem, the eternal present—that he set about redeeming through his tenacious pursuit of consciousness and a rendering of that consciousness in a language as pure and refined as it could be. In the end, he would have this poem—this arduous exercise, this autobiography of "la conscience consciente"—to shore against the ruins of the war years. "I sometimes flattered myself," Valéry says, "by trying to believe that I must at least perform a work on behalf of our language as a substitute for fighting for our land; I thought to erect a minor monument, perhaps a tombstone, to that language, composed of its purest words and its noblest forms—a small, dateless monument—on the menacing shores of the Ocean of Gibberish."[13] In the outcome *La Jeune Parque* was a monument not only to the French language but also to the self shaping and shaped by that language, and I think we would be as wrong to tell Valéry that his poem is not an autobiography merely out of generic squeamishness as we would be to tell him that his autobiography is not a poem. Autobiography is what genius makes of it.

---

[12] "J'ajoute . . . que j'ai trouvé après coup dans le poème fini quelque air d' . . . autobiographie (intellectuelle s'entend . . .)." From the *Correspondance d'André Gide et de Paul Valéry* (Paris, 1955), p. 448; the letter was dated 14 June 1917.

[13] "Je me flattais parfois en essayant de me faire croire qu'il fallait au moins travailler pour notre langage, à défaut de combattre pour notre terre; dresser à cette langue un petit monument peut-être funéraire, fait de mots les plus purs et de ses formes les plus nobles,—un petit tombeau sans date,—sur les bords menaçants de l'Océan du Charabia" (*Oeuvres*, 1: 1630).

Plotinus tells us that every man has two souls, a lower and a higher, and that "each of the two phases of the Soul . . . possesses memory." As to the kinds of memory proper to the higher and lower souls, Plotinus continues:

> But the memory of friends, children, wife? Country too, and all that the better sort of man may reasonably remember? All these, the one (the lower man) retains with emotion, the authentic man passively. . . . The lower soul must be always striving to attain to memory of the activities of the higher. . . . The loftier, on the contrary, must desire to come to a happy forgetfulness of all that has reached it through the lower. . . . The more urgent the intention towards the Supreme, the more extensive will be the Soul's forgetfulness. . . . In this sense we may truly say that the good soul is the forgetful. It flees multiplicity; it seeks to escape the unbounded by drawing all to unity, for only thus is it free from entanglement, light-footed, self-conducted.[14]

If Plotinus was right, then W. B. Yeats's was a good soul indeed, for it was capable of forgetting everything that the lower man "retains with emotion" (as well as myriad facts that even a lower man could scarcely get emotional about) and capable of remembering all sorts of things that only the higher man could be supposed to attain to. According to all testimony, Yeats tolerated a miserably bad memory for names, dates, and facts, but while this might stand him in good stead with the Plotinian Supreme, does it not disqualify him as an autobiographer? Is an autobiographer not utterly dependent on memory for both the shape and the details of his recitation? Yes, he is, if the autobiographer is Richard Wright; but no, he is not, if the autobiographer is Paul Valéry; and both yes, he is, and no, he is not, if the autobiographer is W. B. Yeats.

For memory was as much a double phenomenon for Yeats as it was for Plotinus—a faculty for remembering, balanced and inverted by a faculty for forgetting. Of this faculty and antifaculty, Yeats wrote to Joseph Hone: "What I do not see but may see or have seen, is perceived by another being. In other words is part of the fabric of another being. I remember what he forgets, he remembers what I forget."[15] We can call these the lower man and the

[14] *Enneads*, translated by Stephen MacKenna; Fourth *Ennead*, Third Tractate, 31 and 32.

[15] Allan Wade, ed., *The Letters of W. B. Yeats* (London, 1954), p. 728.

higher man with Plotinus; or the self and the antiself, the man and his daimon, with Yeats. But however we name these two opposed beings who bear reversed, mirror-image likenesses to one another, we can imagine them locked in the complicated dance of antinomic opposites that Yeats alludes to in *A Vision*: "a being racing into the future passes a being racing into the past, two footprints perpetually obliterating one another, toe to heel, heel to toe."[16] Dancing this intricate dance of forgetting/remembering with his daimon, Yeats obliterates memory-traces of this world so that he may recall the forms of another world; he forgets what passes in time so that he may remember what does not pass in eternity; and misremembering, with a fine disregard, the names, dates, and places of a merely individual life, he seeks to embody in the archetypal portraiture and the anecdotal artistry of the *Autobiographies* the very essence of being, purified now of what he in one place calls the "accident and incoherence" of existence. While Wright redeems the time by discovering some sort of meaning in his past and while Valéry redeems the time by creating a monument to language and consciousness in an eternal present, Yeats redeems the time by simply abolishing it in favor of eternity, for, as he says through one of his shadow men (John Aherne), "I think that Plato symbolized by the word 'memory' a relation to the timeless" (*Vision*, p. 54). Plotinus did the same in the philosophy of the *Enneads*; Yeats does the same in the performance of the *Autobiographies*.

"Faces and names are vague to me," Yeats admits in *The Trembling of the Veil*, the second volume of his *Autobiographies*; but then, giving us an insight into his own special performance of autobiography, he goes on to say that "while faces that I met but once may rise clearly before me, a face met on many a Sunday [at W. E. Henley's gatherings] has perhaps vanished."[17] There is no sense of regret on Yeats's part for the vanished, forgettable faces because those more memorable faces seen once only (and seen, I should imagine, by a Plotinian higher, rather than lower, man) have vastly more importance for the Yeatsian autobiographer than do those people who, by being recurrent facts of mundane experience, were at best recalcitrant material to the artist's purpose. Yet, having said this, one must admit that in his *Autobiographies* Yeats did write of those whom he saw often: Lady Gregory, Maud Gonne, Lionel Johnson, John Synge, and many more. He did indeed; but by the

[16] W. B. Yeats, *A Vision* (New York, 1937), p. 210.

[17] W. B. Yeats, *Autobiographies* (London, 1955), p. 128. All subsequent references are to this edition and will be given in the text.

time they reach the page of Yeats's autobiography, these real people have been changed, changed and transformed utterly, so that a great beauty, not terrible but ideal, has been born out of the meeting of the historic facts of their existence and the artist's shaping vision.

Yeats's autobiography is more anecdotal than almost any other that comes to mind—certainly more anecdotal than *Black Boy*, for example (and Valéry, of course, cannot even be brought into the picture). It is composed of a string of more or less factual stories about people, both the famous and the not-so-famous, whom Yeats had known either slightly or well; and on first glance this might seem to go right against the grain of the Plotinian dual memory. What was Yeats doing remembering "friends, children, wife" (actually his children and wife do not really get into the *Autobiographies*, but his friends certainly do) and "country too" if such remembering is the characteristic activity of the lower man and made up of details that would be conscientiously forgotten by the higher man? The answer is that these anecdotes are something other and more than simply historical or factual: in them Yeats seeks to capture character at its most typical, thus catching a glimpse of the essence that lies behind (or, in the spatial metaphor of Plotinus, above) the accident. This is to look with the physical eye on all the sideshow offered to us by *bios*, "the historical course of a lifetime," and yet to see behind and above that *bios* with the intellectual eye, *Bios*, the eternal paradigm, archetype, or idea that is alone capable of conferring upon *bios* the lower, lesser reality that may be ascribed to it. It is to look so intently upon time that you succeed in stilling its movement and thus seeing eternity in and through it (for as Plato's Timaeus said, time is but a moving image of eternity). The ontology of Yeats's autobiography is a thoroughly Platonic one. As Plotinus puts it, "When the two souls chime each with each, the two imaging faculties [i.e., memories] no longer stand apart; the union is dominated by the imaging faculty of the higher soul, and thus the image perceived is as one; the less powerful is like a shadow attending upon the dominant, like a minor light merging into a greater."[18]

Yeats gives us the clue himself when he calls the third of his autobiographical volumes *Dramatis Personae*: the title refers not only to Yeats's involvement in theatrical activity during those years (1896-1902) but also, and more importantly, to the fact that these

---

[18] Fourth *Ennead*, Third Tractate, 31.

people were characters in the drama of Yeats's life—a drama that (especially in the *Autobiographies*) was scripted by himself. When they turn up in *The Trembling of the Veil* or *Dramatis Personae* or *The Death of Synge*, each of them (as Yeats also says of the artist in his work) "has been reborn as an idea, something intended, complete"—they are symbolic, contributive elements in the artist's whole makeup and self-expression. This may seem a rude treatment of history and one's friends, but Yeats could always plead a weak factual memory coupled with a strong creative forgetfulness: he might forget names and faces, but even as they slipped from him, his daimon was busy recalling the ideas lying behind those names and faces, for Yeats liked to agree with what he thought Plotinus (in a different *Ennead*) had said—that there is a unique archetype for every individual soul. And it was the type and the archetype that Yeats sought to capture in the *Autobiographies*. Hence he replaces Lady Gregory, the woman, with Lady Gregory, the ideal aristrocrat (that the living woman was not quite what Yeats saw her to be and made of her we may surmise from the fact that others—Frank O'Connor and George Yeats, for example—found her very different from the ideal that Yeats imagined; indeed, they found her quite impossible); he replaces John Synge the living/ dying man with John Synge the ideal artist; all through the book he replaces individual men and women with types and then, going the last logical step, replaces those types with their full-blown archetypes.

The volumes of Yeats's autobiography are spotted throughout with "I forget when it was," and "I forget who it was," and "I cannot remember where it was," and "I do not recall who was present." But these local lapses are all subsumed, explained, and justified by the preface to the first of the volumes (*Reveries over Childhood and Youth*) that disarms in advance all possible criticism of historical error: "I have changed nothing to my knowledge; and yet it must be that I have changed many things without my knowledge; for I am writing after many years and have consulted neither friend, nor letter, nor old newspaper, and describe what comes oftenest into my memory" (p. 3). Or, as happens so often in the performance of the *Autobiographies*, Yeats is describing what *fails* to come into his memory, for what he is writing is that which comes into his daimonic, higher memory rather than his quotidian, lower memory. "I say this," Yeats concludes, "fearing that some surviving friend of my youth may remember something in a different shape and be offended with my book." Yet, for all the admissions of forgetfulness and the disarming of factual criticism, the *Autobiographies* are full of anecdotal brilliance, as if Yeats were possessed of total recall. One after another, he creates a whole series of richly realized scenes—virtually set pieces—fitted out with detailed, telling descriptions of personalities, events, conversations of years earlier.

A great many (I should say most, if not all) of the anecdotes in the *Autobiographies* are too good to be (literally) true. Already from the preface, however, we should be aware that very little in any of the volumes is intended to be taken as factual or incontrovertible. Yeats presents us instead with a truer truth than fact, a deeper reality than history. This, he says by implication, is how various people would speak and act *if* their speech and action were always in keeping with their deepest character, and that deepest character, which may not have been apparent to anyone else in the drama, is what Yeats as autobiographer has his eye on at all times. In life no one succeeds in fully living out a deep coherent character in every action; hence the necessity for Yeats to forget what "really" happened, to "remember" something that didn't happen (at least not just like this, not with this patina of artistic finish on it) and to create a past that accords less with history than with his present vision of himself and of all the constitutive others.

Very briefly, I am going to offer three typical/archetypical portraits from the *Autobiographies* as evidence of what I have been saying—portraits of figures whose lives, in one way or another, had gone to "ruin, wreck and wrack," as Yeats phrases it in the poem called "The Results of Thought," but whose "wholesome strength" the poet summons back in his book: namely Oscar Wilde, John Synge, and Maud Gonne.

The first use to which Yeats puts Wilde in "The Tragic Generation" is as a type opposed to the type of George Bernard Shaw. According to Yeats, Wilde was all style while Shaw had no style at all. Wilde "had turned his style to a parade as though it were his show, and he Lord Mayor" (p. 284); of Shaw, on the other hand, Yeats says, "I had a nightmare that I was haunted by a sewing-machine, that clicked and shone, but the incredible thing was that the machine smiled, smiled perpetually" (p. 283). The conclusion to Wilde's story, though tragic, finds him still in character, still typical—the stylized protagonist of one of Yeats's finest anecdotes. After his conviction for sodomy, Wilde turned up in Dieppe where

Ernest Dowson was then drunkenly resident, and there, in order to repair his reputation, it was decided that Wilde should visit the local whorehouse. Here is Yeats's account of the incident:

> Wilde had arrived in Dieppe, and Dowson pressed upon him the necessity of acquiring "a more wholesome taste." They emptied their pockets on to the café table, and though there was not much, there was enough if both heaps were put into one. Meanwhile the news had spread, and they set out accompanied by a cheering crowd. Arrived at their destination, Dowson and the crowd remained outside, and presently Wilde returned. He said in a low voice to Dowson, "The first these ten years, and it will be the last. It was like cold mutton"— always, as Henley had said, "a scholar and a gentleman," he now remembered that the Elizabethan dramatists used the words "cold mutton"—and then aloud so that the crowd might hear him, "But tell it in England, for it will entirely restore my character." (Pp. 327-328)

As Yeats tells Oscar Wilde's story, his ruling passion, his rage for style, was fully evident even in that most trying moment when, for sweet reputation's sake, he had to dine on cold mutton, and he remained OSCAR WILDE, his own archetype, right to the bitter end. But Yeats, of course, was not in Dieppe; he was not one of those who cheered Wilde on to the brothel. So where did he get the story with all its scenic particulars, its precise details, and its dialogue certified as accurate by the use of quotation marks? Well, Yeats introduces the story with this sentence: "Then there came a wonderful tale repeated by Dowson himself, whether by word of mouth or by letter *I do not remember*" (p. 327; italics added). In other words, this is exactly the way it happened, or should have happened; and if it happened otherwise—if, for example, there were no such incident—then I have forgotten one thing, remembered another, and created a super-typical scene from my imagination. Anyone foolish enough to reject Yeats's story merely because it comes from a memory for types and archetypes rather than a memory for historic fact is going to miss most of the greatness of the *Autobiographies* and will never gain entry into the higher world of Plotinus and Yeats.

As to John Synge, I think his case was much the same as Standish O'Grady's. "When I try to recall his physical appearance," Yeats says of O'Grady in *Dramatis Personae*, "my father's picture in the Municipal Gallery blots out my own memory" (p. 425). I daresay that the highly wrought portrait of John Synge executed by Yeats himself in the *Autobiographies* subsequently blotted out his own memory of Synge's appearance also, for the description that Yeats gives of his first encounter with Synge suggests just such a blotting out as it proceeds by a series of memory blanks: "I cannot remember," Yeats says, why "I was at the Hôtel Corneille instead of my usual lodging"; and "I forget" who "told me" that Synge was in the same hotel. "I almost forget the prose and verse he showed me in Paris," and "indeed, I have but a vague impression, as of a man trying to look out of a window and blurring all that he sees by breathing upon the window" (pp. 343-344). The key to all this vagueness and memory failure comes in the next sentence where Yeats reveals what his memory for eternal things rather than his forgetfulness of temporal things told him about Synge: "According to my Lunar parable, he was a man of the twenty-third Phase." This is to view Synge from beyond the recall of a trivial daily memory; it is to see him *sub specie æternitatis*, through the spectacles of a memory adjusted to vision in an eternal rather than in a temporal realm. "A writer," Yeats remarked, "must die every day he lives, be reborn, as it is said in the Burial Service, an incorruptible self," and in his *Autobiographies* Yeats performs this service for his friend Synge, and simultaneously for himself, letting mundane memories of accident die ("I forget") that eternal memories of essence may be reborn ("a man of the twenty-third Phase")—in other words, letting John Synge the man die that John Synge the type and archetype may be reborn.

Anne Yeats once remarked to me that she thought that all of her father's references to Maud Gonne as the great, lost love, as Helen of Troy, as the consuming passion of his life, were in the end little more than habit—a sort of unthinking and unmeaning but somehow necessary reflex. To a large extent I think Miss Yeats was right, and there is certainly something willed about what Yeats says of Maud Gonne in *Dramatis Personae*. But after all, a lyric poet of Yeats's persuasion requires an image of perfected, transcendent beauty toward which his poetry may yearn, and if it is not in fact there (and it never can be there in fact, in life) then, if the poet be Yeats, he must will it into existence. The consequence of this is that the Maud Gonne of Yeats's *Autobiographies* is more image than woman, more type than image, and more archetype than either. After describing the great effect that she had on the crowds that she was wont to harangue, Yeats says:

> Her beauty, backed by her great stature, could instantly affect an assembly, and not as often with our stage beauties, because obvious and florid, for it was incredibly distinguished, and if—as must be that it might seem that assembly's very self, fused, unified, and solitary—her face, like the face of some Greek statue, showed little thought, her whole body seemed a master-work of long labouring thought, as though a Scopas had measured and calculated, consorted with Egyptian sages, and mathematicians out of Babylon, that he might outface even Artemisia's sepulchral image with a living norm. (Pp. 364-365)

Need I point out that this is not the way a lover talks or thinks about a real, living, flesh-and-blood beloved? No—this is a poet's description of Beauty with a capital "B." Yeats reveals it all when he concludes this section with a fragment of poetry:

> How many centuries spent
> The sedentary soul
> In toils of measurement
> Beyond eagle or mole,
> Beyond Archimedes' guess,
> To raise into being
> That loveliness?
>
> (P. 365)

Many, many centuries is the obvious answer to the rhetorical question, for a paradigm, an archetype, a Platonic idea—the Idea of Beauty—is not the creation of a lifetime or of several lifetimes but, if a human creation at all, is the creation of many centuries, even aeons, of experience. Nor is it something grasped by a memory that functions in time but only by one like Yeats's Plotinian memory (which on its other face is a capacity for forgetting) that recalls such forms as those of Beauty, Truth, and Goodness viewed in the paradigmatic *Bios* of eternity.

There are doubtless other possible *bioi* and attendant varieties of memory than the three that I have sketched here, but I think that in Richard Wright's two-fold *bios*, his double-referent "I," and his retrospective/projective memory; in Paul Valéry's *bios* of consciousness and his scorning of memory in favor of an eternal present; and in W. B. Yeats's eternal *Bios*, composed of paradigms and archetypes to which the poet and autobiographer has access by way of a memory symbolizing a relation to the timeless—in these three examples I believe we have a sufficient demonstration of the rich variousness of autobiography and clear evidence of the stubborn reluctance of autobiography to submit to prescriptive definitions or restrictive generic bounds. And if they do not exhaust the possibilities, yet the performances of Wright, Valéry, and Yeats at least hint at how various are the different *bioi* that may inform autobiographies by way of as many different exercises of memory.

The Veto of the Imagination:
A Theory of Autobiography

Louis A. Renza

In an autobiography one cannot avoid writing "often" where truth would require that "once" be written. For one always remains conscious that the word "once" explodes that darkness on which the memory draws; and though it is not altogether spared by the word "often," either, it is at least preserved in the opinion of the writer, and he is carried across parts which perhaps never existed at all in his life but serve him as a substitute for those which his memory can no longer even guess at.—Franz Kafka

I say "memory" and I recognize what I mean by it; but where do I recognize it except in my memory itself? Can memory itself be present to itself by means of its image rather than by its reality?
—St. Augustine

I did begin [my autobiography] but the resolve melted away and disappeared in a week and I threw my beginning away. Since then, about every three or four years I have made other beginnings and thrown them away.—Mark Twain

Perhaps more than any other literary concept, autobiography traps us into circular explanations of its being. Is it an indeterminate mixture of truth and fiction? Is it based essentially in fact rather than self-invention? Or is it a full-fledged "literary" event whose primary being resides in and through the writing itself—in the "life" of the signifier as opposed to the life being signified?

James M. Cox doubtless expresses our common-sense response to such questions when he claims that autobiography is basically a factual rather than a fictional "narrative of a person's life written by

---

himself."[1] But as we learn from instances where fiction mimics autobiography, the narrative by itself formally determines and so takes precedence over the putative, factual orientation of autobiographical references. Moreover, along with Northrop Frye and other critics we can stress that in selecting, ordering, and integrating the writer's lived experiences according to its own teleological demands, the autobiographical narrative is beholden to certain imperatives of imaginative discourse. Autobiography, in short, transforms empirical facts into *art*ifacts: it is definable as a form of "prose fiction."[2] Cox himself examines particular autobiographies less as a neutral rendering of facts than as a charged, condensed narrative through which the autobiographer symbolically reckons with his life as it was lived in socially dramatic situations, in revolutionary periods, for example, "when politics and history become dominant realities for the imagination" (p. 252).

In practice, at least, Cox's "factual" conception of autobiography agrees with Frye's and indeed with the theoretical bias of contemporary critics, namely that the writing of autobiography entails a unique act of imagination and not simply the writer's passive negotiation of the constraints and/or compulsions native to any act of self-publication. Various ways exist to reinforce this "imaginative" conception. Perhaps the most obvious way involves citing the presence of explicit fictional techniques or elements in specific autobiographies.[3] But the presence of such elements only shows that autobiography self-consciously borrows from the methodological procedures of imaginative fiction, not that autobiography is founded on the immediate requisites of imaginative discourse. A more cogent way to "prove" the imaginative quality of autobiog-

[1] James M. Cox, "Autobiography and America," *Virginia Quarterly Review* 47 (1971): 254.

[2] Northrop Frye, *Anatomy of Criticism* (Princeton, 1957), pp. 307-308.

[3] The problematic presence of fictional techniques and/or elements in autobiographical works has often been cited but no less often qualified in order to argue for autobiography's generic difference from overt works of fiction: A. M. Clark, *Autobiography: Its Genesis and Phases* (1935; reprint ed., London, 1969), pp. 10-21; Roy Pascal, *Design and Truth in Autobiography* (Cambridge, Mass., 1960), pp. 162-178 and 185-195; Alfred Kazin, "Autobiography as Narrative," *Michigan Quarterly Review* 3 (1964): 210-216; Barrett J. Mandel, "The Autobiographer's Art," *Journal of Aesthetics and Art Criticism* 27 (1968): 215-226; and Stephen Shapiro, "The Dark Continent of Literature: Autobiography," *Comparative Literature Studies* 5 (1968): 421-454. Also cf. Georg Misch, *A History of Autobiography in Antiquity*, trans. E. W. Dickes (Cambridge, Mass., 1951), 1: 1, 4.

raphy is to keep in mind, as does Georges Gusdorf, that the auto-biographical act spontaneously generates epistemological ambiva-lence. The autobiographer of necessity knows as well as writes about his past from the limiting perspective of his present self-image—*ce qu'il est devenu*. Wanting to express the "truth" about this past, he thus adopts specific verbal strategies in order to transcend such limitation.[4] But if we wish to argue for the artistic constitu-tion of autobiography, the writer's self-cognitive dilemma must be seen to permeate the composition of his text. Contrary to what Roy Pascal implies about the function of autobiography when he describes it as a mutually delimiting mixture of "design" and "truth," autobiography must not preexist the act of composition by a separate act of self-reflection.[5]

So we are theoretically led to a third "imaginative" conception of autobiography: the dynamics or drama of autobiographical cogni-tion occurs in terms of the written performance itself. According to this conception, a given autobiographical text normally manifests the writer's spontaneously "ironic" or experimental efforts to bring his past into the intentional purview of his present narrative proj-ect.[6] The autobiographer cannot help sensing his omission of facts from a life the totality or complexity of which constantly eludes him—the more so when discourse pressures him into ordering these facts. Directly or indirectly infected with the prescience of in-completeness, he concedes his life to a narrative "design" in tension with its own postulations, the result being an autobiographical text whose references appear to readers within an aesthetic setting, that is, in terms of the narrative's own "essayistic" disposition rather than in terms of their nontextual truth or falsity. Thus, apparent

---

[4] Georges Gusdorf, "Conditions et limites de l'autobiographie," in *Formen der Selbstdarstellung: Analekten zu einer Geschichte des literarischen Selbstportraits*, ed. Günther Reichenkron and Erich Haase (Berlin, 1956), pp. 116-119.

[5] See Pascal, *Design and Truth*, especially pp. 83 and 188. It should be noted that Pascal and Gusdorf primarily stress the "formal" limitations of autobiography; they do not wish to claim, finally, that autobiography *is* what Pascal terms "imaginative art."

[6] See Francis R. Hart, "Notes for an Anatomy of Modern Autobiography," *New Literary History* 1 (1970), especially pp. 490-491 and 500-506. A clear statement of the autobiographer's "restlessness" with respect to his autobiographical efforts is given by Michael G. Cooke, "Modern Black Autobiography in the Tradition," in *Roman-ticism: Vistas, Instances, Continuities*, ed. David Thorburn and Geoffrey Hartman (Ithaca, 1973), p. 259.

discrepancies between the life being signified and the mode of its signification can "[render] suspect," as Jean Starobinski says, "the content of the narrative, setting up a screen between the truth of the narrated past and the present of the narrative situation."[7]

But while some autobiographies seem to exhibit or evince "ironic" discrepancies such as Starobinski perceives (for example, Rousseau's *Confessions*), it is also true that in most autobiographies instances of tension between the act and object of signification are unequally distributed throughout the narrative: they are inconsistent with or inessential to the narrative as a whole. Moreover, though this conception manages to suspend the so-called "truth" import of autobiographies, it fails to argue for the full aesthetic accessibility of an autobiographical text. Being mentally closer to his past than the reader, the writer can best appreciate its anxious complication of his present narrative and vice versa; the reader can only "suspect" this temporal dialectic. Clearly, we can argue for autobiography as a genuine, imaginative enterprise only if we adopt the reader's a posteriori relation to the text and insist that the writer's references to his past are subordinate to (as though they were a mere contingent source of "life-images") a narrative essentially representing the writer's present self-identity as seen also in the light of his future.[8] Here the immediately accessible narrative *is* the autobiography; in other words, autobiography is the writer's de facto attempt to elucidate his present rather than his past.

Thus, Barrett John Mandel tells us in effect that it is the autobiographer's present that spawns the aforementioned drama of self-cognition, for no one can "talk about the present at all but . . . by distancing and fictionalizing it." Speaking as a would-be autobiographer, Mandel argues that his *present* creates his past "by inspiring meaningless data with interpretation, direction, suggestiveness—life. But as long as I live, my past is rooted in my present and springs to life with my present. . . . I cannot fully give my past to

[7] Jean Starobinski, "The Style of Autobiography," *Literary Style: A Symposium*, ed. Seymour Chatman (New York, 1971), p. 186. Cf. Erik H. Erikson, *Young Man Luther* (New York, 1962), p. 54.

[8] Gusdorf, "Conditions et limites," pp. 120-123, is also willing to see that the autobiographer's present consciousness of himself is incomplete since it is exposed toward his future. Also see Mandel, "The Autobiographer's Art," pp. 221 and 225, and Burton Pike, "Time in Autobiography," *Comparative Literature* 28 (1976): especially 327-328, and 337-339.

the page because it flows mysteriously out of the incomprehensible moods of the present. And as new moods come upon me, my past comes upon me differently."[9] This almost Coleridgean isolation of the writer's creative present at the time of writing allows us to view autobiography as a work, like works of poetic fiction, wholly and immediately accessible to readers. But note what we have done: in sacrificing the autobiographer's past to a secondary role vis-à-vis his "incomprehensible . . . present," *any* first-person narrative-of-a-life that necessarily seems to re-present the author's own mental experiences at the time of writing could be termed autobiographical and/or fictive.

Out of a need to justify or "apologize" for placing autobiography in the context of imaginative rather than what Frye would call "descriptive" modes of writing, we are led to accept James Olney's assertion that "autobiography and poetry are both definitions of the [writing] self at a moment and in a place."[10] But ironically, the genre-nominalism of such "apologies" must overlook the fact that allows us to theorize about autobiography in the first place: we have little difficulty recognizing and therefore reading autobiographies as opposed to works of fiction.[11] Second, in having to assume that the desideratum of both modes of writing devolves on the reader's self-effacing participation in the process, his becoming more or less coincident with the writing self as he reads the work, such "apologies" must overlook the fact that most formal autobiographies fail to pass the test of being intrinsic, purely self-referential—"literary"—events.[12] However secondary the role it plays in actual narrative execution, the factual basis of autobiographical references tends to generate texts relatively closed off from rather than wholly open to the muse who speaks in plurisignative tongues. That is why the critic intent on maintaining the aesthetic-intransitive experience of literary texts finds conventional autobiographies to be less appropriate paradigms than novelistic works like Frank Conroy's *Stop-time* (Mandel); or extended lyrical poems like T. S. Eliot's *Four Quartets* (Olney); or even separate es-

[9] Mandel, "Autobiography—Reflection Trained on Mystery," *Prairie Schooner* 46 (1972-1973): 327.

[10] James Olney, *Metaphors of Self: The Meaning of Autobiography* (Princeton, 1972), p. 44.

[11] See Norman Holland, *The Dynamics of Literary Response* (New York, 1968), p. 68, and Barbara Herrnstein Smith, "Poetry as Fiction," *New Literary History* 2 (1971): 259-281.

[12] See Olney, *Metaphors of Self*, especially pp. 30-50, 261-265, and 312-314.

says like Montaigne's that can be transformed by the holistic minded reader into a hypothetical narrative reflecting a discrete, cumulative, yet always present interrogation of the self who is, like a surrogate "everyman," the very narrative(s) we are in the process of reading.[13]

Nostalgic for the presentational powers of imaginative literature, then, and desiring to colonize autobiography in the name of literary art, the apologist for autobiography is apt to fictionalize the object about which he theorizes. He attenuates autobiography's explicit, formal claim to be a legitimate personal-historical document. He underestimates the truism that autobiographical references appear as subject to extrinsic verification (Pascal, p. 188), especially to the autobiographer's contemporaries; or that autobiographies, prone to the rhetorical justifications or ideological assertions of the writing self that specifically pertain to his cultural-historical (and not time-less) milieu, also tend to exclude the immediate participation of a noncontemporary audience. Most important, such an apologist fails to consider the high casualty rate his "literary" standard would effect if it were seriously used as a way to define and judge prima facie autobiographies.

Must we then settle for that compromising, commonplace conception that depicts autobiography as a formal mutation, a hybrid genre, a vague, unresolved mixture of "truth" about the autobiographer's life dyed into the colors of an ersatz, imaginative "design"? Or can we formulate autobiography as a unique phenomenon, definable neither as fiction nor nonfiction—not even a mixture of the two?

Although our recognition of autobiography as a formal genre historically precedes our attempts to explain its constitution, nothing prevents us from exploring the issue of how discrete acts of writing become identifiable as autobiographical to the writing self as he writes.[14] Adopting this perspective, we will soon realize how alienated, how verbally entropic, the autobiographical enterprise is. Unlike the apologist for autobiography, we will find that even in

[13] Olney hardly conceals this attitude throughout his work, but see ibid., especially pp. 79-88 and 299-316. Both Olney and Frye (p. 307) see Montaigne's work as "a confession made up of essays in which only the continuous narrative of the longer form is missing." Also cf. William L. Howarth, "Some Principles of Autobiography," *New Literary History* 5 (1974): especially 377.

[14] The paradox of genre and history is mentioned by René Wellek, "Genre Theory, the Lyric, and Erlebenis," in his *Discriminations* (New Haven, 1970), p. 252.

the heat of writing, the autobiographical enterprise occludes the writer's own continuity with the "I" being conveyed through his narrative performance.

Something of this alienation can be gleaned from thinking about marginally formal instances of autobiographical writing. Diary and journal entries, for example, do not simply signify their referents to the writer who wrote them and now reads them in another present; they also signify to him the absence of his past-present consciousness concerning their genesis, their original urgency or meaningfulness. Written by "another," in this case himself, the journal writer's previous thoughts can return to him with that Emersonian echo of alienated majesty. Such discontinuities or lesions of personal time also occur with specific memory-acts, even when these acts pertain to other memories. Thus, Proust notes that

> between the memory which brusquely returns to us and our present state, and no less between two memories of different years, places, hours, the distance is such that it alone, even without any specific originality, would make it impossible to compare one with the other. Yes: if, owing to the work of oblivion, the returning memory can throw no bridge, form no connecting link between itself and the present minute, if it remains in the context of its own place and date . . . for this reason it causes us suddenly to breathe a new air, an air which is new precisely because we have breathed it in the past.[15]

But Proust himself demonstrates that the writer of fiction casts just such a bridge between two times or that he seeks to find that "new air" of old memories—memories made literally new again by their introduction into the proleptic course of narrative. The fiction writer's intentional act, his "consciousness-of-his-memory" as he signifies it, makes his "actual" memories suitable for fiction by dissolving them into silhouette images, by slipping "often," in Kafka's words, into the setting of a radical "once" or the sheer contingency that one can ascribe to past events. The fiction writer thus effectively displaces the private "darkness on which the memory draws" and reflects the human tendency to universalize, to make public or representable images out of personal memories: "It was true that I had suffered successively for Gilberte, for Mme. de

[15] Marcel Proust, *The Past Recaptured*, trans. Andreas Mayor (New York, 1971), p. 132.

Guermantes, for Albertine. But successively I had also forgotten them, and only the love which I dedicated to different women had been lasting. The profanation of one of my memories by unknown readers was a crime that I myself committed before them" (p. 157).

A fictional text, then, is trained on its own present; it posits a total world composed of setting, characters, and action whose definitive representation is kept in narrative abeyance like the still, unravished bride of imagination. It invites us as readers to fill in the blanks, to supplement its world with our own experiences in order to become simultaneous with its temporality. No less than the writer, we also submit our memories, our pasts, to the "profanation" of the fictional world. In self-conscious fiction, in works like Beckett's *Malone Dies*, for example, we are even asked to assemble the narrative world (and often the narrative itself) that we are intent on imaginatively consuming but which we must endlessly "wait" for, thus prevented from entertaining even the illusion of preterite representation.[16]

Yet the autobiographer's intentional act aggravates the duality inherent in personal memory-acts. This duality goes beyond the epistemological dilemma previously discussed, for it neither precedes the verbal act nor results in the writer's immediate commitment to his narrative. Wanting to verbalize past events, one finds that they appear against a prelinguistic background, a gestalt of pastness, which is at once absent from these signifiable events and in contrast with the "present" orientation of the discursive intention.[17] Moreover, written discourse exacerbates the phenomenological dilemma created by verbal recollection. More than speaking, writing is what "explodes that darkness on which the memory draws." Writing exposes as arbitrary or merely contiguous the relation between the act of signification and the signified past, thus making possible the isolation of pastness vis-à-vis the verbal medium that permits the autobiographical project to be conceived in the first place. Not the omission of facts—this after all implies

[16] Käte Hamburger discusses this notion of poetry and fiction's atemporality, its sheer presence (but not "present"), throughout her *The Logic of Literature*, trans. Marilynn J. Rose (1957; reprint ed., Bloomington, 1973), especially pp. 45-46, 64-98, and 139-140.

[17] See Stephen A. Erickson, "Language and Meaning," pp. 39-57, and Robert R. Ehman, "William James and the Structure of Self," pp. 266-270, in *New Essays in Phenomenology*, ed. James M. Edie (Chicago, 1969). See also Brian Smith, *Memory* (New York, 1966), especially pp. 88-94 and 193-206.

that the past is a hypothetically recoverable totality—but the omission of the past as past stands beyond the pale of spoken recitations of one's life. Augustine's written confessions, for example, lie somewhere between his awareness of his own lacuna-ridden past and his awareness that language displaces this past whenever he speaks of it to others:

> With regard to the past, when this is reported correctly what is brought out from the memory is not the events themselves (these are already past) but words conceived from the images of those events. . . . My boyhood, for instance, which no longer exists, exists in time past, which no longer exists. But when I recollect the image of my boyhood and tell others about it [*cum eam recolo et narro*], I am looking at this image in time present.[18]

"Words" used in telling, while being two removes from the event indicated by "this image," do not provoke the "autobiographical" speaker to focus on their problematic, nonimmediate relation to the remembered event being signified.

Thus the speaker tends not to recognize that the "I" used in his speech act is, as Roland Barthes has said, "always new, even if it is repeated," despite the fact that his interlocutors suppose this "I" to be "a stable sign, product of a complete code whose contents are recurrent."[19] But in writing, this breach between an "always new" narrator and a "stable" one becomes imminent: "When a narrator [of a written text] recounts what has happened to him, the I who recounts is no longer the one that is recounted" (p. 162). Even this recounting "I," composed of what Barthes after Emile Benveniste calls "the instance of discourse," is not the self who writes as long as we take this self to be "an interiority constituted previous to and outside language" (p. 163). As a matter of fact, autobiography here would seem to be guilty of a Barthesian mode of "bad faith," for is not autobiography an attempt to signify the autobiographer's non-textual identity or "interiority"?

But in the previously cited quotation, Augustine not only sug-

---

[18] St. Augustine, *The Confessions*, trans. Rex Warner (New York, 1963), 11: 18. Cf. Eugene Vance, "Augustine's *Confessions* and the Grammar of Selfhood," *Genre* 6 (1973): 1-28.

[19] Roland Barthes, "To Write: An Intransitive Verb?" in *The Structuralists: From Marx to Levi-Strauss*, ed. Richard and Fernande De George (Garden City, 1972), p. 163.

gests but demonstrates—*by* his writing—the capacity of writing to isolate and transcend the way spoken self-references hypostatize images of his past as the events themselves. Writing thus bears metaverbal gifts: in the passage in question it allows Augustine to reflect on its own process of signification and to grasp the nonexistence or absence of his past in relation to both spoken and written self-references. More relevant for a Christian autobiographer, it allows him to "confess," to be a witness or (in the older sense of the word) a "confessor" to his brute "I was" and "I am" apart from what he can record verbally about his life.

The written text consequently functions as a point of meditative departure for Augustine. Desiring to be more and more aware of God's creation, Augustine also desires to interpret his own personal existence as an experienceable sign of this creation. By exposing the discrepancy between the past the autobiographer has lived and his "present" signification of it, autobiographical writing facilitates this interpretation insofar as it elicits a consciousness of self that transcends his "words" and is therefore imageless—just *there* in its absence and pastness. Or for example in Book XI of the *Confessions*, it is precisely through the meditative space afforded by writing that Augustine is enabled to focus on the disjunction between his experience of time as lived versus that experience as knowable. He then proceeds to use the resultant indeterminacy of these juxtaposed "experiences" as testimony to the continuing mystery of God's creation.

Similarly, the image of self propagated by the lexical "I" of his textual present becomes grounds for identifying his present as his own, a mystery to himself, through but finally beyond his discrete textual acts. Focused on himself, the "silence" of the written as compared with the spoken discourse serves as an immediate occasion to apprehend the silent or private identity of his own soul, especially since (as we have already observed) writing has the capacity to unloosen and disrupt the coitions of words, images, and events. Written words recognize their finite status: they essentially signify a higher signifier, the *logos* of human consciousness, which in turn signifies what cannot become signified, the eternal *Logos*. Thus, the words composing Augustine's *Confessions* are imitations, copies, or more precisely, intentional acts whose object (his consciousness of self as such) reduces them to exterior signs concealing (dialectically determined) silent or invisible confessions: "And I do not make my confessions by means of the words and sounds of the flesh, but with the words of the soul and the crying out of my thought which [Your] ear knows" (10:2).

While in Augustine's *Confessions*, ideology and autobiography complement each other, it seems evident from later examples of the genre that such complementarity is due as much to the indefinite intentionality of self induced by autobiographical writing as to the prescriptive demands, say, of Christianity. Thus, self-abnegation—the transcendence of self from an existence named and nameable by discourse—constitutes revelation for Augustine but is a source of anxiety and paranoia for a writer such as Rousseau. At the very least, such transcendence underscores the suicidal implications of the genre. But what we need to stress here is that the written autobiographical act—and not a prior cognitive or methodological dilemma—yields this potential self-abnegation, this divorce between the writing self and his textual rendition. There is no question of "bad faith" with the autobiographical act, only with the ensuing product that presents the writer as he writes with an empty or discursive "self," an "I" never his own because it makes present what remains past to him. It is as if he could communicate his life to others but never to himself: "There's no such thing as the impossibility of communication except in a single case: between me and myself."[20]

The autobiographer thus cannot assume (as can a writer of traditional or self-conscious fiction) that he can elide the gap between himself as he writes and the discursive "I" passing seriatim through any sustained piece of writing. And where spoken discourse minimizes this discontinuity, the ambiguous anonymity of the "I" in a written work radicalizes it and raises the issue of privacy, the pressure of sheer pastness, as imminently invading the autobiographer's necessary acts of recollection. To acknowledge such a pressure and yet to persist in the autobiographical project, the autobiographer must come to terms with a unique pronominal crux: how can he keep using the first-person pronoun, his sense of self-

---

[20] Eugene Ionesco, *Fragments of a Journal*, trans. Jean Stewart (New York, 1968), p. 74. If the medium of writing is essential to the identity of the autobiographical act, are we not forced to question the association of autobiography with cinematic narratives or those told to and scripted by an amanuensis? Autobiographical intention does not constitute autobiographical intentionality. For a further discussion of the semiological significance of the autobiographical "I" that I am about to query, see Michael Ryan, "Narcissus Autobiographer: *Marius the Epicurean*," *Journal of English Literary History* 43 (1976): especially 184–186.

reference, without its becoming in the course of writing something other than strictly his own self-referential sign—a de facto third-person pronoun?

To write autobiographically, then, one has no choice but to engage somehow, in some manner, in the "impersonating" effect of discourse, either to give in to it as Gertrude Stein does in *Everybody's Autobiography*, or to resist it openly as Henry Miller does in *Tropic of Cancer*. Autobiographical intentionality depends on just such diacritical retention of the "I." In this sense, Thoreau's famous assertion at the beginning of *Walden* lends itself to two contexts of interpretation: "In most books, the *I*, or first person, is omitted; in this it will be retained." Formally, this is "apology," an asserted justification of "egotism" or vanity to the self-effacing norms of conventional and literary writing. But phenomenologically it is a self-conscious insistence on the self-referentiality of his "I" made in the face of writing's law of gravity: namely, that writing about his own existence ironically entails a denial of this existence *as* his own and thus as a secure referential source for such writing.

Autobiographical writing thus entails a split intentionality: the "I" becoming a "he"; the writer's awareness of his life becoming private even as he brings it into the public domain and putatively makes it present through his act of writing. This split, peculiar to the autobiographical task, suggests that the project of writing about oneself to oneself is always at the beginning, is always propaedeutic in structure, and is therefore prone to an obsessive concern with method as well as a "stuttering," fragmented narrative appearance.[21] But there are ways to mitigate this split. One can try to suppress the consciousness of pastness; or one can "confess" it openly to oneself; or one can even extol it and emphasize the narcissism proposed by the autobiographical act. If a self-referential privacy defines the autobiographical act as such to the writing self, then how he deals with this self-privacy during the course of his writing also determines the mode of autobiographical statements and the resultant appearance of the "form."

Needless to say, any or all three types of mitigation may occur within particular autobiographical narratives, for with autobiography especially the part at once determines and undermines the

[21] Cf. Hart's quotation from Dillon Johnston's "The Integral Self in Post-Romantic Autobiography" (Ph.D. diss., University of Virginia, 1969) in his "Notes," p. 490.

whole. Despite the fact that the formal identity of a given autobiography tends to be unstable, however, let us transform these three into a typological spectrum, supposing that an autobiographical writer is apt to rely on one of them to the exclusion of the others. Thus in the first type, the memoir mode, the writer in effect tries to suppress his evocation of pastness by surrendering to the present-oriented and public currents of language and literary convention, notably to the way they conspire with the writer's specific historical situation and its ideological parameters of "self" to determine how one tends to represent oneself before contemporaries. The memoir-prone autobiographer uses language to declassify information about his life; he uses language to apprehend his own life as an intersubjective phenomenon. Discourse proffers the impression that his life is transparently accessible to others—to the readers immediately invoked as he writes—and he accedes to this impression in order to distract himself from the margins of pastness that his autobiographical act intentionally sets in motion. Thus, for example, an autobiographer's apostrophic appeal to an indefinite "posterity" not only serves to modify contemporary pressures affecting his act of self-representation, it also serves to defuse, for himself, the issue of pastness the autobiographical act itself brings up.[22] If this issue were pursued further, it could disrupt the project; it could desocialize or declassify, as he writes, whatever intersubjective sense of self the autobiographer has carried into his work.

The "secret" script of Pepys's diaries, for example, serves to secrete from himself his implicit identity as an alienated voyeur or private person in a bourgeois society. Excluding, as it were, this contemporary sense of self (for which nonsecret diaries would have sufficed), his private code "presents" or defines himself to himself before an imagined, unalienated audience "located" in some indefinite future where and when he will be only the self signified by his diaries. Like most diarists, Pepys believes in the magical power of language to banish now—in the present of his discourse—the blank waysides accruing to lived time. For this reason, he writes

---

[22] Wayne Shumaker, *English Autobiography: Its Emergence, Materials, and Forms* (Berkeley and Los Angeles, 1954), p. 35, sees but a formal problem in the fact that "[when an autobiographer] saw, he saw *things*: when he thought, he thought *thoughts*: and these things and thoughts may appear less intimately personal to his reader than to himself." Concerning references to "posterity" in autobiographical works, see *The Autobiography of Benjamin Franklin*, ed. Leonard W. Labaree et al. (New Haven, 1964), p. 43.

"posthumously": in and through a discursive present when his daily experiences, as if already in some future present, will have been saved from becoming irretrievably past.

But language used in this manner is given an overdetermined power of self-revision. The memoir-prone writer relies heavily on preestablished verbal conventions to neutralize, to accommodate self-convincingly, the pressure of a private past that his act intentionally brings up to him. Hence, the formal habits of autobiographies are often strategies to reinforce the line against phenomenological eruptions of private time. The famous res gestae format, for instance, effectively "public-izes" the writer's already public deeds; or it sets up a socially current, ideological framework that makes the writer's "interior" experiences—as with religious autobiographies and their depictions of sins, graces, conversions, and spiritual trials—seem fully accessible to himself as well as others. Similarly, the teleological pattern—the convention of treating one's life as a story—encourages the writer to use socioreligious quotients of success or failure in viewing his life as having a beginning, middle, and end.[23]

But the price of such usage can be telling. On the one hand, invoking the spell of intersubjective, verbal conventions, whose intersubjectivity is even underscored by the visual duration of written texts, outlaws the writer's conceiving the possibility of a radically private setting to his experiences. On the other hand, this possibility *becomes* possible as soon as the "I" is written down since now the writing self can "intend" this "I" as leaving behind in its wake references that alter the referents themselves; his signification of the past now can appear to himself *as* an act that conceals or, at the very least, somehow mediates this past.

When and if this possibility takes hold of the autobiographer, the second or "confessional" mode of autobiographical writing becomes a manifest part of the writer's performance of his textual project. In this borderline area between the first two modes, the autobiographical writer no longer fully entrusts his life to the present, organizing thrust of narrative or ideological conventions; rather, he intuits how his writing is a sketchy, arbitrary rendering of his life: "If Suetonius by any chance could have noted the method of this

---

[23] For the res gestae formulae in spiritual autobiographies, see Roger Sharrock's introduction to John Bunyan's *Grace Abounding to the Chief of Sinners* (Oxford, 1962), and also Paul Delany, *British Autobiography in the Seventeenth Century* (London, 1969), pp. 89-92.

chapter," Cardano writes near the beginning of his autobiography, "he might have added something to the advantage of his readers; for there is nothing . . . which may not in some manner be unified."[24] Whenever the autobiographer simply senses that his narrative "I" belongs to language, that it constitutes a "secondary revision" of his life, or that it is and can only be a mask of himself, he may still use this apperception of his act to filter out the pastness the act itself evokes; he may still present his references so as to be the accessible self, the anyone, that they signify. But any such declaration of independence from one's past would be self-conscious—it must be chosen continually—and hence tends to occur "here and there" rather than as a whole throughout the work. Short of aborting the autobiographical project itself, how else could it be? To identify with or certify an arbitrary rendition of oneself leads at one extreme to hagiography and at the other to a fictive suspension of the writer's distance from his written "I."

Dwelling in the present afforded by this memoir-confessional type of writing is thus bound to seem deliberate as well as tentative. For example, in his *Autobiography* Franklin employs writing as a technological medium that lets him "intend" his past as a repeatable, revisable text: "I should have no Objection to a Repetition of the same Life from its Beginning, only asking the Advantage Authors have in a second Edition to correct some Faults of the first" (p. 43). One could argue that the *Autobiography*, written, in fact, in moments of leisure, is an *act* of leisure strategically tied more to Franklin's present, his busy career as a revolutionary and diplomat, than to his past.[25] But there is sufficient reason to suppose that the casual, nondialectical prose of the work belies the easy givenness of his past. I would argue that his prose strives to turn past "faults" into mere "errata" because the former constitute indelible points of friction in Franklin's consciousness of his past. In this sense, even his famous effort at moral reformation, his "bold but arduous Project of arriving at moral Perfection" (p. 148), indicates his overdetermined equation of verbal prescription with consciousness of self. Franklin's "arduous Project" dovetails into his *Autobiography* as a whole since the latter too entails a project of self-trans-

[24] Jerome Cardan[o], *The Book of My Life*, trans. Jean Stoner (New York, 1930), p. 9.

[25] This is basically James Cox's view of Franklin's *Autobiography* in "Autobiography and America," pp. 256-262.

formation—of converting the private self into a wholly public one by means of language.

Yet the pull of the past is always a latent issue abrogating this autobiographical project. Specific memories that in "content" seem laden with affectivity are muffled by the momentum of his self-evidently emotionless prose:

> We both [Denham and himself] were taken ill. My Distemper was a Pleurisy, which very nearly carried me off: I suffered a good deal, gave up the Point in my own mind, and was rather disappointed when I found my Self recovering; regretting in some degree that I must now some time or other have all that disagreable work to do over again. I forget what his Distemper was. It held him a long time, and at length carried him off. He left me a small Legacy in a nuncupative Will . . . and he left me once more to the wide World. (p. 107)

Here particularly, Franklin's casual style belies the affective implication of his memory, namely that his present success was nearly nullified by this past event. Thus, he manages to convert this memory, which could signify for him the contingency of his origins and therefore of his present self-identity, into the present of serially disposed, oblique verbal images like "suffered *a good deal*," "*very nearly* gave up *the Point*," and "in *some degree*." By his defused language, by the ease with which he surrenders this incident to the linear momentum of his narrative, and by his rather cursory allusion to a teleological future ("left me once more to the wide World," that is, leading to his self-certain present) Franklin cancels his own latent "distemper" in recollecting a specific scene charged with social impotence and even a suicidal inclination. Language not only allows him to mitigate personal as well as social friction; as the arbiter of his own self-consciousness, it allows him to do so arbitrarily.[26]

With its concealment of the writing self's distance from his written "I" as it appears through the autobiographical act, Franklin's

---

[26] Franklin himself tells us that he disliked using language that "tends to create Opposition" (p. 65). But compare this attitude with the frequently cited description of his first trip to Philadelphia (pp. 70–75), where a memory laden with affectivity, signaled by the hectically detailed narrative, leads to his arbitrary and self-disarming justification of such details. Compare also Robert F. Sayre in *The Examined Self: Benjamin Franklin, Henry Adams, Henry James* (Princeton, 1964) pp. 19–21.

Autobiography shows us that the exemplary motif common to autobiographies is not simply reducible to a determinate ideology preceding the work. The exemplary or model "I" in autobiography ipso facto belongs to writing: it is an explicit "dummy" ego by which the autobiographer is kept aware of or acknowledges the discrepancy between his "life" and life. In more definitive cases of the confessional mode of writing, the autobiographer explicitly testifies or "confesses" to his own separation both from his written "I" as he writes and from the intersubjective imperatives incurred by this act of writing. St. Teresa openly confesses, for example, how the authority of the Church is submerging, as she writes, the actual appearance of her thus privately constituted experiences behind the verbal persona of her life: "I wish I had also been allowed to describe clearly and in full detail my grave sins and wicked life. . . . [But] I have been subjected to severe restrictions [by my confessors] in the matter."[27] Teresa's *Life* is being written, then, *as* a secondary revision, a public version, of a "life" being silently and conterminously traced in her mind. What would otherwise be a repressive dilemma, however, works in Teresa's favor here. The socioreligious prescriptions forcing her to write as a spiritual persona for lay and clerical members of the Church help her determine the privacy of her past and present existence, which she can then—again, privately—sacrifice to God, offering Him, in effect, the untouched because unsignified "virginity" of her being. Thus, toward the end of her *Life*, she willingly embraces her social isolation and, by analogy, chooses to exclude the socially discursive aspect of her written *Life*: "His Majesty [God] has put me in this little corner, where I live in such strict enclosure, and where I am so much like a dead thing that I once thought nobody would ever remember me again. But this has not been so to the extent I should like, as there are certain people to whom I am obliged to speak" (*Works*, 1:297-298). Encased within the intersubjective walls of language, her autobiography, like the cloister, paradoxically excludes her sense of others.

Teresa's withdrawal from life is also, then, a withdrawal from the public aspect of her *Life*. She converts the latter into a radically private prayer, a monological text, a secret expression of her own self, which she can do only by silently writing in reverse—toward

---

[27] St. Teresa, *The Life* in *The Complete Works of St. Teresa*, 3 vols., ed. and trans. E. Allison Peers (London, 1946), 1: 9.

herself alone—in order to experience what remains a project (not a realization) of religious self-abnegation. Teresa's Christian orientation, of course, invites her to use in a positive way the duality inherent in autobiographical intentionality. But in secular autobiographies such as *The Education of Henry Adams* where no single sanctioned ideology, religious or otherwise, immanently seems to circumscribe the autobiographical act, this duality results in an outright alienation from the text, in a fixation on the unresolved discrepancy between the way writing "public-izes" the autobiographer to others and the way it signifies himself to himself.

Thus Adams sees his *Education* as a "failure," an arbitrary document per se, reflecting neither his intersubjectively accessible life and times nor his own existence as he lived it to himself. On the one hand, he writes as an exemplary "he" caught within the teleological trappings of a narrative of "education"; yet he restricts the value and immediate availability of his work to a privileged audience that is already familiar with his life and times—and even to this audience, Adams defamiliarizes his persona by reducing it to a dumb "manikin" or an explicit, abstract, anonymous "he" subject to inexpressible "supersensual" forces. On the other hand, his own past appears to him through the gap pervading the middle of his life as he writes his "life." He literally leaves out his marital life from *The Education* not because it has little to do with the topic but because his wife's suicide permeates his recollections with inexpressible pastness, that is, it signifies his own immediate absence, his present discontinuity, from a life he nevertheless lived.[28] Unable to see himself as a representative persona for anyone and yet also unable to "intend" his own past except in the context of a dissipating gestalt, Adams writes an autobiographical work that is, to himself, thoroughly incomplete—an "education" that leads him out of the accountable into the unaccountable aspect of his past life.

[28] Howarth, "Some Principles of Autobiography," p. 369, does not question that Adams is one of those autobiographers who "carve public monuments out of their private lives. This didactic purpose . . . explains Adams's choice of 'Education' as a metaphor for his life." But in Adams's letters (the relevant ones of which have been appended to the Riverside Edition of *The Education of Henry Adams*, ed. Ernest Samuels [Boston, 1973]), Adams refers to his masochistic resistance to having his text made public ("I . . . send it out into the world only to be whipped," p. 510), and he alludes to its being no more than a failed experiment (p. 512). For Adams, *The Education* "at least served one purpose—that of educating *me*" (p. 511): distinctly a private rather than a public effect.

Significantly, like Teresa's *Life*, Adams's *Education* indicates that the locus of autobiographical "texts" is beyond the writing *through* the writing. Moreover, the confessional mode shows us that the autobiographer's split from his persona not only creates the possibility—for the writer, not the reader—of an alternative text to which the written version is but an oblique "prelude" or indecisive "failure," it also denominates the autobiographical act *as such* to the writing self. But here another problem presents itself: how can the autobiographer prevent the autobiographical act, with its call for textual disaffection, from inhibiting the actual execution of the autobiographical project as a whole?

Nothing plays more havoc with the continuity of autobiographical narrative than this dilemma. Given his separation from his persona, the autobiographer, in order simply to perform his task, must make his language refer to himself allegorically, must invert the public or "present" direction of discourse so that it will not seem at odds with the residual consciousness of self it itself exposes.[29] Yet it is precisely his own narrative activity that tempts him to forget his constitutive separation from the "I" of his discursive acts. To write autobiographically, to limit the presentational effect of his narrative on himself, the writer will often "jam" his narrative's totalizing unity (with its promise of an unselfconscious transcription of his life) by overdetermining its parts. For this reason as much as any other, a given autobiographical work tends to be a composite, an eclecticism, of distinct verbal moments. It tends to accrue discrete pockets of verbal irrelevancies such as casual or ironic self-references; compressed or abbreviated narratives within—and redundantly digressing from—the major narrative line; letters substantiating the factuality of the narrative's references, the former which thus "frame" the narrative so as to place its textual priority into question; journal and/or diary entries that in effect displace the narrative's present by evoking a past-present verbal act; and especially imaginative ramblings, digressions, "visions," reveries, unusual or drawn-out depictions of other persons—all "spots of time," in other words, that seem complete or sufficient by themselves.[30]

---

[29] Fredric Jameson defines allegory this way in *Marxism and Form: Twentieth-Century Dialectical Theories of Literature* (Princeton, 1971), pp. 71-72. See also Paul de Man, "The Rhetoric of Temporality," in *Interpretation: Theory and Practice*, ed. Charles S. Singleton (Baltimore, 1969), especially p. 197.

[30] An "exemplary" text in this regard is Thoreau's *A Week on the Concord and Merrimack Rivers*. Most of the works cited in this essay "use" at least several such types

Each and all of these allow the autobiographer to evade, at least temporarily, *his* displacement of himself through narrative and thus promote the monological appearance of his writing to himself.

Such eclecticism, no doubt, could be construed as simple mimetic strategy. We could take Rousseau at his word, for example, and view the shifting "styles" in his *Confessions* as ways to depict himself according to his past life: "I may omit or transpose facts, or make mistakes in dates; but I cannot go wrong about what I have felt, or about what my feelings have led me to do; and these are the chief subjects of my story."[31] More likely, however, these eccentric swerves from self-sustaining narrative compression indicate the autobiographer's anxiety over the way writing channels his existence into a progressive self-image not his own. Unlike the memoir mode where they serve as temporary substitutes for the perpetually inadequate self-image writing presents via autobiographical intentionality, and unlike the confessional mode where they signify a resigned or willing concession to the intersubjective limits imposed on self-expression, in various autobiographies of the narcissistic mode these eccentric verbal moments act as signs of vigilance, guarding the writer's consciousness of himself, his self-identity, from slipping into whatever norms of self-reference he is aware of, if only subliminally, at the time of writing. In this sense Rousseau's "mimetic" explanation for his stylistic pluralism in the *Confessions* should be weighed against his conscientious resistance to writing about himself according to the pressures and habits of those modes of self-representation with which he was familiar before writing his work. Thus he abjures the tempting but (to himself) self-distorting routes of apologetics, religious narratives of conversion, also "des histoires, des vies, des portraits, des caractères. . . . des romans ingenieux bâtis sur quelques actes extérieurs, sur quelques discours qui s'y rapportent, sur de subtile conjectures où l'Auteur cherche bien plus à briller lui-même qu'a trouver la vérité"—he even ab-

---

of verbal overdetermination. Even Augustine's latter discursive ruminations in his *Confessions*, especially on time, can be interpreted as a spiritual re-vision of his "life," a self-conscious repetition of his work's process or method. It merits speculation that what we might term the autobiographical "repetition compulsion," the actual rewriting or just going into greater detail and/or abstraction over previously signified material (cf. textual histories of autobiographies by Wordsworth, de Quincey, Nabokov, and Henry Miller), also suggests the incompleteness, the "prelude" appearance, of autobiographical works to their authors.

[31] Jean-Jacques Rousseau, *The Confessions*, trans. J. M. Cohen (Baltimore, 1954), bk. 7, p. 262.

jures the method of what to him are the quasi-autobiographical revelations of Montaigne, claiming it only gives us a "profile" of the person, an artistic portrait of Montaigne's self ensconced in the chiaroscuros of language.[32]

Rousseau thus envisions *his* autobiographical project as a first in literary history. It is a project in every sense of the word, for to write with an ever-vigilant awareness of the distinction between personal and person without at the same time being able to accommodate this gap, as Augustine could by trusting in the redemptive value of verbal silence, requires an endless and taxing alertness to the monistic wiles of discourse. Using stylistic shifts to alert him, using them as if they were diacritical signals of autobiographical intentionality per se, Rousseau can withdraw from the persona being propagated at any given point in his writing and conversely experience the verbal execution of his project as phenomenologically "truthful" to his own existence or as signifying his life to himself with a minimum of mediational interference. The honesty that Rousseau wants to claim for his *Confessions* belongs as much to his determination to be honest with the autobiographical act as to the referential accuracy or frankness of his revelations.

For Rousseau, then, to write autobiographically means to react consistently and aggressively against self-forgetfulness through the discursive act—against, in other words, fictional intentionality. It also means to assert and experience his self-identity by excluding the presence of others "who" appear immediately, as a presupposition of writing, and otherwise distract him from his task to *write* about his life as accessible to and hence assessable by himself alone: "I shall continue just the same faithfully to reveal what J. J. Rousseau was, did, and thought, without inquiring whether any others have thought like him" (*Confessions*, bk. 12, p. 595). Incessantly protesting too much, he sees himself always plotted against: the autobiographical act with its intrinsic suspicion of discourse's tendency to present the self before others and make present—mediate—a consequently evermore inviolable pastness, condenses the object of Rousseau's paranoia into the plot-ridden traps of language itself. Thus, even those reveries included in the *Confessions*,

---

[32] "Histories, lives, portraits, characters—all of them nothing but clever fictions built on some external acts, some relevant speeches, and some ingenious conjectures wherein the Author is much more concerned to shine himself than he is to discover the truth." From Rousseau, "Ébauches des *Confessions*," *Oeuvres complètes* (Paris, 1959), 1: 1149-1150. Translation by James Olney.

in spite of their seemingly random, relatively timeless and de-pressurized "this, then that happened" appearance, can be con-strued as aggressive responses to his anxiety over being "fixed" in a narrative as well as existential sense at the time of writing.[33] Feeling plotless himself, Rousseau *looks for* plots outside of himself so that he can view himself as, in every meaning of the pronoun, the *first* person of his life, an idiosyncratic "moi, moi seul" ("Ebauches," p. 1149) concealed between the lines of each narrative moment. In the invisible recesses of his text, Rousseau retains the "I-ness" of his written "I" the more he reveals it self-consciously before his antici-pated readers.

Rousseau finally disdains the possibility of balancing the dualistic appearance of persona and person; rather he "intends" himself mostly as an illicit person and crosses over into what I heuristically term the narcissistic mode of autobiographical writing. In this mode, the writing self tries to transform the self-privacy yielded by the autobiographical act into a sui generis principle of self-identity. It is here that we encounter the provocative association of autobi-ography and paranoia, an association touched upon by Freud in his psychobiographical revision of Schreber's *Memoirs of My Nervous Illness*.[34] I would like to suggest that a metafather image, mediated, yet not finally expressible by literal and figurative father images (cf. Franklin's Denham and Teresa's confessors), generates the writer's need to assert his self-identity repetitively or else as a once-and-for-all conversion.

Psychologically fatherless and ideologically (if not in his literal discourse) godless, Rousseau the autobiographer evokes through his autobiographical act the chaos of absence, the equivalent of Kafka's "that darkness on which the memory draws." He brings up his own discontinuous, arbitrary origins—his pastness—which

---

[33] In one of his "reveries" in *The Confessions*, Rousseau, rowing on the lake, expe-riences a joy he cannot "really understand . . . unless it was perhaps some secret self-congratulation at being thus out of the reach of the wicked" (bk. 12, p. 594). Because of their eccentric positioning with the main narrative, reveries included in *The Confessions* are not the lyrical "presents" that they apparently represent when recorded by themselves. See Christie Vance, "Rousseau's Autobiographical Ven-ture: A Process of Negation," *Genre* 6 (1973): 108-112. Rousseau's paranoiac sense of others observing his act of writing occurs explicitly in bk. 12, p. 574 of *The Con-fessions*.

[34] Sigmund Freud, "Psychoanalytic Notes Upon an Autobiographical Account of a Case of Paranoia," in *Three Case Histories*, ed. Philip Rieff (1963; reprint ed. New York, 1972), pp. 103-186.

he tries to convert into being the fatherlike source of himself. This is why he excludes "others" from the consciousness of his act, for "they" distract him, in effect, from the self-privacy elicited by his act. So too his confessions of masturbation and general sense of betrayal by others not only signify his aggressive exclusion of others, his rejection of "social" intercourse, sexual, discursive, and otherwise; they also mirror his autobiographical act in that they represent withdrawals of affect from others (in autobiographical terms, the "others" attached to discourse and the eventual destiny of his text) so as to effect a wholly private, autoeroticized consciousness of self. Similarly, in many Puritan autobiographies of the seventeenth century, the self-abasing "I," the writer's narrative inflation of himself as the "chief of sinners," serves as a ruse by which he "elects" idiosyncrasy—spiritual uniqueness—or strives to realize a definitive experience of his own spiritual identity beyond that of others and in the paranoid context (here evoked by the desire for a special self-conversion) of an arbitrary God.[35]

There is no question but that a spirit of anarchism is bred within the autobiographical act. Such anarchism is frequently mitigated in works where the writer blends the exclusive sense of self disclosed through his act into an exclusive, though collective, "minority" persona. A black autobiographer defining himself over and against what to him is an arbitrary yet pervasive system of white values— values synonymous with the very language he is writing in; Franklin casually asserting his American independence from the arbitrary tyranny of English political and cultural life by infiltrating the homonymic English language; homosexual autobiographies or autobiographical works like Whitman's or Genet's, written in the immediate context of heterosexual "others" and disguised as such for the writing self by their socially privy ("in drag") pronominal references—these are common examples of how the writing, revolutionary self, already predisposed to resist linguistic usage that is phenomenologically occupied by a given social establishment, coincides with and at least temporarily realizes the narcissistic trend

---

[35] See Delany, *British Autobiography*, p. 60. Teresa's inability to predict and sometimes to authenticate "visions" that are beyond her control, visited upon her by the unknowable discretions of God, may "explain" the self-abasements she propagates on herself in *The Life*. This feminine or passive relation to an arbitrary God is matched by Freud's observation in "Psychoanalytic Notes," p. 129, that Schreber's delusions took the form of his assuming "a feminine attitude towards God; he felt that he was God's wife."

of autobiographical intentionality. But it is also clear that any sustained autobiographical project, predicated as it is on the duality inherent in its intentional acts, inevitably tends to expose the writing self's distance from even his revolutionary persona, as in the case of *The Autobiography of Malcolm X*. Or else it leads to its own abandonment in fact if not in literal performance; for in repressing this incurred duality, the writer forfeits his textual performance as signifying *his own* self in favor of *a* self at once continuous with others and in accord with the idealism of an omniscient discourse.

The pull toward anarchic privacy, the consciousness of one's life as one's own exclusive of others in and through discourse, this is both the self-experiential signal and latent direction of autobiographical writing to the self as he writes: "This then? This is not a book, in the ordinary sense of the word. No, this is a prolonged insult, a gob of spit in the face of Art, a kick in the pants to God, Man, Destiny, Time, Love, Beauty . . . what you will."[36] The "this" here is the narcissistic extreme of autobiographical writing. It lasts, however, only as long as the autobiographical act is performed, for only in this act can the writer suspect the ethical, psychological, and linguistic priorities engaged, to employ a quotation from Wallace Stevens, "merely in living as and where we live." It is only in the autobiographical act that the writer can "intend" the narcissistic trend of self-consciousness as a truth as opposed to a fiction of consciousness. Continued beyond this act, the autobiographer's apperceived insulation from others can go the way of mysticism or its dubious double—the translation of the autobiographical act into the supreme fixation of solipsism.

Needless to say, the typologies of autobiographical writing that I have tried to elucidate in this essay refer to autobiography's "idea," to how we can think of its verbal identity from the imagined perspective of the writer immediately situated in the act of writing. For as actual readers—readers at a second remove from the text's genesis—we are fated to be voyeurs or "biographers" of the writer's "life." We ask the narrative to be primary; whether in content (his past) or in style (his present), the "life" necessarily appears as comparable or substantially continuous with the writer's life. But although we are bound to lend narrative totality to autobiographical significations, they intentionally reside, as I have tried to

[36] Henry Miller, *Tropic of Cancer* (1934; reprint ed., New York, 1961), p. 2.

argue, beyond the narrative they are set in, and as a consequence they tend to *de*totalize—make contingent—this narrative.

Thus, as A. M. Clark suggested in 1935, autobiographical narratives are apt to seem two dimensional, since the autobiographer conscientiously needs "to be aware of and then to resist the temptation to create" (p. 20). Clark's observation is accurate as long as one keeps in mind that the autobiographer's awareness of and resistance to narrative fixation are not reflective but intentional acts. Except as inoperative concepts, such awareness and resistance do not preexist the writing; rather, they signify the writer's immediate consciousness of the relation of his writing with the "time" of his time. The autobiographical act discloses a spontaneous, an unsought-for intentionality, a "calling" uncalled for that requires different responses from the writer at explicitly different intervals in the evolution of his text.

The nature of the autobiographical act thus precludes the possibility that the writer can deliberately adopt a persona behind which he conceals references to his own life. So-called "autobiographical fiction" and/or "incognito" autobiographies (Gusdorf, p. 121) are essentially quasi-autobiographical insofar as they presuppose the writer's having determined the privacy of his materials through a constantly prior "autobiographical" use of language—a prior as well as nonreflective mental-scriptural act. But even granting the possibility of such an act and of its unmediated textual transcription, here again we are reminded that the text the reader reads is at odds with the text the autobiographer writes. On the one hand, the "I" of written discourse can never in itself signify the writer's self-presence. In fact, according to Jacques Derrida, it signifies his absence from being present to himself, for the writer can declare "I am also 'alive' and certain about it" only "as something that comes over and above the appearance of the meaning."[37]

On the other hand, the autobiographer is separated from this "I" not only because of his absence from its present but also because of the potential unverifiability of his material or references vis-à-vis the presence of the reading "other" whom he "intends" as he writes. "The child," Emerson writes in one of his journal entries,

---

[37] Jacques Derrida, *Speech and Phenomena and Other Essays on Husserl's Theory of Signs*, trans. David B. Allison (Evanston, Ill., 1973), p. 96. On the writer's "private" relation to his use of language, see Roland Barthes, *Writing Degree Zero and Elements of Semiology*, trans. Annette Lavers and Colin Smith (Boston, 1967), pp. 10-18.

"is sincere, and the man when he is alone, *if he be not a writer* [my italics], but on the entrance of the second person hypocrisy begins."[38] We need not reduce his insight to a purely cognitive issue, namely that in writing about himself with the foreknowledge and immediate expectation that others will read it, the writer tends to put his best or worst face forward; or conversely, that the task of the autobiographer is a privileged matter since he alone was the eyewitness of his life, he was closest to it, he alone can verify the authenticity of his references. Emerson's entry suggests, rather, that discourse itself spontaneously bears the stamp of verifiability, for since the "reader" is implicitly continuous with all utterances, anything to which language *can* refer is already de facto verifiable. This truism, however, poses a special problem for the autobiographer. Whereas even in spoken memory-acts the listener is, in effect, presently witnessing and procreating the objects being signified with the speaker, in autobiographical acts this present "other" appears to the writer as having been absent from the objects being signified. In autobiographical writing the intuited "reader" is phenomenologically absent from the signified references—the writer himself thus cannot immediately apprehend the verifiability of his own references.

To mitigate his alienation from his own activity brought about by the intentionality of his absent readership, the autobiographer is likely to employ measures like the ones discussed in the previous section of this essay. In particular, this issue of the "absent reader" helps explain why autobiographers commonly resort to writing in terms of autobiography's version of a muse: an anticipated, intimate, familial or familiar reader or group of readers such as Franklin's son; Adams's close circle of friends (to whom *The Education* was first exclusively available); or Wordsworth's "Friend" addressed in *The Prelude*. Such invocation periodically serves to contain the severe objectification with which the split between the signifying memory and its signified referent presents the writing self.

But the fact remains that in no other discursive project does the "reader" so crucially aggravate the project's realization. Documented or not, biographical and historical materials are intersubjective through and through. Their intentional presupposition is that

[38] Ralph Waldo Emerson, *The Journals and Miscellaneous Notebooks of Ralph Waldo Emerson*, ed. William H. Gilman, Alfred R. Ferguson et al. (Cambridge, Mass., 1964), 4: 314.

others were or could have been present at their making. And biographical as well as historical narratives reinforce this presupposition by seeming to act as transparent relayers of information to "others" that in effect are already present at the time of writing, already underwriting, in other words, the verifiability of the references being made. Similarly, fictive (including poetic) writing projects its materials via a "reader" conterminous with its occurrence. These materials are thus constituted through "the instance of discourse" or as if they were immediately accessible and *imaginatively* verifiable to this apparitional yet inescapable "reader" that designates discourse as an explicit enterprise of communication. The imagined, even imaginary world of the writer of fiction is always a "sharable" proposition.[39]

But in autobiographical writing, materials seeming verifiable at first turn out to be unverifiable as they are written. Except by an act of will, which already implies a separation from his act of writing, the autobiographer cannot depend on the "others" of discourse to substantiate his references in a phenomenological sense. Writing raises the possibility that these "others" could have "existed" the writer's existence—and raises it as he writes. But in doing this, writing also estranges him from his signified referents—his "life"—an estrangement moreover that he alone is privy to as he writes since he is, quite literally, the only one who can *signify* his life to *himself*.

There is no escaping this vicious circle. As estranged, autobiographical referents tend to appear within a dreamlike setting to the writing self; and here, at least, autobiographical writing seems to resemble fictional more than biographical or other "factual" modes of discourse. But even this resemblance must be qualified. The autobiographer cannot refer to his life *as* a dream without losing the *autobiographical* consciousness of his "life"; he cannot efface himself through a dream-narrative except, again, by a willful act that denotes itself as such as he writes; nor can he fully commit himself to writing about writing's inability to signify his life as he tries, nevertheless, to do so, for this would entail conceding his discursive act

[39] E. D. Hirsch discusses this issue in his *Validity in Interpretation* (New Haven, 1967), especially in his first chapter and particularly pp. 14–19. Contrary to my position, Howarth argues for the reader's constitutive continuity with the autobiographical text in "Some Principles of Autobiography," especially pp. 366, 371, 373, 374, 379, 381. Also cf. Elizabeth W. Bruss, *Autobiographical Acts: The Changing Situation of a Literary Genre* (Baltimore, 1976), especially pp. 1–32.

to the consciousness of "others." Each of these tacks would essentially abort the autobiographical project itself, a project paradoxically structured on the "reader's" absence and hence predicated on the veto of all modes of imaginative intentionality.

We might say, then, that autobiography is neither fictive nor nonfictive, not even a mixture of the two. We might view it instead as a unique, self-defining mode of self-referential expression, one that allows, then inhibits, its ostensible project of self-representation, of converting oneself into the present promised by language. We might also say that its logical extreme would be the conception of a private language, although as we know from Wittgenstein no such thing exists. At this extreme, the autobiographer's life appears like a daydream that at first seems recordable, but then, when the attempt is made to record it, eludes the word. "All we communicate to others," says Bachelard concerning such attempts, "is an *orientation* towards what is secret without ever being able to tell the secret objectively."[40] Thus we might conceive of autobiographical writing as an endless prelude: a beginning without middle (the realm of fiction) or without end (the realm of history); a purely fragmentary, incomplete literary project, unable to be more than an arbitrary document like the one Wordsworth, in Book VII of his autobiographical poem, recalls having seen appended to the person of a blind beggar, signifying for all of its verbal brevity and plainness

> . . . the utmost we can know,
> Both of ourselves and of the universe.

[40] Gaston Bachelard, *The Poetics of Space*, trans. Maria Jolas (New York, 1964), p. 13.

Eye for I:
Making and Unmaking
Autobiography in Film

Elizabeth W. Bruss

It is only natural that most writing about autobiography should be concerned with its "appearance"—when and how it first emerged, its shifting forms and emphases over time, the miracle and paradox of its elasticity, its capacity to capture what is most individual about each writer while remaining recognizably the same activity for them all. But it is equally interesting, and perhaps more timely, to ponder its "disappearance." How does a genre like autobiography, a genre characterized by its durability and flexibility, disappear? Not, I would propose, all at once, in a flaming apocalypse. Not with a melodramatic bang, not even (necessarily) with a whimper, not with clear symptoms of internal decay, disaffection, or cynicism. The disappearance of a genre is both subtler and more gradual; it is not a change in one genre alone but a change of the total environment, especially in the relative strength of alternative modes of expression. An activity that was once central and pervasive continues to have its practitioners and its audience, but they are fewer and their interests are more specialized. Such a displacement may even now be underway for autobiography, as part of a larger displacement (a change in the dominant systems of communication) affecting our culture as a whole. If film and video do come to replace writing as our chief means of recording, informing, and entertaining, and if (as I hope to show) there is no real cinematic equivalent for autobiography, then the autobiographical act as we have known it for the past four hundred years could indeed become more and more recondite, and eventually extinct.

But there is more at stake than the loss of a single genre. First there is what the "intranslatability" of autobiography implies about language and film as semiotic institutions. All of the extant attempts at autobiographical film seem to run afoul of the same problems and end by becoming indistinguishable from biography, on the one hand, or expressionist cinema, on the other. The unity of subjectivity and subject matter—the implied identity of author, narrator, and protagonist on which classical autobiography depends—seems to be shattered by film; the autobiographical self decomposes, schisms, into almost mutually exclusive elements of the person filmed (entirely visible; recorded and projected) and the person filming (entirely hidden; behind the camera eye). Of course, this schism might be only a contingency, a failure peculiar to the group of filmmakers who happen to have made the effort. But when one considers how various these would-be cinematic autobiographers are—ranging from Cocteau to Woody Allen, from the documentary *Joyce at 34* to the hallucinatory *Chapaqua*—and notes how persistently, in spite of such variety, the same problems recur, coincidence hardly seems a satisfactory explanation. It must instead be something in the medium itself, something inherent in the organized set of practices that together constitute the institution we call cinema. The question then becomes what (conventionalized) understandings have been erected around the making and the viewing of films—assumptions embodied in the structure of participation associated with film and embedded in its very machinery—that interfere with the translation of autobiography from one medium to another. And what, in turn, is there in language to explain its peculiar fitness for autobiographical expression? The problems posed by autobiography thus show that the differences between the media are more than formal, that the most important distinction is not between images and sentences but between "signifying practices"—what these forms are organized to do, why they are so organized, and the consequences (social, epistemological, aesthetic) that these differences could have.[1]

---

[1] I borrow the phrase "signifying practice" from Julia Kristeva, although I extend it slightly to include pragmatic and social conventions as well as the logical principles that are Kristeva's chief concern. Cf. William F. Van Wert and Walter Mignolo, "Julia Kristeva: Cinematographic Semiotic Practice," *Sub-stance* 9 (1974): 97-114, and other arguments against purely formalistic criticism such as Marie-Christine Ques-

Film appears to lack the same capacity for self-observation and self-analysis that we associate with language and literature. We have grown so accustomed to this kind of introspective activity that it is difficult for us to appreciate its fragility—the peculiar combination of assumptions and prerogatives upon which it relies. What, then, are the implications for our notions of the self and of human subjectivity if the autobiographical "I" cannot survive the move from text to film intact—if there is no "eye" for "I"? We were apt to take autobiography, for all its local variations of design and reticence, as at least expressive of a common underlying reality—a self existing independently of any particular style of expression and logically prior to all literary genres and even to language itself. First, we have selfhood, a state of being with its own metaphysical necessity; and only then autobiography, a discourse that springs from that state of being and gives it voice. Such was the line of reasoning that Descartes used for his famous autobiographical demonstration of his own existence. The more radical the doubts expressed in the course of the *Meditations*, the more certain the being of the doubter. Descartes never considered whether the apparent order of cause and effect might not be reversed, whether the "doubter" might not be the product rather than the producer of the doubt. Perhaps subjectivity takes shape by and in its language rather than using language as a "vehicle" to express its own transcendental being.[2] This is certainly what the problematic status of autobiographical films seems to suggest. For if it is impossible to characterize and exhibit selfhood through film, then the apparent primacy of the self—its very existence—is called into question. The discourse that had seemed a mere reflection or instrument of the self becomes its foundation and sine qua non.

It has been said that "the world seen cinematically" is "the world seen without a self."[3] In the pages that follow I shall discuss why and how this is so. In addition I will try to suggest what this loss of self might ultimately mean. Indeed it need not be a loss at all but the beginning of a new enterprise that will transform classical autobi-

---

terbert, "Ideological Resistances Barring the Reading of Film as Text," *Enclitic* 1 (1977): 7-12, and Rosalind Coward, "Class, 'Culture,' and the Social Formation," *Screen* 18, no. 1 (1977): 75-105.

[2] Such is the brunt of the various assaults mounted in recent years on the Cartesian "cogito" by Foucault, Lacan, and Derrida—from whom I depart insofar as I treat the self as an arbitrary cultural fact but *not* a delusion.

[3] Frank D. McConnell, *The Spoken Seen* (Baltimore, 1975), p. 113.

ography into something else and will transform along with it the organization of experience that autobiography both presupposes and helps to maintain. As a new signifying practice, film is (potentially) capable of reordering our expectations and channeling our experience in new and fruitful ways, altering old ideas about the nature of character and individual identity. There is, of course, no guarantee that these possibilities will be exploited; in fact, a good deal of popular film seems to be devoted to salvaging familiar notions and reassuring us that they are still adequate for the way we live now. Nor are all the foreseeable consequences of this reordering of experience equally palatable. Instead of overcoming the old antagonisms between self and other, mind and matter, film might only exaggerate them, or fuel the tendency toward passive consumption and a sense of individual powerlessness that already threaten us. But it is premature to speak of possible effects until we have the causes more fully in view.

The problems of film autobiography are many. Several logically separate issues are involved—our notions of authorship, the difference between narrating (on the one hand) and perceiving or "focalizing" (on the other), the conventions of representational realism—issues that must be unraveled before one can understand the various ways in which cinematic autobiography can fail. The power of film to depict most aspects of character is indisputable, and it is clearly capable of rendering narrative sequence as well as language. It is not, then, the auto*biography* that is the source of the difficulties but the circumstances under which that *auto*biography is told. The generic "force" of autobiography and the leading features that have distinguished it throughout its history from other kinds of discourse are contextual rather than formal. There is no narrative sequence, no stipulated length, no metrical pattern, and no style that is unique to autobiography or sufficient to set it apart from biography or even fiction. To count as autobiography a text must have a certain implicit situation, a particular relationship to other texts and to the scene of its enactment. Three parameters define this situation and give classical autobiography its peculiar generic value:

Truth-value.   An autobiography purports to be consistent with other evidence; we are conventionally invited to compare it with other documents that describe the same events (to determine

its veracity) and with anything the author
may have said or written on other occasions
(to determine its sincerity).

Act-value.   Autobiography is a personal performance,
an action that exemplifies the character of the
agent responsible for that action and how it
is performed.

Identity-value.   In autobiography, the logically distinct roles
of author, narrator, and protagonist are con-
joined, with the same individual occupying a
position both in the context, the associated
"scene of writing," and within the text itself.[4]

The correlation of text to situation seems obvious enough, but it
might seem far more contrived were we not already so familiar
with the contextual implications that regularly accompany all our
uses of language.[5] As initiates to language as an institution, we are
already accustomed to the power of words to express propositions,
assert truths, imply beliefs, and encode subtle changes in the contexts that surround the production and the reception of sentences.
Above all else, we do not find it remarkable to expect that for every
utterance there must be a speaking subject, one and only one authorizing source who is responsible for what is said and done. Autobiography simply exploits more general conventions that apply
to language as a whole, especially the established structure of participation that defines the relevant roles of those who use language,
isolating certain key positions (for example, speaker, listener) and
stipulating the powers that they putatively possess. Equally important for autobiography is the fact that language practice commonly
allows the same individual who plays the role of speaker to serve as
his own referent as well. The English pronoun "I" is the extreme
example of this practice, simultaneously *indicating* the subject of the
act of speaking and *designating* the subject of the sentence that is
spoken. In this way "I" becomes both the potential bearer of qual-

---

[4] This version of my earlier work in *Autobiographical Acts: The Changing Situation
of a Literary Genre* (Baltimore, 1976), pp. 9-18, has been revised to stress that "action," "actor," and "identity" are defined by the rules of speaking and rely on such
conventions for their existence.

[5] Cf. J. L. Austin's *How to Do Things with Words* (New York, 1968) and J. R.
Searle's extension of that work in *Speech Acts* (Cambridge, 1969).

ities and the agent of actions that go beyond the immediate act of speaking, making the otherwise spectral and barely differentiated speaking subject into a more palpable and powerful figure.[6]

Thus the structure of autobiography, a story that is at once by and about the same individual, echoes and reinforces a structure already implicit in our language, a structure that is also (not accidentally) very like what we usually take to be the structure of self-consciousness itself: the capacity to know and simultaneously be that which one knows. Like the speaking subject, the classical epistemic subject is both the site or source of consciousness and the subject matter of its own reflections. Indeed to be a "self" at all seems to demand that one display the ability to embrace, take in, one's own attributes and activities—which is just the sort of display that language makes possible. This fundamental identification (or conflation) of two subjects—the speaking subject and the subject of the sentence—is, then, crucial to the autobiographical project, to the unity of observer and observed, the purported continuity of past and present, life and writing.[7]

Just how delicate this balance is becomes apparent when one turns from language to film, where the organizing assumptions are no longer the same. Film upsets each of the parameters—"truth-value," "act-value," and "identity-value"—that we commonly associate with the autobiographical act to such an extent that even deliberate attempts to re-create the genre in cinematic terms are subtly subverted. As a result, the autobiographical self begins to seem less like an independent being and more like an abstract "position" that appears when a number of key conventions converge—and vanishes when those conventional supports are removed.

"Truth-value" would seem to present the least difficulty for film, but even this is not quite what it was in language. Images lack the articulation and, hence, the selectivity of sentences; they do not distinguish between subjects and predicates in a way that allows us to

---

[6] Maureen O'Meara, "From Linguistics to Literature: The Un-time-liness of Tense," *Diacritics*, (Summer 1976), p. 68, has further words on this topic with respect to fiction in particular.

[7] The charge of conflation is Lacan's, for whom there is always a "disjunction of the *sujet de l'énoncé* and the *sujet de l'énonciation*. . . . The 'I' cannot lie on both planes at once," and hence "the simple identity of the subject" is a "constitutive impossibility." See Ben Brewster et al., "Comment on Julia Lesage, 'The Human Subject—You, He, or Me?'," *Screen* 16, no. 2 (1975): 83-90, and Jeffrey Mehlman's full-length study of French autobiographies from this perspective, *A Structural Study of Autobiography: Proust, Leiris, Sartre, Lévi-Strauss* (Ithaca, 1974).

discriminate between the essential and the accidental. Are we meant
to notice the gun in the felon's hand or the felon who is holding the
gun? For would-be autobiographers this means the possibility of
misplaced emphases and misunderstood claims. Does the figure on
the screen look like the artist as a young man or only behave like
him? Granted, because of the sequencing and editing of images in
film there is greater opportunity for control, but the dream of capturing on film the world in all its density and contingency is equally
compelling. Even the possibility of using language—an accompanying voice—to direct attention to certain aspects of a shot must
be weighed against the possibility of recording human sounds that
are more elusive, such as the inarticulate or polyphonic tonalities in
the sound track of an Altman film. To re-create the more selective
truth of the autobiographical text might, then, appear to diminish
the truthfulness that is peculiarly cinematic.

Over the years, film has managed to establish its own generic
distinction between fiction and fact. But the situation is complicated by a further subdivision of "truth-telling" films into those
that are unstaged, "documentary" recordings of actual events and
those that are openly staged representations of actual events (with
"staging" here embracing not only script and artificial *mise en scène*
but postproduction optical effects as well). In the first case, we read
the film as a mechanical imprint, its truth depending on the accuracy, completeness, and purity of that imprint in addition to its
freedom from contamination or human interference. In the second
case, we judge the film as a depiction rather than as evidence, and
we assess its truthfulness according to canons of resemblance.[8] Film
therefore introduces a new variable that autobiographers have not
heretofore had to contend with—the choice between staging "the
truth" or recording it directly. Language, of course, offers no way
of recording without also staging—a diary is no more a direct
transcription, in this sense, than the memoirs of a septuagenarian.
Thus, although the truth of both documentaries and staged reenactments depends on conventional assumptions (whether about
photographic processes or about resemblance), the need to choose
remains. It seems almost inevitable that the choice of staging over
recording will suggest a greater need for intervention or even provoke suspicions that the autobiographer "has something to hide."

[8] Umberto Eco, "On the Contribution of Film to Semiotics," *Quarterly Review of
Film Studies* 2, no. 1 (1977): 1-14.

Moreover veracity is only part of the "truth-value" we expect from autobiography, the other being its purported "sincerity." But under what conditions would we call a film sincere or say that it expresses a belief in, a commitment to, the images it presents—the very wording sounds bizarre. There are cases, to be sure, where a voice-over accompanying an image casts doubt on the status of that image, but without such accompaniment nothing in the shot itself—not even gross distortion or sudden loss of focus—could identify it unambiguously as an expression of doubt. Shots may differ in their pacing, composition, lighting, focus, and so forth, but these differences have no fixed significance, as is apparent from the way the meaning of slow motion changes from film to film according to the context in which it appears. There is no way of filming that conventionally counts as wishing or grieving in the same manner as ways of speaking count as the ritual expression of grief, or belief, or need—yet another barrier to the self-expression autobiography traditionally requires.

We read attitudes and judgments in prose because we accept language as a mode of action, by definition an attempt to effect some end and therefore presupposing (if only by the same definition) an agent with certain abilities and psychological capacities. But our sense of film as a mode of action is relatively weak; we have only a few vague notions of what films "do" beyond such broad categories as "report," "entertain," and "advertise." In fact, many film theorists have claimed that what is most characteristic about film is precisely its power to constrain human agency, to limit selectivity, temper will, and blunt authority. In André Bazin's famous words: "For the first time, between the originating object and its reproduction there intervenes only the instrumentality of a non-living agent. For the first time, an image of the world is formed automatically, without the creative intervention of man."[9] This is "the myth of total cinema," the effortless magic of something that happens of its own accord. But the automatic undoes the autobiographic; we no longer need to infer the presence of a human agent, nor by the same token can filmmakers entirely control what will be filmed. Thus ends the hope of either discovering or demonstrating personal capacities in the act of filming.

[9] "The Ontology of the Photographic Image," in *What is Cinema?*, trans. Hugh Gray (Berkeley, 1967), p. 13. Cf. also McConnell, *The Spoken Seen*; Alan Spiegel, *Fiction and the Camera Eye* (Charlottesville, 1976); and Stanley Cavell, *The World Viewed* (New York, 1971).

Film disrupts the "act-value" necessary for autobiography in other ways as well. Where the rules of language designate a single source, film has instead a disparate group of distinct roles and separate stages of production. Even if a single individual should manage to be scriptwriter and director, cameraman, set designer, light and sound technician, and editor to boot (and few "auteurs" in fact manage to do them all), the result would be a tour de force and not the old, unquestionable integrity of the speaking subject. An auteur is never quite the same thing as an "author" because of the changes film effects in the nature of authority itself. Authors must exercise their own capacities where auteurs are free to delegate; authors actually possess the abilities that auteurs need only oversee, and they fabricate what filmmakers may only need to find. This indirection and multiplicity, the fact that we cannot confidently treat everything in a film as the product of a single source or expect the same intimate involvement of the maker in the texture of what is finally made, leads to autobiographical paradox. In a film like *The Rose*, for example, the protagonist (whom we see actually giving birth) is partly responsible for making the film as well: she works as the sound technician, while her husband acts as the director of the film. Since autobiography is predicated on sole authorship, the classical definitions no longer seem to fit. Indeed, it is hard to know what to call such an effort, especially if we continue to accept the traditional division between self and other, and remain convinced that one and only one person can have authentic knowledge of that self (and, in turn, that my own self is the only self I can ever really know). It was paradox like this that two decades ago led Merleau-Ponty to declare that film confronts us with the need for a new epistemology and a renovated psychology:

> We must reject the prejudice which makes "inner realities" out of love, hate, or anger, leaving them accessible to one single witness: the person who feels them. . . . They [films] directly present to us that special way of being in the world, of dealing with things and other people, which we can see in the sign language of gestures and gaze and which clearly defines each person we know.[10]

Not every commentator is so sanguine, however, and many find in film not a new psychology but the end of psychology, a "dehu-

---

[10] "The Film and the New Psychology," *Sense and Non-sense*, trans. Hubert L. Dreyfus and Patricia Allen Dreyfus (Evanston, 1964), pp. 52, 58.

manized . . . depthless treatment . . . [that] not only distances seer and reader from the character but usually makes this character impervious to further inspection."[11] Whichever conclusion one draws, it is clear that film is—from the vantage point of the old, language based psychology—more or less "impersonal." There is no way of marking a personal attachment to one image rather than another, no way of discriminating a shot of the director from a shot of any other, indifferent individual. This is not a deficiency in the medium but the consequence of longstanding practices of representational realism, which allow no distinctive position for the "I" of the depictor as opposed to the "You" of the spectator—the realistic illusion thus depending on conflating these points of view and making them appear identical. Moreover, representation requires that the vantage point be situated "out of frame," rendered as unobtrusive as possible, a necessary blind spot that might otherwise destroy the seeming self-sufficiency of the view.[12] To the extent that the filmmaker accepts the conventions of pictorial realism (and it is these conventions that underlie the "truth-value" of film), he must avoid unusual or unexpected points of observation that might not be immediately accessible to the "average viewer"—avoid anything, in fact, that betrays the work of filming and indicates that it exceeds the mere passive reception of images (or sounds). Bazin's innocent formula—"between the *originating* object and its reproduction there intervenes only the instrumentality of a non-living agent"—gives it all away. The epistemology of representation that film adopts and extends to its logical limit is the epistemology of spectatorship—the object originates what the perceiving subject only absorbs and thereafter tries to copy. The camera perfects this process by making the copying automatic—free from the fallibility of human inattention, beyond the distorting intervention of human artifice that cannot compete with the original and, since it involves effort, challenges the impression that the perceiver merely *re*produces what the object itself produces.

Of course, there are films that flaunt their "infidelity" through the opulence of their staging and cinematic effects, repudiating the conventional passivity of representation. Yet so powerful is the myth of total cinema, the ideal of automatic reproduction, that to be distinctive a filmmaker must be exceptional, a violator of norms. We assume that each text has its author, but we credit the

---

[11] Spiegel, *Fiction and the Camera Eye*, p. 146.
[12] Jean-Louis Comolli, "Le passé filmé," *Cahiers du Cinéma* 277 (1977): 13.

existence of an auteur only when there is something odd, exceptional, idiosyncratic in the composition—for much the same reason
that the so-called "subjective shots" in film (which send us scurry-
ing in search of a particular sensibility to whom we can attribute
them) are those that are blurred, or slowed, or oddly angled.[13] If
cinema is "personal" only when it is somehow "private" or "ab-
normal," only when something disrupts the representational illusion and prevents the audience from automatically assuming the
spectator's position, then it is clear why film has so much difficulty
in re-creating the balance autobiography requires. For the autobiographical act must be at once expressive and descriptive; the two
are not mutually exclusive in language where truth is acknowledged to be a construction (an assertion that the speaker makes)
rather than a reflection. Thus we do not immediately assume that
statements delivered *in propria persona* must be distorted or vague or
unverifiable, whereas in film expressive and descriptive shots seem
almost mutually exclusive. It is surreal and stylized cinema like
Cocteau's *Testament* that is called "personal." But if so, then the
more a film succeeds as an expression of the autobiographer's personal vision, the less it can claim to be an undistorted record or representation of that person.

Moreover, even at their most extreme, it is doubtful that the effects of shooting, editing, and staging are capable of expressing
what we conventionally call "personality" to the degree that language can. The "subjective camera" can exploit proximity, angle,
focus, and mobility to make its presence felt, but these are poor
substitutes for the array of modal qualifiers and performatives that
define the speaker's subjective position vis à vis his subject matter.
What students of literature usually refer to as "point of view" is
rarely limited to geometry or strictly visual information. Indeed
Mieke Bal has recently proposed a separate category, a "focalizer"
as distinct from the "narrator," to make the different qualities of
these vantage points more clear.[14] The need for such a category is
especially apparent in assessing those films that attempt to re-create
a first-person narrator, such as the notorious *The Lady in the Lake*.
The film adopted the hero's point of view quite literally—director-
star Robert Montgomery wearing a camera strapped to his chest

[13] According to Christian Metz, "The Imaginary Signifier," *Screen* 16, no. 2
(1975): 56, "The uncommon angle makes us more aware of what we had merely
forgotten. . . . The ordinary framings are finally felt to be non-framings."
[14] Mieke Bal, "Narration et focalisation," *Poétique* 29 (1977): 107-127.

throughout the filming—but the effect was not at all what he had hoped. As George Wilson describes it:

> The movie gives one the impression that there is a camera by the name of "Philip Marlowe" stumbling around Los Angeles passing itself off as the well-known human being of the same name. We do not (cannot?) naturally see the moving camera as corresponding to a continuous re-orientation in space of the visual field, and . . . we don't see a cut, even within a scene, as representing a shift in a person's visual attention. . . . There may be a sense in which film delivers a series of views of a world, but it is only in restricted circumstances that these will be *someone's views*.[15]

Given the cinematic conventions outlined above, we are not likely to seek a "focalizer" for what appears on the screen (that is, ascribe it to a particular observer) unless there are exceptional reasons for doing so. And even when we do, there is little in the shot itself to characterize the focalizer; usually we must refer to prior events and images to tell who is viewing and the motive and manner of his view.[16] Since the powers of the perceiving subject are fewer and weaker than those of the speaking subject, the first-person focalizer lacks the distinctive attributes and behavior that we expect of the autobiographical first-person, even when we are aware of some intervening presence.

Another and final factor that makes the cinematic subject seem so much more shadowy than the speaking subject is the total absence of "identity-value" in film. In speaking "I" merge easily, almost inextricably, with another "I" whose character and adventures I am claiming as my own. But the spectator in film is always out of frame, creating an impassible barrier between the person seeing and the person seen. To merge them into a single figure would be equivalent to admitting the possibility of being in two places at the same time—a clear violation of governing geometric and optical codes. The trick comes off in language where the position of the speaker is already marked and the "frame" of the speech act offi-

---

[15] "Film, Perception, and Point of View," *Modern Language Notes* 91, no. 5 (1976): 1042. See also Metz's treatment of the subject camera in "Current Problems of Film Theory," *Screen* 14, nos. 1 and 2 (1973): 47, 69.

[16] See Edward Branigan, "Formal Presentation of the Point of View Shot," *Screen* 16, no. 3 (1975): 54-64, and Nick Browne, "The Spectator-in-the-Text," *Film Quarterly* 39, no. 2 (1975-1976): 26-44.

cially recognized. More important is the fact that the mode of existence that the speaker putatively shares with the figure he speaks about need not be temporal or spatial. Language tolerates more difference in identity and affords more grounds for saying that separate instances are "the same"—perhaps the only grounds in some cases, such as the case of the otherwise impalpable, unobservable but not unspeakable sense of a persisting "self."

The impersonality of the cinematic eye, its lack of density and individuation, its relative passivity and the eternal separation of the seer from the seen—all these create the impression of a subjectivity that is "too pure" for autobiography. As Christian Metz explains:

> The perceived is entirely on the side of the object, and there is no longer any equivalent of the own image, of that unique mix of perceived and subject (of other and I). . . . it is always the other who is on the screen; as for me, I am there to look at him. I take no part in the perceived, on the contrary, I am the *all-perceiving*. . . . the spectator . . . [is] a pure act of perception (as wakefulness, alertness): as condition of possibility of the perceived and hence as a kind of transcendental subject, anterior to every *there is*.[17]

The perceiver can never hope to catch a glimpse of himself; the figure that he sees before him on the screen cannot be his own, for he is somewhere else watching it. Like frames around a picture, screens are simply the concrete manifestation of a barrier between the site of the perceptual stimulus and the site of the response; their presence underscores the cinematic lesson that objectivity ends where subjectivity begins. Language has no such absolute dichotomy—neither uncontaminated objectivity nor pure subjectivity. In reading autobiography, we accept this from the start and know that we will get no more than a description filtered through the speaker's subjectivity. But film makes us impatient for a direct transcription—an actual imprint of the person, unmediated and "uncreated." Yet at the same time, it ironically forbids that the same person can be both the figure on the screen and the one whose consciousness is registering that figure.

There are still cases, to be sure, where a single auteur is recognized as the creator of the film and yet appears "in person" in the film. This would preserve the proprieties of classical autobiog-

---

[17] Metz, "The Imaginary Signifier," pp. 49-51.

raphy, were it not for a latent inconsistency. We are usually willing to allow that someone could first plan a shot and then edit the results, but when that same person passes into view, purporting to give his whole person over to "the side of the object," there comes a flash of vertigo, an eerie instant when "no one is in charge" and we sense that a rootless, inhuman power of vision is wandering the world—"les trajets d'un regard sans nom, sans personne."[18] At this juncture as at perhaps no other all our traditional verbal humanism temporarily breaks down and we are forced to acknowledge that this cinematic subjectivity belongs, properly, to no one: "Personnages, acteurs, spectateurs, opérateur et réalisateur y sont impliqués, de diverses façons, mais ce n'est proprement celui d'aucun: il manque à chacun."[19]

It should now come as no surprise that turning to particular films we find a tendency for them to fall into two opposing groups—those that stress the person filmed and those that stress the person filming—replicating the split between the "all-perceived" and the "all-perceiving." The problem for the first group of films, as I suggested at the outset, is how to indicate that the life we see is an act of self-perception, an autobiography and not just a biography. For the second group, the problem is how to make the film express the personality of a particular perceiver without at the same time allowing it to collapse in the opposite direction, into abstract expressionism, fantasy, or surrealism. A look at individual experiments will illustrate how great the dilemmas faced by aspiring cinematic autobiographers actually are.

First come those films where autobiography almost merges with biography or even realistic fiction: Gordon Park's *The Learning Tree*, for example, or Nadine Marquand Trintignant's *Ça n'arrive qu'aux autres*. Neither of these staged productions with their professional casts and their polished but "unmarked" style would immediately strike us as personal reminiscence. It is only after we have learned in some other way that the events the films depict are very like events in the lives of the directors themselves that we begin to speak of autobiography. More than the absence of marked eccentricities of style, however, it is the way these films adhere to the

[18] P. Bonitzer, "Les deux regards," *Cahiers du Cinéma* 275 (1977): 41.

[19] "Characters, actors, spectators, cameraman, and director are in various ways involved in it, but it doesn't properly belong to any one of them: each somehow falls short" (ibid.).

so-called "tutor code of classical cinema" that makes them so difficult to recognize as personal accounts.[20] This "sutured" cinema, with its seamless and always logical transitions, its camera work and editing scrupulously subordinate to the progression of the plot, deliberately effaces the act of observation and makes the story seem to tell itself. Far from presenting self-images, then, such cinematic practices seem designed to disown images, to make the audience forget the camera and even their own intrusive glance.

But it is equally possible that a more marked style, where open framing and rhythm no longer conceal the work of the camera and the editor, will still fail to communicate that a film is autobiographical. Truffaut's *The 400 Blows* is proof of this, although Truffaut also took certain steps of his own to "estrange" his represented self behind another name and allowed the already ambiguous figure of "Antoine Doinel" to stray even further from his own life in succeeding films. (Thus, though Jean-Pierre Léaud literally grew up in the role of Doinel, he has ultimately come to represent not Truffaut but the spirit of the *Nouvelle Vague*, making allusive appearances as such in films by Godard and Bertolucci.) One could, of course, learn a great deal about how an autobiographer sees or wishes to see himself from the actor he chooses to embody his self-image— provided that one can be sure about the generic status of the film and certain too of *whose* autobiography it is and how much control he had over the casting. None of these doubts attend us when we read autobiographies, nor do writers have to contend with "self-images" who have life histories of their own, who age and reappear in different roles, and even add their own, independent interpretation to the self they body forth. Then too, the rules of similitude being what they are, we can never know precisely the degree or kind of resemblance we are asked to see—does it extend to Léaud's physique, his particular physiognomy, his very gestures and tone of voice? A writer who ventures into self-description can be far more discriminating and many autobiographers never refer to their physical appearance at all. Unlike the cinematic eye that becomes diffuse and indistinct without an accompanying image, the "I" of prose can act, think, and even love without it. Indeed to dwell on one's own appearance in a book has a ludicrous effect, a hint of nar-

[20] Daniel Dayan, "The Tutor-Code of Classical Cinema," *Film Quarterly* 28, no. 1 (1974).

cissism, even if it is the body-image (as the French suggest) to which we owe our first presentiment of an integrated ego.[21]

No matter how much attention the camera lavishes on Léaud it is not this in itself that brings *The 400 Blows* so close to autobiography but the fact that Antoine Doinel functions as a focalizer as well as a focus. Doinel is, in fact, the only figure whose glances the camera regularly follows, to the extent of occasionally imitating the low-angle perspective of a child. Much of the pathos of the film derives from this, the demonstrated inability of others, particularly adults, to see what and how the child sees, and his own inability to communicate his perceptions in a language they will understand. Yet as the famous freeze-frame that concludes the film makes clear, Doinel is ultimately more seen than seeing, caught within a power of vision that cannot be his own, that even robs him in the end of his power of movement. He is left standing inert before a transfixed gaze that struggles to preserve him from his fate, preferring to embalm him rather than allow something to befall him that the gazer evidently cannot bear to watch. We could ascribe this euthanasiac glance to Truffaut himself were we not already so deeply implicated in it, experiencing it as the projection of our own troubled regard for the child. Our interest in the ending of *The 400 Blows* is not a product of our curiosity about Truffaut's idiosyncratic perspective or his private attachment to the child that he once was. It is because the film's autobiographic claims are so tenuous that we feel free to claim as our own the position of the perceiving subject.

Another group of films replace the focalizer with a narrator—a disembodied voice—rather than the image of a character to accompany the shots as they unfold. The result approximates first-person narration far more closely, making what we see someone's vision of the world and at the same time filtering it through all those parameters peculiar to language—tense, modality, mood—that give an otherwise neutral image the quality of a memory, a supposition, an expression of desire. But interestingly, we are not willing to call a film autobiographical on the basis of the narrating voice alone. In *Antonia: A Portrait of the Woman*, we hear the protagonist's voice describing scenes from her own past, yet the fact that she did not control the shooting or the editing of these scenes makes them part

---

[21] Jean Laplanche, *Life and Death in Psychoanalysis*, trans. Jeffrey Mehlman (Baltimore, 1976), develops the work of Freud and Lacan on the introjection of the ego (pp. 80-84).

of a documentary life, an unstaged portrait but not a self-portrait. There are also films where the voice does belong to a member of the crew, as in *Phantom India* where Louis Malle's own commentary penetrates the exotic footage until India, like Levi-Strauss's sad tropics, seems almost to become the phantasm of the explorer's mind. It is tempting to construe this commentary as somehow responsible for what we see, but logically we know this cannot be the case. What we hear issues from within the film, just another part of the cinematic record. As with the camera, so too with the microphone; the voice comes to us automatically with no way of knowing who transcribed it and no necessary link between the one who speaks and the one who then records. Thus there still remains the stubborn impersonality of the machinery itself and a process of recording whose presumed fidelity depends on that impersonality.

The same misgivings must attend those more ambitious efforts to put the autobiographer himself on film, to place him bodily before the camera and record his every word and mannerism. These may range from staged reenactments to *cinéma verité* and involve various levels and kinds of collaboration. In *Chapaqua*, the writer, Conrad Rooks, also stars in the evocation of his own drug addiction and subsequent withdrawal, but the direction is by another hand; in *Joyce at 34*, the protagonist is the codirector of a film that evolves without a prior script. An especially interesting example of the perplexities autobiographical film can provoke is Kenneth Anger's *Fireworks*. Anger writes, directs, and plays the principal role in a story set in his own home and concerned with his own confessed homosexuality. Yet the particular events the film depicts are entirely fictitious, albeit therapeutic—"imaginary displays offer temporary relief," as a headnote to the film explains. The encounter with an ideal lover never really happened, and many of the film's striking optical effects (a Roman candle bursting from an open fly, to take one familiar image) are blatantly staged. The mixture of real bodies and artificial members, actual settings and imaginary events, literal desires with figurative fulfillments is dizzying and badly skews our usual assumptions about the self-evidence of visual information and the coherence of the visible person. In writing, the appearance, character, and identity of the person are normally indivisible, if not completely isomorphic. Even in theater, the dichotomy of appearance and character as opposed to actual identity is still relatively clear. But film separates them all, giving us actual ("unretouched") appearances in the role of unreal characters—the distinctive "individuality" of a star apart from his individual identity.[22] Hence the complexity of *Fireworks*, a film in which Anger actually appears but not in his own character, where he impersonates his own person accomplishing what he himself cannot.

If there is a single filmmaker whose work best summarizes the problematic character of autobiographical film, it is Federico Fellini. Few commercial directors have been more persistently autobiographical and none more resourceful in trying to translate the classical formula into cinematic terms. On closer inspection, however, one sees not uniformity but a series of shifting approximations that alternate (as one might expect) between an investment in the person before the camera and the personal qualities of the filming itself. Fellini's oeuvre thus could almost serve as an anthology of all the different strategies an aspiring autobiography might employ. There is the staged reminiscence and the dramatized self of *Amarcord*, the first-person focalizer of *8 1/2*, the unseen narrator at the opening of *The Clowns*, and the personal appearances of the director himself later in the same film, as well as in *Roma* and the *Director's Notebook*. In addition, there are those extravagant "signed creations"—*Fellini-Satyricon* and *Fellini-Casanova*—where we witness the imperial staging of personal fantasies against the background of already established works, the better to display the workings of his own imagination. Apparently the constraints of autobiographical truth are too great to permit the fullest exhibition of Fellini's subjectivity; the recollections in *Amarcord* are filmed with far less of the personal whim one finds in *Casanova*, and the films where Fellini appears "in person" are always those where the shooting and montage are most "realistic." Fellini's own assessment of the generic status of his work is equally inconsistent—"I am my own still-life."/"I am a film."/"Everything and nothing in my work is autobiographical."[23]

This indecisiveness is half playful and half a response to some permanent ambiguities in autobiographical film itself. Typical of this are the arguments over whether *8 1/2* should be taken as an autobiography or not. It is not that the film fails to render "inner life" convincingly or falls hopelessly short of the first-person narration necessary for autobiography. Indeed it is a triumph of sustained

[22] See Cavell's discussion in *The World Viewed*, pp. 36–37.

[23] *Fellini on Fellini*, ed. Anna Keel and Christian Stritch, trans. Isabel Quigley (New York, 1976), Preface.

focalization and proof of the depths that it can achieve. It is instructive to compare its famous silent opening in a dream *ex nihilo* with the more literal minded use of the subjective camera in *Lady in the Lake*. Why does the opening of *8 1/2* immediately compel us to see it as "someone's view," when we have as yet to encounter an eligible viewer? In part it is simply its obscurity, the disorientation we feel in the absence of an establishing shot to tell us where these cars are going or why the traffic has stalled, the nervous motion of the camera itself, the milk and murk of the lighting, the exaggerated pettiness of the occupants of the other cars surrounding the focal car, and, of course, the ultimate violation of the laws of gravity when the figure in the focal car ascends and flies from the tunnel. We are plunged into a mystery and reach out for an explanation—as we would not if the scene maintained the decorums of cinematic realism: stable camera, lighting wholly subservient to the demands of recognition, clearly delineated planes of foreground and background that correspond to the logic of the narrative.[24] To restore our own equilibrium we must reduce the sequence to a dream and then seek out the dreamer whose subjective distortions are responsible for what we see.

An additional clue to the mediated nature of the opening is the odd way the figure in the focal car is filmed. This we quickly grasp must be the embodiment, the self-image, of the dreamer himself, a focalizer whom we both do and do not see, since the camera will not confront him directly, face to face. Thus there is a margin of invisibility reserved—a blind spot that remains irrevocably on the side of the viewer and cannot enter the field of vision. This is perhaps as close as the "eye" of filming can ever come to the "I" of writing, a "shifter" (as Jespersen called the personal pronouns) that is seemingly both inside and outside the frame at once, both the subject and the object of perception. The film preserves this facelessness until Guido is fully awake and stands before his bathroom mirror, where the vague silhouette and the jumble of limbs that we have previously seen at last compose themselves into an integrated reflection, and Guido's own anxious gaze sees in the glass the coherent image of a middle-aged man. The reenactment of the *stade du miroir* is brilliant but inconclusive insofar as settling the question of whether the film is truly autobiographical. It is Guido,

---

[24] Raymond Williams, "A Lecture on Realism," *Screen* 18, no. 1 (1977): 61-74.

after all, and not Fellini whose face emerges in the mirror, and it is as much our gaze as Fellini's own that watches this take place.

Guido may well be a director of Fellini's age and very much in Fellini's mold, his childhood memories and his adult crises may overlap at every point with Fellini's own, and his ninth (unmade) film may even coincide with Fellini's ninth success so perfectly that the resulting film is somewhere in between, a teasing eight and one-half. The resemblance may be remarkable, but resemblance in itself is not enough. It will never add up to autobiographical identity (which is what makes it resemblance in the first place) nor establish beyond contention that Guido is Fellini's own image. No matter how narrow it becomes, the gap between the person filming and the person filmed remains.

Why should the organizing assumptions be so different in language and in film? Why should self-reference and even selfhood be so ingrained in one set of practices and not the other? The origins of language and even writing are too remote to do more than speculate, but the rise of film is relatively recent. Here one can say something about the conditions that surround the emergence of a signifying practice and about how that practice, in turn, becomes intelligible—"thinkable" and "experienciable"—for those who use it. By examining the ideological milieu and historical moment that gave rise to film, we can better understand why it should be so resistant to autobiography.

The first sustained impetus for film came from the natural sciences (although there were also certain toys—projection devices and instruments to make still images appear to move—that also anticipated film, and the potential for using film to produce sheer spectacle and optical illusions rather than more accurate visual records was quickly recognized). As scientific documents, films were closely associated with contemporary positivist assumptions about the nature of knowledge, the most reliable evidence, and the most valid methods of proof. The only good evidence was "objective"—that is, independent of any particular observer. Whatever could not be reproduced at another time, in another place, for another observer was untestable and therefore either suspect or irrelevant. The "subjective" side of knowledge was confined to widely shared responses, hence to those perceptual judgments that unlike value judgments or emotional reactions no one would be inclined to dispute. Ideally, the perceiving subjects were therefore interchangeable.

At its most extreme, in the late nineteenth and early twentieth centuries (coinciding with the rise of cinema), this was a science that rejected theory and put all its faith in methodology, impatient to reduce discovery to a system and limiting the role of the "discoverer" as far as possible to a series of prescribed, repetitive motions. Later scientific (and cinematic) practices have no doubt called much of this program into question, particularly its faith in unmediated observation. In retrospect, the strictures of positivism may even seem defensive, a response to growing uncertainties about what was "real" or knowable or subject to human control. None of these uncertainties needed to be confronted if the area of inquiry were sufficiently circumscribed. The greater the power of the discoverer, the less the apparent power and autonomy of the evidence. The implicit fear, as Stanley Cavell names it, is that "ours is an age in which our philosophical grasp of the world fails to reach beyond our taking and holding views of it."

> How do movies reproduce the world magically? Not by literally presenting us with the world, but by permitting us to view it unseen. This is not a wish for power over creation (as Pygmalion's was), but a wish not to need power. . . . It is as though the world's projection explains our forms of unknowness and of our inability to know.[25]

Hence the prestige of perceptual evidence and the erosion of autobiography. "Seeing is believing" because of what it is not: it is not an exertion that requires singular powers or a fabrication of something that might not otherwise exist—in a word, it is not an action some particular agent must perform but an event that simply happens to anyone who occupies a specified position. All of this has been built into film, incorporated in its machinery and in the role it assigns to the spectator. In the words of George Wilson, "film technique presupposes quite definite assumptions about the audience's perceptual relationship to the natural significance of phenomena."[26]

But perhaps the change in consciousness is less drastic than it seems. It is a very small step from the private autobiographical self,

---

[25] Cavell, *The World Viewed*, pp. xiii, 40-41.
[26] Wilson, "Film, Perception, and Point of View," p. 1028.

inaccessible to public scrutiny, to the anonymous public person, interchangeable with any other.[27] Both heir and enemy of autobiography, the signifying practices of film have contradictory implications. On the one hand, they simply expose certain tendencies already implicit in writing. In the words of Derrida:

> We are witnessing not an end of writing that would restore, in accord with McLuhan's ideological representation, a transparency or an immediacy to social relations; but rather an increasingly powerful historical expansion of general writing. . . . To write is to produce a mark that will constitute a sort of machine which is productive in turn, and which my future disappearance will not, in principle, hinder in its functioning, offering things and itself to be read and to be rewritten. . . . Cut off from all absolute responsibility, from consciousness as the ultimate authority . . . the intention animating the utterance will never be through and through present to itself.[28]

Writing may be figuratively a machine, a "speech" that continues to operate in the absence of any speaking subject, but the machinery of film is literal and unavoidable. Thus one potential effect of film is to "deconstruct" the autobiographical preoccupation with capturing the self on paper, demonstrating the delusion of a subjectivity trying to be "through and through present to itself" in the very writing that is the mark of its own absence. The ideal of self-possession—the reifying desire for mastery over an essential self—might then give way to both an identity that could not be possessed and a more playful and disenchanted autobiographical quest.

But if film does dismantle certain key effects of language (such as self-consciousness) and reveal their dependence on a particular set of semiotic conventions, it surely has its own conventional effects and its own characteristic blind spots as well. The absence of any particular "source" that is responsible for what we see becomes

[27] "In viewing films, the sense of invisibility is an expression of modern privacy or anonymity. . . . Our condition has become one in which our natural mode of perception is to view, feeling unseen. We do not so much look at the world as look *out at* it, from behind the self." See Cavell, *The World Viewed*, pp. 40 and 102. The connection to economic and social history and especially to the place of the individual in advanced bourgeois societies where certain sentiments are confined to private life and isolated from the values of the public marketplace is obvious enough.

[28] Jacques Derrida, "Signature Event Context," *Glyph* 1 (1977): 180-181, 194-195.

confused with the total absence of intervention or control: thus, the myths of total cinema, of "positive" knowledge purged of all impurities of human will and imagination, of an Edenic eye. The exaggerated claims once made for individual genius then give way to equally exaggerated claims for (and hence fears of) impersonal technology—machines that not only operate automatically but actually control their operators. In place of the old imperial author (when no special effort is made to maintain that position for the auteur) there emerges a system of concealed authority, a denial of responsibility, a helplessness made legitimate for filmmaker and spectator alike. Surely this powerless cinematic subject is no less chimerical than either the speaking subject or a fixed belief that passive spectatorship is the inevitable form of consciousness no less "ideological" than an uncritical acceptance of the masterful cogito.[29]

Thus while it is clear that film must effect some changes in our familiar notions of personal identity, selfhood, and individuality, it is less clear what direction these changes will ultimately take or how consistent they will be. In the absence of an authoritative self, what will film make of personal identity? It could reduce it to a type, a set of distinctive mannerisms and nothing more,[30] but it could also lay bare a more radical mystery beyond the limits of self-awareness. There are no doubt films that simplify and submerge the individual in the collective, but there are also those like Anger's *Fireworks* that unearth a delicate polyphony within the apparent unity of a single existence. When cinematic autobiographers join with others in a collaborative "self-study" or simply submit themselves to the camera, they acknowledge that they are no longer "lords and owners of their faces." And how they manage this confrontation—whether they deliberately exhibit themselves or only await the alien gaze—is as rich an illustration of their personal idiosyncracies as most written confessions and apologies provide. Such films cannot produce the old self-knowledge (nor the old self-deceptions) of classical autobiography, but they can do

[29] See Coward's "Class, 'Culture,' and the Social Formation" for a more extended discussion of the relationship between the "mechanist" and the "idealist" subjects of empiricism (pp. 75-79).

[30] A number of writers treat the tendency of film to "typify" rather than "individualize" characters: Walter Benjamin, "The Work of Art in the Age of Mechanical Reproduction," in *Illuminations* (New York, 1969); McConnell, *The Spoken Seen*, Chapter 6, passim; and Cavell, *The World Viewed*, Chapters 4 and 5, passim.

something else: they can take identity beyond what one consciousness can grasp, beyond even what the unaided human consciousness can encompass. "The camera," in Benjamin's well-known formulation, "introduces us to unconscious optics as does psychoanalysis to unconscious impulses."[31] Filmed, the unowned image of the body becomes a locus of identity rather than its mask, an expression of personality rather than an encumbrance. Nor is this image of the body the same crude, undifferentiated whole of the *stade du miroir*, but a new, articulate assemblage, a fresh construction of elements never before juxtaposed where voice may stray away from body, the whole diffuse and fuse again into yet other configurations.

In the process of revealing how precarious these perceived configurations are, however, film also challenges the presumed integrity of the perceiving subject. For the eye of cinema is itself a composition made up of the separate elements of staging, lighting, recording, and editing; it is subjectivity released from the ostensible temporal and spatial integrity of the speaking subject. Such freedom, multiplicity, and mobility could not occur without mechanical assistance. The cinematic subject cannot, then, precede the cinematic apparatus, meaning that even the most "personal" film is logically the product of a person whom the film itself creates. Fellini's paradox—"I have invented myself entirely: a childhood, a personality, longings, dreams, and memories, all in order to enable me to tell them"—begins to sound less extreme.[32] In fact, it is not extreme enough, for the "teller" is also an invention.

No doubt this was also the case with those earlier instruments of consciousness, speech and writing; contemporary autobiography in particular (Nabokov's *Speak, Memory* or Barthes' *Roland Barthes by Roland Barthes*) often takes as both its burden and its liberation the power of the autobiographical text to extend and utterly transform the person of its author. But the heterogeneity of the edited image goes even further toward expressing a manufactured subjectivity, an artifact that has no single site, no inherent unity, no body where it is "naturally" confined. Thus the assertion that "the world seen cinematically is the world seen without a self" actually has a double meaning. It could mean either a new way of experiencing ourselves or an exacerbation of the worst tendencies in the old modes of

[31] Benjamin, "The Work of Art in the Age of Mechanical Reproduction," p. 237.
[32] Keel and Stritch, eds., *Fellini on Fellini*, p. 51.

perception—the Cartesian split made absolute at last, leaving only reified appearances, a "world" devoid of human agency, on one side, and a disembodied power of vision, all transcendental voyeurism, on the other. "A world complete without me." According to Cavell, "this is an importance of film—and a danger. It takes my life as my haunting of the world."[33]

But to say this is to treat film as a metaphysical essence rather than as a set of signifying practices—an institution capable of bearing those meanings that Cavell (and not Cavell alone) finds in it but capable as well of bearing other meanings according to the uses that filmmakers and financiers, audiences and critics ultimately make of it. In this respect, film simply shares—or better, articulates—the dilemmas of an entire culture now irrevocably committed to complex technologies and intricate social interdependencies. To make the meanings of film human without falling back on an outworn humanism, to achieve more fluid modes of collaboration and diversity rather than standardized expression, to establish practices in which "I" may no longer exist in the same way but nonetheless cannot escape my own participation—these concerns are not unique to film but among the most fundamental problems that confront "the age of mechanical reproduction" as a whole.

One thing is therefore certain: if film is gradually displacing other modes of communication, it is no alien invasion. The popularity of film and video could only come about because the way they position us in relation to each other and to our common world is somehow familiar to us, closer to the way we live than the linguistic and literary practices they supplant—autobiography, in particular. They must make sense of us or we could never make sense of them.

---

[33] *The World Viewed*, p. 160. It may be the fact that Cavell retains traditional notions of the self that makes him see film as "a world complete without me."

Fictions of the Self:
The End of Autobiography

Michael Sprinker

Seul ce qui ressemble diffère,
seules les différences se ressemblent.
—Gilles Deleuze

A photograph is a secret about a
secret. The more it tells you, the
less you know.
—Diane Arbus

Near the end of *Gravity's Rainbow*, it is reported that the supposed
hero of the book, Tyrone Slothrop, appears to have been dispersed
by some inexplicable means into countless fragments throughout
postwar Europe. He has been transformed from a single identity, a
seemingly ordinary American soldier, into a kind of ubiquitous
presence that crops up periodically in improbable places:

> Some believe that fragments of Slothrop have grown into con-
> sistent personae of their own. If so, there's no telling which of
> the Zone's present-day population are offshoots of his original
> scattering. There's supposed to be a last photograph of him on
> the only record album ever put out by The Fool, an English
> rock group—seven musicians posed, in the arrogant style of
> the early Stones, near an old rocket-bomb site, out in the East
> End, or South of the River. . . . There is no way to tell which
> of the faces is Slothrop's: the only printed credit that might
> apply to him is "Harmonica, kazoo—a friend."[1]

[1] Thomas Pynchon, *Gravity's Rainbow* (New York, 1973), p. 742.

© 1980 Princeton University Press *Autobiography: Essays Theoretical and Critical*
0-691-06412-1/80/0321-022$01.10/1 (cloth)
0-691-10080-2/80/0321-022$01.10/1 (paperback)
For copying information, see copyright page

This passage presents an instance of a pervasive and unsettling feature in modern culture, the gradual metamorphosis of an individual with a distinct, personal identity into a sign, a cipher, an image no longer clearly and positively identifiable as "this one person." A few years ago, American popular culture underwent a minor crisis when it was learned that Paul McCartney of the Beatles had died a few years previously and had been replaced in the singing group by the winner of a Paul McCartney look-alike contest. The scandal died quietly after a few months, probably because "Paul McCartney" had long since ceased to have any significance as an individual and had become, as far as anyone besides his wife and children was concerned, simply a face and a voice. As long as the face and the voice remained essentially the same, it mattered little whether this was the real Paul McCartney or some impostor. In fact, the idea of an impostor had little relevance to the case, since all that mattered was the music that the Beatles produced, and no one was willing to argue that it had diminished in quality since McCartney's alleged demise.

The same problem crops up when one attempts to talk about "the author of *Gravity's Rainbow*." Very little is known about Thomas Pynchon, and almost nothing—save that his name has appeared on the title page of three novels, several short stories, and at least one essay published in the *New York Times Magazine*—of his life, his physical appearance, or his whereabouts during the past decade. Such studied anonymity is bound to provoke speculations like the recent piece by John Batchelor in the *Soho News*, which improbably asserts that "Thomas Pynchon" is a fraud, that the name is merely the pseudonym assumed by J. D. Salinger in the late 1950s in order that he might continue his writing career in seclusion and anonymity. Who is Thomas Pynchon? This apparently innocent question conceals an intricate web of related problems about the concept of the author (and of authority itself), about the ways in which texts are constituted, and about notions of consciousness, of self, of personality, and of individuality as categories applicable to authors of texts.

What is an author? Michel Foucault's recent essay on this topic outlines some of the crucial questions for literary criticism posed by the notion of the author. Foucault argues, persuasively, that the concept of the author as subject, as one who authorizes, gives authority to, is responsible for a text (or series of texts), is of comparatively recent invention and may no longer be useful or even tenable: "Finally, one comes to the conclusion that the author's name does not refer to a real person but that it exceeds the limits of the texts, that it organizes them, that it reveals their mode of being, or at least characterizes them. Though it clearly points to the existence of certain texts, it also refers to their status within a society and within a culture. . . . The function of the author is thus characteristic of the mode of existence, circulation, and operation of certain discourses within a society."[2]

Here Foucault is thinking primarily of the legitimation and proliferation of scientific discourse, which in its purer forms has no authorizing subject, since its very goal is to remove the subject from the text and to replace him (it?) with a discourse descriptive of what *is*—the results of an experiment, a hypothesis, some facet of the empirical world. But as Foucault is quick to point out, this absence of the authorizing subject from the text is equally characteristic of nonscientific discourse as well—of literature, philosophy, psychology, and history. Novels, poems, plays, philosophical works, essays in experimental psychology, historical writing—all the forms of discourse in modern intellectual life circulate quite independently of the personality and even the authority of the writer (plagiarism and modern photoreproduction are two of the most obvious examples). The author of a piece of writing has only the most attenuated existence for the majority of his audience—the signature that he affixes to his work, his name on the title page.[3]

The concept of the author as a subjective presence who originates and is thus responsible for a discourse or a piece of writing has re-

[2] Michel Foucault, "What is an Author?," trans. James Venit, *Partisan Review* 42 (1975): 608. Foucault contends that the concept of author as "real person," that is as a thinking and morally active subject responsible for the text, arose in Western culture "at the end of the eighteenth and the beginning of the nineteenth centuries" as a result of certain economic and social responsibilities connected with the production and dissemination of texts: "Texts, books, discourse, really began to have authors (other than mythic personages or sanctified and sanctifying figures) to the degree to which the author could be punished. Historically, discourse was a gesture charged with risks before it became a commodity included in the general circulation of property" (p. 608).

[3] This signature itself is not without certain inherent ambiguities, as Jacques Derrida has shown. See his essay, "Signature Event Context," trans. Jeffrey Mehlman and Samuel Weber, *Glyph* 1 (1977): 172-196; especially the note appended to the final paragraph, in which Derrida draws attention to his own signature (photographically reproduced on the page) as a counterfeit. The problem is also treated, amusingly, by Hugh Kenner as part of the "aesthetics of simulation" in *The Counterfeiters: An Historical Comedy* (1968; reprint ed., Garden City, New York, 1973).

cently been the object of much rigorous critical reexamination, particularly in France. Much of Foucault's recent work, beginning
with the concluding chapters of *Les mots et les choses*, has been a direct assault against the sovereignty of the individual author over a
text or discourse and against all the attendant anthropological
values implied in this high valuation of the individual subject.[4]
Over the past ten years, Roland Barthes, Jacques Derrida, and the
Tel Quel group have produced a ceaseless torrent of writing in an
effort to establish the primacy of what Jean Thibaudeau has called
the "textual, non-subjective 'I' " as the creator/originator/producer
of a discourse.[5]

Among the important motivating forces in this movement in
contemporary French intellectual life has been Jacques Lacan,
whose "return to Freud," announced in the *Discours de Rome* in
1953 and elaborated in his seminars in the ensuing years, has repeatedly and trenchantly denied the transparency of the Cartesian
cogito (and the related formulations of the *moi* in Sartre and the *per-
cipio* in Husserl and Merleau-Ponty). For Lacan, the subject is never
sovereign by itself but only emerges in an intersubjective discourse
with the Other: "the condition of the subject S (neurotic or psy-
chotic) depends on what is being unfolded in the Other A. What is
being unfolded there is articulated like a discourse (the unconscious
is the discourse of the Other)—a discourse whose syntax Freud first
sought to define for those fragments of it which come to us in certain privileged moments, dreams, slips of the tongue or pen, flashes

---

[4] See *The Order of Things: An Archaeology of the Human Sciences*, a translation of *Les
mots et les choses* (New York, 1973), pp. 303-387; *The Archaeology of Knowledge*, trans.
A. M. Sheridan Smith (New York, 1976); and *L'ordre du discours* (Paris, 1971). An
excellent discussion of Foucault's conception of the text, the archive, and the changing concept of the author is Edward Said's "An Ethics of Language," *Diacritics* 4
(1974): 28-37. Said's own recent theoretical work, *Beginnings: Intention and Method*
(New York, 1975) and "Orientalism," *Georgia Review* 31 (1977): 162-206, shows the
clear imprint of Foucault's inquiries into the production and dissemination of discourse.

[5] See Roland Barthes, *Sade, Fourier, Loyola*, trans. Richard Miller (New York,
1976), *S/Z*, trans. Richard Miller (New York, 1974), and *The Pleasure of the Text*,
trans. Richard Miller (New York, 1975); Jacques Derrida, *L'écriture et la différence*
(Paris, 1967), and *Of Grammatology*, trans. Gayatri Chakravorty Spivak (Baltimore
and London, 1976); and *Théorie d'ensemble* (Paris, 1968). The latter is a collection of
essays by people associated with *Tel Quel* in the 1960s, including Barthes, Derrida,
Foucault, Thibaudeau, and Philippe Sollers. The phrase I have taken from
Thibaudeau is from his essay in this collection, "Le roman comme autobiographie,"
p. 214.

of wit."[6] In short, the self can no more be author of its own discourse than any producer of a text can be called the author—that is
the originator—of his writing. "To write," as Barthes has cleverly
shown, can be conceived as an intransitive verb with an impersonal
subject, in the same sense as in the French idiom *il pleut*.[7] Every text
is an articulation of the relations between texts, a product of intertextuality, a weaving together of what has already been produced
elsewhere in discontinuous form; every subject, every author,
every self is the articulation of an intersubjectivity structured
within and around the discourses available to it at any moment in
time. It is in the context of this critique of the subject that the investigation of autobiography as a particular species of writing can
most fruitfully be undertaken.

The history of the word *autobiography* itself poses this problematic of the author. The birth of the word at the end of the eighteenth
century (the OED credits Southey with the first usage in 1809;
Pierre Larousse attributes the French form to a derivation from the
English; Herder is generally cited as the originator of the German
Selbstbiographie) coincides with the beginning of what Foucault has
called "the anthropological sleep" in Western culture. Autobiography and the concept of the author as sovereign subject over a discourse are products of the same *episteme*. Prior to the end of the
eighteenth century, works that are today labelled autobiographies
were known as confessions, memoirs, *journaux intimes*. When Vico
was asked to write what has come to be known as his *Autobiography*, he did so under the title of "The Life of Giambattista Vico
written by himself." In the opening paragraph of the *Confessions*,
Rousseau went so far as to claim that he was inaugurating an entirely new species of writing: "I have begun on a work which is
without precedent, whose accomplishment will have no imitator. I
propose to set before my fellow-mortals a man in all the truth of

[6] Jacques Lacan, *The Language of the Self: The Function of Language in Psychoanalysis*, trans. Anthony Wilden (Baltimore and London, 1968), p. 107. The importance
of Lacan in contemporary French thought is intelligently discussed in the translator's
introduction to this volume. Lacan's insistence on the constitutive function of intersubjective relations in the formation of the subject is nicely summarized in a remark
on the misconceived objectivity of scientific discourse: "Ce qu'il faut dire, c'est que
le je de ce choix naît ailleurs qua là où le discours s'énonce, précisément chez celui
qui l'écoute." Lacan, "La métaphore du sujet," in *Écrits* (Paris, 1966), p. 892.

[7] Barthes, "To Write: An Intransitive Verb?," in *The Structuralist Controversy: The
Languages of Criticism and the Sciences of Man*, ed. Richard Macksey and Eugenio
Donato (Baltimore and London, 1972), pp. 134-145.

nature; and this man shall be myself."[8] Rousseau's characteristically egotistical assertion has often been echoed by historians of autobiography, who have credited him with inaugurating the genre in its modern form.[9] What remains true in this generalization is the foundation of autobiography as a literary genre in the historical conditions that gave rise to the concepts of subject, self, and author as independent sovereignties. But Rousseau is probably not the only candidate one might offer as the father of autobiography. Vico is such another.

Like his other writings, Vico's *Autobiography* is a text about texts, a book that originates in other discourses, an original work that cannot claim originality in the sense of independence from other works. It is a book permeated by the problems and contradictions inherent in the concepts of author and self. Though certainly not unique in this respect among autobiographies, Vico's account of his life is marked by his always referring to himself in the third person. In this way he effectively displaces himself as author from the hero of his narrative and allows his personality, his selfhood, to emerge in the act of writing that constructs the *Autobiography*. At least in part, Vico's purpose is to distinguish himself from the dominating figure of Descartes, whose *Discourse on Method* provides the principal model for Vico's own text. Vico was profoundly suspicious of the Cartesian *cogito*, hence of all thought that takes as its point of origin the subjective consciousness. One of Vico's goals in the *Autobiography* was to controvert the subjective side of Cartesian dualism:

> We shall not here feign what René Descartes craftily feigned as to the method of his studies simply in order to exalt his own philosophy and mathematics and degrade all the other studies included in divine and human erudition. Rather, with the candor proper to a historian, we shall narrate plainly and step by step the entire series of Vico's studies, in order that the proper and natural causes of his particular development as a man of letters may be known.[10]

[8] *The Confessions of Jean-Jacques Rousseau*, trans. W. Conyngham Mallory (New York, 1928), p. 3.

[9] See, for example, Philippe Lejeune, *L'autobiographie en France* (Paris, 1971). Recently, however, Lejeune has modified this formulation somewhat. See Lejeune, "Autobiographie et histoire littéraire," *Revue d'histoire littéraire de la France* 75 (1975): 903-936.

[10] *The Autobiography of Giambattista Vico*, trans. Max Harold Fisch and Thomas Goddard Bergin (Ithaca, 1944), p. 113.

Vico's history of his own intellectual development, he claims, is not so much an account of himself as it is a narrative of the works that combined to make him "a man of letters." The book is properly a history of the origin and growth of the *New Science*. The *Autobiography* comments upon and attempts to justify the text toward the writing of which Vico believed his entire life was directed. This facet of the *Autobiography* becomes more pronounced in the "Continuation by the Author" (1731), in which Vico responds to the criticisms of the first edition of the *New Science* (1725): "[Vico] however blessed all these adversities as so many occasions for withdrawing to his desk, as to his high impregnable citadel, to meditate and to write further works which he was wont to call 'so many noble acts of vengeance against his detractors.' These finally led him to the discovery of his *New Science*. And when he had written his work, enjoying life, liberty and honor, he held himself more fortunate than Socrates."[11] Vico's writings, particularly the *New Science* and the *Autobiography*, are generated by other texts: the works of other writers whom Vico opposes (Descartes, Lucretius, his contemporary Neapolitan and Venetian critics), works from which Vico claims to have drawn inspiration (Bacon, Plato, Tacitus, and Grotius), and works that Vico himself had previously written (*On the Method of the Studies of Our Time*, *The Most Ancient Wisdom of the Italians*, "the new science in negative form," the first edition of the *New Science*, and the *Autobiography*— the latter two must be read together and in conjunction with subsequent editions of the *New Science*). As he depicts it in the *Autobiography*, Vico's life is a long series of revisions of previously written texts, culminating in the *New Science*, which went through three editions (each a revision of the previous one) in the author's lifetime.

Vico's relation to his precursors (even to those whom he acknowledges favorably) is complicated by his belief that he was, in the words he attributes to his friend Caloprese, "the 'autodidact' or 'teacher of himself.' "[12] In the *Autobiography*, he is at great pains to portray his independence from other thinkers, to establish the originality of his thought, to depict his works as the product of a unique authorizing intention. He claims, for example, that he had no mentor to guide him through his life except the lights of his own intelligence: "Vico blessed his good fortune in having no teacher whose words he had sworn by, and he felt most grateful for those woods

[11] Ibid., p. 200.   [12] Ibid., p. 136.

in which, guided by his good genius, he had followed the main course of his studies untroubled by sectarian prejudice."[13] Even Bacon, whom Vico names as one of four authors from whom he derived the principles underlying the *New Science*, is not granted immunity from Vico's attempts to liberate himself from the fetters of intellectual influence: "And his slight satisfaction with Bacon's book attempting to trace the wisdom of the ancients in the fables of the poets, was a sign of the source whence Vico, also in his latest works, was to recover principles of poetry different from those which the Greeks and Latins and the others since them have hitherto accepted."[14] Everywhere in the *Autobiography* Vico asserts his originality, his uniqueness, his authority. It is as if he sees his own intellectual development in light of his apodictic aphorism in the *New Science*: "for purposes of this inquiry, we must reeckon as if there were no books in the world."[15]

The paradoxical originality that Vico asserts for himself depends upon his famous theory of history, reiterated again and again in the *New Science*. For Vico, history is repetition, an endless fluctuation of *corsi* and *ricorsi* repeating each other in slightly modified form. Every epoch of what Vico calls gentile history recapitulates the passage of men from barbarism, to civilization, to decadence, but with differences that stamp each epoch as individual at the same time that each produces a recurrence of the universal pattern. This admittedly problematic concept of repetition is neatly captured in the passage from Deleuze's *Logique du sens* cited at the beginning of this paper: "Seul ce qui se ressemble diffère, seules les différences se ressemblent."[16] Vico's own texts can thus be seen as repetitions of previous works—his own and the works of others—but only in the

---

[13] Ibid., p. 133.   [14] Ibid., p. 153.

[15] *The New Science of Giambattista Vico*, trans. Thomas Goddard Bergin and Max Harold Fisch (Ithaca, 1948), p. 85.

[16] Gilles Deleuze, *Logique du sens* (Paris, 1969), p. 302. As Edward Said has noted, in Vico's theory of history "epistemologically the status of repetition itself is uncertain." "On Repetition," in *The Literature of Fact: Selected Papers from the English Institute*, ed. Angus Fletcher (New York, 1976), p. 138. Both Vico and Deleuze (and for that matter Nietzsche when he imagines the eternal recurrence) attempt to confront the paradoxical condition of repetition in reality: namely, that recurrence of the same cannot account for historical change, while theories of historical progress cannot encompass the typical and (for Vico at least) apparently providential repetitions of universal patterns of human conduct. "The status of repetition" is "epistemologically uncertain" in part because the perception of recurrence is always a retrospective act bidding for proleptic powers.

sense that each repetition constitutes a unique and individual articulation of the pattern. Each text repeats others by producing difference. Repetition is a function of memory understood in the special
sense that Vico gives it: "Memory has thus three different aspects:
memory when it remembers things, imagination when it alters or
imitates them and invention when it gives them a new turn or puts
them into proper arrangement and relationship."[17] Vico's *Autobiography* and *New Science* are products of memory in all three senses of
the term. They resemble each other and the works from which they
derive only by differing from them.

Repetition and memory are surely among the most crucial
categories to any consideration of autobiography, a fact that Kierkegaard, more than any thinker, knew well. His book *Repetition*
(1843) is a searching critique of the similarities and differences between recollection and repetition, couched in a form that Freud was
to make famous—the case history. In the book's opening paragraph, the pseudonymous author, Constantine Constantius, defines the relation of recollection to repetition in a decidedly Vichian
manner: "Repetition and recollection are the same movement, only
in opposite directions; for what is recollected has been, is repeated
backwards, whereas repetition properly so called is recollected
forwards."[18] Kierkegaard's championing of the instantaneous, the
momentary, the disruptive against the Hegelian concept of media-
tion is well known. As Constantius later affirms, the paradox of
repetition lies in its simultaneous confirmation of similarity and
discontinuity: "The dialectic of repetition is easy; for what is repeated has been, otherwise it could not be repeated, but precisely
the fact that it has been gives to repetition the character of novelty.
When the Greeks said that all knowledge is recollection they
affirmed that all that is has been; when one says that life is a repetition one affirms that existence which has been now becomes."[19]

Repetition is what the nameless young man, vainly in love, longs
for, and it is what he achieves, though hardly in a way he could
have anticipated. His final letter to Constantius reveals the dialectic
that the book has explored in the startling announcement that the
woman whom the young man has abandoned has married another.
The nameless lover has achieved his repetition, in the same way as

[17] Vico, *New Science*, p. 280.
[18] Søren Kierkegaard, *Repetition: An Essay in Experimental Psychology*, trans. Walter Lowrie (1941; reprint ed., New York, Evanston, and London, 1964), p. 33.
[19] Ibid., p. 52.

Job had everything he had lost "doubly restored," though with an interesting twist: "Only his children Job did not receive again double, because a human life is not a thing that can be duplicated. In that case only spiritual repetition is possible, although in the temporal life it is never so perfect as in eternity, which is the true repetition."[20] Outwardly the young man has lost all; inwardly all is recovered. Only by creating the discontinuity of losing her, only by engendering the difference in their external relationship can the young man recover the young woman inwardly. As Constantius earlier remarks: "It indubitably is not possession in the strictest sense which concerns him, or the content which develops from this situation; what concerns him is *return*, conceived in a purely formal sense. . . . The girl is not a reality but a reflection of the movements within him and their exciting cause."[21] Repetition is a strange kind of metaleptic movement of the spirit in which two conditions seemingly not at all alike become equivalent in a relation of temporal difference. Unlike recollection, which "begins with the loss,"[22] repetition is a plenitude, a recovery of what recollection has lost by means of a transumption of the recollected object into an atemporal order—"eternity, which is the true repetition."

But the text accomplishes more than this lucid exposition of a problematic concept. *Repetition*, like its companion piece *Fear and Trembling* (both texts were published on the same day), is also a covert autobiography, an attempt by Kierkegaard to explain to himself and to Regina Olsen the reasons that had compelled him to break off their engagement. Both books present imaginative retellings of the major events of Kierkegaard's romance—*Fear and Trembling* through a re-creation of Abraham's sacrifice of Isaac, *Repetition* through the fictional narrative of the relations between Constantius and the nameless young lover. Outwardly, no two books could be more dissimilar; inwardly their resemblance is precise. Johannes de silentio, the narrator of *Fear and Trembling*, proceeds by way of a meditation and commentary upon the story of Abraham and Isaac, just as Constantius takes as the occasion for his discourse the relations between the two young lovers. Both stand outside the intersubjective relations they encounter, just as Kierkegaard assumes the position of neutral observer with respect to the relations that are figuratively represented by the lovers and by Abraham and Isaac. In both cases, Kierkegaard has covertly repre-

---

[20] Ibid., p. 126.   [21] Ibid., pp. 88–89.   [22] Ibid., p. 39.

sented his own relationship to Regina, whom he has sacrificed but believes he will recover, as Abraham wills to do with Isaac and the young man with his lover. What fascinates Kierkegaard and his pseudonymous narrators is the inner dialectic of Abraham, the young man, of Kierkegaard himself—a dialectic that simultaneously wills the loss and the recovery of the object of passion (Isaac, the young woman, Regina). This incomprehensible movement of the spirit occasions the discourses of de silentio and Constantius (a fact that they both aver), just as Kierkegaard himself is prompted to create these two pseudonymous authors by the pressure of his own spiritual life.

Near the end of *Repetition*, Constantius draws attention to the fictional content of his work by confessing that he has imagined the figure of the young man in order to illuminate the exceptional case of the poet. The young man represents an ideal figure upon which Constantius can exercise his psychological investigations. Constantius confesses that "every word of mine is either ventriloquism or is uttered with reference to him."[23] But the relationship is not simply that of a puppet to his master, for Constantius himself is produced as a writer only in relation to the young man: "My personality is a presupposition psychologically necessary to force him out."[24] The existences of Constantius and the young man are mutually constitutive, as each repeats the words of the other in a different form. The letters that the young man supposedly writes must have been composed by Constantius himself, just as the words that Constantius writes must have taken their origin in the words and deeds of the young man. The text of *Repetition*, if Constantius's account of it is to be believed, originates in an intersubjectivity in which two imagined characters talk to each other by repeating what the other has not said.[25]

Kierkegaard himself, seemingly not implicated in this dialogue between the two characters in the book (his name appears nowhere in the original edition), nevertheless cannot be omitted from the discussion. That Kierkegaard was "the author, as people would call it" of *Repetition* and of all the pseudonymous works, he later admitted publicly in a note appended to the *Concluding Unscientific Post-*

---

[23] Ibid., p. 134.   [24] Ibid., p. 137.

[25] This situation corresponds closely to Lacan's account of the psychoanalytic interview. See *The Language of the Self*, pp. 3–87, passim; and "Seminar on 'The Purloined Letter,' " trans. Jeffrey Mehlman, in *French Freud: Structural Studies in Psychoanalysis, Yale French Studies* 48 (1972): 38–72, passim.

script (1846), thereby bringing to an end his "pseudonymity or polynymity." But he continued to maintain that the words uttered in these works were not his but the words of the pseudonymous authors, that the opinions and ideas expressed by these imagined persons were entirely their own: "So in the pseudonymous works there is not a single word which is mine, I have no opinion about these works except as third person, no knowledge of their meaning except as a reader, not the remotest private relation to them."[26]

Kierkegaard here refuses to assume the traditional responsibility of an author for his text, and in so doing he undermines the conventional notions of author and text, self and discourse. The "I" who writes these sentences is an altogether different subject from Johannes Climacus, Johannes de silentio, Victor Eremita and all the other authors whose names were affixed to the series of works that had come from Kierkegaard's prolific pen over the previous three years. Insofar as he is a subject at all responsible for the pseudonymous works, Kierkegaard achieves authority over the texts only conditionally, in the form of an intersubjectivity generated by the confrontation between the discourse of the pseudonymous author and the interpretative responses (silent for the most part) made by Kierkegaard as reader of that discourse. In a sense, while writing the pseudonymous works, Kierkegaard is not a subject at all, or rather, he is a multiplicity of subjects who constitute in the intersubjective relations that any act of reading constructs among them an authorizing figure whose presence/absence one might designate "Kierkegaard." But care must be taken always to distinguish him from the other "Kierkegaard" who affixed his name to *The Concept of Irony, Edifying Discourses*, and the numerous works written between 1846 and his death in 1855. This most radical expounder of "truth as subjectivity" is also among the most suspicious questioners of the authority of the subject over his discourse. In this the Kierkegaardian discourse resembles nothing more closely than the Nietzschean text of *The Will to Power*.

Despite the determined efforts of some of his recent commentators to minimize and circumscribe the importance of *The Will to Power*, it remains one of Nietzsche's most interesting and significant texts.[27] As a text, it raises in its own mode of production and

---

[26] Kierkegaard, *Concluding Unscientific Postscript to the Philosophical Fragments*, trans. David F. Swenson and Walter Lowrie (Princeton, 1941), p. 551.

[27] See, for example, the "Editor's Introduction" to *The Will to Power*, trans. Walter Kaufmann and R. J. Hollingdale (New York, 1967).

in numerous observations within its limits the question of the ground of authority over discourse. As everyone knows, the book was first published by his sister Elisabeth Förster-Nietzsche in the year after Nietzsche's death. It comprises a collection of late notes and fragments written between 1883 and 1888. The order of the entries and the authenticity of at least some of them has long been a matter of dispute. That Nietzsche at one time intended to publish a book under the title *The Will to Power* is clear; that he intended anything like the text that has been circulated for three-quarters of a century under that title is not at all certain. Nietzsche's authority over *The Will to Power* is problematic; his responsibility for its contents, for its circulation, and for the influence it exercised over a generation of German thinkers cannot be determined, for he never authorized its publication, not even in the "juridical and literary sense" for which Kierkegaard assumed responsibility for the pseudonymous works.[28] But *someone* wrote *The Will to Power*, or perhaps it would be more correct to say that it (the book, the text, the notes and fragments) was written, that by means of certain familiar modes and procedures of publication *The Will to Power* simply came into existence and assumed its place in that discursive practice that subsequent readers have labelled Nietzschean. To say so is to repeat the very essence of *The Will to Power* itself.

As Foucault has shown, the fundamental Nietzschean question is, "Who is speaking?" But Foucault's analysis of Nietzsche's discourse is inadequate to the crucial text, *The Will to Power*, in which this question is posed most forcefully and paradoxically. According to Foucault, "Nietzsche maintained his questioning as to who is speaking right up to the end, though forced, in the last resort, to irrupt into that questioning himself and to base it upon himself as the speaking and questioning subject: *Ecce homo*."[29] In contrast to this interpretation based upon the confessedly autobiographical *Ecce Homo*, one can present the following observations made by Nietzsche himself: "The 'subject' is not something given, it is

---

[28] Kierkegaard, *Concluding Unscientific Postscript*, p. 552.

[29] Foucault, *The Order of Things*, pp. 305-306. In fairness to Foucault, it should be said that he is perfectly aware of the ambiguous concept of authorship in relation to Nietzsche's (and all) texts, despite the apparent false step in the passage cited. The problem is confronted in *The Archaeology of Knowledge* (p. 24) and "What is an Author?" In the latter he explicitly treats the difficulty encountered in *Les mots et les choses* by the attribution of proper names (Buffon, Cuvier, Ricardo, Marx, Darwin) to "certain discursive practices" (p. 603).

something added and invented and projected behind what there is";
" 'The subject' is the fiction that many similar states in us are the
effect of one substratum: but it is we who first created the 'similarity' of these states; our adjusting them and making them similar
is the fact, not their similarity (—which ought rather to be denied—)"; " 'Subject,' 'object,' 'attribute'—these distinctions are
fabricated and are now imposed as a schematism upon all the apparent facts. The fundamental false observation is that I believe it is
I who do something, suffer something, 'have' something, 'have' a
quality."[30]

In *The Will to Power* Nietzsche is not "himself the speaking and
questioning subject," for no such subject exists, except, as the text
asserts, fictively. What thinks, organizes, writes the text before us
is something nonsubjective, impersonal, beyond the authority and
control of any individual. It is the will to power: "All 'purposes,'
'aims,' 'meaning' are only modes of expression and metamorphoses of one will that is inherent in all events: the will to
power."[31] Nietzsche obliterates the authority of the subject by exposing it as a deception, as merely the figurative expression of a
conditioned activity: "[. . . What I demand is] that one should take
the doer back into the deed after having conceptually removed the
doer and thus emptied the deed; that one should take doing *something*, the 'aim,' the 'intention,' the 'purpose,' back into the deed
after having artificially removed all this and thus emptied the
deed."[32] If autobiography can be described as the self's inquiry into
its own history—the self-conscious questioning of the subject by
itself—then Nietzsche offers the most fearful warning for any autobiographical text: "The danger of the direct questioning of the subject *about* the subject and of all self-reflection of the spirit lies in this,
that it could be useful and important for one's activity to interpret
oneself *falsely*."[33] In the present century no one has taken this ad-
monition more seriously than Freud.

The crucial Freudian concepts—repression, the unconscious,
narcissism, the phenomenon of countertransference—are all profoundly Nietzschean (and Schopenhauerian) in the manner in
which they question the ontological status of the subject. Freud was
acutely aware of his debt to Nietzsche and Schopenhauer and attempted to deny it: "The large extent to which psychoanalysis

---

[30] Nietzsche, *The Will to Power*, pp. 267, 269, 294.   [31] Ibid., p. 356.
[32] Ibid. Brackets in the text.   [33] Ibid., p. 272.

coincides with the philosophy of Schopenhauer . . . is not to be traced to my acquaintance with his teaching. I read Schopenhauer very late in my life. Nietzsche, another philosopher whose guesses and intuitions often agree in the most astonishing way with the laborious findings of psycho-analysis, was for a long time avoided by me on that very account; I was less concerned with the question of priority than with keeping my mind unembarrassed."[34] Quite the contrary, Freud was perpetually (one might say without injustice, pathologically) concerned with the question of priority. In his *Autobiographical Study* (1925) as in the earlier *History of the Psycho-Analytic Movement* (1914), Freud's anxious assertion of his originality in, authority over, and complete responsibility for the doctrines of psychoanalysis is everywhere apparent. The opening sentences of the latter work are characteristic: "No one need be surprised at the subjective character of the contribution I propose to make here to the history of the psycho-analytic movement, nor need anyone wonder at the part I play in it. For psycho-analysis is my creation."[35] Acting like the tyrannical father figure in the family romance, Freud cast Adler and Jung into the psychological darkness beyond the boundaries of psychoanalysis, while at the same time defending himself against the charges of having plagiarized his ideas from a variety of contemporary sources: Charcot, Breuer, Popper-Lynkeus, and Janet. Safe from the dangers presented by apostates within and hostile critics outside the movement, Freud could assess his achievement with a deceptive modesty:

> Looking back, then, over the patchwork of my life's labours, I can say that I have made many beginnings and thrown out many suggestions. Something will come of them in the future, though I cannot myself tell whether it will be much or little. I can, however, express a hope that I have opened up a pathway for an important advance in our knowledge.[36]

As Lacan and others have shown, the proper approach to understanding Freud's discourse is to subject it to the same techniques of interpretation that Freud employed in analyzing the discourse of

---

[34] Sigmund Freud, *An Autobiographical Study*, in *The Standard Edition of the Complete Psychological Works of Sigmund Freud*, 24 vols., trans. James Strachey (London, 1953), 20: 59-60.

[35] *Standard Edition*, 14: 7.   [36] *Standard Edition*, 20: 70

neurotics.[37] To turn Freud back upon himself is to discover a discourse trapped in its own discursiveness, or to put it another way, it is to discover in Freud a neurotic impulse to uncover the secrets and the mechanisms of neurosis. It is not unfair to suggest that the passage just quoted sounds remarkably like a description of the way in which the unconscious operates in mental life, and, conversely, remarkably like the techniques employed by the analyst to interpret the symptoms and dreams of his patients. In presenting this account of his life, Freud's discourse has no more (or less) privileged status than the discourse of the neurotic in the psychoanalytic interview, as a passage from the Postscript (1935) to the *Autobiographical Study* makes apparent:

> And here I may be allowed to break off these autobiographical notes. The public has no claim to learn any more of my personal affairs—of my struggles, my disappointments, and my successes. I have in any case been more open and frank in some of my writings (such as *The Interpretation of Dreams* and *The Psychopathology of Everyday Life*) than people usually are who describe their lives for their contemporaries or for posterity. I have had small thanks for it, and from my experience I cannot recommend anyone to follow my example.[38]

Like a neurotic patient, Freud resists the reader's advances and deflects further inquiry into his "personal affairs." At the same time, he gives the reader the crucial information necessary to pursue the investigation further—examine my other texts, he says. Freud refers the curious reader to *The Interpretation of Dreams*, his true autobiography and a key text in any discussion of autobiographical writing. Freud recognized the central place of *The Interpretation of Dreams* for his own life and for the body of his psychoanalytic work. In the Preface to the second edition (1908), he observed: "For this book has a further subjective significance for me personally—a significance which I only grasped after I had completed it."[39] Years later, in the Preface to the third English edition, he judged this work "the most valuable of all the discoveries it

---

[37] See, for example, Derrida, "Freud and the Scene of Writing," trans. Jeffrey Mehlman, in *French Freud*, pp. 73-117; Jeffrey Mehlman, "How to Read Freud on Jokes: The Critic as *Schadchen*," *New Literary History* 6 (1975): 439-461; and Hélène Cixous, "Fiction and Its Phantoms: A Reading of Freud's *Das Unheimliche* (The 'uncanny');" trans. Robert Dennomé, *New Literary History* 7 (1976): 526-548.

[38] *Standard Edition*, 20: 73.   [39] *Standard Edition*, 4: xxvi.

has been my good fortune to make. Insight such as this falls to one's lot but once in a lifetime."[40] The book is thus both an autobiography and the foundation of all Freud's theoretical writing. Autobiography and theory confront each other in the production of the text; the life and the thought are, in fact, produced in the writing. To understand how this can be so, one must interpret the *Interpretation*.

The famous dream of "Irma's Injection" is a place to begin. Freud offers it as an exemplary case of the method of dream interpretation that he has discovered. Presenting his own mental life for examination, he demands of the reader an intimate participation in the interpretative process: "And now I must ask the reader to make my interests his own for quite a while, and to plunge, along with me, into the minutest details of my life; for a transference of this kind is peremptorily demanded by our interest in the hidden meaning of dreams."[41] As both patient and analyst Freud creates, through the complicity of the reader, an intersubjective discourse in which the text of the dream and its interpretation constitute one element and the reader's response to text and interpretation, the other. The ordinary dialectic between the speaking patient and the listening analyst collapses into a univocal discourse uttered by Freud for the benefit of the readers who have been tricked into believing for the moment that they are receiving a privileged glimpse of the mental life of the master. The illusion is short-lived. Freud breaks off the interview abruptly at its most interesting juncture when he has discovered in his own dream the motive of revenge:

> I will not pretend that I have completely uncovered the meaning of this dream or that its interpretation is without a gap. I could spend much more time over it, derive further information from it and discuss fresh problems raised by it. I myself know the points from which further trains of thought could be followed. But considerations which arise in the case of every dream of my own restrain me from pursuing my interpretative work. If anyone should feel tempted to express a hasty condemnation of my reticence, I would advise him to make the experiment of being franker than I am. For the moment I am satisfied with the achievement of this one piece of fresh knowledge.[42]

[40] Ibid., p. xxxii.
[41] Ibid., pp. 105-106.
[42] Ibid., pp. 120-121.

For "reticence," one might more accurately read "resistance" here. As with the hysteric Dora whom he was to treat not long after writing this passage, Freud breaks off the analysis when it verges on uncovering the truth. In a remarkable transference of responsibility, he then lays the blame for the termination at the feet of the reader, who, Freud knows well, is scarcely likely "to make the experiment of being franker than I am." Freud's text thus reaches the impasse of the recalcitrant patient and the inept analyst; it enacts the very process of repression that it has sought to illuminate.

The curious reader, like the resourceful analyst (cleverly represented by Freud himself in the Dora analysis), can of course go elsewhere for information: to other dreams reported by Freud in *The Interpretation of Dreams*, to other of Freud's published writings, above all to the correspondence with Fliess that coincided with the period of writing *The Interpretation of Dreams*. In his early *Project for a Scientific Psychology* (1895), Freud refers to the dream of "Irma's Injection" in explaining the mechanisms of dream displacement and mentions the "friend" (the editor of the *Standard Edition* identifies him in a footnote) to whom he had referred in the analysis of one segment of the dream as one "who had for many years been familiar with all my writings during the period of their gestation, just as I had been with his."[43] The friend of course is Fliess, to whom Freud wrote on 12 June 1900 (apropos of a visit to Bellevue, where Freud had originally dreamt of "Irma's Injection"):

Do you suppose that some day a marble tablet will be placed on the house, inscribed with these words:

> IN THIS HOUSE ON JULY 24TH, 1895,
> THE SECRET OF DREAMS WAS REVEALED TO
> DR. SIGMUND FREUD

At this moment I see little prospect of it. But when I read the latest psychological books (Mach's *Analyse der Empfindungen*,

---

[43] Ibid., p. 116. The passage from the *Project* can be found in Freud, *The Origins of Psychoanalysis: Letters to Wilhelm Fliess, Drafts and Notes—1887-1902*, ed. Marie Bonaparte, Anna Freud, Ernst Kris, trans. Eric Mosbacher and James Strachey (New York, 1954), p. 403.

second edition, Kroell's *Aufbau der Seele*, etc.) all of which have the same kind of aims as my work, and see what they have to say about dreams, I am as delighted as the dwarf in the fairy tale because "the princess doesn't know."[44]

More information—the dream played a crucial role in Freud's discovery of the mechanism of dreams; it is linked to his friendship with Fliess; Freud indulges in a childlike delight over his discovery of "the secret of dreams"—and yet no key to unlock the secret of Freud's reticence/resistance. Later in *The Interpretation of Dreams*, Freud returns to this dream to analyze further what he refers to as its "Otto" and "Wilhelm" groups of associations—the images of hostile opponents and sympathetic friends respectively.[45] Though many more details are elaborated, he does not give further insight into the source of the dream. He simply repeats the already proffered interpretation that the dream content compensated for certain feelings of inadequacy. The dream becomes one of the touchstones of Freud's text, by far the one most often cited in the book. Nowhere, however, is the interpretation carried beyond the point at which he abruptly brings it to a halt in the initial analysis. In a reading of Freud's text, "Irma's Injection" becomes a node of resistance, a knot of uninterpretability, what Freud called a "navel":

> There is often a passage in even the most thoroughly inter-preted dream which has to be left obscure; this is because we become aware during the work of interpretation that at that point there is a tangle of dream-thoughts which cannot be un-ravelled and which moreover adds nothing to our knowledge of the content of the dream. This is the dream's navel, the spot where it reaches down into the unknown. The dream-thoughts to which we are led by interpretation cannot from the nature of things, have any definite endings; they are bound to branch out in every direction into the intricate network of our world of thought. It is at some point where this meshwork is particularly close that the dream-wish grows up, like a mushroom out of its mycelium.[46]

The point of origin for the dream-wish marks a limit, the point at which interpretation turns back upon itself to reconstitute the

---

[44] *The Origins of Psychoanalysis*, p. 322.
[45] *Standard Edition*, 4: 294-295.   [46] *Standard Edition*, 5: 525.

same meanings already discovered by tracing the meandering course of the dream-wish back to its source (the navel) via different paths. Throughout *The Interpretation of Dreams*, Freud repeats in various guises this model of the dream as a multilayered text structured by repetition and difference. When confronted, as he often is, with two seemingly opposed interpretations of a dream, he asserts that "the two interpretations are not mutually contradictory, but both cover the same ground; they are a good instance of the fact that dreams, like all other psychopathological structures, regularly have more than one meaning."[47] In other places, he regularly appeals to information not presented in the dream itself: "I was able to [give the interpretation of the dream] because I was familiar with the whole of the dreamer's previous history."[48] As texts, dreams present a model of intertextuality in which interpretation depends upon the ability to articulate a structure inscribed by the juxtaposition of differing texts. Hence, Freud's approving citation of James Sully in a footnote added to *The Interpretation of Dreams* in 1914: "Like some palimpsest, the dream discloses beneath its worthless surface-characters traces of an old and precious communication."[49] Superimposition, contiguity, juxtaposition, repetition—these are the characteristic features of Freud's textual model generated in *The Interpretation of Dreams*. They are, moreover, the constitutive techniques of *The Interpretation of Dreams* itself.[50]

If dream interpretation returns again and again to the same point—the navel of the dream—it can also be said that *The Interpretation of Dreams* returns again and again to the same nodes of uninterpretability (among them the dream of "Irma's Injection") that always leave the text somewhat mystified about its own meaning. Freud's discourse often defers the solution of a problem until a later chapter (the reader is aided in following this aspect of the text by the carefully cross-referenced notes in the *Standard Edition*), as, for example, in the first chapter when the problem of typical dreams comes up in a discussion of the sources and stimuli of dreams: "I

---

[47] *Standard Edition*, 4: 149.   [48] Ibid., p. 152.

[49] Ibid., p. 135.

[50] Edward Said has brilliantly discussed the place of *The Interpretation of Dreams* in the history and theory of Western narrative, arguing that Freud's text displaces the "genealogical, hierarchical, and consecutive conventions" of the classical nineteenth-century novel with a narrative structure based on a theory of interpretation "in which statements are dispersed but whose positions can be determined with regard only to certain (but not all) other statements." *Beginnings: Intention and Method*, pp. 163, 169. For Said, *The Interpretation of Dreams* presents a model of textual interpretation by generating the text to which such a model could apply.

shall later have occasion to return to the question of typical dreams and their origin."[51] The question is then treated at length in Chapter 5. Or in the case of dream distortion (which can only be understood in the context of the structure of the entire mental apparatus), Freud announces that he will have to "postpone [the discussion of this topic] until a later stage."[52] Frequently, the text promises more than it will deliver: "Anxiety-dreams are dreams with a sexual content, the libido belonging to which has been transformed into anxiety. There will be an opportunity later to support this assertion by the analysis of some neurotic patients' dreams."[53] As the editor's note indicates, this "assertion" is nowhere "supported" later in the book, though Freud does return to the subject of anxiety-dreams without resolving the problems they raise for his theory.

Thus Freud's text is an intricately constructed web of concepts, motifs, and images that repeat without resolving the theoretical problems he attributes to the dream-work. Just as the metaphor of the journey dominates much of his discussion of the work of dream interpretation, so the same metaphor controls Freud's presentation of the structure of his own text:

> When the analysis of the dream of Irma's injection showed us that a dream could be the fulfillment of a wish, our interest was at first wholly absorbed by the question of whether we had come upon a universal characteristic of dreams, and for the time being we stifled our curiosity about any other scientific problems that may have arisen during the work of the interpretation. Having followed one path to its end we may now retrace our steps and choose another starting-point for our rambles through the problems of dream-life: for the time being, we may leave the topic of wish-fulfillment on one side, though we are still far from having exhausted it.[54]

Freud's text enacts the process it describes by tracing and retracing the paths of its own discourse. Moreover, as the passages quoted earlier from the 1935 Postscript to his *Autobiographical Study* and the Preface to *The Interpretation of Dreams* show, this text is the locus of all the significant themes of his later work. Like the dream of "Irma's Injection," which constitutes a kind of dream-navel at

[51] *Standard Edition*, 4: 38.   [52] Ibid., p. 144.

[53] Ibid., p. 162.

[54] Ibid., p. 163. That Freud intended the metaphor of the journey to govern the structure of his text is made clear in a letter to Fliess. See *The Origins of Psychoanalysis*, p. 290.

the heart of Freud's text, *The Interpretation of Dreams* stands at the center of Freud's writing as a "tangle of thoughts," a point where "the meshwork" of the Freudian discourse is "particularly close." *The Interpretation of Dreams* produces the very resistance it identifies as the core of all dreams, indeed of all mental activity; as a text, it constitutes the navel of Freud's writing, the point to which all interpretations of the Freudian discourse must inevitably return again and again.

Freud's theoretical discourse thus presents an exemplary instance of the general theory of autobiographical writing explored in this essay through a reading of certain texts by Vico, Kierkegaard, and Nietzsche. Just as Freud establishes a limit beyond which dream interpretation cannot pass and to which interpretation always returns to confirm itself, so autobiography, the inquiry of the self into its own origin and history, is always circumscribed by the limiting conditions of writing, of the production of a text. Vico, Kierkegaard, and Nietzsche all contend that the self is constituted by a discourse that it never completely masters. Freud reaffirms this belief and adumbrates the mechanisms that produce this discourse: displacement, condensation, secondary revision—all the mechanisms of the dream-work. In so doing, he is led to the boundaries of the self, the point at which the discourse of dreams touches the unconscious. What he discovers is that the self is always already in existence, that each dream, each slip of the tongue or lapse of memory, each flash of wit illuminates a prior discourse, a text elaborated long ago that governs all subsequent moments of textual making. But what he also discovers is that this master text, the unconscious, is perpetually changing—that each dream, each slip of the tongue, each witticism alters in some small way the configuration of the unconscious. Like Vico's theory of history, Freud's theory of the unconscious rests on the concept of repetition conceived as the production of difference in the generation of a text. The writing of autobiography is a similar act of producing difference by repetition. Just as dream interpretation returns again and again to the navel of the dream, so autobiography must return perpetually to the elusive center of selfhood buried in the unconscious, only to discover that it was already there when it began. The origin and the end of autobiography converge in the very act of writing, as Proust brilliantly demonstrates at the end of *Le temps retrouvé*, for no autobiography can take place except within the boundaries of a writing where concepts of subject, self, and author collapse into the act of producing a text.

Bibliography

A select list of books and articles that give a critical or theoretical treatment of autobiography

Arensberg, Liliane K. "Death as Metaphor of Self in *I Know Why the Caged Bird Sings.*" *College Language Association Journal* 20 (1976): 273-291.

Baker, Houston A., Jr. "The Problem of Being: Some Reflections on Black Autobiography." *Obsidian* 1 (1975): 18-30.

Bates, E. Stuart. *Inside Out: An Introduction to Autobiography.* New York: Sheridan House, 1937.

Bell, Robert. "Metamorphoses of Spiritual Autobiography." *Journal of English Literary History* 44 (1977): 108-126.

Bergonzi, Bernard. "Retrospect I: Autobiography." *Heroes' Twilight: A Study of the Literature of the Great War.* New York: Coward-McCann, 1966.

Berthoff, Warner. "Witness and Testament: Two Contemporary Classics," *New Literary History* 2 (1971): 311-327.

Blanchard, Jean Marc. "Of Cannibalism and Autobiography." *Modern Language Notes* 93 (1978): 654-676.

Blasing, Mutlu Konuk. *The Art of Life: Studies in American Autobiographical Literature.* Austin: Univ. of Texas Press, 1977.

Blassingame, John W. "Black Autobiographies as Histories and Literature." *Black Scholar* 5 (1973-1974): 2-9.

Bloom, Lynn Z. "Gertrude Is Alice Is Everybody: Innovation and Point of View in Gertrude Stein's Autobiographies." *Twentieth Century Studies* 24 (1978): 81-93.

Borel, Jacques. "Problèmes de l'autobiographie." *Positions et oppositions sur le roman contemporain.* Edited by Michel Mansuy. Paris: Klincksieck, 1971.

Bottrall, Margaret. *Every Man a Phoenix: Studies in Seventeenth-Century Autobiography.* Chester Springs, Pa.: Dufour, 1958.

Bowen, Elizabeth. "Autobiography as an Art." *Saturday Review of Literature* 34 (1951): 9-10.

Brée, Germaine. "The Break-up of Traditional Genres: Bataille, Leiris, Michaux." *Bucknell Review* 21, no. 2 (1973): 3-13.

Brignano, Russell C. *Black Americans in Autobiography: An Anno-*

*tated Bibliography of Autobiographies and Autobiographical Books
Written Since the Civil War*. Durham: Duke Univ. Press, 1974.

Bruchac, Joseph. "Black Autobiography in Africa and America."
Black Academy Review 2 (1971): 61-70.

Bruss, Elizabeth W. *Autobiographical Acts: The Changing Situation of
a Literary Genre*. Baltimore: Johns Hopkins Univ. Press, 1976.

Buell, Lawrence. "Transcendentalist Self-examination and Autobiographical Tradition." *Literary Transcendentalism: Style and
Vision in the American Renaissance*. Ithaca: Cornell Univ. Press,
1973.

Burr, Anna Robeson. *The Autobiography: A Critical and Comparative
Study*. Boston: Houghton Mifflin, 1909.

Butler, Lord Richard. *The Difficult Art of Autobiography*. Oxford:
Clarendon Press, 1968.

Butterfield, Stephen. *Black Autobiography in America*. Amherst:
Univ. of Massachusetts Press, 1974.

Church, Richard. "The Art of Autobiography." *Cornhill* 171
(1960-1961): 469-480.

Clark, A. M. *Autobiography: Its Genesis and Phases*. Edinburgh:
Oliver and Boyd, 1935.

Coirault, Yves. "Autobiographie et mémoires (XVIIe-XVIIIe siè-
cles) ou existence et naissance de l'autobiographie." *Revue
d'histoire littéraire de la France* 75 (1975): 937-953.

Cooke, Michael G. " 'Do You Remember Laura?' or, The Limits
of Autobiography." *The Iowa Review* 9, no. 2 (1978): 58-72.

———. "Modern Black Autobiography in the Tradition." *Romanticism: Vistas, Instances, Continuities*. Edited by David Thorburn
and Geoffrey Hartman. Ithaca: Cornell Univ. Press, 1973.

Cooley, Thomas. *Educated Lives: The Rise of Modern Autobiography
in America*. Columbus: Ohio State Univ. Press, 1976.

Couser, G. Thomas. *American Autobiography: The Prophetic Mode*.
Amherst: Univ. of Massachusetts Press, 1979.

———. "Of Time and Identity: Walt Whitman and Gertrude Stein
as Autobiographers." *Texas Studies in Language and Literature*
17 (1976): 787-804.

———. "The Shape of Death in American Autobiography." *Hudson Review* 31 (1978): 53-66.

Cox, James M. "Autobiography and America." *Virginia Quarterly
Review* 47 (1971): 252-277.

———. "Autobiography and Washington." *Sewanee Review* 85
(1977): 235-261.

————. "Jefferson's *Autobiography*: Recovering Literature's Lost Ground." *The Southern Review* 14 (1978): 633-652.

Curtin, John Claude. "Autobiography and the Dialectic of Consciousness." *International Philosophical Quarterly* 14 (1974): 343-346.

Delany, Paul. *British Autobiography in the Seventeenth Century*. London: Routledge & Kegan Paul, 1969.

Dilthey, Wilhelm. *Selected Writings of Wilhelm Dilthey*. Selected, translated, and introduced by H. P. Rickman. Cambridge: Cambridge Univ. Press, 1976.

Donato, Eugenio. "The Ruins of Memory: Archeological Fragments and Textual Artifacts." *Modern Language Notes* 93 (1978): 575-596.

Downing, Christine. "Re-Visioning Autobiography: The Bequest of Freud and Jung." *Soundings* 60 (1977): 210-228.

Eakin, Paul John. "Malcolm X and the Limits of Autobiography." *Criticism* 18 (1976): 230-242.

Earle, William. *The Autobiographical Consciousness: A Philosophical Inquiry into Existence*. Chicago: Quadrangle Books, 1972.

Ebner, Dean. *Autobiography in Seventeenth-Century England: Theology and the Self*. The Hague: Mouton, 1971.

Erikson, Erik H. "Gandhi's Autobiography: The Leader as a Child." *The American Scholar* 35 (1966): 632-646.

Fendelman, Earl. "Toward Walden Pond: The American Voice in Autobiography." *Canadian Review of American Studies* 8 (1977): 11-25.

Frye, Northrop. *Anatomy of Criticism*. Princeton: Princeton University Press, 1957.

Gelpi, Barbara C. "The Innocent I: Dickens' Influence on Victorian Autobiography." *The Worlds of Victorian Fiction*. Edited by Jerome Buckley. Cambridge: Harvard Univ. Press, 1975.

Gasché, Rodolphe. "Self-engendering as a Verbal Body." *Modern Language Notes* 93 (1978): 677-694.

Goldberg, Jonathan. "Cellini's *Vita* and the Conventions of Early Autobiography." *Modern Language Notes* 89 (1974): 71-83.

Gossman, Lionel. "The Innocent Art of Confession and Reverie." *Daedalus* 107 (1978): 59-77.

Gottfried, Rudolf. "Autobiography and Art: An Elizabethan Borderland." *Literary Criticism and Historical Understanding: Selected Papers from the English Institute*. Edited by Phillip Damon. New York: Columbia Univ. Press, 1967.

Greene, Donald. "The Uses of Autobiography in the Eighteenth Century." *Essays in Eighteenth-Century Literature*. Edited by Philip B. Daghlian. Bloomington: Indiana Univ. Press, 1968.

Gunn, Janet Varner. "Autobiography and the Narrative Experience of Temporality as Depth." *Soundings* 60 (1977): 194–209.

Gusdorf, Georges. "Conditions et limites de l'autobiographie." *Formen der Selbstdarstellung: Analekten zu einer Geschichte des literarischen Selbstportraits* (Festgabe für Fritz Neubert). Edited by Günther Reichenkron and Erich Hasse. Berlin: Duncker & Humblot, 1956.

———. *La découverte de soi*. Paris: Presses Universitaires de France, 1948.

———. "De l'autobiographie initiatique à l'autobiographie genre littéraire." *Revue d'histoire littéraire de la France* 75 (1975): 957–994.

Harbert, Earl N. "Henry Adams's *Education* and Autobiographical Tradition." *Tulane Studies in English* 22 (1977): 133–141.

Hart, Francis R. "Notes for an Anatomy of Modern Autobiography." *New Literary History* 1 (1970): 485–511.

Hoggart, Richard. "A Question of Tone: Some Problems in Autobiographical Writing." *Critical Quarterly* 5 (1963): 73–90.

Howarth, William L. "Some Principles of Autobiography." *New Literary History* 5 (1974): 363–381.

Howells, W. D. "Autobiography." *Harper's Monthly* 107 (1904): 478–482.

———. "Autobiography, a New Form of Literature." *Harper's Monthly* 119 (1909): 795–798.

Ilie, Paul. "Franklin and Villarroel: Social Consciousness in Two Autobiographies." *Eighteenth Century Studies* 7 (1974): 321–342.

Kaplan, Louis, et al. *A Bibliography of American Autobiographies*. Madison: Univ. of Wisconsin Press, 1961.

Kazin, Alfred. "Autobiography as Narrative." *Michigan Quarterly Review* 3 (1964): 210–216.

Kent, George E. "Maya Angelou's *I Know Why the Caged Bird Sings* and Black Autobiographical Tradition." *Kansas Quarterly* 7, No. 3 (1975): 72–78.

Landow, George P. *Approaches to Victorian Autobiography*. Athens, Ohio: Ohio Univ. Press, 1979.

Langbaum, Robert. "Autobiography and Myth in *Out of Africa*." *Virginia Quarterly Review* 40 (1964): 64–80.

Lehmann, Paul. "Autobiographies of the Middle Ages." *Transactions of the Royal Historical Society*. Vol. 3. London: Offices of the Royal Historical Society, 1953.

Leigh, James. "The Figure of Autobiography." *Modern Language Notes* 93 (1978): 733-749.

Lejeune, Philippe. *L'autobiographie en France*. Paris: A. Colin, 1971.

———. "Autobiography in the Third Person." *New Literary History* 9 (1977): 27-50.

———. *Lire Leiris, autobiographie et langage*. Paris: Klincksieck, 1975.

———. *Le pacte autobiographique*. Paris: Editions du Seuil, 1975.

Lerner, L. D. "Puritanism and the Spiritual Autobiography." *Hibbert Journal* 55 (1957): 373-386.

Levin, David. *In Defense of Historical Literature: Essays on American History, Autobiography, Drama, and Fiction*. New York: Hill & Wang, 1967.

Lillard, Richard G. *American Life in Autobiography: A Descriptive Guide*. Stanford: Stanford Univ. Press, 1956.

MacCannell, Juliet Flower. "History and Self-Portrait in Rousseau's Autobiography." *Studies in Romanticism* 13 (1974): 279-298.

McDonnell, James. "Success and Failure: A Rhetorical Study of the First Two Chapters of Mill's Autobiography." *University of Toronto Quarterly* 45 (1976): 109-122.

Mandel, Barrett J. "The Autobiographer's Art." *Journal of Aesthetics and Art Criticism* 27 (1968): 215-226.

———. "Autobiography—Reflection Trained on Mystery." *Prairie Schooner* 46 (1972-1973): 323-338.

———. " 'Basting the Image with a Certain Liquor': Death in Autobiography." *Soundings* 57 (1974): 175-188.

———. "Bunyan and the Autobiographer's Artistic Purpose." *Criticism* 10 (1968): 225-243.

———. "Darwin's Crisis with Time." *Soundings* 60 (1977): 179-193.

———. "The Didactic Achievement of Malcolm X's Autobiography." *Afro-American Studies* 2 (1972): 269-274.

———. "Problem of Narration in Edward Gibbon's Autobiography." *Studies in Philology* 77 (1970): 550-564.

Mansell, Darrel. "Unsettling the Colonel's Hash: 'Fact' in Autobiography." *Modern Language Quarterly* 37 (1976): 115-132.

Marin, Louis. "The Autobiographical Interruption: About Stendhal's 'Life of Henry Brulard.'" *Modern Language Notes* 93 (1978): 597–617.

Matthews, William. *British Autobiographies: An Annotated Bibliography of British Autobiographies Published or Written before 1951.* Berkeley: Univ. of California Press, 1955.

Maurois, André. *Aspects of Biography.* New York: D. Appleton & Co., 1929.

May, Georges. *L'autobiographie.* Paris: Presses Universitaires de France, 1979.

Mazlish, Bruce. "Autobiography and Psycho-analysis: Between Truth and Self-Deception." *Encounter* 35 (1970): 28–37.

Mehlman, Jeffrey. *A Structural Study of Autobiography: Proust, Leiris, Sartre, Lévi-Strauss.* Ithaca: Cornell Univ. Press, 1974.

Miller, Ross. "Autobiography as Fact and Fiction: Franklin, Adams, Malcolm X." *Centennial Review* 16 (1972): 221–232.

Misch, Georg. *Geschichte der Autobiographie.* 4 vols., 8 tomes. Bern: A. Francke, 1949–1950 (vol. 1) and Frankfurt-am-Main: G. Schulte-Bulmke, 1955–1969 (vols. 2–4).

———. *A History of Autobiography in Antiquity.* Translated by E. W. Dickes. 2 vols. Cambridge, Mass.: Harvard Univ.Press, 1951.

Morris, John N. *Versions of the Self: Studies in English Autobiography from John Bunyan to John Stuart Mill.* New York: Basic Books, 1966.

Neumann, Bernd. *Identität und Rollenzwang: Zur Theorie der Autobiographie.* Frankfurt: Athenæum, 1970.

O'Brien, William J. "Toward Understanding Original Sin in Augustine's *Confessions.*" *Thought* 49 (1974): 436–446.

Ohmann, Carol. "*The Autobiography of Malcolm X*: A Revolutionary Use of the Franklin Tradition." *American Quarterly* 22 (1970): 131–149.

Olney, James. "Autos★Bios★Graphein: The Study of Autobiographical Literature." *South Atlantic Quarterly* 77 (1978): 113–123.

———. "Experience, Metaphor, and Meaning: *The Death of Ivan Ilyich.*" *Journal of Aesthetics and Art Criticism* 31 (1972): 101–114.

———. *Metaphors of Self: The Meaning of Autobiography.* Princeton: Princeton Univ. Press, 1972.

———. *Tell Me Africa: An Approach to African Literature.* Princeton: Princeton Univ. Press, 1973.

Osborn, James M. *The Beginnings of Autobiography in England.* Los Angeles: Univ. of California Press, 1959.

Pascal, Roy. *Design and Truth in Autobiography*. Cambridge, Mass.: Harvard Univ. Press, 1960.

Perloff, Marjorie G. "Tradition of Myself: The Autobiographical Mode of Yeats." *Journal of Modern Literature* 4 (1975): 529–573.

Peyre, Henri. *Literature and Sincerity*. New Haven: Yale Univ. Press, 1963.

Pike, Burton. "Time in Autobiography." *Comparative Literature* 28 (1976): 326–342.

Pison, Thomas. "Wordsworth's Autobiography: The Metonymy of Self." *Bucknell Review* 23, no. 2 (1977): 78–95.

Porter, Laurence M. "Autobiography versus Confessional Novel: Gide's *L'immoraliste* and *Si le grain ne meurt*." *Symposium* 30 (1976): 144–159.

Porter, Roger J. "Edwin Muir and Autobiography: Archetype of a Redemptive Memory." *South Atlantic Quarterly* 77 (1978): 504–523.

———. "Gibbon's Autobiography: Filling Up the Silent Vacancy." *Eighteenth Century Studies* 8 (1974): 1–26.

———. "The Singer in the Song: Autobiography and Time in *The Odyssey*." *Massachusetts Review* 18 (1977): 801–820.

———, and Wolf, H. R. *Voice Within: Reading and Writing Autobiography*. New York: Knopf, 1973.

Rendall, Steven. "The Rhetoric of Montaigne's Self-Portrait: Speaker and Subject." *Studies in Philology* 73 (1976): 285–301.

Renza, Louis A. "The Veto of the Imagination: A Theory of Autobiography." *New Literary History* 9 (1977): 1–26.

Rinehart, Keith. "The Victorian Approach to Autobiography." *Modern Philology* 51 (1954): 177–186.

Robinson, Philip. "Jean-Jacques Rousseau and the Autobiographical Dimension." *Journal of European Studies* 8 (1978): 77–92.

Rosenblatt, Roger. "Black Autobiography: Life as the Death Weapon." *The Yale Review* 65 (1976): 515–527.

Rosenfeld, Alvin H. "Inventing the Jew: Notes on Jewish Autobiography." *Midstream* 21 (1975): 54–67.

Ross, Morton L. "Form and Moral Balance in Franklin's Autobiography." *Ariel: A Review of International English Literature* 7, no. 3 (1976): 38–52.

Ryan, Michael. "The Question of Autobiography in Cardinal Newman's *Apologia pro vita sua*." *Georgia Review* 31 (1977): 672–699.

Salaman, Esther P. *The Great Confession: From Aksakov and De Quincey to Tolstoy and Proust*. London: Allen Lane, 1973.

Sayre, Robert F. "Autobiography and Images of Utopia." *Salmagundi* 19 (1972): 18–37.

————. *The Examined Self: Benjamin Franklin, Henry Adams, Henry James*. Princeton: Princeton Univ. Press, 1964.

————. "The Proper Study—Autobiographies in American Studies." *American Quarterly* 29 (1977): 241–262.

Schultz, Elizabeth. "To Be Black and Blue: The Blues Genre in Black American Autobiography." *Kansas Quarterly* 7, no. 3 (1975): 81–96.

Shapiro, Stephen A. "The Dark Continent of Literature: Autobiography." *Comparative Literature Studies* 5 (1968): 421–454.

Shea, Daniel B., Jr. *Spiritual Autobiography in Early America*. Princeton: Princeton Univ. Press, 1968.

Shumaker, Wayne. *English Autobiography: Its Emergence, Materials, and Forms*. Berkeley and Los Angeles: Univ. of California Press, 1954.

Smith, Sidonie A. "The Song of a Caged Bird: Maya Angelou's Quest after Self-Acceptance." *Southern Humanities Review* 7 (1973): 365–375.

————. *Where I'm Bound: Patterns of Slavery and Freedom in Black American Autobiography*. Westport, Conn.: Greenwood Press, 1974.

Spacks, Patricia M. *Imagining a Self: Autobiography and Novel in Eighteenth-Century England*. Cambridge: Harvard Univ. Press, 1976.

————. "Reflecting Women." *Yale Review* 63 (1973): 26–42.

————. "Stages of Life: Notes on Autobiography and the Life Cycle." *Boston University Journal* 25, no. 2 (1977): 7–17.

————. "Women's Stories, Women's Selves." *Hudson Review* 30 (1977): 29–46.

Spender, Stephen. "Confessions and Autobiography." *The Making of a Poem*. New York: W. W. Norton & Co., 1962.

Spengemann, W. C., and Lundquist, L. R. "Autobiography and the American Myth." *American Quarterly* 17 (1965): 501–519.

Starobinski, Jean. "The Style of Autobiography." *Literary Style: A Symposium*. Edited by Seymour Chatman. New York: Oxford Univ. Press, 1971.

Starr, George A. *Defoe and Spiritual Autobiography*. Princeton: Princeton Univ. Press, 1965.

Stone, Albert E. "After *Black Boy* and *Dusk of Dawn*: Patterns in Recent Black Autobiography." *Phylon* 39 (1978): 18-34.

———. "Autobiography and American Culture." *American Studies: An International Newsletter* 11 (1972): 22-36.

———. "Cato's Mirror: The Face of Violence in American Autobiography." *Prospects: An Annual of American Cultural Studies*. Vol. 3. Edited by Jack Salzman. New York: Burt Franklin, 1977.

———. "Identity and Art in Frederick Douglass's *Narrative*." *College Language Association Journal* 17 (1973): 192-213.

———. "The Sea and the Self: Travel as Experience and Metaphor in Early American Autobiography." *Genre* 7 (1974): 279-306.

Sturrock, John. "The New Model Autobiographer." *New Literary History* 9 (1977): 51-63.

Szávai, János. "La place et le rôle de l'autobiographie dans la littérature." *Acta Litteraria Academiae Scientiarum Hungaricae* 18 (1976): 398-414.

Tayler, J. Lionel. *The Writing of Autobiography and Biography*. Hull: printed for the author, 1926.

Taylor, Dennis. "Some Strategies of Religious Autobiography." *Renascence* 27 (1974): 40-44.

Taylor, Rodney L. "The Centered Self: Religious Autobiography in the Neo-Confucian Tradition." *The History of Religions* 17 (1978): 266-283.

Thibaudeau, Jean. "Le roman comme autobiographie." *Tel Quel* 34 (1968): 67-74.

Thomas, William. "John Stuart Mill and the Uses of Autobiography." *History* 66 (1971): 341-359.

Tintner, Adeline R. "Autobiography as Fiction: The Usurping Consciousness as Hero of James's Memoirs." *Twentieth Century Literature* 23 (1977): 239-260.

Vance, Eugene. "Augustine's *Confessions* and the Poetics of the Law." *Modern Language Notes* 93 (1978): 618-634.

Vitz, Evelyn Birge. "Type et individu dans 'l'autobiographie' médiévale." Translated by Philippe Lejeune. *Poétique* 24 (1975): 426-445.

Voisine, Jacques. "De la confession religieuse à l'autobiographie et au journal intime: entre 1760 et 1820." *Neohelican* 2, nos. 3-4 (1974): 337-357.

———. "Naissance et evolution du terme littéraire 'autobiographie.' " La littérature comparée en Europe orientale. Budapest: Akademiai Kiado, 1963.

Webber, Joan. The Eloquent "I": Style and Self in Seventeenth-Century Prose. Madison: Univ. of Wisconsin Press, 1968.

Weintraub, Karl J. "Autobiography and Historical Consciousness." Critical Inquiry 1 (1975): 821–848.

———. The Value of the Individual: Self and Circumstance in Autobiography. Chicago: Univ. of Chicago Press, 1978.

Wethered, H. N. The Curious Art of Autobiography. New York: Philosophical Library, 1956.

Whitfield, Stephen J. "Three Masters of Impression Management: Benjamin Franklin, Booker T. Washington, and Malcolm X as Autobiographers." South Atlantic Quarterly 77 (1978): 399–417.

Wu, Pei-yi. "Self-Examination and Confession of Sins in Traditional China." Harvard Journal of Asiatic Studies 39 (1979): 5–38.

Wuthenow, Ralph-Rainer. Das erinnerte Ich: Europäische Autobiographie und Selbstdarstellung im 18. Jahrhundert. Munich: C. H. Beck, 1974.

Zimmerman, T. C. Price. "Confession and Autobiography in the Early Renaissance." Renaissance: Studies in Honor of Hans Baron. Edited by Anthony Molho and John A. Tedeschi. DeKalb: Northern Illinois Univ. Press, 1971.

Zumthor, Paul. "Autobiography in the Middle Ages?" Genre 6 (1973): 29–48.

Index

LIBRARY OF CONGRESS CATALOGING IN PUBLICATION DATA

Main entry under title:

Autobiography, essays theoretical and critical.
  Includes index.
  1. Autobiography—Addresses, essays, lectures.
I. Olney, James.
CT25.A95   809   79-17556
ISBN 0-691-06412-1
ISBN 0-691-10080-2 pbk.